658.45
D29m

143203

DATE DUE			

Management Information Systems

McGRAW-HILL SERIES IN MANAGEMENT INFORMATION SYSTEMS

Gordon B. Davis, Consulting Editor

Davis   Management Information Systems:
Conceptual Foundations, Structure,
and Development

Management Information Systems: Conceptual Foundations, Structure, and Development

Gordon B. Davis

Professor of Management Information Systems
Director, The Management Information Systems Research Center
University of Minnesota

McGraw-Hill Book Company

New York
St. Louis
San Francisco
Düsseldorf
Johannesburg
Kuala Lumpur
London
Mexico
Montreal
New Delhi
Panama
Paris
São Paulo
Singapore
Sydney
Tokyo
Toronto

Library of Congress Cataloging in Publication Data
Davis, Gordon Bitter.
Management information systems.
(McGraw-Hill series in management information systems)
Includes bibliographies.
1. Management information systems. I. Title.
T58.6.D38   658.4'5   74-2037
ISBN 0-07-015827-4

Management Information Systems: Conceptual Foundations, Structure, and Development

1234567890DODO7987654

This book was set in Times Roman by Black Dot, Inc.
The editors were Kenneth J. Bowman and Joseph F. Murphy;
The designer was Anne Canevari Green;
the production supervisor was Joe Campanella.
The drawings were done by Graphics Arts International.
R. R. Donnelley & Sons Company was printer and binder.

Contents

v

Preface

A management information system, or MIS, is an information system that, in addition to providing all necessary transaction processing for an organization, provides information and processing support for management and decision functions. The idea of such an information system preceded the advent of computers, but computers made the idea feasible. Organizations have always required systems for collecting, processing, storing, retrieving, and distributing information. The computer has added a new and powerful technology to information systems, so that computer-based information systems can be radically different from systems using manual or electromechanical processing. And while organizations are changing their information systems in response to this technology, frequently their adjustment lacks an inadequate understanding of the nature of the changes being made. To use the computer to do clerical processing is a fairly simple matter; to apply the computer to provide support for management functions is more complex. Indeed, the latter application is so challenging that it has been identified by the Association for Computing Machinery as a new academic discipline.

The field of study known as MIS—organizational information systems, computer-based information systems, etc.—is so new that the available text material is not well defined as to content and coverage. This text is unique in its attempt to provide a comprehensive conceptual and structural foundation for the study of the area. It is, in a sense, a first approximation to what is needed. It is difficult to make a satisfactory text until many different students, professors, and practitioners have had a chance to use the material. The publication of the text is therefore a step in defining the content required for an introduction to management information systems. The text could have been delayed for several more years of testing by the author and his colleagues. The "fine tuning" that could have resulted was considered less important than providing a broader use of the text in its current state of development. Comments and suggestions are therefore solicited from all readers and adopters of the text. A possible second edition would be able to reflect the suggestions, insights, references, etc., that are received. This process should have a significant impact in improving quality of text material in the information system area.

The text has been used in draft form by several professors at the College of Business Administration at the University of Minnesota. Students have been varied as to background and preparation: undergraduate and graduate students, MIS majors and nonmajors, business and non-business majors, students with good computer backgrounds and students with little or no knowledge of computers, regular degree students and evening continuing education students. The reaction of the students has been excellent. Students with little mathematics or statistics tend to have difficulty with the mathematical theory of information (in Chapter 2) and the value of information (Chapter 7). However, it is satisfactory to survey these topics for an intuitive understanding without attempting to learn the topics in depth. Students tend to have a better understanding of the material if they have had some introduction to computers. The content of most introductory texts is sufficient background (such as Gordon B. Davis, *Computer Data Processing*, 1973, or *Introduction to Electronic Computers*, 1971, both published by McGraw-Hill Book Company). However, some students have had good success in learning the material with no previous coursework in computers.

Although the text may be used as an introduction to computer-based organizational information systems without prerequisite coursework or background, it is most appropriate as the text for a second or third course in information systems. Two possible sequences in which the text is used are:

Sequence 1	*Sequence 2*
Introduction to computers	Introduction to computers
Introduction to MIS	Development of an information system
Development of an information system	Introduction to MIS

Sequence 1 is currently the approach used at the University of Minnesota.

The text has been used in the Minnesota courses in the order followed in the text. However, an alternative order of use is possible.

Chapter 1 Overview
Section 2 Structure
Section 3 Development and management
Section 1 Conceptual foundations

In other words, the structure and development of an information system may be presented prior to describing the conceptual foundations. There are some references in Sections 2 and 3 back to Section 1, but these are not critical.

There are exercises at the end of each chapter but no cases. A case-oriented instructor would need to provide supplementary cases. A set of references at the end of each chapter provides for supplementary reading if desired. A separate instructor's guide contains instructional suggestions.

The pioneering nature of the text makes feedback from users very important. Comments and suggestions can be sent to:

College of Business Administration
University of Minnesota
Minneapolis, Minnesota 55455

Gordon B. Davis

Management
Information
Systems

An Overview
of Management
Information Systems

In 1954 the first computer was installed for a business application: processing of payroll. By 1974, only 20 years later, there were over 100,000 computers in the United States and a like number in the rest of the world. Payroll processing by computer, which was a revolutionary idea in 1954, is now considered a rather routine application. Today the frontiers in information processing are systems which also provide information resources in support of managerial and decision-making functions. Such a system is commonly called a *management information system* or MIS. This chapter provides an overview of MIS and issues related to it. The topics will be discussed in more detail in subsequent chapters.

DEFINITION OF A MANAGEMENT
INFORMATION SYSTEM

There is no agreement on the term "management information system." Some writers prefer terms such as "information processing system," "information/decision system," or simply "information system" to refer to computer-based information processing systems which are designed to support the operations, management, and decision functions of an organization. This text uses MIS because it is descriptive and generally understood.

An organization has transactions that must be processed in order to carry out its day-to-day activities. The payroll must be prepared, sales and payments on account must be posted: these and others are data processing activities and might be termed clerical in nature; they follow rather standard procedures. The computer is useful for these clerical data processing tasks, but a management information system performs other tasks as well and is more than a data processing system. It is an information processing system applying the power of the computer to provide information for management and decision making. The management information system has been described as a pyramid structure (Figure 1-1) in which the bottom layer consists of the information for transaction processing, status inquiries, etc.; the next level consists of

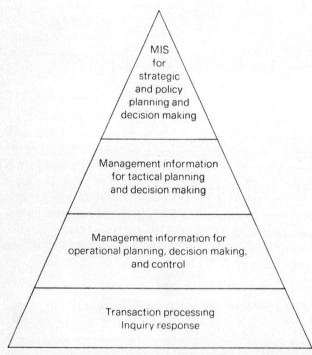

Figure 1-1 Management information system. (*Adapted from Robert V. Head, "Management Information Systems: A Critical Appraisal,"* Datamation, *May 1967, p. 23.*)

information resources in support of the day-to-day operations management; the third level consists of information system resources to aid in tactical planning and decision making for management control; and the top level consists of information resources in support of the planning and policy making by higher levels of management.

A definition of a management information system, as the term is generally understood, is an integrated, man/machine system for providing information to support the operations, management, and decision-making functions in an organization. The system utilizes computer hardware and software, manual procedures, management and decision models, and a data base.

Computer-based Man/Machine System

One can conceptually discuss management information systems without computers, but it is the power of the computer which makes MIS possible. The question is not whether a computer shall be used in management information systems, but the extent to which various processes should be computerized. The idea of a computer-based information/decision system does not mean complete automation. The man/machine system concept implies that some tasks are best performed by man, while others are best done by machine. For many problems, the man and machine form a combined system with results being obtained through a set of dialogs and interactions between the computer and a human processor.

The man/machine interaction is enhanced by online operations in which input/output terminals are connected to the computer to provide immediate input and immediate output for applications which can benefit from it. Online operation is required for man/machine dialog, but many clerical processing tasks are more efficiently done without terminal input or output.

The fact that an MIS is computer-based means that designers must have a good knowledge of computers and their use in information processing. The man/machine concept means that the designer of management information systems should understand human capabilities as information processors and human behavior in decision making.

Integrated System with Data Base

Most early computer processing systems followed the manual processing system approach in which each application is processed separately by use of separate files. This method has processing and control efficiencies; however, it leads to duplication of files and to separate files, some having the same data fields but with the data frequently not in agreement. Also, in this approach each application is restricted to the data planned for it. An analytical application using data from many applications would need to build a new file from parts of separate files.

An integrated system is based on the concept that there should be integration of data and processing. Data integration is accomplished by the data base. For an information processing system, this consists of all data that can be accessed by the system. In a computer-based MIS, the term *data base* is usually reserved for data that can be readily accessed by the computer. The management of the data base is by a computer software system known as a *data base management system.* Any application using a data item accesses the same data item, which is stored only once and made available to all applications. A single updating of a data item updates it for all uses.

Integrated processing is accomplished by an overall system plan. The system is usually designed as a federation of subsystems rather than a single system. This system design may mean a large central computer, or it can involve a network of smaller computers. The main idea is the planned integration of applications where this is feasible and effective.

Operations Support

The advanced information processing system must still provide for processing of transactions. In fact, the processing of transactions (payroll, sales, accounts receivable, and others) provides input for the data base that is vital to advanced applications. The trend in transaction processing in advanced systems is toward online data collection and online inquiry. The updating of files may also be performed immediately, although other approaches are also used.

The online inquiry capability is very significant in operational support. It means that any authorized employee may obtain immediate response to an inquiry such as the current balance in a customer account or the inventory on hand for an item.

Utilization of Management and Decision Models

It is insufficient for human recipients to receive only raw data or even summarized data alone. There needs to be a way of processing and presenting data so that the result is directed toward the decision to be made. The result should be decision-impelling. The method for doing this is processing data in terms of a decision model. For example, an investment decision relative to new capital expenditures might be processed in terms of a model of capital expenditure based on rate of return subject to constraints related to size and risk.

The decision-assisting models used in the system can be intelligence models to find problems; decision models to identify and analyze possible solutions; and various choice models such as optimization models that provide an optimal solution or satisficing methods for deciding on a satisfactory solution. In other words, there is a need for a variety of analytical and modeling approaches to meet a variety of decision situations. The following are some examples of problems and the type of model that might be included in an MIS to meet the need:

Problem	Example of model
Amount of inventory safety stock	Inventory model which computes safety stock
Personnel selection	Personnel search and selection model
New product pricing	New product introduction model
Expenditure control	Budgetary control model

The variety of decision models required means that an MIS has a set of general decision models useful for many types of analysis and decision situations plus a set of very specific models useful for restricted types of decisions. This is the model base or model bank[1] for the MIS.

In addition to decision models, there should be planning models and planning model software to assist managers in the planning function. These are generally most effective when the manager can use online man/machine dialog to build a plan.

Control models are included to report actual performance compared with planned or standard performance and to analyze the reasons for significant differences.

The Minimum MIS

An MIS is an organizational information system which supports not only operations but also the management processes. Since every MIS will perform transaction processing as one of its elements, a rather mundane data processing system might be identified as an MIS by the addition of a simple data base, retrieval capabilities, and one or two planning or decision models. Is this an MIS? This is not a useful question. MIS is a concept and an orientation toward which an information system design moves rather than being an absolute state. What is most significant is the

[1]For a discussion of model bank concept, see Hartmut J. Will, "MIS—Mirage or Mirror Image?," *Journal of Systems Management*, September 1973, pp. 24–31.

extent to which an information system adopts the MIS orientation or an information system supports the management functions of an organization. The answer is usually a matter of degree rather than a simple "yes" or "no."

It is difficult to support management and decision-making needs without technical capabilities for information retrieval upon request. But this need not be online with immediate response. Immediate response is an enhancement rather than a fundamental requirement for many situations. A variety of analytical and decision-making models need to be available if management is to receive useful information. An MIS should, however, not be measured by the complexity and sophistication of its model base. Fairly simple models are often more useful and more used—depending on the organization and the experience of its executives in using such models.

EVOLUTION OF THE MIS CONCEPT

The idea of an information system to support management and decision making predates the use of computers, which have extended the organizational capabilities for implementing such a system. This extension of capabilities is so significant that MIS is new in the sense that it is now feasible. Many of the ideas which are part of MIS evolved as part of other disciplines. Four major areas of concept and system development are especially significant in tracing the evolution of the MIS concept: managerial accounting, management science, management theory, and computer processing. The MIS concept may be viewed as a substantial extension of the concepts of managerial accounting taking into consideration the ideas and techniques of management science and the behavioral theories of management and decision making. The capabilities of computers have added to the development of the MIS concept because new hardware and software have offered new dimensions to be considered in conceptualizing the information system for an organization.

Managerial Accounting

It is useful to think of the field of accounting as being divided into two major areas, financial and managerial accounting. Financial accounting is concerned with measurement of income for specific periods such as a month or a year (the income statement) and reporting of financial status at the end of the period (the balance sheet). Since an organization operates continually through time, the measurement of income for a period involves questions of measuring revenues applicable to a period and identifying and matching the applicable expenses to arrive at a profit. The need for investors to receive this information and for the reports to be relied upon by parties not connected with the accounting process means that the basis for measuring income and financial condition should be as free as possible from personal bias, speculation, and forecasts. The primary set of users for financial accounting results can be thought of as investors outside the firm. As a result, financial accounting has limited usefulness for managerial decision making. Managerial accounting, on the other hand, is concerned with cost behavior and other analysis useful for managerial decisions.

The rise of the large corporations in the late 1800s created a need for an information system larger and more complex than systems designed for the fairly small enterprises existing prior to that time. Early efforts at managerial control concentrated on simple cost accounting and budgeting. The movement to business budgeting and cost control developed strength during the 1920s and 1930s.[2] The simple cost computations of the early 1900s were often found lacking in terms of management decision making. The 1930s and 1940s saw theoretical work related to costs for decision making and the use of decision-making models. Much of this work was from the field of microeconomics (also termed "economies of the firm" or "managerial economics"), but it was through managerial accounting that these conceptual developments were implemented in organizations. The changes resulted in improved cost analysis and in improved reporting methods.

The reporting systems for organizations developed by managerial accountants have generally reflected the idea of responsibility[3] and profitability[4] accounting. In these approaches, each manager receives reports covering his or her responsibility. The report is organized to identify variations from planned performance and the reasons for the variations. Lower-level reports are summarized to provide summary reports to the next level of management, etc., until the top management receives summary reports which identify problem areas and causes, but not in the same detail as for lower-level managers.

Cost analysis is used in managerial accounting to determine the most relevant cost for decision making. Relevant cost may be full cost, direct

[2]The first book on business budgeting did not appear until 1922 (James O. McKinsey, *Budgetary Control*, The Ronald Press Company, New York, 1922).

[3]John A. Higgins, "Responsibility Accounting," *The Arthur Andersen Chronicle*, April 1952.

[4]Robert Byer and Donald J. Trawicki, *Profitability Accounting for Planning and Control*, 2d ed., The Ronald Press Company, New York, 1972.

cost, marginal cost, replacement cost, opportunity cost, or others. Managerial accounting also employs cost-oriented decision techniques such as capital budgeting, breakeven analysis, and transfer pricing. The idea of providing relevant costs based on the decision to be made rather than providing a single cost figure for all uses is similar to the MIS concept of relevant information tailored to the use for which it is needed.

The short-term planning activity of organizations has generally been part of the accounting department in terms of the processing, review, etc., of the budget figures prepared by organizational budgetary units. Variable budgeting techniques are often used to develop a budget figure based on actual level of activity. This planning supports control reporting which consists of a comparison of planned or budgeted performance with actual performance and an analysis of reasons for variations.

In summary, financial accounting is an information system with rules and processes oriented toward supplying information suited to investors and creditors. Managerial accounting is an information system oriented toward internal management and control and is therefore closely identified with MIS.

Management Science

Management science (or operations research) is the application of the scientific method and quantitative analysis techniques to management problems. Some of its key concepts are:

1 Emphasis on systematic approaches to problem solving and application of scientific method to investigation
2 Use of mathematical models and mathematical and statistical procedures in analysis
3 Goal of seeking optimal decision or optimal policy

Management science solutions have tended to use economic or technical criteria rather than behavioral criteria with an emphasis on technical methods for solving problems. The success of management science in organizations has been most apparent in operational problems and tactical decisions. Inventory management, for example, has received considerable attention, as have problems such as production scheduling, plant location, transportation routing, and investment analysis.

The model building for analysis of organizational problems generally involves the use of sets of mathematical statements or of computational procedures such as a computer program. A common advantage of a model in analysis is the ability of the researcher to examine the behavior of the system over time and under a variety of conditions. Alternative strategies can be compared by simulating the effects of each strategy.

The manipulation of a model and the use of mathematical and statistical procedures generally depend on the computer. Many techniques, including simulation and linear programming, are essentially impractical without the computer. Some of the common techniques associated with management science are:

Linear programming
Integer programming
Dynamic programming
Queueing theory
Game theory
Decision theory
Simulation

Management science is an important development relative to computer-based management information systems because management science has developed procedures for the analysis and computer-based solution of many types of decision problems. The systematic approach to problem solving, use of models, management science techniques, and computer-based solution algorithms are generally incorporated in the MIS design.

Management Theory

Recent developments in management theory are significant in understanding the evolution of the MIS concept. Whereas management science developments have emphasized optimizing as a goal, recent management theory (see Chapter 6 for a further description) has emphasized *satisficing* (i.e., reaching a satisfactory solution) and has pointed out the human limitations on the search for solutions. A number of management researchers have concentrated on the behavioral and motivational consequences of organizational structure and systems within organizations. These developments in management theory are important in MIS design because they aid in understanding the role of man/machine systems and in developing decision models.

Computer Processing

Computers were not originally planned for information processing, but this is now the major use to which they are applied. The technical requirements for a computer-based management information system will be surveyed in Chapter 9. In summary, these requirements (assuming some online operations) are:

Element	Requirement for MIS
Hardware	Central processor capable of online operations. Relatively high processing speed.
	Large primary storage. Large, fast access, online storage.
	Hardware/software storage management method such as virtual memory.
	Input/output peripherals.
	Terminals for online inquiry and response.
	Data communications.
Software	High-level languages.
	Data base management system.
Operating system	Online operations. Multiprogramming.

lot of std'ization

These computer system features have been developed over the 20 years between the use of the first computer in 1947 and the development of early management information systems in the late 1960s. Although an MIS was technologically feasible at a very high cost before 1965, it is difficult to conceive of a large cost/effective MIS before that time.

Computer technology has been a major factor in inducing MIS development, but also a major inhibitor of progress. Without the capabilities of the computer, the concept of an MIS could not be implemented. The very existence of hardware and software capabilities induces their use in information system design. At the same time, hardware and software developments do not occur uniformly. For example, a hardware development allowing online inquiry may cause the design of an information system using these capabilities, but the initial system may have poorer performance than expected because of inadequate software. This causes improvements in software until the initial expectations are more nearly achieved. However, the difficulties in the software cause hardware changes in the next-generation computer, etc.

Software is now a greater problem than hardware with respect to MIS development. For every organization developing an MIS to design and program all software modules would be too costly. For cost/effective MIS, much of the software must be available as standard packages. This requires a fairly general agreement on the software needed. These developments are now in progress, and some MIS software packages are available from software vendors. *[handwritten: much standardization because of high software cost otherwise.]*

MIS AS SEEN BY THE USER

The major users of a computer-based management information system are the following:

User	Uses
Clerical personnel	Handling transactions, process data, and answer inquiries.
First-level managers	Obtaining operations data. Assistance with planning, scheduling, identifying out-of-control situations, and making decisions.
Staff specialists	Information for analysis. Assistance with analysis, planning, and reporting.
Management	Regular reports. Special retrieval requests. Special analyses. Special reports. Assistance in identifying problems and opportunities. Assistance in decision-making analysis.

[handwritten: much clerical work initially in gathering all data at its source]

   Clerical personnel may notice increased requirements for input when an MIS effort is begun and a data base is being established. New procedures for data control will be instituted. Clerical processes may be altered to utilize online devices such as CRTs, typewriters, and data entry devices. Personnel through the organization will be asked to report information they formerly kept in their own files or "little black books."

   The first-line supervisors will have additional data input requirements but will find information retrieval greatly improved. Status information is likely to be much easier to obtain. Decision models may provide first approximation solutions to problems such as scheduling. Reports will tend to be more meaningful and to arrive with less delay. Special analyses and reports will be more readily available. Feedback on performance variables will be more frequent.

   The staff specialist assisting higher levels of management makes substantial use of the capabilities of the MIS. The data base is searched for problems. The data is analyzed to find possible solutions. The planning

[handwritten: dec models give good 1st approx if not ideal solution]

models are utilized to arrive at first approximation of plans for the manager to examine. The model base provides the means for intelligence and design as the staff specialist formulates the data for managerial use.

Managers at all levels have new retrieval capabilities to obtain information relevant to their functions. For decision making, the system may provide the suggested optimal solution directly or may provide man/machine analysis and decision procedures to aid in achieving a good decision. For example, a manager for an inventory will have programmed the decision making in many cases such as order quantity. In complex situations such as the order of a carload lot to achieve purchase economies, an optimizing algorithm is probably not used, but instead a decision procedure is provided to assist the manager in arriving at a satisfactory solution. Planning is assisted by planning models plus a man/machine dialog to perform the testing of solutions.

The higher levels of management are affected by MIS through improved response to inquiries, continuous monitoring rather than periodic reporting, and improved capabilities for identification of problems or opportunities. Management control is enhanced by planning models and analytical models. For the highest level of management, strategic planning is aided by strategic planning models and analysis which supports their use. The highest-level manager is not likely in most cases to use online devices personally but is more likely to depend on his staff specialists to do the man/machine interaction.

In summary, routine processing is least affected by adoption of the MIS approach. Clerical personnel will prepare much of the same data, but new data requirements will be added, and more online devices may be utilized. The data requirements throughout all levels of personnel will be expanded, but there will be an increased availability of current, accurate information. Reports, responses to information requests, analysis, planning, and decision making receive improved processing and information support.

UNDERLYING CONCEPTS

A management information system is more than a technological development. It is related to the organization and to human processors. A complete understanding of computer-based organizational information systems should therefore include an understanding of the concepts related to information, information use, and information value. Section 1 of the text (Chapters 2 to 7) is devoted to a survey of concepts. The following comments introduce briefly the major concepts to be covered in Section 1.

Concept	Comments
Information	Information is that which adds to a representation. It has attributes of age and quality.
Humans as information processors	The capabilities of humans as information processors impose limitations on information systems and suggest principles for their design.
System concepts	Because a management information system is a system, the concepts of systems are useful in understanding and designing approaches to information system development.
Organization and management concepts	An information system exists within an organization and is designed to support management functions. Information is an important determinant of organizational form.
Decision-making concepts	MIS design should reflect not only rational approaches for optimization but also the behavioral theory of organizational decision making.
Value of information	Information changes decisions. The changes in the value of the outcomes determine the value of information.

An underlying assumption is that information systems add value to an organization. Information is viewed as a resource much like land, labor, and capital. It is not a free good. It must be obtained, processed, stored, retrieved, manipulated and analyzed, distributed, etc. An organization with a well-designed information system will generally have a competitive advantage over organizations with poorer systems.

OUTLINES OF AN MIS

A management information system contains the following physical elements:

1 Computer hardware
2 Software
   a Generalized system software
   b Generalized application software
   c Application programs
3 The data base (data stored on computer storage media)

— forms, instructions, layouts etc

4 Procedures
5 Operating personnel

In terms of applications, a complete application subsystem consists of:

The programs to perform computer processing
The procedures to make the application operational (forms, instructions for operators, instructions for users, etc.)

The application subsystems can be described in terms of the organizational functions they support (marketing, production, etc.) or in terms of the type of activities being performed.

Organizational Function Subsystems

Because organizational functions are somewhat separable in terms of activities and are defined managerially as separate responsibilities, an MIS may be viewed as a federation of information systems—one information system for each major organizational function. There may be common support systems used by more than one subsystem, but each functional system stands alone as to the procedures, programs, models, etc., unique to it. Typical major subsystems for a business organization engaged in manufacturing would be (Figure 1-2) as follows:

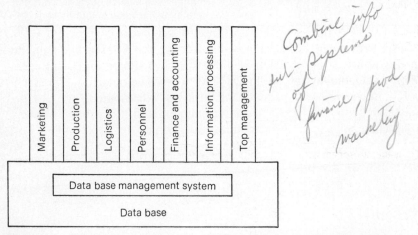

Combine info of systems... ful-... of... finance, prod, marketing

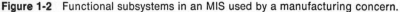

Figure 1-2 Functional subsystems in an MIS used by a manufacturing concern.

The subsystems will vary among organizations; the basic idea is the same—to identify major functions around which subsystems may be designed. These subsystems may be subdivided into smaller subsystems.

Major functional subsystem	Some typical uses
Marketing	Sales forecasting, sales planning, customer and sales analysis
Manufacturing	Production planning and scheduling, cost control, cost analysis
Logistics	Planning and control of purchasing, inventories, distribution
Personnel	Planning personnel requirements, analyzing performance, salary administration
Finance and accounting	Financial analysis, cost analysis, capital requirements planning, income measurement
Information processing	Information system planning, cost/effectiveness analysis
Top management	Strategic planning, resource allocation

For example, the personnel subsystem may be subdivided into personnel procurement, personnel records, personnel evaluation, and payroll administration.

Activities Subsystems

Combine activity sub-systems

Another approach to understanding the structure of an information system is in terms of the subsystems which perform various activities. Some of the activities subsystems will be useful for more than one organizational function subsystem; others will be useful for only one function. Examples of major activities subsystems are:

Activity subsystem	Some typical uses
Transaction processing	Processing of orders, shipments, receipts
Operational control	Scheduling of activities and performance reports
Management control	Formulation of budgets and resource allocation
Strategic planning	Formulation of objectives and strategic plans

These activities subsystems utilize the data in the data base and the capabilities of retrieval contained in the data base management system.

The relation of the activities subsystem to the functional subsystems is illustrated in Figure 1-3.

PROCESS OF MIS DEVELOPMENT

A management information system is a large undertaking—completion of the basic system will usually require several years. After completion there will be additions. The size and complexity of the system demand that it be carefully planned and controlled.

The first step is to establish a master development plan for the MIS. This defines the expected structure and establishes a schedule for the development. This plan will be revised periodically as priorities change and new conditions occur. The current state of MIS planning requires considerable judgment.

The development of each application in the MIS is controlled by applying the concept of a system development life cycle. The basic idea of the life cycle is that all applications essentially must go through the same process when they are conceived, developed, and implemented.

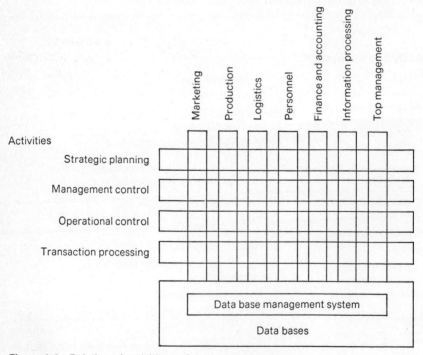

Figure 1-3 Relation of activities to functional subsystems.

Neglecting any portion of the development process may have serious consequences for the end result.

The life cycle concept gives structure to a creative process. In order to control the development effort, it is necessary to know what has been done and what has yet to be accomplished. The stages in the development life cycle provide the basis for this control because the stage of a project can be identified by both the work being performed and the documents produced.

The life cycle is consistent with the idea of planning. If an application cannot be planned by means of the development life cycle, it probably cannot be accomplished at all. The stages and phases in the life cycle of information processing systems are described differently by different writers,[5] but the differences are primarily in amount of detail and manner of categorization. All agree on the essential flow of development steps and the necessity for tight control over development. The major states are definition, programming, and implementation. The development life cycle is explained in more detail in Chapter 15.

THE MIS PROFESSIONAL

The field of computing did not, in the beginning, emphasize formal education as a preparation. This was beneficial in that there was no barrier to entry, but it meant that the background for advanced information system design was often lacking. Now there is a trend toward more formal academic preparation for persons planning a career in information processing.

The academic field concerned with scientific, algorithmic, or mathematically oriented computing is generally termed "computer science." A different curriculum is needed for the management information system specialist. A base of organizational understanding (marketing, finance, manufacturing, accounting, management, etc.) is as important as computer knowledge. An understanding of decision making and human behavior in systems is as important as knowledge of programming.

An example of academic preparation suitable for MIS is the curriculum proposal of the Association for Computing Machinery (ACM) for those who wish to specialize in computer-based organizational information systems.[6] The curriculum is a post-bachelor's degree program for

[5]See Robert Benjamin, *Control of the Information Systems Development Cycle*, Wiley-Interscience, a division of John Wiley & Sons, Inc., New York, 1971, p. 29, for a tabular presentation of different categorizations of the life cycle.

[6]R. L. Ashenhurst (ed.), "A Report of the ACM Curriculum Committee on Computer Education for Management," *Communications of the ACM*, May 1972, pp. 363–398.

fairly high-level educational preparation for a career in organization information processing. Figure 1-4 shows the basic structure of the proposed curriculum. A similar, but scaled down, curriculum has been proposed for undergraduates.[7]

The ACM curriculum is intended as academic preparation for two types of information processing professionals: the information analyst who works with users to define information requirements and the system designer who specifies hardware and software requirements. The distinction between information analyst and system designer is an emerging one

[7]Daniel Couger (ed.), "Curriculum Recommendations for Undergraduate Programs in Information Systems," *Communications of the ACM*, December 1973.

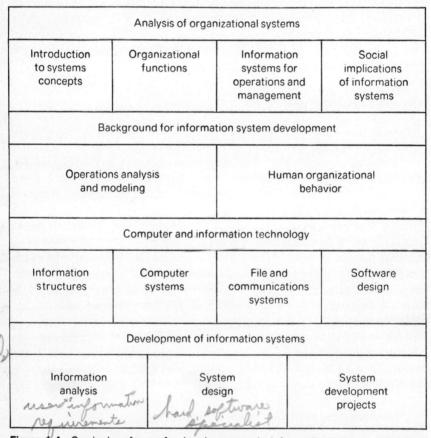

Analysis of organizational systems			
Introduction to systems concepts	Organizational functions	Information systems for operations and management	Social implications of information systems
Background for information system development			
Operations analysis and modeling		Human organizational behavior	
Computer and information technology			
Information structures	Computer systems	File and communications systems	Software design
Development of information systems			
Information analysis		System design	System development projects

Figure 1-4 Curriculum for professional program in information systems. [*Based on R. L. Ashenhurst (ed.), "A Report of the ACM Curriculum Committee on Computer Education for Management,"* Communications of the ACM, *May 1972, pp. 363–398.*]

and reflects the differing interests of these specialists. The information analyst is concerned with organizational information needs, organizational forms, and the human use of information, whereas the system designer is computer-oriented or technology-oriented. Both need a similar, basic background, although subsequent career emphasis may differ.

CONTROVERSY ABOUT MIS

The application of computer technology and MIS concepts has produced some spectacular successes and also some rather expensive failures. The reasons for the failures are generally associated with inadequate hardware/software (application attempted too much), inadequate MIS development personnel and procedures, or the lack of readiness of the user personnel and user function for the new system. The evolution of the computer-based systems has produced conflicting ideas. Some of these areas of controversy are:

1 A total system versus a federation of subsystems
2 Centralized information system resources versus decentralized processing
3 A terminal for computer access in every executive office versus staff-operated terminals
4 Readiness of managerial functions to accept and use advanced information system technology

Soon after the first use of computers for information processing (say, in the late 1950s), the idea of a total system was proposed. This was to be a single, unified system for handling all information processing and storing all information resources. The concept was similar to such MIS features as the data base system, but the current thinking in MIS is to reject the complete integration proposed by the total system as being too difficult to implement and maintain. The alternative view is a federation of subsystems which can be developed and maintained somewhat independently.[8]

The issue of centralization of information system resources is affected by computer technology, economics of centralization versus organization. Each of the following alternative views finds its advocates:

1 Centralization of all information resources

[8]H. Schwartz, "Computer Project Selection in the Business Enterprise," *Journal of Accountancy*, April 1969, pp. 35–43.

  2 Centralization of computing; decentralization of systems analysis and design

  3 Decentralization of information resources but interconnected computers (distributed systems)[9]

  4 Decentralization of information resources

Computer technology has tended, in the past, to support centralized computing, but current technology will support either centralized computing, distributed processing, or independent, decentralized computing. The economics of computing has generally favored centralized computing, but analysis of some new systems using distributed processing and systems of small, independent computers suggests that economics may not always be in favor of large, centralized computers. This point will be explored further in Chapter 9.

  Another early idea which evoked considerable discussion was for each manager to have a terminal such as a typewriter or CRT in his office to use in interrogating the computer, interacting on decision making, etc. A few systems were attempted with mixed results, but a common report was a lack of direct management use of the terminal. Managers appear to view their role as working through people.[10] By way of contrast, systems in which the terminal is used by the executive's secretary or assistant have received greater acceptance.

  The management information system is an application of new technology to the organizational problems of transaction processing and of providing information for organizational use. There is no question but that the technology has improved both the transaction processing and also much of the clerical-level handling and use of information. There are some who question whether it is desirable or even possible to design and maintain adequate computer-based information systems to support the various management planning and decision-making functions, especially strategic planning.[11] They question the value of applying advanced information technology to an ill-defined judgmental process in a primitive state of development.

  [9]Distributed systems represent decentralized activity within a network. This approach is used for processing, communication, and data bases.

  [10]Robert A. Dunlop, "Some Empirical Questions on the Man-Machine Interface Question," in Kriebel, Van Horn, and Heames, *Management Information Systems: Progress and Perspectives*, Carnegie Press, Carnegie-Mellon University, Pittsburgh, 1971, pp. 219–252.

  [11]John Dearden, "MIS Is a Mirage," *Harvard Business Review*, January–February 1972, and "Myth of Real-Time Management Information," *Harvard Business Review*, May-June 1966, pp. 123–132.

This introduction to controversy highlights the fact that MIS is an evolving concept. Many proposals have had to be altered when implemented in the imperfect world of organizations. The application of technology to information processing has achieved mixed results depending somewhat on the readiness of the organization and on the function involved to use it. There is a period of severe adjustment when an advanced technology is applied to an area having a primitive or poorly developed process. Some adaptation is necessary for both the information system and the user system. A useful historical analogy is the experience with the first application of the computer to data processing—the processing of a factory payroll. The application had severe problems because the payroll system was poorly defined and because the computer processing routines attempted to handle too many exceptions. But in a short time payroll processing became an "easy" application. The MIS for managerial planning and decision-making support is having a similar (although lengthier) experience, and there is reason to expect a similar result, which would mean that a rather complete MIS could be implemented in almost any organization.

[handwritten margin notes: MIS now at same stage as early attempts to computerize payroll with all its problems]

SUMMARY

Information is a vital ingredient to management. The information system in an organization is limited by the data that can be obtained, the cost of obtaining, processing, storing, etc., the cost of retrieval and distribution, the value of the information to the user, and the capability of humans to accept and act on the information. A computer-based management information system generally has both reduced the costs and increased the capabilities and performance of the information system. Many of the ideas of MIS are an extension of ideas proposed by managerial accounting and management science. The MIS concept extends the function of the information system well beyond the operational level to a system for providing information resources in support of the management decision and planning areas. The user of an MIS has access to an extensive data base and to a model bank consisting of analysis models, processing models, decision models, planning models, and others. The access is, for many applications, online so that response is immediate and there is a possibility of "conversation" between the user and the computer application.

[handwritten margin notes: MIS goes beyond operational areas to mgt. decision-making areas]

An MIS can be viewed structurally as consisting of hardware, software, data base, procedures and operating personnel. Subsystems can be described in terms of organizational functions (such as marketing and production) or in terms of subsystems for activities such as planning. Each functional subsystem can be viewed as containing activities subsystems related to that function.

The MIS development generally follows a master plan. Individual applications follow a development life cycle of definition, programming, and implementation. MIS development methodology is primarily trial and error. Because of the complexity of the process and use for judgment, there is a need for comprehensive academic training for MIS designers. An example of such a curriculum was presented.

There is not complete agreement as to the structure or even the value of an MIS. A few critics have labeled the systems as not cost/effective or desirable. The chapter summarized some of the controversy.

EXERCISES

1 Read several articles on MIS and develop a definition of MIS.
2 Describe the effect of applying computer technology to information systems in terms of:
    a Speed of processing and retrieval
    b Scope of information system
    c Complexity of system design and operation
3 How does MIS differ from:
    a Managerial accounting?
    b Management science?
4 Why is a data base generally a feature of an MIS?
5 Read the two articles by John Deardon (see Selected References below) and write an analysis covering the following points:
    a Valid objections
    b Irrelevant points
    c Invalid objections
    (Hint: You may wish to read the Letters to the Editor following the article "MIS Is a Mirage.")
6 Some critics of the MIS concept (see John Deardon, "Myth of Real-Time Management Information") say that management does not generally need completely up-to-date information and therefore online systems for management cannot be justified. Comment.
7 Give examples of analysis and decision models.
8 Why is the MIS developed as a federation of systems rather than as a single or total system?
9 MIS has been "pushed" by the computer technology. Explain.
10 How might the following employees be affected by a comprehensive MIS:
    a Accounts receivable clerk?
    b Sales representative?
    c Sales manager?

    d Plant manager?
    e Staff analyst for financial vice-president?
    f President?
11 What are the functional modules commonly found in an information system for:
    a A manufacturing company?
    b A department store?
12 What management activity modules might one find in a rather complete MIS?
13 Explain the difference between information analyst and computer systems designer. (Hint: Read "Curriculum Recommendations for Graduate Professional Programs in Information Systems," *Communications of the ACM*, May 1972, pp. 368–369.)
14 A person who understands all about computer hardware, software, and programming may not be suited to design a computer-based management information system. Why?
15 Summarize the alternative views of MIS with respect to:
    a Total system
    b Centralization
    c A terminal on every executive desk

SELECTED REFERENCES

report on one of these.

Aaron, J. D.: "Information Systems in Perspective," *Computing Surveys*, December 1969, pp. 213–236.

Ackoff, R. L.: "Management Misinformation Systems," *Management Science*, December 1967, pp. B.147–B.156.

Blumenthal, Sherman: *MIS—A Framework for Planning and Development*, Prentice-Hall, Inc., Englewood Cliffs, N.J., 1969.

Deardon, John: "MIS Is a Mirage," *Harvard Business Review*, January-February 1972, pp. 90–99.

———: "Myth of Real-Time Management Information," *Harvard Business Review*, May-June 1966, pp. 123–132.

Dickson, Gary W.: "Management Information Decision Systems," *Business Horizons*, December 1968, pp. 17–26.

Diebold, John: "Bad Decisions on Computer Use," *Harvard Business Review*, January-February 1969, pp. 14–28, 176.

Drucker, Peter F.: "What the Computers Will Be Telling You," *Nation's Business*, August 1966, pp. 84–90.

Gale, John R.: "Why Management Information Systems Fail," *Financial Executive*, August 1968.

Hanold, Terrance: "The Executive View of MIS," *Datamation*, November 1972.

Head, Robert V.: "Management Information Systems: A Critical Appraisal," *Datamation*, May 1967, pp. 22–27.

———: "The Elusive MIS," *Datamation*, Sept. 1, 1970, pp. 22–27.

Kelly, Joseph F.: *Computerized Management Information Systems*, The Macmillan Company, New York, 1970.

Krauss, Leonard I.: *Computer-based Management Information Systems*, American Management Association, Inc., New York, 1970.

Kreibel, C. H., R. L. Van Horn, and T. J. Heames (eds.): *Management Information Systems: Progress and Perspectives*, Carnegie Press, Carnegie-Mellon University, Pittsburgh, 1971.

Leavitt, Harold J., and Thomas L. Whisler: "Management in the 1980s," *Harvard Business Review*, November-December 1958, pp. 41–48.

Li, David H. (ed.): *Design and Management of Information Systems*, Science Research Associates, Inc., Palo Alto, Calif., 1972.

Schwartz, M. H.: "MIS Planning," *Datamation*, September 1970, pp. 28–31.

Unlocking the Computer's Profit Potential, McKinsey & Company, Inc., New York, 1968. Reprinted in *Computers and Automation*, April 1969.

"What Is a Management Information System?," research report no. 1, Society for Management Information Systems, Chicago, June 6, 1970.

"What's the Status of MIS," *EDP Analyzer*, October 1969.

Will, Hartmut J.: "MIS—Mirage or Mirror Image?," *Journal of Systems Management*, September 1973, pp. 24–31.

Withington, Frederic G.: *The Real Computer: Its Influence, Uses, and Effects*, Addison-Wesley Publishing Company, Inc., Reading, Mass., 1969.

Zani, William M.: "Blueprint for MIS," *Harvard Business Review*, November-December 1970, pp. 95–100.

Zannetos, Zenon S.: "Toward Intelligent Management Information Systems," *Industrial Management Review*, vol. 9, no. 3, 1968, pp. 21–37.

Chapter number and title	Notes on content
2 Concepts of Information	Describes various concepts relating to the meaning of information and explains attributes of information such as age and quality.
3 Humans as Information Processors	Explains a model of the human information processing system and describes various factors affecting performance.
4 System Concepts and Information Systems	A survey of system concepts with an emphasis on those concepts significant to information systems.
5 Concepts of Organization and Management Relevant to Information Systems	Highlights of major concepts of management and organization and their implication for information systems.
6 Decision-making Concepts for Information Systems	A survey of models of decision making and methods for deciding among alternatives and a discussion of their relevance to information system design.
7 Value of Information for Decision Making	A mathematical approach to the value of perfect and imperfect information.

Section One

Conceptual Foundations

What good are theories and concepts? Why not get to the part where we learn "how"? There is a very practical need for concepts and theory for problem solving. They provide a framework for thinking about and simplifying a problem. The framework assists in structuring the problem for solution and in choosing among available alternatives. Theory and concepts are very valuable in education and training. They aid in generalizing past experience and condensing it for transmission to others.

The concepts and theories underlying information systems are sometimes imprecisely defined, and the relevance of the concepts to information system analysis and design ranges from weak to strong. However, the field of information systems is embryonic, and the connection between the theoretical and the practical will certainly be strengthened as additional experience is gained and additional research is performed on the connection between theory and practice.

The section on conceptual foundations contains six chapters. For a few comments about each chapter that will aid in understanding the scope of the section, see the table on the facing page.

Chapter 2

Concepts
of Information

Management information systems deal with information, but what is information? How much information does an information system provide? There is no method for measuring the information from an information system, and the complexity of information makes it unlikely that there will ever be a formula or algorithm for computing content. However, several concepts and analogies are useful in partially answering these questions. This chapter describes various concepts related to the meaning of information and the attributes of information. It is one of three chapters dealing with information. Chapter 3 explores the capabilities of humans as information processors, and Chapter 7 explains quantitative assessment of the value of information.

DEFINITION OF INFORMATION

"Information" is an imprecise term as commonly used. It can refer to raw data, organized data, the capacity of a communication channel, etc.

info reduces uncertainty and adds value to the decision process.

However, underlying the use of the term "information" in information systems are several ideas: information adds to a representation, it has surprise value, or it tells something the receiver did not know or could not predict. In a world of uncertainty, information reduces uncertainty. It changes the probabilities attached to expected outcomes in a decision situation and therefore has value in the decision process. These statements about information are explained in this and subsequent chapters.

A useful general definition of *information* for information systems purposes is the following: *Information is data that has been processed into a form that is meaningful to the recipient and is of real or perceived value in current or prospective decisions.*

The relation of data to information is defined as that of raw material to finished product (Figure 2-1). In other words, the information processing system processes data into information. Or more precisely, the processing system processes data in unusable form into usable data that is information to the intended recipient. The analogy of raw material to finished product illustrates the concept that information for one person may be raw data for another—just as the finished product from one manufacturing division may be the raw material for another division. For example, shipping orders are information for the shipping room staff, but they are raw data for the vice-president in charge of the inventory (Figure 2-2). Because of this relation between data and information, the two words are used somewhat interchangeably.

The value of information is related to decisions. If there were no choices or decisions, information would be unnecessary. The decisions can range from simple, repetitive decisions to long-range strategic ones. The value of the information is described most meaningfully in the context of a decision. For example, the characters 3109.49 cannot be judged as to value unless the decision affected by them is known.

Data, the raw material for information, is defined as groups of

Information has value in decision-making process.

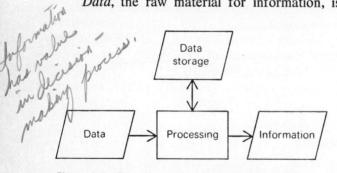

Figure 2-1 Transformation of data to information.

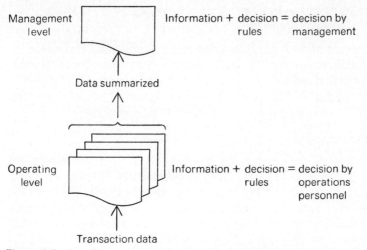

Figure 2-2 Data for one level of an organization may be information for another.

nonrandom symbols which represent quantities, actions, things, etc. Data is formed from characters. These may be alphabetic, numeric, or special symbols such as *, $, and ∼. Data is organized for processing purposes into data structures, file structures, and data bases. These concepts are reviewed in Chapter 13.

Information, in the information system sense, may have several attributes:

1 True or false. It may coincide with reality or not. If the receiver of false information believes it to be true, the effect is the same as if it were true.

2 New. It may be completely new and fresh to the recipient.

3 Incremental. It may update or add new increments to information already available.

4 Corrective. It may be a correction of past false information.

5 Confirmatory. It may confirm existing information. This is still valuable because it increases the recipient's perception of the correctness of the information.

In summary, then, the terms "data" and "information" are often used interchangeably, but there is a distinction in that data is the raw material that is processed to provide information. Information is associated with decision making, and for this reason information can be considered as at a higher, more active level than data.

INFORMATION IN THE MATHEMATICAL THEORY OF COMMUNICATION

[handwritten annotation: Info theory is the math theory of communication or how accurately it can be transmitted]

The term "information theory" is often used to mean the mathematical theory of communication. The mathematical theory has direct applications in mechanical and electronic communication systems. It is limited in its practical use for management information systems. Nevertheless, the theory does provide insight into the nature of information.

Historical Development

Information theory was suggested by Norbert Weiner, a well-known mathematician, as a result of his study of cybernetics.[1] Weiner's contention was that any organism is held together by the possession of means for acquisition, use, retention, and transmission of information. Claude Shannon of Bell Laboratories developed and applied concepts to explain communications systems, such as the telephone systems.[2] In the context of the Shannon work and most subsequent study, information theory has developed primarily as a mathematical theory of communication.

The problems of information communication in information systems can be considered in terms of three levels:

1 Technical level. How accurately can information be transmitted?
2 Semantic level. How precisely do the transmitted symbols convey the desired meaning?
3 Effectiveness level. How suitable is the message as a motivation of human action?

The mathematical theory of communication deals with the technical level and does not consider meaning or effectiveness.

Model of a Communication System

A simple model of a communication system takes the following form:

There is a transmitter which provides coded symbols sent through a channel to a receiver. The message which comes from a source to the

[1]Norbert Weiner, *Cybernetics, or Control and Communication in the Animal and the Machine*, John Wiley & Sons, Inc., New York, 1948.
[2]Claude E. Shannon, "A Mathematical Theory of Communication," *Bell System Technical Journal*, 1948, pp. 379–423, 623–659.

transmitter is generally encoded by a transmitter before it can be sent through the communications channel and must be decoded by a receiver before it can be understood by the destination. The channel is not usually a perfect conduit for the coded message because of noise and distortion. These features are shown in the following expanded diagram of a communications system:

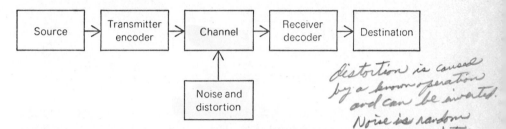

Distortion is caused by a known operation and can be inverted.

Noise is random interference.

There is a distinction between noise and distortion. Distortion is caused by a known (even intentional) operation and can be corrected by an inverse operation. Noise is random or unpredictable interference. The purpose of a communications system is to reproduce at the destination a message selected at the source. There is a set of possible messages to be transmitted. For example, each of the letters and numerals is a possible message to be transmitted by a Teletype. Each sound, inflection, pitch, etc., of the human voice is a message in the telephone system. Suppose a message, "Now is the time for all good men to pray," is spoken over the telephone and also sent by Teletype. The message is the same, but the information transmission capacity required is substantially different (probably by a factor of over 500 to 1). The meaning of information in the theory of communication will help explain this difference.

Mathematical Definition of Information

As used in the mathematical theory of communication, information has a very precise meaning. It is the average number of binary digits which must be transmitted to identify a given message from the set of all possible messages to which it belongs. In other words, the theory says that there are a limited number of messages which may need to be transmitted. It is therefore possible to devise a different code to identify each message. The message to be transmitted is encoded, the codes are sent over the channel, and the decoder identifies the message intended by the codes. Messages can be defined in a variety of ways. For example, each alphanumeric character may be a message or complete sentences may be messages if there is a limited, predefined number of such sentences to be transmitted.

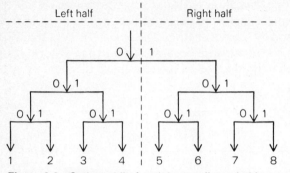

Figure 2-3 Code mobile for eight equally probable messages.

The size of the code is of course dependent on the coding scheme and the number of possible messages. The coding scheme for information theory is assumed to be binary. This is convenient for several reasons including the fact that most machine communication uses a binary code based on two states of the signal being transmitted. One bit is defined as the amount of information required to identify one of two equally probable messages. In other words, if the communication system is required to respond to only two messages, "yes" or "no," then the system needs to transmit only two possible signals, which can be represented by 1 and 0, the two values in the binary system. As another example, assume a system used to transmit only birthday greetings. However, the sender may not write his own greeting—he may select from only several standard messages such as "Wishing you happiness on your birthday." Now, assuming that there are eight such messages, the information content to identify the message for the receiver is 3 bits. This is shown by a code mobile in Figure 2-3. Note that the first bit identifies the message as being in the left half or the right half. The second bit identifies the half of the half identified by the first bit, etc. The resulting codes are:

Message no.	Bits
1	000
2	001
3	010
4	011
5	100
6	101
7	110
8	111

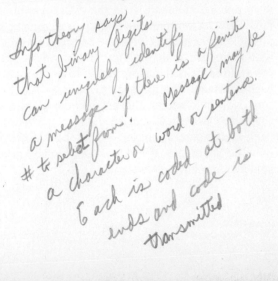

Note that a separate unique code of three 0s and 1s identifies each message and distinguishes it from the other seven, and that the decoder receives the bits from left to right.

The information content (or code size in bits) may be generalized as: *required bit code size*

$$I = \log_2 n \qquad log_2 n \; says \qquad n = 2^I$$

where n = the number of possible messages and all messages are equally
        likely

To understand the application of this formula, consider some examples
where n = 8
    n = 2
    n = 1
    n = 27

(1) n = 8 $I = \log_2 8 = 3$

This is the same as the example of eight birthday greetings where it was shown that 3 bits would be needed.

(2) n = 2 $I = \log_2 2 = 1$

If there are only two outcomes, a single bit (0 or 1 value) can identify which of the two is intended.

(3) n = 1 $I = \log_2 1 = 0$

If there is only one message to select from, there is no need to transmit anything because the answer is already known.

(4) n = 27 $I = \log_2 27 = 4.75$

If the set of messages is the alphabet plus a space symbol, the minimum code will average 4.75 bits per letter, assuming all letters to be equally probable.

The last example of the information content of a code for the alphabet can be used to illustrate the effect on the code when the messages (alphabetic characters plus space in this case) to be transmitted are not equally likely. If each of the 27 characters were equally likely, each would appear 1/27 of the time or with a probability of .037. But letters do not occur with equal frequency. The probability of occurrence for a few letters illustrates the wide difference in English text:

Letter	Probability
A	.0642
B	.0127
E	.1031
J	.0008
Space	.1859

Use of a short code for common letters and the space and a longer code for the letters occurring less frequently (much like the Morse code) reduces the average code size (average information) required to transmit alphabetic text. A code for the five characters in the example is shown in Figure 2-4 by an asymmetrical code mobile.

If the messages are not equally likely, as in the case of the alphabet, the information required to identify a message will be different for each one—short codes for common characters and long codes for uncommon characters. The information (average) is the sum of the probability times the $\log_2$ of 1/probability for each item. This is stated as:

$$I = \sum_{i=1}^{n} p_i \log_2 \frac{1}{p_i}$$

A computationally equivalent form is $I = -\sum_{i=1}^{n} p_i \log_2 p_i$

As an example, assume four messages. If they were all equally likely, the

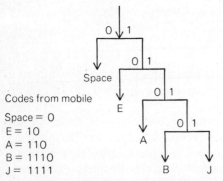

Codes from mobile

Space = 0
E = 10
A = 110
B = 1110
J = 1111

Figure 2-4 Asymmetric code mobile to provide shorter codes for more common characters.

formula $\log_2$ n would yield an answer of 2. If the probabilities were unequal (say, .50, .25, .15, and .10), the computation would be as follows:

Event	Probability of the event	$\log_2 p_i$	$p_i \log_2 p_i$
1	.50	−1.00	− .50
2	.25	−2.00	− .50
3	.15	−2.74	− .41
4	.10	−3.32	− .33
			= −1.74

$$I = -\sum p_i \log p_i = 1.74$$

Even though there are still four messages, the average number of bits needed is less than if they are equally probable. This is intuitively correct.

The emphasis so far has been on the coding scheme, but notice that the formula for information specifies how much information is required to tell something the receiver did not already know or could not predict with certainty. Information in this sense might be termed as having "surprise" or "news" value.

Information reduces uncertainty. Given a set of messages, the receiver does not know which one (is uncertain) until information is received. Partial information will reduce the uncertainty but not eliminate it. For example, in the case of the eight birthday messages, 3 bits are required to eliminate uncertainty completely by identifying the exact message. However, a single bit reduces the number of possible messages to be considered and therefore reduces uncertainty. In the case of eight codes, four will start with 0 and four with 1. A single bit reduces the possibilities from eight to four.

Another example may assist in understanding the effect of partial information. If a decision maker has 10 courses of action (say, 10 job

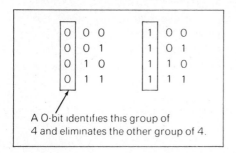

A 0-bit identifies this group of
4 and eliminates the other group of 4.

applicants to choose from)[3] and they all appear to be equally qualified, the probability that a single individual is most qualified is 1/10, or .10. Information which positively identifies the best candidate has a value of 3.32 bits ($\log_2$ 10). However, a message such as an aptitude test which reduces the selection from 10 candidates to 4 has an information value of 1.32. This is computed as the difference between the information needed to select from 10 (3.32) and the information needed to select from 4 (2.0).

The more uncertainty exists, the more information is required. For example, a message consisting of random alphabetic characters contains more information than an English text because the random set is completely unpredictable (I = 4.75) and the English text is somewhat predictable. Shannon estimated that the average number of bits required to encode English text would be only 1 bit per letter if each code was based on groups of letters rather than single letters.

Entropy

The term *entropy* has been borrowed from thermodynamics. It describes the relative disorder or randomness in a system. Information is a measure of order in a system and is the opposite of entropy; it reduces uncertainty and therefore reduces entropy. However, the formula for information is frequently termed the "entropy function." The reason is that since information is required to reduce uncertainty (disorder), the amount of information required is also a measure of the disorder or entropy to be reduced. *if greater level of entropy, more information required*

Redundancy

A communication is rarely if ever completely composed of information. There are usually redundant elements. Redundancy sounds bad because it indicates unnecessary elements. However, some redundancy is desirable for error control. In the model of a communication system, there was noise in the channel. This means that the received message may not be exactly as sent. The transmission of redundant data allows the receiver to check whether the received message is correct and may allow him to reconstruct the correct message. Suppose, for example, a message dealing with the history of the United States was partially intermixed with noise so that only the following came through to the receiver (* stands for an undetermined character):

T** F**ST PR***DE*T O* THE UN***D S**T** *E**** **SH*NG***

[3]Example adapted from Charles L. Bostwick, "The Use of Information Theory in Accounting," *Management Accounting*, June 1968, pp. 11–17.

The fact that the reader immediately perceives the sentence as reading "The first president of the United States George Washington" indicates that the original message was highly redundant. In fact, the garbled message is still redundant. The redundancy means that the listener need not hear and decode every sound in order to understand the message.

Error-detecting codes using parity bits make use of redundancy to detect and also to correct errors in transmission (Figure 2-5). There are a large number of possible codes so that the communication engineer can design the codes to achieve a specified level of accurate transmission.

Redundancy in coding is easily computed as the percentage of the information coding capability not being used.

$$R = 1 - \frac{I_n}{I_m}$$

n = # of messages to code

where I_n = information capacity needed $= \log_2 n$
I_m = information capacity of code

For example, a code of 6 bits which can code 64 possibilities might be used even though there are only 16 possibilities to code.

$I_n = \log_2 16 = 4$ *only need 4 bits to encode 16 messages*
$I_m = \log_2 64 = 6$ *use 6, so get 2/6 redundancy*
$R = 1 - \dfrac{4}{6} = \dfrac{1}{3}$ or .33 redundancy

Suppose there are four equally likely possibilities. A selection requires an average of 2 bits ($\log_2 4 = 2$). However, if they are not equally likely, a 2-bit code would be slightly redundant.

Outcome	P_i	$\log p_i$	$P_i \log_2 p_i$
1	.20	−2.32	− .46
2	.30	−1.74	− .53
3	.40	−1.32	− .53
4	.10	−3.3	− .33
			= −1.85 I = 1.85

redundancy in code used for parity/error checking in transmission.

$R = 1 - \dfrac{1.85}{2.00} = .08$ or
8 percent redundancy in
use of 2-bit code
for this data

Case 1 Simple parity bit to detect errors

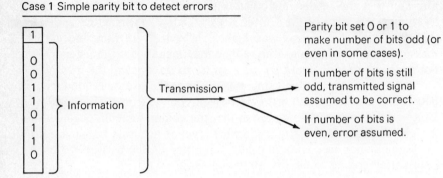

Parity bit set 0 or 1 to make number of bits odd (or even in some cases).

If number of bits is still odd, transmitted signal assumed to be correct.

If number of bits is even, error assumed.

Case 2 Row and column parity to detect and correct errors

Longitudinal parity check by character

1	1	0	1	0	0
0	0	0	1	1	1
0	1	1	0	0	1
1	0	1	0	0	1
1	0	0	1	1	0
0	1	1	0	1	0
1	1	0	1	0	0
1	0	1	0	1	0
0	1	1	1	1	1

Row parity check of block

Combination of row and longitudinal parity. This allows specific error bit to be isolated and corrected.

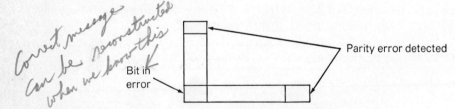

Correct message can be reconstructed when we know this

Bit in error

Parity error detected

Figure 2-5   Use of parity bits in error detection and correction.

DATA REDUCTION

The constraints on information systems and on humans as data processors require that various means be used to reduce the quantity of data stored or presented for human use (Figure 2-6). These methods are classification and compression, organizational summarizing and filtering, and inference.

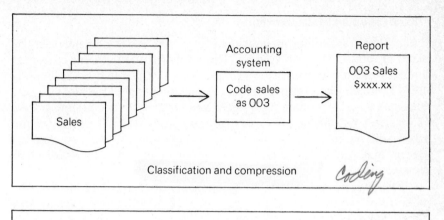

Classification and compression   *Coding*

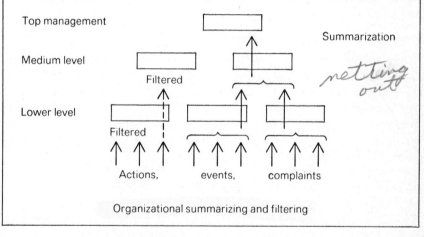

Organizational summarizing and filtering

netting out

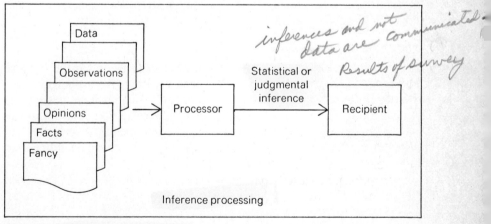

Inference processing

inferences and not data are communicated. Results of survey

Figure 2-6 Data reduction methods.

Classification and Compression

amt of compression depends on level of decision-maker

Rather than transmitting all individual data items, the system may classify items to reduce the data volume. The totals for the different classifications represent a compression of data. This is illustrated by accounting classifications. The president of an organization cannot normally review each sale to get information for decisions. Instead, the accounting system summarizes all sales into a "sales for the period" total. This may be too gross and obscure the information for decision purposes so that the system may provide sales by product group, geographical area, or other classification.

The level of summarization is dependent on the level of the decision maker. For example, the president may need only the total sales by area but the sales manager for the area may need sales by sales representative and sales by product.

Organizational Summarizing and Filtering

do not want signals filtered out by intermediaries but do want org. filt. & summing to take place

The accounting system classifies and compresses transaction data required for accounting purposes, but many other transactions and events have a bearing (i.e., are information) for decision making. Customer attitudes as perceived by the salesmen, changing policies of government regulatory agencies, and financial condition of major suppliers are examples. These "messages" are summarized in various ways as they move up the organization, the efficiency of communication depending on the organizational methods for eliciting the data and the communication channel provided for them. Unless there is a formal procedure to classify, summarize, and transmit them to the decision makers, the signals may be filtered out by intermediate organizational elements. For example, customer complaints of salesmen's tactics in a sales district may be blocked by the district sales manager who does not wish the criticism to reflect on him and who may feel he can remedy the situation himself.

Need summary but do not want "filtering" out of messages imp to decisions want filter to reduce load to next level if dec can be made at this level

Inferences

eliminate individual data variances and make assertions about the groups.

March and Simon[4] use the term *uncertainty absorption* for the form of data reduction that occurs when inferences are drawn from a body of data and the inferences instead of the data itself is communicated in the organization. This results in substantial data reduction. The inference may be based on quantitative data such as information from questionnaires on employees or may be more subjective inferences reflecting a set

[4]James G. March and Herbert A. Simon, *Organizations*, John Wiley & Sons, Inc., New York, 1958, pp. 164–169.

receiver ~~and tool~~ must have some confidence level in inferences from raw data

of nonreproducible inputs to the inferential process. An example of the latter might be an inferential message regarding the anticipated role of the Federal Antitrust Division in mergers during the coming period. The reason for terming this "absorption of uncertainty" is that the data has uncertainty associated with it, but the recipient of the inference information is removed from the original data and must, for practical purposes, rely on the inference itself. However, note that he or she may have a subjective estimate of the confidence to be placed in the inference based on knowledge of the source, methods, etc.

QUALITY OF INFORMATION   *affected by bias and error*

In a study by Adams[5] of management attitudes toward information systems, 75 managers rated quantity and quality improvements as nearly identical in terms of impact on job performance; yet given a choice 90 percent preferred an improvement in quality of information over an increase in quantity. Information varies in quality because of bias or errors. Bias is illustrated by the example of a sales representative who tends to overestimate expected sales or who quotes unrealistic delivery dates. If the bias is known to the receiver of the information, he or she can adjust for it. The problem is to detect the bias; the adjustment is generally fairly simple.   *Can adjust for bias if known;*

Error is a more serious problem because there is no simple adjustment for it. Errors may be a result of: *error adjustment usually not possible.*

6 major sources of data error

1 Incorrect data measurement and collection methods
2 Failure to follow correct processing procedures
3 Loss or nonprocessing of data
4 Wrong recording or correcting data
5 Incorrect history (master) file (or use of wrong history file)
6 Mistakes in processing procedure (such as computer program mistakes)
7 Deliberate falsification   *good syst design should attack these sources of error*

In most information systems, the receiver of information has no knowledge of either bias or errors that may affect its quality. The measurement processes which produce reports and the precision of data in the reports imply a precision that is not warranted. For example, an

[5]Carl R. Adams, "Attitudes of Top Management Users toward Information Systems and Computers," working paper 73-07, The Management Information Systems Research Center, University of Minnesota, Minneapolis, September 1973, p. 4.

inventory report may indicate that there are 347 widgets in stock. However, this figure is probably based on a perpetual, book inventory; various errors in recording inventory issues, receipts, etc., mean that in a significant number of cases there is a small error, and in a few cases, a large error. This is the reason for periodic physical counts to correct the book inventory. The difficulties due to bias may be handled in information processing by procedures to detect and measure bias and to adjust for it. The difficulties with errors may be overcome by:

1   Internal controls to detect errors
2   Internal and external auditing
3   Addition of "confidence limits" to data
4   User instruction in measurement and processing procedures so users can evaluate possible errors

auditing and controls help to limit errors in data

There is a difference in the effect of the first two and the last two error remedies. The last two remedies attempt to provide the user with confidence limits, whereas the first two methods attempt to reduce the uncertainty about the data and therefore increase the information content. Internal controls and auditing can be thought of in this context as adding value to the information being provided by the information system by reducing the uncertainty about the existence of most errors. The control and audit procedures do not tend to affect either bias or the errors due to the methods of measurement and data collection.

The way that data is presented will influence or bias the way it is used. For example, if a portfolio manager requests lists of stocks with rates of return greater than 5 percent, the stocks may be presented in different ways. The manager's approach to decision making is likely to be influenced by the presentation. To illustrate, consider three alternatives and possible biases to decision making.

often list is used in sequence printed and "top" of list gets more attention

Form of presentation	Decision bias caused by data presentation
Alphabetical order	In an alphabetical list of any length, the first items will tend to receive more attention than the later items.
Order by rate of return	The items with the highest rate of return will be emphasized with less regard for industry, size, etc.
Order by rate of return within industry	Rate of return and industry will be emphasized. Size, etc., will have less influence.

AGE OF INFORMATION

This section explores the attribute of age of information with respect to information contained in periodic reports,[6] such as the monthly operating report and the statement of financial position at the end of a period. Two types of data are defined:

1 Condition data which pertains to a point in time such as December 31. An example is the inventory at 12/31/73 as reported on the balance sheet.

2 Operating data which reflects changes during a period of time. Examples are inventory used during a month or sales for a week.

An information interval (i) is defined as the interval between reports. For weekly reports, the information interval is one week; for monthly reports, one month. The reporting delay (d) is defined as the processing delay between the end of the information interval and the issuance of the report for management use. By use of these two variables, the maximum, average, and minimum age of information in management reports is defined as follows and in Figure 2-7:

[handwritten annotations: a point in time; continuous period; d is delay between end of interval i and date report is issued for use.; age depends on type of info whether condition or operating and d and i.]

	Condition information	Operating information
Maximum age	$d + i$	$d + 1\frac{1}{2} i$
Average age	$d + \frac{1}{2} i$	$d + i$
Minimum age	d	$d + \frac{1}{2} i$

where i = information interval between reports
      d = processing delay

The formulas for condition information say that the minimum age is the processing delay. If the delay is five days, the inventory figure for September 15 will be at least five days old before it is received on September 20. The maximum age of condition information is the delay plus the processing interval. If the inventory reports are issued weekly (the information interval is seven days) and the processing delay is five days, the age of the information on hand just prior to receiving a new

---

[6]This section is based on an article by Robert H. Gregory and Thomas V. V. Atwater, Jr., "Cost and Value of Management Information as Functions of Age," *Accounting Research*, vol. 8, no. 1, January 1957, pp. 42–70. The journal is no longer published.

reports issued

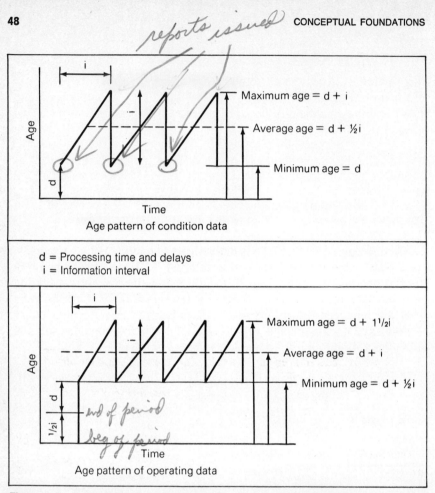

Figure 2-7 Patterns for age of information. (*Adapted from Robert H. Gregory and Thomas V. V. Atwater, Jr., "Cost and Value of Management Information as Functions of Age,"* Accounting Research, *vol. 8, no. 1, January 1957, pp. 49, 51.*)

report is 7 + 5. In other words, the September 15 inventory figure must be used until a new report is issued for the 22d (but not available until the 29th). The average age of the condition information is the processing delay plus one-half of the information interval. Since the inventory report in the example is in use from the 20th to the 29th and it was five days old when received, the average age during its use was 5 + (7/2) = 8½.

The operating information is accumulated during a period of time. For example, the sales for a period consist of those made the first day of the period, the second day, etc. The average age of operating information accumulated during an information interval is therefore one-half of the

operating information represents a period of time (accumulated) from beg to end of period and is always ½ i or period "old". with delay d min age is d + ½ i

operating ~~data~~ info always $\frac{1}{2}i$ > condition data

interval. The operating information for a 10-day period thus has an average of five days ($\frac{1}{2}i$) at the close of the interval. Since it will be d days (the processing delay) until the information is available, the minimum age is d + $\frac{1}{2}i$. The age of operating data under these assumptions is always half an interval greater than the age of condition information.

The practical processing limitations under manual and electromechanical data processing systems made it desirable to use regular information intervals, such as a month, for the major financial reports and a shorter period, such as a week, for some operating reports. The computer removes many of the processing restrictions on both the interval and the delay. Note that the age of information available to management can be altered by changing i, d, or both.

computer can reduce both

The delay for computer processing depends on the methodology. For batch processing, the batch may be accumulated for a day, a week, or other period before being processed. It may be possible to obtain some condition data such as inventory balance with very little delay, but it is out of date; i.e., it has an age equal to the time since the last update. On the average, this will be half of the batch processing interval. So, for inquiry access to condition data under batch processing, the average age will be one-half batch interval plus delay in processing the inquiry. Given this analysis, a system of immediate access to a data base updated weekly does not seem to make sense. The age of condition data on regular, periodic reports will be the same as previously explained.

d and i in information systems

small i large d no good in inquiry

For online processing, there is no batch delay. Data is processed as received, which usually is when the transaction is occurring. The batch delay is therefore 0. An inquiry for condition data is generally processed with very little delay so that d is very small. Technically, the computer system allows i to be varied for operating data and allows condition data to be available at any point in time subject only to very small processing delays. The fact that regular reports are issued at regular intervals even when these capabilities exist is probably due to reasons such as the following:

1 Management decisions are not sensitive to short intervals.
2 The capabilities for irregular intervals have not been implemented.
3 Management personnel find periodic reports more useful.

The most important concept for information system design relative to the age of information is the impact of both the information interval and the processing delay. Much attention has been focused on the minimum age of information, but the average age is probably more

re-read

significant. Computer data processing has concentrated to a great extent on reducing the processing delay by realtime processing while not much emphasis has been placed on the impact of the information interval.

APPLICATION OF INFORMATION CONCEPTS
TO INFORMATION SYSTEM DESIGN

The chapter has outlined the concept of information in information theory, data reduction, quality of information, and age of information. This section summarizes the application of these concepts to information system design.

The mathematics of information theory has been applied in communication system design. The mathematics does not apply in the more complex management information system environment, but the insights provided by the theory are several:

1 Information has surprise value.
2 Information reduces uncertainty.
3 There is no information unless there is choice. *has decision value; no choice — no decision*
4 Not all data that is communicated has information value.
5 Redundancy is useful for error control of communication.

The basic model of a communication system in information theory is more complicated when humans are included. The humans are goal-directed self-adaptive systems, which, of course, makes them more difficult to describe than a hardware communication system.

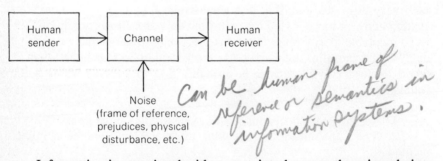

Human sender → Channel → Human receiver

Noise *Can be human frame of reference or semantics in information systems.*
(frame of reference, prejudices, physical disturbance, etc.)

Information is associated with uncertainty because there is a choice to be made and the correct choice is uncertain. The reason for having information is to reduce uncertainty so the correct choice can be made. If there is no uncertainty, there would not be a need for information to influence the choice. The basis of choice is the relative efficiency of alternative courses of action. Information received will modify the choice by altering the subjective estimate of the probability of success.

If a receiver is in a decision-making situation, it is easy to understand the definition of information as being messages which modify the decision maker's probabilities as to the success of possible actions. But much data is received and stored without reference to decisions being made. Mathematical information theory has no explanation for data not related to a choice. Two views are possible: (1) There is no information content until there is a choice, or (2) there is information content if there is expected use for potential choice. The second view is close to the information system view that information is data that is meaningful to the recipient and is of real or perceived value in current or prospective decisions. *— There must still be choice*

The existence of noise is explicitly defined in communication theory. Redundancy is used to ensure correct receipt of the transmitted message. In management information systems, there is substantial noise due to the differing backgrounds of humans, differing frames of reference, varying prejudice, level of attention, physical differences in ability to hear, see, and other causes. Redundancy can be effectively used to overcome noise and improve the probability of the message being received and interpreted correctly.

The need for data reduction has resulted in various mechanisms, all of which are relevant to the design of processing systems—classification and compression, organizational summarizing and filtering, and inferences. These methods reduce the volume of data storage and especially reduce the amount of data transmitted to human receivers.

The information quality concepts apply to information system design in the provision of methods to detect and adjust for bias and methods to detect, control, and reduce errors.

The concepts relating to age of information introduce the idea of condition data measured at a point in time and operating data which cover a period of time. The concepts of an information interval plus a processing delay are important to information system design because the age of information is related to both factors and not just to the processing delay. The concept of information interval is also a useful one when considering more flexible computer-based systems.

SUMMARY

This chapter has been devoted to exploring concepts of information. Information theory is more properly termed the mathematical theory of communication, but it does provide some useful insights for management information systems. It emphasizes the fact that the need for information arises from uncertainty and choice and the role of information is to reduce uncertainty.

Methods of data reduction were described. These are classification and compression, organizational summarizing and filtering, and inferences. The quality of information is affected by bias and error. Information systems can be designed to detect and adjust for bias and to detect, control, or compensate for error.

The concepts of age of information point out the relation of information interval, the type of data, and the processing delay in determining the age of information.

The relevance of the information concepts to information system design is primarily in the insight which they provide. The state of the theory does not provide quantitative application of the ideas.

EXERCISES

1   The code of Paul Revere was "one if by land and two if by sea." Changing the conditions slightly, assume that Paul Revere had lanterns which could show either red or green. He would have then used one lantern and "red if by land and green if by sea." If the British could take many routes, tell how many lanterns (each with red and green) he would need to signal the route taken if there were:

[handwritten: $i = 2$]
[handwritten: $i = 4.39$]
[handwritten: $i = 4.91$]

   a   4 routes.   *[handwritten: $i = \log_2 m$]*
   b   20 routes.   *[handwritten: 5 lanterns   some redundancy because $2^5 = 32$]*
   c   30 routes.
   Show codes for each.

2   Assume the same facts as in question 1 but that Paul Revere and the receiver agree to include some redundancy in the message so that the receiver could make sure he has received it properly. Indicate how an additional lantern could serve this purpose. (Hint: This can be a parity-type code.)

[handwritten: use 3 lanterns, first as parity, always done, even # of green (4 possibilities)]

3   Assume a set of six possible messages identified by the letters A, B, C, D, E, or F.

   a   Develop a minimum-size binary code to identify the six messages. (Hint: Make a code mobile.)

   b   What is the average number of bits which must be transmitted to select from the six messages using the code from (a)?   *[handwritten: $16/6 \cdot = 2.67$]*

   c   Assuming that the six messages are equally probable, use the formula $H = \log_2 n$ to determine the average information required. The $\log_2$ for 1 to 8 are given below for your use. If your answers to (b) and (c) are different, account for the difference.   *[handwritten: log formula contemplates continuous not discrete]*

[handwritten: $i = \log_2 6$ $i = 2.58$]

No.	$\log_2$	No.	$\log_2$
1	0.2	5	2.32
2	1	6	2.58
3	1.585	7	2.81
4	2.0	8	3.0

[handwritten diagram: a binary tree mobile]

[handwritten tree showing branches labeled 0 and 1 leading to leaves A, B, C, D, E, F]

[handwritten: $A = 000$]
[handwritten: $B = 001$]
[handwritten: $C = 01$ etc]
[handwritten: $D = 10$]
[handwritten: $E = 110$]
[handwritten: $F = 111$]
[handwritten: 16 bits in set]

d Assume that the probabilities of the different messages are not the same; develop the most efficient code. (Hint: Make an asymmetrical code mobile.)

Message	Probability
A	.10 _/ / / 0_
B	.25 _10_
C	.40 _short code_ 0
D	.20 _/ / 0_
E	.03 _/ / / / 0_
F	.02 _long code_ / / / / /

e What is the average information that must be transmitted using the revised code in (d)?

f Apply the formula for unequal probabilities to compute the average information required to identify the messages:

$$I = -\sum_{i=1}^{n} p_i \log_2 p_i$$

The base-2 logs of the probabilities are:

Probability	log$_2$	Probability	log$_2$
.10	−3.32	.20	−2.32
.25	−2.00	.03	−5.06
.40	−1.32	.02	−5.64

Account for differences between the answer obtained for H and the answer in (e).

4 Define the following terms as used in information theory:
  a Information. _Data with decision value_
  b Channel. _Carrier of coded messages_
  c Noise. _random interference_
  d Redundancy. _elements not required to understand message_
5 Explain how information reduces uncertainty.
6 How can a transmission of a set of random digits contain more information than a transmission of text from a book? _text is predictable and somewhat redundant_
7 How is entropy related to information? Why is the formula $I = -\sum p_i \log_2 p_i$ often referred to as the "entropy function"?
8 Assume a parlor game in which you are trying to guess the content of a short English language sentence. The sentence is not gibberish but neither is it a well-known sentence. Just pick sentences from a textbook or a novel. For (a) and (b) the letters should be mixed up rather than being asked in word order. You are allowed to ask questions that can be answered with only "yes" or "no." Play the game with three different strategies:

a Attempt to learn each letter without regard to the context. In effect, assume that the letters are random and all occur with the same probability. (Hint: Ask questions such as, "Is the letter before M and after G?")

b Assume that the letters occur randomly but with the probability found in English given below. Alter the questioning to take this into account.

		Total
Over 8%	Space, E	29%
5 to 8%	A, I, N, O, S, T	38%
3 to 4.9%	D, H, L, R	16%
Less than 3%	15 others	17%

c Assume the frequencies in (b) above plus a meaningful text.

(1) Write down the questions you should ask (in order of use) for each of (a), (b), and (c).

(2) Keep statistics on the number of questions required to obtain an answer.

(3) What is the theoretical average number of questions for (a) and (b), assuming that probabilities and logs are:

	Probability	$\log_2$
Space	.18	−2.5
E	.10	−3.3
A, I, N, O, S, T	.07 each	−3.8
D, H, L, R	.04 each	−4.7
Others	.01 each	−6.6

9 The game of Twenty Questions is based on "yes" and "no" answers. Assuming equal probability, how many different items can there be for which 20 questions will allow one of the items to be identified?

10 Compute redundancy in the following cases:

a An 8-bit code is used to encode 58 alphanumerics ($\log_2 58 = 5.86$).

b A 3-bit code is used to encode five possibilities with the following probabilities. The logs of the probabilities are also given.

Outcome	P	$\log_2 P$
A	.10	−3.32
B	.25	−2.00
C	.40	−1.32
D	.15	−2.74
E	.10	−3.32

11 The double-entry system of accounting records the dual effect of transactions. It is said to be quite redundant. If it is really redundant, what kind of system performance would be expected with regard to (a) error detection and (b) ability to reconstruct results from partial records? How do the expected characteristics compare with actual characteristics of accounting?

12 What assumption about flow of data is necessary to have the age of operating data equal $1/2i$ at the end of the information interval? *Constant over interval i*

13 Write formulas for minimum, average, and maximum age of inquiry data obtained from a file that is updated by periodic batch processing. The inquiry may specify either operating or condition data and may specify the information interval for operating data.

14 How does online realtime updating affect age of information for monthly reports? *Is reduced to 0 or negligible but i unaffected* *min = 0 ave = 1/2 i max = i*

15 When asked where Bill was, John answered, "He is pressing a suit." Explain what Bill is doing if (a) he is a tailor or (b) he is a lawyer. Explain how frame of reference affects our perception, using this case as an example. *introduces bias and may block or filter info*

16 Why do errors in perception have the opposite effect as information?

17 Are individual filters (i.e., filters by individuals) good or bad for an organizational information system? Explain. *reduces info load to next level up - good may stop important decision info - bad* *increase uncertainty*

18 What are the advantages and the disadvantages for information communication of the following:
a Classification and compression.
b Organizational summarizing and filtering.
c Inferences.

19 A detailed examination was made of 1,000 credit histories. The analysis of the data is reported to management in the following statements: "There is a .95 probability of a credit applicant becoming a delinquent account if he receives less than a score of 50 on the credit application rating. Only 1 percent of those scoring 64 or above become delinquent. . . ." Explain why these inferences constitute uncertainty absorption. *(also reduction) many data elements in a few info messages, eliminate individual variances and make group assertions*

20 Explain how the concepts of this chapter apply to (or explain) the following situations:
a A decision maker who says, "Don't bother me with the facts; my mind is made up."
b A decision maker who will not make a decision without more information.
c A president of a company who feels the need to go out and mingle with customers and suppliers in order to make good decisions.
d A president who complains that he is receiving much data from his government intelligence office which does not make sense—it does not seem to apply to him and his company.

SELECTED REFERENCES

Bedford, N. M., and M. Ousi: "Measuring the Value of Information—An Information Theory Approach," *Management Services*, January-February 1966, pp. 15–22

Bello, Francis: "The Information Theory," *Fortune*, December 1953, pp. 136–141.

Broadbent, D. E.: *Decision and Stress*, Academic Press, London, 1971.

Cherry, Colin: *On Human Communication*, The M.I.T. Press, Cambridge, Mass., 1957. Discusses information concepts in broader context.

Emery, James C.: *Organizational Planning and Control Systems*, The Macmillan Company, New York, 1969.

Etz, D. V.: "The Marginal Utility of Information," *Datamation*, August 1965, pp. 41–44.

Feltham, Gerald A.: "The Value of Information," *The Accounting Review*, October 1968, pp. 684–696.

———, and Joel S. Demski: "The Use of Models in Information Evaluation," *The Accounting Review*, October 1970, pp. 623–640.

Gilbert, E. N.: "Information Theory after Eighteen Years," *Science*, vol. 152, April 1966, pp. 320ff.

Goldstein, H. S.: "Information Theory," *Science*, vol. 133, May 1961, pp. 1395–1399.

Gregory, Robert H., and Thomas V. V. Atwater, Jr.: "Cost and Value of Management Information as Functions of Age," *Accounting Research*, vol. 8, no. 1, January 1957, pp. 42–70.

Peterson, Wesley W.: "Error-correcting Codes," *Scientific American*, vol. 206, May 1963, pp. 96–108.

Raisbeck, Gordon: *Information Theory*, The M.I.T. Press, Cambridge, Mass., 1964. Good, short coverage. Moderately mathematical.

Shannon, Claude E., and Warren Weaver: *The Mathematical Theory of Communication*, The University of Illinois Press, Urbana, 1962.

Chapter 3

Humans as Information Processors

Management information systems are man/machine systems. The MIS designs tend to tie the decision maker very closely to the machine processing system, and clerical functions are performed in a manner dictated by computer requirements. The human is thus a significant element in the information processing system. An understanding of human capabilities as information processors is important to information system design. This chapter describes both a general model and the Newell-Simon model of the human as an information processor. It also describes some tentative limits on human processing and on human perception of differences. A discussion of the effect of data compression on human performance and the psychological value of unused data furnishes a possible explanation of otherwise irrational data use, data collection, and storage.

BASIC MODEL

A simple model of the human as an information processor consists of sensory receptors (eyes, ears, nose, etc.) that pick up signals and transmit

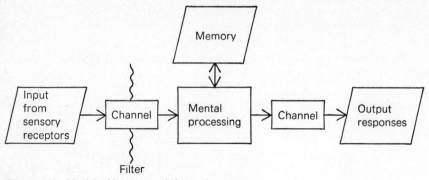

Figure 3-1 Model of human as information processor.

them to the processing unit (brain with storage). The results of the processing are output responses (physical, spoken, written, etc.). This model is diagrammed in Figure 3-1.

The capacity of the human to accept inputs and produce outputs (responses) is limited. When the human processing system is overloaded, the response rate can decrease. A simple experiment of human ability to respond to musical tones resulted in Figure 3-2. Note that up to the information overload point, each input resulted in an output. For exam-

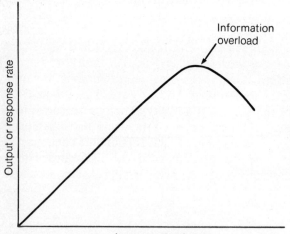

Figure 3-2 Performance of human as information processor. (*Adapted from Harry H. Good, "Greenhouse of Science for Management,"* Management Science, *July 1958, p. 3.*)

ple, 10 inputs resulted in 10 outputs during the time allowed. When overload was reached, performance began to decrease. If the overload point, for example, was 40 inputs (with 40 outputs), then 45 inputs resulted in less than 45 outputs. This experiment would suggest that for job situations involving the possibility of overload, the optimal staffing is a workload a little less than overload rather than a little over the overload condition. A telephone switchboard operator illustrates such a condition. If the number of calls to handle exceeds her ability to respond, performance will drop below the maximum response rate.

The world provides more input than the human processing system is able to accept. The human reduces this input to a manageable quantity by a filtering or selection process. Some inputs are blocked and prevented from entering processing through the use of a filter which blocks them. The filter is normally based on the probability of a stimulus being important (Figure 3-3). The filter may result from:

1 Frame of reference of the individual
2 Normal decision procedure
3 Decisions under stress

Individuals establish importance filters based on their experience, background, custom, etc. Decision procedures identify relevant data and therefore provide a filter to screen factors unnecessary to the decision. The filtering mechanism may be changed by decision-making stress; i.e., the stress of making decisions under time measure will cause filtering to increase, thereby reducing the data to be processed by the decision maker. For example, a production line supervisor will, during a period of crisis and stress, concentrate on the most important problems and will not accept stimuli that are related to less important problems.

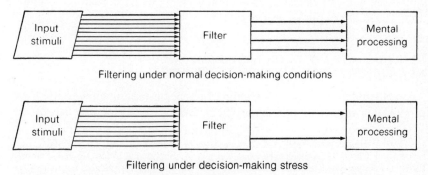

Filtering under normal decision-making conditions

Filtering under decision-making stress

Figure 3-3   Filtering of information to reduce processing requirements.

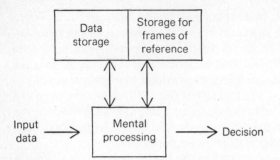

Figure 3-4 Use of input data, stored data, and frame of reference to process a decision.

The frame of reference concept applies to both input and processing. To develop a new processing routine for each new stimulus would reduce the stimuli that could be processed. Over an extended period of time, and on a continuing basis, the brain establishes patterns or categories of data which define the human understanding of the nature of the environment. These patterns or frames of reference are called into use in processing the input (Figure 3-4), thereby reducing processing requirements.

Filtering may reduce or block unwanted data. It may also work to block data that is inconsistent with an established frame of reference. This and the natural limits on the human sense receptors lead to information perception errors. The writer of a report may mean one thing; the reader may perceive another. These errors of perception increase uncertainty which, as explained in Chapter 2, is the opposite of the effect of information.

An organization is made up of individuals, and therefore the limitations of individuals as information processors is also reflected in organizations. The organization develops certain forms to handle this limitation, such as decision programs, division of work, and data reduction. These are explored in Chapter 5.

NEWELL-SIMON MODEL OF THE HUMAN AS AN INFORMATION/DECISION PROCESSOR

Allen Newell and Herbert A. Simon of Carnegie-Mellon University[1] have proposed a model of human problem solving which makes use of the

[1]Allen Newell and Herbert A. Simon, *Human Problem Solving*, Prentice-Hall, Inc., Englewood Cliffs, N.J., 1972. See also Herbert A. Simon and Allen Newell, "Human Problem Solving: The State of the Theory in 1970," *American Psychologist*, February 1971, pp. 145–159.

analogy between computer processing and human information processing. This is not to say that humans solve problems like computers, but that the analogy is very useful in understanding human information processing. Figure 3-5 compares the Newell-Simon model of information processing with a general model of a computer processing system.

Human Information Processing System

The human information processing system consists of a processor, sensory input, motor output, and three different memories: long-term memory (LTM), short-term memory (STM), and external memory (EM). The processing system operates in serial fashion rather than in parallel. This means that the human can perform only one information processing task at a time, whereas a computer may operate in serial or parallel for three significant operations. A good example of computer parallel processing is the simultaneous addition of all pairs of bits in two computer

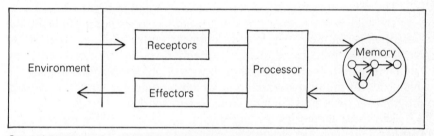

General structure of a human information processing system *(Allen Newell and Herbert A. Simon,* Human Problem Solving, *Prentice-Hall, Inc., Englewood Cliffs, N.J., 1972, p. 20.)*

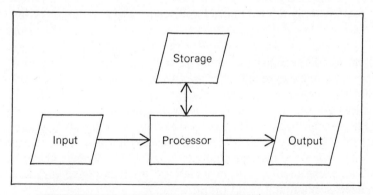

General model of computer information processing system

Figure 3-5 Comparison of Newell-Simon model and model of computer system.

Operation	Serial design	Parallel design
Data transfer	Data transferred a bit or a byte at a time.	Data transferred a word at a time (e.g., 32 bits).
Arithmetic on one data item	One adder/comparator. Operations on pairs of bits or bytes from right to left.	One adder/comparator for each set of bits. Operations on all pairs of bits simultaneously.
Processing of several data items	One processor. Processing one item at a time.	CPU consists of several small processors. Several items processed concurrently.

data words. Humans add serially a pair of digits at a time from right to left. The three operations are described above and in Figure 3-6.

The fact that a human is a serial processor does not mean he or she cannot work on more than one task concurrently. While not part of the Newell-Simon model, the human probably does this by rapid switching from one task to another with short bursts of processing for each. This is analogous to multiprogramming in which a computer works on several programs at once by switching from one to another.

The three memories are significant to the model (Figure 3-7). The long-term memory has essentially unlimited capacity. Its content consists of symbols and structures of symbols. Storage may be quite compact such that an entire configuration of stimuli may be designated by a single symbol. It requires only a few hundred milliseconds to read (recall) from long-term memory, but the write time (commit to memory) is fairly long (say, $5K$ to $10K$ seconds for K symbols). This means that it requires an average of 50 to 100 seconds to memorize a 10-digit number, but once stored in memory, one can recall it for use in a few hundred milliseconds.

The short-term memory is part of the processor and is quite small. It holds only five to seven symbols. However, only about two can be retained while another task is being performed, which suggests that part of the short-term memory is used for input and output processing. Read and write time are very fast. A computer analogy is register storage, scratch pad, or cache memory, all of which are small and have very fast processing access, read, and write times.

The external memory consists of external media such as a pad of paper or a chalkboard that act as a memory. The access time for the eye to

locate the symbols at a known location is quite high (say, 100 milliseconds), and read times are estimated at about 50 milliseconds. The
write times (say, 1 second per symbol) are much less than the write times

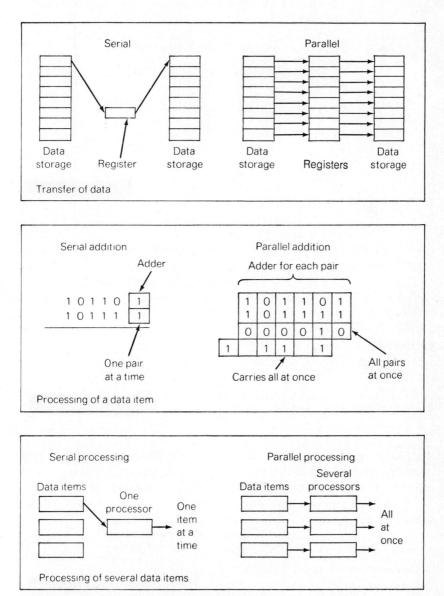

Figure 3-6 Examples of serial and parallel processing in computers.

Internal

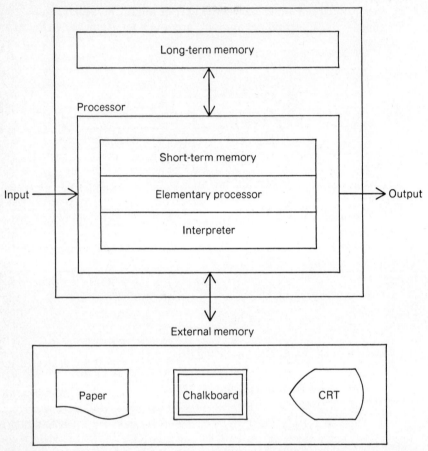

Figure 3-7 The three memories of the Newell-Simon model.

for long-term memory, which accounts for the efficiency of using external memory in problem-solving procedures. For example, if two 10-digit numbers are to be added, the following approximate times are required by long-term and external memories.

	Seconds using long-term memory	Seconds using external memory
Accept numbers	Same	Same
Write numbers to memory	50.0 to 100.0	10.0
Read numbers to		

	Seconds using long-term memory	Seconds using external memory
add	1.0 to 2.0	0.6
Process (add digits a pair at a time,	Same	Same
Write result to memory	50.0 to 100.0	10.0
Total	101.0 to 202.0	20.6

Even if large errors are assumed in the estimated times for reading and writing, the point about the operating efficiency of external memory is easily seen. By way of contrast, the retrieval, processing, and storage of results by computer would require a few millionths of a second.

The elementary processes of the information processing system are such operations as *compare* and *replace*. The processor contains three parts: the elementary processor, the short-term memory, and the interpreter which interprets (and perhaps holds) part of or all the program of instructions for problem solving (Figure 3-7). Goal structures are used to help organize problem solving. The program used by an individual will depend on a number of variables such as task or intelligence of problem solver.

Problem Space

Another Newell-Simon concept useful in understanding human information/decision processing is that of task environment and problem space. The *task environment* is the problem as it exists; the *problem space* is the way a particular decision maker represents the task in order to work on it. In other words, confronted by a problem, the problem solver formulates a representation to use in working on the problem. This representation is the conceptual space where problem solving takes place. The problem space is determined by the task environment (but is not identical to it).

The structure of the problem space (how the problem solver represents the task) determines the processes that can be used for problem solving. The problem space can be thought of as a network of knowledge state nodes; each node describes what the problem solver knows at a moment in time. A knowledge state will consist of a few dozen or perhaps a few hundred symbols. Problem solving takes place by a search process in the problem space until a desired knowledge state is reached. Problem solving thus consists of constructing a problem space and processing in the problem space until a solution is found.

Structure in a problem space is equivalent to redundancy. This means that information in one part of the problem space is, by means of the structure, predictive of properties in another part of the space. It thus permits a more efficient search process.

A concept related to the problem space is bounded rationality. Man has a limited capacity for rational thinking; he must generally construct a simplified model of the real situation in order to deal with it. The behavior with respect to the simplified model may be rational. However, it does not follow that the rational solution for the simplified model is rational in the real situation. Rationality is restricted or bounded by limitations on human processing capabilities but also by such factors as training, prejudice, custom, and attitude.

TENTATIVE LIMITS ON HUMAN PROCESSING

The Newell-Simon model suggests limitations on the ability of humans as information processors. There is some empirical evidence relating to these limits. One set of limits relates to the processing of data and is directly related to short-term memory. Another set of limits is the ability of humans to detect differences. Humans are also limited in their ability to generate, integrate, and interpret probabilistic data.

Processing of Data

Miller coined the phrase, "the magical number seven, plus or minus two"[2] to describe human capability for processing information. His survey, supported by empirical research, shows in essence that the number of symbols humans can hold in short-term memory and process effectively is from five to nine but with a common limit of seven.

The limits of 7 ± 2 are more appropriate for codes, quantities, and other data rather than for a language text. In language text, a word or even a group of words probably utilizes one symbol in short-term memory, whereas each character in a code may utilize one symbol of storage space.

The application of the limits 7 ± 2 to codes is important because information processing depends heavily on the use of codes. The following summary of some studies indicates the validity of the Miller limits:

Study	Object of study and results
Crannell and Parrish[3]	Immediate oral recall of orally presented numeric data. Span for immediate recall

[2]George A. Miller, "The Magical Number Seven, Plus or Minus Two: Some Limits on Our Capability for Processing Information," *The Psychological Review*, vol. 63, no. 2, March 1956, pp. 81–97.

[3]C. W. Crannell and J. M. Parrish, "A Comparison of Immediate Memory Span for Digits, Letters, and Words," *The Journal of Psychology*, vol. 44, October 1957, pp. 319–327.

Study	Object of study and results
	slightly better than seven digits.
Conrad[4]	Telephone operators memorizing telephone numbers and then recalling them. Error rates on recall were:

Digit length	Percent in error
8	30
9	44
10	54

Study	Object of study and results
Chapdelaine[5]	Error rate for transferring coded data from one form to another for codes from 5 to 15 digits in length. The frequency of errors from least to highest was 5, 6, 7, 8, 10, 11, 13, 9, 14, 12, 15. The differences were significant. Note that 9 and 12 are out of order. A 12-digit code had almost double the error rate of a 13-digit code.
Owsowitz and Sweetland[6]	Error rates for codes composed of mixed alphabetic and numeric characters. Error rates increase when alphabetic characters are mixed with numeric characters. Codes with one part (say, half) alpha and the other part numeric had lower error rates than codes with alpha, numeric, alpha, etc.

In the light of the Newell-Simon model and the Miller limits, the Chapdelaine result of increasing errors with length except for 9 and 12 may be explained by the human subjects treating short codes as a set to be processed, and the limit of 9 (7 + 2) introduced greater error for the 9-digit numbers. For numbers greater than 9 it may be that humans must divide the code into two parts, thus accounting for greater error at the breakpoint. The explanation for the unusual error frequency of 12 digits is not easily explained. The explanation may be that the break into two parts uses up part of the processing capability such that the limit tends to drop to 5 or 6 symbols for each part (certainly consistent with 7 ± 2). The 12-digit length would then be a breakpoint for changing to a three-part processing for lengths 12 and greater than 12. The lower rate for codes with grouped alphabetics and numerics, compared with mixed, suggests a

[4]R. Conrad, "Errors of Immediate Memory," *The British Journal of Psychology*, vol. 50, no. 4, November 1959, pp. 349–359.

[5]P. A. Chapdelaine, *Accuracy Control in Source Data Collection*, Headquarters, Air Force Logistics Command, Wright-Patterson Air Force Base, Ohio, 1963.

[6]S. Owsowitz and A. Sweetland, *Factors Affecting Coding Errors*, Rand Memorandum RM-4346-PR, The Rand Corporation, Santa Monica, Calif., 1965.

processing by subgroups when the code becomes too long or too complex. A mixed alphabetic-numeric code increases the information requirements to process the code. According to the information theory concept described in Chapter 2, more information is required to identify a character from the set of 36 alphanumerics compared with the 10 numerics.

Just Noticeable Differences

An important question in information processing is the ability of human processors to identify differences. This ability may be important in detecting errors (i.e., noticing difference between correct and incorrect data) and also in the reaction of receivers to variations in the data values received. In other words, how do human receivers evaluate the significance of differences such as profit differences and cost differences? A law developed in the field of psychology may be useful for this question. Weber's law[7] of just noticeable difference is a psychologic law developed with respect to judgments of physical stimuli such as the brightness of light, the loudness of sounds, and the heaviness of weights. The law says that the difference that is noticeable is a constant proportion of the physical dimensions or stimulus. In other words, if C denotes a criterion and ΔC is the just noticeable difference, then:

$$\frac{\Delta C}{C} = k \qquad \text{for all C}$$

This means that as C changes, ΔC changes in order to hold k as a constant. If, for example, a variation of 1/5 pound is sufficient difference to distinguish between two 5-pound weights, then

$$\frac{1/5}{5} = \frac{1}{25}$$

For a 20-pound weight, the difference must be 4/5 pound to hold the ratio constant.

$$\frac{4/5}{20} = \frac{1}{25}$$

In essence, a larger weight difference is required to distinguish between heavier objects, but the relation is the same.

[7]R. S. Woodworth and Harold Schlosberg, *Experimental Psychology*, rev. ed., Henry Holt and Company, Inc., New York, 1955, pp. 192–233.

There is some evidence[8] to suggest that Weber's law holds also for data differences. In other words, the reader of a financial report considers differences to be significant as judged by their size relative to the base rather than the absolute amount. A 10 percent variation in budgeted sales of $100,000 (variance of $10,000) has the same significance in terms of noticeable difference as a 10 percent variation in selling expense of $10,000 (variance of $1,000).

Handling Probabilistic Data[9]

Decision makers are frequently required to perceive, process, and evaluate the probabilities of uncertain events. There is evidence of serious deficiencies in human performance as an intuitive statistician. These deficiencies are significant because an information/decision system can be designed to compensate for them. Some of the deficiencies identified by research are:

1 Lack of intuitive understanding of the impact of sample size on sampling variance
2 Lack of intuitive ability to identify correlation and causality
3 Biasing heuristics for probability estimation
4 Lack of capability for integrating information

Sampling variance decreases in proportion to sample size. In other words, if a sample of 10 manufactured parts is examined for defects and 2 are found defective, the meaning is different from 20 defects in a sample of 100. In a study of psychology research practices, Tversky and Kahneman[10] found that the investigators did not seem to perceive correctly the error and unreliability inherent in small samples. Other studies with students suggest humans do not have an intuitive understanding of the effect of sample size on variance. This results in unwarranted conclusions from small samples.

It is important in decision making to identify correlation and causality because this allows a prediction of the value of one variable from the value of another. There is research which suggests that causality is frequently intuitively identified with joint occurrence. However, the occurrence of two things at the same time does not demonstrate causality.

[8]J. Dickhout and V. Eggleton, "An Application of Weber's Law in an Accounting Setting," *Proceedings of 4th Annual Midwest AIDS Regional Conference*, April 1972, pp. J15–J18.
[9]The following two sections are based on Paul Slovic, "From Shakespeare to Simon: Speculations—and Some Evidence—about Man's Ability to Process Information," research monograph, vol. 12, no. 12, Oregon Research Institute, University of Oregon, April 1972.
[10]A. Tversky and D. Kahneman, "The Belief in the Law of Small Numbers," *Psychological Bulletin*, vol. 76, 1971, pp. 105–110.

Also, organizational events may occur at a fairly low rate and in a variety of contexts, so that correlation and causality are obscured.

As pointed out earlier, humans operate with bounded rationality. Estimation of probabilities is influenced by a variety of biasing factors, for example, the availability of data. Events that are easily remembered or imagined are assigned a higher probability.

Humans are not usually consistent in patterns of choice when faced with different types of information and values. For example, subjects presented with various gambling situations will demonstrate inconsistent choice between player and dealer information. The difficulty of integrating different types of information and different types of values into an overall consistent judgment prompts the use of judgmental strategies. However, these strategies often yield inconsistent results.

Information Processing Strategies

Humans adopt strategies for dealing with their limitations as information processors and for easing the strain of integrating information. Some examples are concreteness and anchoring and adjustment.

The concept of *concreteness* is that the decision maker tends to use only information he has available and only in the form in which it is displayed. There will be a tendency not to search for data stored in memory or to transform or manipulate the data that is presented. Explicit, available information thus has an advantage over data that must be obtained or manipulated before use.

The idea of *anchoring and adjustment* is that humans tend to make judgments by establishing an anchor point and making adjustments from this point. The anchoring and adjustment behavior reduces information processing requirements. It is a common phenomenon in budgeting, planning, and pricing. The adjustments tend to be inadequate when dealing with probabilistic estimates.

EFFECT OF DATA COMPRESSION
ON HUMAN PERFORMANCE

In Chapter 2, methods of data reduction were described. Earlier in this chapter it was explained that humans have limits to their processing capabilities. This suggests the use of compressed or summary data which reduces the volume of data to be processed by the receiver. A question that then arises is the effect of compressed data on human performance. Does decision performance improve with summarized data compared with raw data not summarized?

In a research study performed at the Management Information

Systems Research Center at the University of Minnesota,[11] subjects were asked to perform decision tasks. One group was provided with summarized data; the other was given raw transaction data. The results were interesting for information system design. The group with summarized data made better decisions but were less confident of their decisions. This may explain the reluctance of some managers to eliminate detailed transaction listings. Scanning the raw data may not improve a manager's decision performance, but it will strengthen his or her confidence in the decision.

A related study performed by Anderson[12] investigated decision maker response to probabilistic information. Decision makers were presented with one, two, or three types of data for a series of capital budgeting decisions:

1 Mean value
2 Mean value plus ranges
3 Probability distributions

Decision makers provided with all three data items were more confident of their decisions but were less consistent in decision making than when they received only the first item.

NEED FOR FEEDBACK

The model of input, processing, and output implies that the human can accept input, process, and provide output without additional system elements. In computer systems, various mechanisms are used to determine that the output has been received. The printer returns a signal to the central processor to indicate the fact that the transmitted data has activated the printer. A data terminal returns a signal to indicate receipt of a block of data. Similar feedback mechanisms must be provided in human processing situations not only for error control but also to meet the psychological needs of human processors. Feedback will be described further in Chapter 4.

The importance of the need for feedback to satisfy human needs was

[11]Norman L. Chervany and Gary W. Dickson, "An Experiment Evaluation of Information Overload in a Production Environment," working paper 71-14, The Management Information Systems Research Center, University of Minnesota, Minneapolis, August 1972.

[12]John C. Anderson, "Decision-Maker Response to Probabilistic Information in the Capital Investment Decision Process," unpublished doctoral dissertation, University of Minnesota, Minneapolis, 1973.

illustrated by a system that used a source data recorder.[13] The employee entered data which was transmitted to a central location, but the device returned no response, such as a light, hum, or buzz, to indicate that the input was recorded. The result was duplicate entry of data and frustrated employees. Another illustration was an incident connected with the installation of a nationwide online airline reservation system.[14] The computer load was estimated at 85 percent of capacity but was immediately overloaded. An analysis revealed that the reservation operators did not trust the computer. After entering reservation data, they immediately entered an inquiry to see if the system had the data. This effectively doubled the load on the computer system. The solution was to provide a feedback signal confirming that the message had been received. In this case the feedback was to wiggle the typewriter ball.

In everyday conversation, it is customary to make some signal to indicate receipt of spoken communication. The receiver will nod or say uh-huh. Some languages provide a special sound; for example, spoken Swedish has a sound like a short, quick intake of air which the listener repeats at fairly frequent intervals to indicate continued receipt of the communication.

PSYCHOLOGICAL VALUE OF UNUSED DATA

A common phenomenon in organizations is the accumulation and storage of data that has very little probability of being used. Using a cost/benefit analysis, the value of the data would be calculated as follows:

$$\text{Value of data} = \text{probability of use} \begin{bmatrix} \text{average} \\ \text{economic benefit} \\ \text{from use} \end{bmatrix} - \begin{bmatrix} \text{cost of} \\ \text{obtaining} \\ \text{and storing} \end{bmatrix}$$

Because the probability of use is low, the value of the data is likely to be negative. For example, two data items with the same cost (say, $10) and the same use benefit (say, $50) but different probabilities (say, .1 and .5) will have different values.

Value of data with probability of .5 = .5 ($50) − 10 = $15
Value of data with probability of .1 = .1 ($50) − 10 = −$5

[13]J. Anderson, G. Dickson, and J. Simmons, "Behavioral Reactions to the Introduction of a Management Information System at the U.S. Post Office: Some Empirical Observations," working paper 72-05, The Management Information Systems Research Center, University of Minnesota, Minneapolis, March 1973.

[14]Reported by C. Dudley Warner, "System Performance and Evaluation—Past, Present, and Future," *Proceedings of the Fall Joint Computer Conference*, 1972, p. 962.

There are many explanations for uneconomic accumulation and storage of data. One explanation may be the increased confidence decision makers appear to obtain from added data, even if unnecessary. Another useful explanation is the concept of the value of unused opportunities.

The basic theory says that people attach a significant value to the existence of unused opportunities. This phenomenon was demonstrated in a recent investigation into the reasons people liked living in the New York City area. The responses typically included a substantial listing of cultural facilities such as museums, art galleries, and theaters. Yet the people who listed these factors did not, in general, use them—they did not go to the theater, art galleries, or museums. The value of the cultural facilities was not related to actual use. Having them there in case they ever did want to go appeared to be the significant value.

The theory of unused opportunities may be applied to explain the phenomenon of apparent uneconomic accumulation and storage of data. The value is not the actual use, given any expected frequency of access, but in the unused opportunity. The value of unused opportunities is a psychological response rather than an economic response and cannot be traced to the income statement.

If the psychological value of unused opportunities applies to the value of unused data, this has implications for information systems design. Individual users may request data that will receive little use and have little value but a psychological one. The information system cost/benefit analysis should detect these situations in order to apply organizational criteria rather than individual criteria. The principle can also influence storage structures since low-cost storage can be used to satisfy the psychological need.

IMPLICATIONS FOR INFORMATION
SYSTEM DESIGN

The chapter has presented concepts and research evidence about humans as information processors. This is useful background material for information system designers. It also has direct relevance for information system design. Some of the implications are:

Concept	Implications for Information System Design
Information overload	Input to humans and responses required should be kept below the overload point.
Filtering	Information systems should be designed to filter irrelevant data and to provide increased filtering for stress decisions. System should attempt to

Concept	Implications for Information System Design
	override undesirable frame of reference filters by reinforced display of relevant data.
Newell-Simon model	Information system should assist in defining problem space and in the search process for a solution. The information format should attempt to expand the limits of bounded rationality. Systems should use the memory that is suited to the task.
Magical number 7 ± 2	Codes for human use should not exceed 5 to 7 symbols or be subdivided into segments of 5 or less. Systems should not have humans do significant, unaided processing.
Just noticeable differences	Systems should highlight significant differences rather than assuming humans will notice them.
Human as intuitive statisticians	The information system should provide statistical analysis of data—sample variance, correlation, probability estimates, etc. Decision algorithms should provide a consistency check of various information sources. Data generation procedures should be designed to assist in eliminating bias such as recency of events.
Concreteness	The information needed should be presented in the form needed. No added processing should be required.
Anchoring and adjustment	Information/decision system should be designed to assist in setting a suitable anchoring point and for prompting adequate adjustments from it.
Effect of data compression	Information systems should present summarized data in a decision-impelling format, but the system should allow browsing through the raw data.
Feedback	Systems should provide feedback to indicate data has been received, processing is taking place, etc.
Value of unused data	Explains some of pressure for data with no apparent utility. Suggests storage and retrieval strategies to reduce cost.

These examples illustrate the importance of understanding the capabilities of the human portion of the man/machine system. In some cases, the connection between theory and practice is strong; in other instances, the implications are not so clear. The latter suggest the need for further research in this area.

SUMMARY

The basic model of the human as an information processor consists of input from sensors, a processing unit, and output responses. Inputs are too numerous for all to be accepted, so a filtering mechanism is applied to screen input. The Newell-Simon model focuses on three types of memory used in human information processing: short-term, long-term, and external storage. The varying read and write speeds for the different storages plus the differences in capacity explain many characteristics of human processing.

Some tentative limits on humans as information processors are expressed by the "magical number seven, plus or minus two." Another limit is the amount of difference that is noticed or considered significant by a receiver. Humans are also not good intuitive statisticians.

Data compression is necessary because of storage and processing considerations, but research suggests it may have a dual effect. Decision performance may improve with summarized data, but confidence in the decisions decreases. Another human response is a need for feedback which indicates to the human sender that the message has been received.

A well-known phenomenon is the processing and storage of data that receives very little use. One explanation for this is the psychological value that is attached to unused opportunities.

EXERCISES

1   Describe the Newell-Simon model of the human as an information processor.
2   Explain the effect of too much input on performance.
3   Explain the filtering process. How is it affected by stress? What are the implications for information system design?
4   Explain how patterns or frames of reference are used by human processors.
5   Compare the access, read, and write speeds estimated for the Newell-Simon model to the speeds of any modern computer system.
6   What are the implications for information system design of the statement that humans are serial rather than parallel processors?
7   Explain multiprogramming. How might this concept be used by humans in processing?
8   What are the parts of the Newell-Simon processor?
9   What is problem space?
10   Explain the implications of "the magical number seven, plus or minus two" for information processing system design.
11   Explain Weber's law of just noticeable differences. Describe its implication for information processing.

12 In terms of the research reported in the chapter, what is the effect of data compression on human performance? What are the implications of this finding for information system design?

13 Do research on output feedback mechanisms in computer hardware systems. Define the major mechanisms used for:
  a Printer
  b Card punch
  c Data communication terminal

14 What are the implications for information systems design of the psychological need for feedback?

15 Explain the value of unused opportunities. What are the implications for information system design?

16 How does the model of human processing assist in explaining the decision maker who makes decisions more easily under stress, apparently with very little information?

SELECTED REFERENCES

Conrad, R.: "Errors of Immediate Memory," *The British Journal of Psychology*, November 1959, pp. 349–359.

Crannell, C. W., and J. M. Parrish: "A Comparison of Immediate Memory Span for Digits, Letters and Words," *The Journal of Psychology*, vol. 44, October 1957, pp. 319–327.

Miller, George A.: "The Magical Number Seven, Plus or Minus Two: Some Limits on Our Capability for Processing Information," *The Psychological Review*, vol. 63, no. 2, March 1956, pp. 81–97.

Moskowitz, Herbert, and Richard O. Mason: "Accounting for the Man/Information Interface in Management Information Systems," working paper 374, Institute for Research in the Behavioral, Economic, and Management Sciences, Krannert School of Industrial Administration, Purdue University, Lafayette, Ind., September 1972.

Newell, Allen, and Herbert A. Simon: *Human Problem Solving*, Prentice-Hall, Inc., Englewood Cliffs, N.J., 1972.

Simon, Herbert A., and Allen Newell: "Human Problem Solving: The State of the Theory in 1970," *American Psychologist*, vol. 26, February 1971, pp. 145–159.

Slovic, Paul: "From Shakespeare to Simon: Speculations—and Some Evidence—about Man's Ability to Process Information," research monograph, vol. 12, no. 12, Oregon Research Institute, University of Oregon, April 1972.

Chapter 4

System Concepts and Information Systems

The term "system" is in common use. One speaks of an educational system, computer system, software system, solar system, system of theology, and many others. This chapter surveys system concepts with an emphasis on those concepts that are significant for the designer of management information systems.

DEFINITION OF A SYSTEM

Systems can be abstract or physical. An *abstract system* is an orderly arrangement of interdependent ideas or constructs. For example, a system of theology is an orderly arrangement of ideas about God, man, etc. A *physical system* is a set of elements which operate together to accomplish an objective. A physical system may be further defined by examples:

Physical system	Description
Circulatory system	The heart and blood vessels which move blood through the body.
Transportation system	The personnel, machines, and organizations which transport goods.
Weapons system	The equipment, procedures, and personnel which make it possible to use a weapon.
School system	The buildings, teachers, administrators, textbooks, etc., that function together to provide instruction for students.
Computer system	The equipment which functions together to do computer processing.
Accounting system	The records, rules, procedures, equipment, and personnel which operate to record data, measure income, prepare reports.

Characteristics of a System

From the examples, it is possible to discern certain characteristics of systems. A system is composed of interacting parts that operate together to achieve some objective or purpose. In other words, a system is not a randomly assembled set of elements, but consists of elements which can be identified as belonging together because of a common purpose, goal, or objective. Physical systems are more than conceptual constructs; they can display activity or behavior.

A further restriction on types of systems to be studied in information system analysis and design is that the system must be under human control, which may be exercised in the ordering of the elements or in the rules for system operation. This restriction does not apply to physical systems such as the solar system and animals because these are not under human control.

General Model of a System

A general model of a system is input, processor, and output. This is, of course, very simplified because a system may have several inputs and outputs (Figure 4-1). The features which define and delineate a system form its *boundary*. The system is inside the boundary; the *environment* is outside the boundary. In some cases, it is fairly simple to define what is part of the system and what is not; in other cases, the person studying the system may arbitrarily define the boundaries. Some examples of boundaries are:

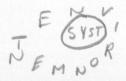

System	Boundary
Human	Skin, hair, nails, and all parts contained inside form the system; all things outside are environment.
Automobile	The automobile body plus tires and all parts contained within form the system.
Production	Production machines, production inventory of work in progress, production employees, production procedures, etc., form the system. The rest of the company is in the environment.

The production system example illustrates the problem of the boundary concept. Is raw material inventory included in the production system? One system may include it because it is necessary for the system being studied; another use may exclude it.

Each system is composed of *subsystems* which in turn are made up of other subsystems, each subsystem being delineated by its boundaries. The interconnections and interactions between the subsystems are termed *interfaces*. Interfaces occur at the boundary and take the form of inputs and outputs (material, energy, or information). Figure 4-2a and b shows examples of subsystems and interfaces at boundaries.

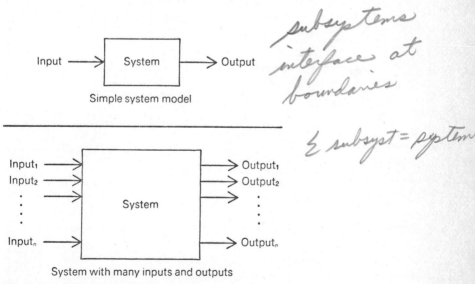

Simple system model

System with many inputs and outputs

Figure 4-1 General models of a system.

System	Subsystems	Interface at boundary
Computer	Central processing unit (CPU) Input units Output units Auxiliary storage	Channels
Central processing unit	Arithmetic unit Control unit Storage unit	Connection wires
Batch processing with separate runs	Edit run Sort run Update run Output run	Run-to-run data transfer (say, data tape)

Computer configuration as system

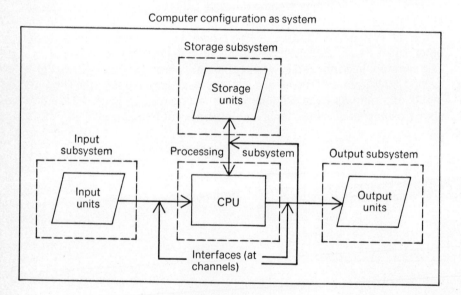

Central processing unit as system

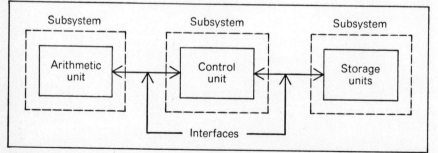

Figure 4-2a and b   Above and facing page: Examples of subsystems and interfaces.

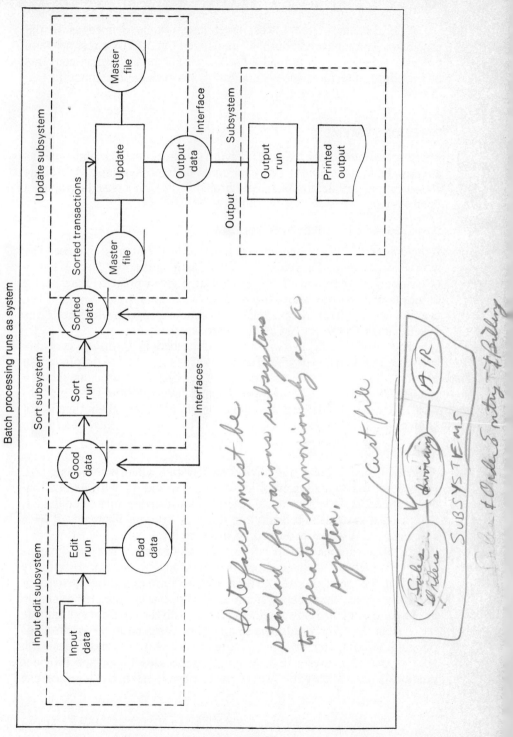

Batch processing runs as system

A subsystem at the lowest level may not be defined as to the processor. The inputs and outputs are defined but not the transformation process. This system is termed a *black box*. The major system concepts of boundary, interface, subsystem, and black box are illustrated in Figure 4-3.

TYPES OF SYSTEMS

There are a number of ways of viewing systems. One classification has already been mentioned: physical and abstract systems. Additional classifications are deterministic and probabilistic systems and closed and open systems.

Deterministic and Probabilistic Systems

A *deterministic system* operates in a perfectly predictable manner. The interaction among the parts is known with certainty. If one has a description of the state of the system at a given point in time plus a description of its operation, the next state of the system may be given exactly, without error. An example is a computer program which performs exactly according to the set of instructions.

The *probabilistic system* can be described in terms of probable behavior, but a certain degree of error is always attached to the prediction of what the system will do. An inventory system is an example of a probabilistic system. The average demand, average time for replenishment, etc., may be defined, but the exact value at any given time is not known.

Closed and Open Systems

A *closed system* is defined in physics as a system which is self-contained. It does not exchange material, information, or energy with its environment. An example is a chemical reaction in a sealed, insulated container. Such closed systems will finally run down or become disorganized. This movement to disorder is termed an *increase in entropy.*

In organizations and in information processing, there are systems that are relatively isolated from the environment but not completely closed in the physics sense. These will be termed closed systems or relatively closed systems. Systems in manufacturing are, for example, designed to minimize unwanted exchanges with the environment outside the system. In other words, the systems are designed to be as closed as possible. A computer program is a relatively closed system because it accepts only previously defined inputs, processes them, and provides previously defined outputs. The relatively closed system is, therefore, one

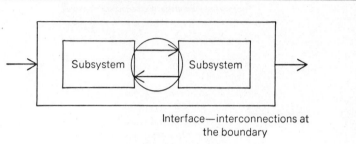

The boundary concept

Interface—interconnections at
the boundary

Interface

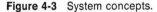

Simple case of subsystems operating in serial
fashion

System factored into subsystems

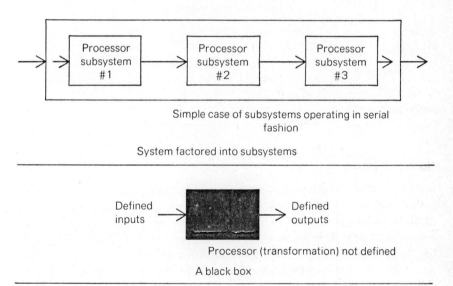

Processor (transformation) not defined

A black box

Figure 4-3 System concepts.

that has only controlled and well-defined inputs and outputs. It is not
subject to disturbances from outside the system (Figure 4-4).

Open systems exchange information, material, or energy with the
environment. The exchanges may include random and undefined inputs.
Examples of open systems are biological systems (such as man) and

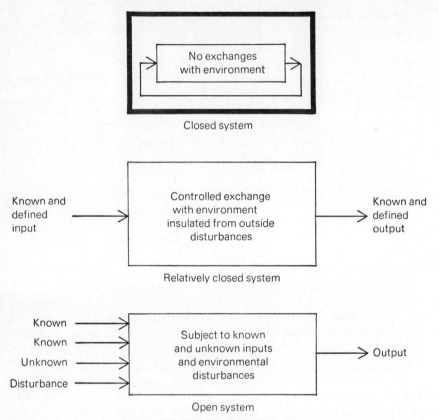

Figure 4-4   Concept of open and closed systems.

organizational systems. Open systems tend to have a quality of adaptation which means they can adapt to changes in their environment in such a way as to continue their existence. The system is self-organizing and changes its organization in response to changing conditions. Organizational systems usually have this capability for adaptation. In fact, this adaptation is required by business organizations in the face of changing competition, changing markets, etc. Firms which fail to adapt cease to exist. A design objective in most organizational systems, including information systems, is to provide adaptive capabilities in the system. An important method in adaptive responses is feedback, to be described later.

When a system is put into operation, there may be a period of activity before the system achieves the steady state which is the expected or normal level of operation. Whereas the completely closed system is at the steady state when it achieves maximum entropy (is run-down or disorganized), the open system receives an inflow of material, energy, and information so that it does not run down or disorganize. In the terminology of physics, it receives negative entropy from the environment. The steady state for an open system might be better described as a dynamic equilibrium in which the various subsystems are operating to achieve the objective, but are also adapting to environmental forces and performing self-organization to adjust its internal forces. As an example, a new data processing application achieves steady state when all subsystems are debugged and it is processing within the limits of the processing volume intended for it. The addition of program maintenance keeps the application system from running down or becoming disorganized.

Man/Machine Systems

The system designer usually prefers a relatively closed, deterministic system—in other words, a stable, predictable system which always performs exactly as it is supposed to do. These systems are generally easier to design than open, probabilistic systems because they are predictable in behavior. They are also easier to regulate or control.

In the area of information systems, the machine elements such as computer and computer programs are relatively closed and deterministic, but the human elements are open systems and probabilistic. The use of both man and machine in the system forms a man/machine system. Various combinations of man and machine are possible. Man/machine systems can emphasize the machine and use the human only as a monitor of the machine operation. Or, at the other extreme, a system may emphasize the human so that the machine performs only a supporting role such as to provide computation or search for data.

SUBSYSTEMS

Factoring

The concept of a system requires the designer to consider the system as a whole. But the entire system may be too large for detailed analysis. Therefore, the system is divided or factored into subsystems. The boundaries and interfaces are carefully studied to make sure the relations among subsystems are clearly defined and that the sum of the subsystems is the entire system. This process of *factoring* is continued with the subsystems which are divided into smaller subsystems until the subsystems are of manageable size. The subsystems resulting from this factoring process generally form hierarchical structures (Figure 4-5).

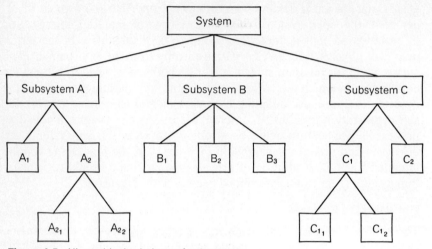

Figure 4-5 Hierarchical relations of subsystems.

An example of the factoring process is an information processing system. Although the system for study is the information system, there are too many details in the system to study them carefully all at once. Therefore, the breakdown into subsystems is used. One approach to factoring might proceed as follows:

1 Information system divided into subsystems such as:
   a Sales and order entry
   b Inventory
   c Production
   d Personnel and payroll
   e Purchasing
   f Accounting and control
   g Planning
   h Environmental intelligence
2 Each subsystem divided further into subsystems. For example, the personnel and payroll subsystem might be divided into the following smaller subsystems:
   a Personnel records input data preparation
   b Personnel-payroll file update
   c Personnel reports
   d Payroll input data preparation
   e Hourly payroll
   f Salaried payroll
   g Payroll reports—management
   h Payroll reports—government
   i Personnel and payroll audit

3 If the task is to design and program a new system, the subsystems defined in (2) might be further subdivided into smaller subsystems or modules. For example, the hourly payroll might be factored into processing modules such as input edit, calculation of gross pay, calculation of deductions and net pay, check printing, payroll register and audit controls preparation, and register output.

Simplification

The process of factoring a system into subsystems is important in problem simplification, but since each subsystem is defined as to inputs, outputs, and interfaces with other subsystems, a large number of subsystems could lead to a large number of interfaces to define. For example, four subsystems interacting with each other will have six interconnections; a system with 20 subsystems each interacting will have 190 interconnections. The number can rise quite quickly as the number of subsystems increases.

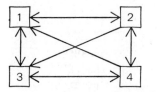

The number of interconnections is in general $\frac{1}{2}n(n-1)$, where n = number of subsystems. Each interconnection is a potential interface for communication among subsystems. Each interface implies a definition of the communication path.

Fortunately, not all subsystems interconnect with all others. This reduces substantially the interconnections. There are also other possibilities for simplification of interfaces and communication among subsystems. Some of these are:

1 Clusters of subsystems are established which interact with each other and then define a single interface path from the cluster to other subsystems or clusters of subsystems (Figure 4-6). An example is a data base which is interfaced by many programs, but the communication is only through a data base management interface. The data items are not accessed directly.

2 Methods are established for decoupling systems to make precise interaction analysis unnecessary.

Decoupling

If two different subsystems are connected very tightly, a very close coordination of the two subsystems is required. For example, suppose

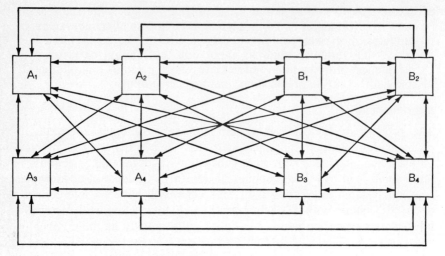

All systems interconnected

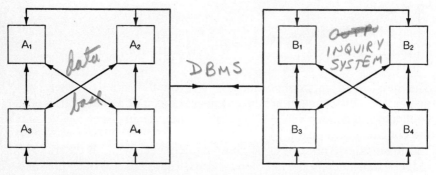

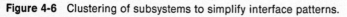

Systems connected within cluster, and clusters interconnected
with single interface

Figure 4-6 Clustering of subsystems to simplify interface patterns.

that raw material is put directly into production the moment it arrives at the factory; then the raw materials system can be said to be tightly coupled. Under these conditions, raw material delivery (input to production system and output from raw material system) must be precisely timed in order to avoid delays in production or to prevent new material from arriving too soon with no place to be stored.

Such tight coupling generally places too great a coordination and timing requirement for the two systems. Because they are somewhat independent, it is difficult to make them operate completely in synchronized fashion. Random events make delivery times uncertain, and so expected arrival times vary. Likewise, the production process can experience random or unplanned delays. The solution is to decouple or loosen the connection so that the two systems can operate in the short run with some measure of independence. Some means of decoupling are (Figure 4-7):

1 *Inventories, buffers, or waiting lines.* In the example of the raw material subsystem and the production subsystem, a raw material inventory allows the two subsystems to operate somewhat independently (in the short run). Data buffers are used in some computer systems and some communications systems to compensate for different rates of input and output of data.

2 *Slack and flexible resources.* When the output of one subsystem is the input to another, the existence of slack resources allows subsystems to be somewhat independent and yet each to respond to the demands of *operate at under full capacity for slight variances* the other subsystem. For example, most data processing systems can provide an extra report or extra analysis because they have slack resources. The ability of an organization to respond to variations with the use of slack resources is enhanced if the available resources can be employed for a variety of purposes. An information systems organization

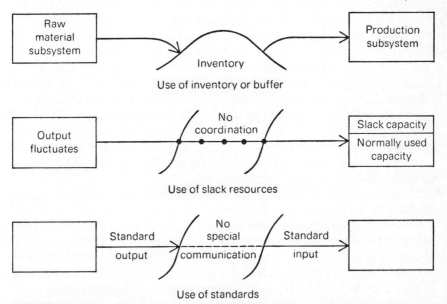

Use of inventory or buffer

Use of slack resources

Use of standards

Figure 4-7 Decoupling mechanisms to reduce need for communication and close connection among subsystems.

that uses the concept of a combination of systems analyst/programmer has more flexibility in meeting increased demand than an organization with the same number of personnel but which uses systems analysts only for analysis and design and programmers only for programming. (But, of course, this is only one consideration in the choice of separate or combined jobs.)

3 *Standards.* Standard specifications, standard costs, and other considerations allow a subsystem to plan and organize with reduced need to communicate with other subsystems. If, for example, the production department wishes to design a data processing module involving finished goods, a standard product code used throughout the organization will eliminate the need to negotiate and inform others about the codes to be used. A standard data base description maintained by the data administrator allows use of the data base without tedious and time-consuming checking with other subsystems also using the data base.

The problems of tight coupling stem not only from the physical problems of coordinating movement of resources but also from the problem of communication. The various methods for decoupling reduce the need for communication and allow the subsystems to communicate on an exception basis. Only if the subsystem begins to operate out of certain limits do the other subsystems with which it interfaces need to be informed. For example, the processing of vendor payments may be handled by a subsystem in accounting and data processing. It may be able to handle an average of 200 payments per day and by using slack resources handle up to 300 payments per day. The purchasing subsystem initiates the orders which result in the processing load in the payments subsystem. Because the payments subsystem can handle up to 300 payments, the purchasing subsystem need not communicate variations in orders placed unless there is an increase beyond 300 per day. The use of decoupling mechanisms may therefore be viewed as an alternative to increased communications. This means that an improved information/communication system may increase the opportunity for tight coupling and may reduce the need for decoupling mechanisms.

The process of decoupling and allowing each subsystem some independence in managing its affairs has many benefits, but it is not without its costs. One of these is the cost of the decoupling mechanism itself (inventory, buffer, waiting line, slack resources, standards, etc.). Another cost stems from the fact that each subsystem may act in the best possible way as a subsystem, but the sum of their actions may not be optimal for the organization. This is the problem of suboptimization.

The issue of alternative structures can be seen in questions of centralized (tightly coupled) versus decentralized (loosely coupled) organizations. As one proceeds from the loosely coupled system to a more tightly coupled one, there are benefits from system-wide optimization, but there are also costs of coordination and communication. The changing level of independent responsibility assigned to each subsystem (generally less in a tightly coupled system) may affect productivity by the human components. Thus, each system structure has advantages and disadvantages. There is no single, general answer. However, the experience of system designers in man-dominated and in man/machine systems suggests the need for at least some decoupling. These types of systems have so many random and probabilistic elements that individual subsystems must have some independence.

CONTROL IN SYSTEMS

The basic model of a system as inputs, process, and outputs does not provide for regulation and control of the system. For control purposes, a feedback loop is added to the basic model (Figure 4-8). In its simplest form, outputs from the system are compared with the desired output, and any difference causes an input to be sent to the process to adjust the operations so that the output will be closer to the standard.

Feedback which seeks to dampen and reduce fluctuations around the norm or standard is termed *negative feedback.* It is used in feedback control loops. *Positive feedback,* on the other hand, reinforces the direction the system is moving. In other words, positive feedback causes the system to repeat or amplify an adjustment or action. For example, a programming supervisor may have learned about use of modular program structure. Trying it on a small project and getting good results (positive feedback), the supervisor tries it on a larger, and again gets good results. He or she may continue this until all programming is done in that way (a steady state) or until projects are found for which it does not work and thus gets negative feedback.

Feedback in which the system changes its operations is not the only

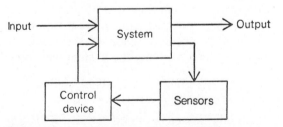

Figure 4-8 Feedback control for a system.

adjustment an organizational system may make. In response to feedback the organization may change its standards (objectives, goals, purposes, etc.). Since organizations are goal-directed and self-organizing, a change in goals may lead to changes in the system to achieve it.

Negative Feedback Control

Control in a system essentially means keeping the system operating within certain limits of performance. A system that is in control is operating within the specified tolerances. For example, an automated production system is in control if inputs of material and energy are being converted to output of produced items by use of a standard amount of material and energy and with the percentage of defective items falling within allowable limits. A system out of control functions outside the allowable limits because the regulatory mechanisms are not operative. Control using negative feedback normally involves four elements:

> **1**   A characteristic or condition to be controlled. The characteristic or condition must be measurable from some output.
> **2**   A sensor for measuring the characteristic or condition.
> **3**   A control unit which compares the measurements with a standard for that characteristic or condition. *Comparator*
> **4**   An activating unit which generates a corrective input signal to the process.

These elements are diagrammed in Figure 4-9. A very common example is the thermostat and heating system. The thermostat measures the temperature of the air (a result of the heating system) and compares it with the thermostat setting. If the temperature drops below the setting (standard), the thermostat switches on the furnace, causing more heat. An organizational example is the use of a budget as a standard and the application of various organizational pressures (including the terminating of employees) to keep income and expenditures close to the budget. The supervision and operation of a system may become more and more expert so that the system achieves a steady state in which it shows only small, random variations around the standard. However, soon some disturbance (change of personnel, change of supervisor, new pay policy, new types of documents) will cause the system to fluctuate again. If the negative feedback and the adjustment system are working, the system will soon stabilize again.

Closed or Open Loops

Feedback control loops are frequently classed as closed or open. A *closed control loop* is an automated control such as a thermostat or computer-

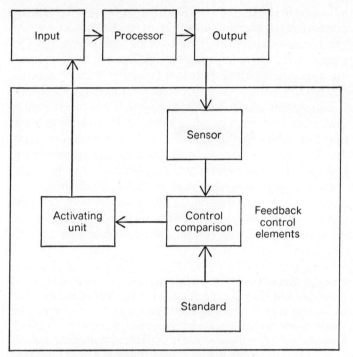

Figure 4-9 Negative feedback control elements.

controlled process. In much the same way that a closed system is insulated from disturbances in the environment, a closed feedback loop is insulated from disturbances in the control loop. An *open control loop* is one with random disturbances, such as those associated with human control elements. There are variations between the two extremes. In other words, human controls tend to make an open system; machine controls tend to make a closed system. A man/machine system is thus an attempt to use the best characteristics of both to make the system as closed as possible.

Law of Requisite Variety

One of the basic notions of system control theory is the need for requisite variety to obtain control. This has various rigorous formulations, but a commonsense understanding is that to control each possible state of the system elements, there must be a corresponding control state; to control a hundred states of system elements, there must be a hundred different states of controls. To view it another way, there must be at least as many variations of controls to be applied as there are ways for the system to get out of control. This means also that the controller for a system must be able to receive information about the output of each element and to transmit each variation of the control input back to each element of the system. This requires substantial information handling and large channel capacity. In human organizational terms, a manager who wishes to control an inventory of 10,000 stockkeeping units would need to be able to receive detailed information on each stockkeeping unit and to generate a different control response for each possible variation in the state of each stockkeeping unit. This is beyond the capabilities of one person—in terms of channel capacity to receive and transmit the data and in processing capability to generate the variety of control responses. The manager handles this by subdividing the system and assigning a subordinate to control the subdivisions. Each subordinate is furnished with decision rules for generating the variety of responses required to control the inventory assigned. An example of a system without requisite variety will illustrate the concept:

> A company making heavy equipment suddenly found its raw materials and in-process inventory climbing, but, at the same time, it was experiencing reduced sales and reduced production. The system was out of control. The cause was traced to the materials analysts who made the detailed inventory decisions. They had been furnished with decision rules for ordering, canceling, etc., under normal conditions, but they had no rules on how to handle the inventory when production was decreasing and production lots were being canceled. In other words, the system did not provide the requisite variety of control responses. In this case, the urgency of remedy did not allow new rules to be formulated and validated. Instead, each materials analyst was treated as a self-organizing system, given a target inventory, and told to achieve it. Given the freedom to generate control responses, they reduced the inventory in a few months.

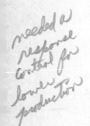

For the information system designer, the law of requisite variety means that for a system to be controlled, every controller (man or machine) must be provided with either (1) enough control responses (what to do in each case) to cover all possible conditions the system may face, (2) decision rules for generating all possible control responses, or (3) the authority to become a self-organizing system in order to generate control responses (Figure 4-10). Enumerating all responses is possible only in simple cases. Providing decision rules works well, but to be all-encompassing when open systems are involved is difficult. Computer-controlled open systems are not feasible because of the law of requisite variety. The solution is the use of man/machine systems in which the computer applies decision rules to generate control responses for ex-

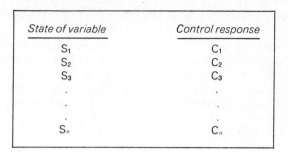

Enumeration

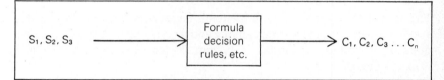

Deterministic control response generator

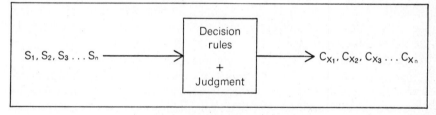

Self-organizing response system

Figure 4-10 Methods for providing sufficient system control responses.

pected cases and a human decision maker is used to generate control responses for the unexpected.

Filtering

Filters are often used for system input and in feedback. A *filter* is essentially a system element which keeps out certain inputs, allowing others to enter the system. The oil filter in an automobile lets the oil through but prevents metal particles, etc., from passing. Filters may be used to:

    1 Reduce the types of input. For example, the secretary to the president of an organization acts as a filter diverting certain types of mail (say, consumer product complaints) from the president and allowing through only the types of letters really requiring the president's cognizance.

2   Reduce the amount of information. A feedback system causes the system to generate corrective responses, but it may not be desirable to have the system respond to small variations. A filter is established to eliminate feedback which does not reach the threshold requiring corrective action. Exception reports in industry which cover only those items which require action (all others are assumed to be within control limits) are an example of a filter.

filter lets only exception reports out

SYSTEM APPROACHES

The concepts associated with systems have been applied in various system approaches to problem solving and management. Two of these are quite significant for information system design—systems analysis and project management.

Systems Analysis

*define problem
determine objectives
evaluate strategies*

The essence of systems analysis is to attempt to look at the entire problem in context, to systematically investigate the objectives of the system and the criteria for system effectiveness, and to evaluate the alternatives in terms of effectiveness and cost. The results of the analysis indicate a re-questioning of the objectives and criteria, formulation of new alternatives, new cost/effectiveness studies, etc., until the problem, the objectives, the assumptions, the alternatives, and the cost/effectiveness of alternatives are clarified for decision making. The cost/effectiveness studies generally include a sensitivity analysis to determine how sensitive the system is to changes in the variables.

Systems analyses can use tools ranging from simple cost behavior analysis to sophisticated computer simulation. The mathematical modeling approach has been used substantially by science and operations research.

To appreciate the value and also the difficulties of the approach, consider the problem of allocating resources to higher education. In the non-system approach, resources (faculty, research funds, buildings, etc.) are allocated to academic departments on the basis of number of students, past allocations, bargaining strengths of department heads, etc. Evaluation is based on a multiplicity of individual, unrelated factors such as reputation of faculty. In the system approach, the departments are defined as systems which receive inputs and are to achieve specified, measurable objectives such as number of graduates. However, this example points up a problem in applying the system approach to areas such as education, namely, the defining of system goals that are measurable. How does one define quality of instruction? The U.S. Office of Education experimented with performance contracts for establishing and running remedial reading programs. In the non-system approach, such projects would have been evaluated in terms of students enrolled, student/teacher ratios, etc. In the system approach used, the projects were evaluated on the basis of measurable change in the ability of the participants to read. The mixed results of the experiment (a few successes, a few failures, most questionable) suggest the embryonic state of the use of such techniques in social service areas.

Project Management

Every organization has times when a special project must be undertaken such as building a new plant, developing a new product, or developing an information system. Some industries, such as aerospace, consist largely of this type of projects. An aerospace firm may have no continuing work of consequence, but may work only on development projects such as a new weapons system or a vehicle for space shuttle use. Other industries have large numbers of projects but only in certain functions such as new product development. The management of such projects may follow many different patterns, but a very successful approach can be termed the system approach to project management. It applies many of the concepts of systems described in this chapter.

The system approach to project management is essentially one of organizing around systems with system objectives. The first step in project management is to define carefully the project and the results expected and to choose a single project manager as responsible for the entire project. The unity or wholeness of the system is recognized by this action of putting a single person in charge of the project.

The manager of the project breaks down (factors) the project system into subsystems. Each subsystem is carefully defined as to its objectives, interfaces it makes with other subsystems, and time for delivery. Each is assigned to a subsystem manager. Each subsystem manager factors that subsystem in like manner with each subsystem being carefully defined as to input, output, interfaces, objectives, and time schedule for delivery. This process continues down to small, manageable elements. These manageable elements may be physical components in the case of a building or a missile, or they can be work units such as program modules in the case of software systems.

A project planning and control system is established to monitor each subsystem. The progress of each subsystem is followed with respect to time schedule, performance of completed system component, etc. As changes are made in specifications or time schedules are altered, the project management system communicates the necessary information to each subsystem that is affected. Planning and control are guided by system objectives. Performance for the project is measured by the system performance rather than by the performance of the separate subsystems.

This concept can be illustrated by a new weapons system such as a truck-mounted missile. A non-system approach might be to establish separate contracts for the missiles, the trucks, the training materials, the testing, etc. The system approach puts one person, a project manager, in complete charge of everything required to make the missile operational. Subcontracts may be let for subsystems, but there is close supervision based on the defined objectives and time requirement for each subsystem. It is, for example, irrelevant how good the truck is by itself. Only the performance of the truck as part of the system is important.

SYSTEM CONCEPTS APPLIED TO
MANAGEMENT INFORMATION SYSTEMS

As a system, the management information system and any of its subsystems may be studied and understood in terms of the system concepts described in the chapter. This section surveys the application of the system concepts to information processing systems.

Information System as a System

The information system receives inputs of data and instructions, processes the data according to the instructions, and outputs the results. The basic system model of input, process, and output is suitable in the simplest information processing system case when all inputs come in at the same time, but this is rarely true. The information processing function frequently needs data that was collected and processed in a prior period. A data file storage is therefore added to the information system model, so that the processing activity has available both current data and data collected and stored previously (Figure 4-11). When the data storage is added, the information processing function includes not only the transformation of data into information but also the storing of data for subsequent use. This basic information processing model is useful in understanding not only the overall information processing system but also the individual information processing applications. Each application may be analyzed in terms of input, storage, processing, and output.

The information processing system has functional subsystems such as the hardware system, the operating system, the communication system, and the data base system. It also has application subsystems such

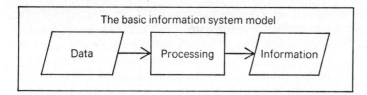

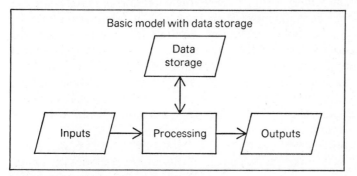

Figure 4-11 Basic information system model.

as order entry and billing, and payroll and personnel. The application subsystems make use of the functional subsystems (Figure 4-12).

System Approach to Information System Analysis and Design

An information system is sufficiently integrated and interconnected that it must be viewed as a single system, but it is also sufficiently complex that it must be broken into subsystems for planning and control of its development and for control of the operations. The system project nature of information processing applications means that the system approach to project control is generally appropriate. This suggests the following application of system concepts in development of information system projects:

    1 Information system is defined and overall responsibility assigned to one person.

    2 Major information processing subsystems are defined. Boundaries and interfaces are carefully specified.

    3 A development schedule is prepared.

    4 Each subsystem, when ready for development, is assigned to a project. The project leader factors the job into subsystems and assigns responsibility for each.

    5 A control system is used to monitor the development process.

The factoring of the information system into subsystems and these subsystems into smaller subsystems is vital because it makes feasible the subdividing of the very complex overall information system into manageable units of work. If each subsystem is carefully specified and carefully designed so that it fits the boundaries set for it and so that it will interface properly, the parts should fit and work together to make the whole.

The concept is very simple; the implementation is more complex. Some operational questions are: How big should a subsystem be? How should interfaces be defined? How can boundaries be defined to make them unambiguous? The problems arising when a subdivided system is put together are usually found at the boundaries and interfaces, so these operational questions are relevant in implementing the concept. The approach of using system, boundary, and interface definitions in planning, assigning, and controlling the design of a system is basic to a well-constructed information system.

A simple order entry system will illustrate the system approach to design. The system may be defined in terms of several subsystems or modules.

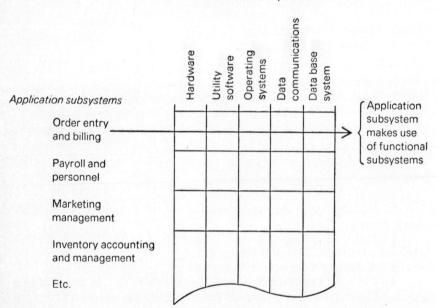

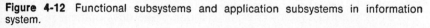

Figure 4-12 Functional subsystems and application subsystems in information system.

Subsystems	
Order entry system	Input procedures Input editing Credit checking Inventory checking and updating Order writing Warehouse picking Pricing and invoicing Error handling

Each of these subsystems of the order entry system can be defined in terms of the boundaries (what it does and does not do) and the interfaces (what it gets from other subsystems in this system or from other systems and what it must provide to other subsystems or systems). For example, the input editing subsystem receives defined inputs from the input procedure and provides defined outputs to the credit checking subsystem. It also interfaces with an error handling routine.

The black box concept is useful when subsystems, boundaries, and interfaces are being defined. Some processing subsystems can be considered as black boxes, and these do not need to be defined completely in order for the information system development to be started. For example, when planning the overall order entry system, credit checking may be viewed as a black box and not defined in terms of the rules, etc., for deciding whether a customer can be given credit. It is defined only as to input and output. The process is considered a black box. Later in the development process a system analyst is provided with the defined inputs and required outputs and assigned to work with the credit department as it defines the rules inside the black box.

Information System Design Concepts Derived from System Concepts

A number of design concepts important in the design of management information systems are derived from the system concepts described in this chapter. These are the use of subsystems, decoupling, feedback, requisite variety, and filtering.

Use of Subsystems The use of subsystems might also be termed a modular or building block concept. The concept of subsystems is used in project management, but it is also used in the design itself. This is illustrated by program design based on this concept. The program is designed as a number of modules or subprograms. Each module performs a program task such as reading input, output of report, or error checking. An executive module or mainline routine consists of the program steps to call the subprograms modules in the correct order. A subprogram module may call other modules (i.e., subsystems may communicate with each other).

The bounding of subsystems is important to system maintenance (i.e., updating and correcting). If a subsystem is clearly bounded and its interfaces clearly specified, a change or correction may be made more easily than if it were imbedded in a larger process because it is easier to evaluate the effects of the changes or corrections and easier to test the alteration.

Decoupling The concept of open system recognizes the certainty of disturbances to the system from the environment. In fact, the existence of an open system is dependent on its ability to adapt to environmental pressures and influences.

The concept of decoupling is based on the premise that systems which are open are difficult or impossible to tightly couple because of the communication requirements or because of the rate by which the coupled subsystems can adjust to each other. The methods of decoupling described earlier were use of inventory or buffers, use of slack resources, and use of standards. All are useful concepts in information system design.

Decoupling mechanism	Application to information processing system design
Inventory, buffer, or waiting line	In computer processing, the input/output systems operate at rates different from those of the processor. A buffer memory concept is used to hold data to compensate for the different rates.
	In a man/machine system, it is not possible for the man to receive or send whenever the computer sends or asks for a response. The computer is not always available to accept messages. This means that there must be a buffer in which to store messages to allow for this difference.
	In a manual system, one clerk may do the checking of invoices for payment and prepare the payment voucher. Another clerk checks the voucher, codes the transaction, and prepares the check. In a tightly coupled system, as soon as the first clerk finishes, the second clerk starts. But even if the average rates of production are the same, the two clerks do not finish each invoice at exactly the same time. Random influences affect one but not the other. The solution is an inventory of invoices to be checked and checks written between the first

Decoupling mechanism	Application to information processing system design
	and second clerk. In cases where prompt service is expected, but there are variations in arrival rates of people or messages, etc., to be serviced, a waiting line provides a decoupling mechanism. For example, in a telephone information service, it would be uneconomical to have sufficient personnel to handle the peak load of tele-phoned information requests. A waiting line is established by asking the person on the tele-phone to wait until an information analyst is free to process the call.
Slack resources	Computer hardware systems are generally designed with slack resources. A computer system is rarely fully loaded with work—some hours are not scheduled. This allows the systems to handle fluctuations in processing load. The accounts receivable department does not need to inform data processing that the number of receivables for processing will be 25 percent above normal. The slack resources of the computer will normally handle this input variation with-out strain. In designing information processing systems, the designer should consider having some slack resources in the system. In man/machine systems, the designer can plan that human processors will be able to respond to substantial short-term variations in activity. For example, a clerk receiving payments may be able to handle an average of 15 per hour. But he or she can probably increase processing to handle an increased demand—say, a doubling of rate for up to one hour at the doubled rate.
Standards	The use of standards can eliminate or reduce the need for communication among infor-mation subsystems. The use of standard methods (say, for handling loop utilization) and standards (say, flowchart standards) reduces the need for communication among programmers and system ana-lysts working on a project. A data base normally represents a simplification of the relations of the program to the data. A programmer does not have to consider all the other programs commu-nication with the data base. A standard method is provided for accessing the data base, thereby eliminating the need for close coordination with other subsystems.

Feedback Feedback requires a quantifiable standard by which to measure output and a method for the control input to affect the process. A budget is a common standard of performance provided by information processing. The feedback to the manager shows deviations from the budget standards. The manager then changes the activities to bring the process within budgetary limits (or may seek to change the standards).

Requisite Variety The essential point for information system design is the need to provide some method of supplying a control response to every possible state of the controlled variable. Since it is often difficult to enumerate all responses, the designer should consider enumerating the major cases in a decision situation and then use a supervisor or other person to generate responses to unusual situations.

Filtering Filters should be used in information systems to reduce unneeded or irrelevant data being accepted for processing or being output for another (perhaps human) subsystem.

SUMMARY

The chapter has described major system concepts with emphasis upon those having relevance for information system design.

A system consists of parts which belong together because of a purpose. The basic model is input, process, and output, but this can be expanded to include storage as well. Systems can be open or closed, but information systems are generally open systems, meaning that they receive some uncontrolled inputs from the environment.

The factoring of systems into subsystems is an important step in simplifying the design of systems. The use of subsystems usually requires some decoupling mechanisms to reduce the complexities of coordination and communication among them.

Control in systems is based on feedback. The loop may be open or closed. Filters may be used to reduce the processing requirements by reducing inputs. The law of requisite variety is important in designing control systems because it states the need for a method of obtaining a control response for every state of the variable being controlled.

The system approach is applied in orderly steps to systems analysis and to project management. The concepts of systems also have direct application to the design of information systems.

EXERCISES

1 Define:
   a System.
   b Subsystem.
   c Interface.
   d Boundary.
   e Black box.
   f Feedback.
   g Filtering.
2 Differentiate between:
   a Open and closed systems.
   b Open and closed loops.
   c Deterministic and probabilistic systems.
   d Negative and positive feedback.
3 Define the inputs, process, and outputs for the following systems:
   a Operating system (software).
   b Accounting system.
   c Heating system (for home).
   d School system.
4 Define the boundaries and interfaces for the following subsystems:
   a Disk storage subsystem.
   b Accounts payable subsystem.
   c Administrative subsystem (of school system).
   d Error analysis subsystem (of operating system).
5 a If there are 21 subsystems and each subsystem must be able to communicate with each other subsystem, how many interconnections must there be?
   b Suppose the 21 subsystems are arranged in three clusters of seven subsystems, each communicating with the others in the cluster and clusters communicating with each other. How many interconnections are required?
6 A student may be considered as a subsystem. Each course may be viewed as a subsystem which provides input and asks for output from the student subsystem. The coursework subsystems are not coordinated to level the student subsystem load. How does a student decouple?
7 How have the following systems handled the problem of decoupling:
   a The telephone system?
   b The computer center at a university?
   c The construction industry?
8 Explain the application of negative feedback in the following:
   a A management reporting system using budgets.
   b A management reporting system using standard costs.
   c A management reporting system reporting actual figures with no comparison.

9 An inventory decision rule is stated as:

$$Q = \sqrt{\frac{24S\ C_o}{C_u\ C_h}}$$

where S = monthly usage in units
C_o = cost of ordering
C_u = cost per unit
C_h = cost of holding as decimal

a Does this have requisite variety?
b Suppose the rule is supplemented by:
  (1) No order greater than 12 months supply.
  (2) No order less than 2 weeks supply.
  Is there still requisite variety?

10 An inventory decision rule is stated as:

Average usage per month	Order quantity
1–5	5
6–10	10
11–15	30
16–25	45

Does this have requisite variety? Explain.
11 What are the essential features of systems analysis?
12 Describe the system approach to project management using the example of preparing a textbook (many people working on it).
13 Explain how system concepts are applied (or are not applied) to management information systems in the following cases:
a Executive wants to see all sales over $50,000.
b Company insists programmers use modules in programming job.
c A data administrator controls all access and change of data base.
d Programming group issues standard programming practices manual.
e Clerk cannot complete unusual transaction. The clerk's instructions are to send the customer to assistant manager.
f The program documentation for a job for several error codes says: "can't happen." They did happen, but operator does not know what to do.
g Hours lost due to computer hardware failure are summarized for management. There is no agreed upon acceptable level.
h A total system idea is to be implemented. All files and processing are to be interrelated. There is immediate input, immediate response, immediate updating of all files, etc.
14 Explain the system objectives and criteria of effectiveness for:

  a A course subsystem (in a university).
  b A police system (in a community).
  c An information system for marketing.
  d An information system for an executive.
15 An analysis of a manufacturing company shows each subsystem operating well but the total operating very poorly as evidenced by:
  a Long delays between receipt of order and delivery.
  b Large inventories of raw material.
  c Large inventories in process.
  Explain this phenomenon in terms of system concepts.

SELECTED REFERENCES

Ackoff, R. I.: "Towards a System of System Concepts," *Management Science*, July 1971, pp. 661–671.

———: "Systems, Organizations, and Interdisciplinary Research," *General Systems Yearbook*, 1960, pp. 1–8. Also reprinted in F. E. Emery (see below).

Beckett, John A.: *Management Dynamics*, McGraw-Hill Book Company, New York, 1971.

Boulding, Kenneth: "General Systems Theory—The Skeleton of Science," *Management Science*, April 1956, pp. 197–208. Widely reprinted.

Buckley, Walter (ed.): *Modern Systems Research for the Behavioral Scientist*, Aldine Publishing Company, Chicago, 1968. Collection of articles.

Churchman, C. W.: *The Systems Approach*, Dell Books, Dell Publishing Co., Inc., New York, 1968.

Cleland, David I., and William R. King: *Systems Analysis and Project Management*, McGraw-Hill Book Company, New York, 1968.

DeGreen, Kenyon B. (ed.): *Systems Psychology*, McGraw-Hill Book Company, New York, 1970.

Emery, F. E. (ed.): *Systems Thinking*, Penguin Books, Inc., Baltimore, 1969.

Emery, James C.: *Organizational Planning and Control Systems*, The Macmillan Company, New York, 1969.

Hare, VanCourt, Jr.: *Systems Analysis: A Diagnostic Approach*, Harcourt, Brace & World, Inc., New York, 1967.

Kast, Fremont E., and James E. Rosenzweig: *Organization and Management, A Systems Approach*, McGraw-Hill Book Company, New York, 1970.

Katz, Daniel, and Robert L. Kahn: *The Social Psychology of Organizations*, John Wiley & Sons, Inc., New York, 1966.

Miller, James G.: *Living Systems*, John Wiley & Sons, Inc., New York, 1972.

———: "Living Systems: The Organization," *Behavioral Science*, January 1972, pp. 1–182.

Optner, Stanford L.: *Systems Analysis for Business Management*, 2d ed., Prentice-Hall, Inc., Englewood Cliffs, N.J., 1968.

————: *Systems Analysis for Business and Industrial Problem Solving*, Prentice-Hall, Inc., Englewood Cliffs, N.J., 1965.

Sayles, Leonard R., and Margaret K. Chandler: *Managing Large Systems*, Harper & Row, Publishers, Incorporated, New York, 1971.

Von Bertalanffy, Ludwig: "General System Theory," *General Systems*, Yearbook of the Society for Advancement of General Systems Theory, 1956, pp. 1–10.

————: *General System Theory: Foundations, Development, Applications*, George Braziller, Inc., New York, 1968.

————: "Theory of Open System in Physics and Biology," *Science*, vol. 111, January 1950, pp. 23–29.

Chapter 5

Concepts of Organization and Management Relevant to Information Systems

An understanding of organization and management is important to the analysis and design of the lowest level information processing systems; this understanding is vital to the design of a management information system.

No single, comprehensive theory of management can be described fully in a few pages. There is some diversity of opinion as to how best to organize and to manage. This chapter highlights the major concepts that are especially relevant to information system design. For the student who has already studied management theory, the chapter can be a review; for the student without prior study of management, the chapter provides background for the remainder of the text and provides an outline of areas for further study.

The implementation of computer-based information systems can have influences on organizational structure, motivation in organizations, management, and decision making. The chapter describes concepts regarding each of these and the implications for information system design.

MANAGEMENT THEORY

There is no single theory of management; rather, there are many theories which are both complementary and contradictory. A traditional starting point especially relevant to the designer of a management information system is to look at the management functions (what managers do).

There are a number of different classifications of management functions based primarily on the orientation of the writer.[1] For the purposes of this survey, a classification of five functions are used. These functions assume an organization with goals and objectives which cannot be achieved without management of the material and human resources.

In carrying out these five functions, the manager engages in structuring activities related to the function, decision making, and human interaction (Figure 5-1). The human interaction is with persons inside and outside the organization and with superiors and subordinates. Both the quality of his decision making and the quality of his interactions with people will affect the effectiveness with which the organization operates. The management functions, decision making, and human interactions are constrained by both the resources available to the organization and the overall environmental constraints for the environment (industry, society, etc.) in which the organization operates.

Management function	Comments
Planning	The selection of goals and defining of policies, procedures, and programs for achieving them.
Organizing	Grouping of activities to be performed and establishment of organizational forms and relations to carry out activities.
Staffing	Selecting and training of people to work in the organization.
Coordinating	Scheduling of activities in proper sequence. Communicating changes in requirements.
Directing	Leading, guiding, directing, and motivating people in the organization.
Controlling	The measurement of performance and performance deviations from the plan. Regulation and correction of activities or correction of policies, procedures, and programs.

[1]See "Management" by Marian V. Sears in Appendix A, "Notes on Terminology," in Robert N. Anthony, *Planning and Control Systems: A Framework for Analysis*, Harvard University Press, Cambridge, Mass., 1965.

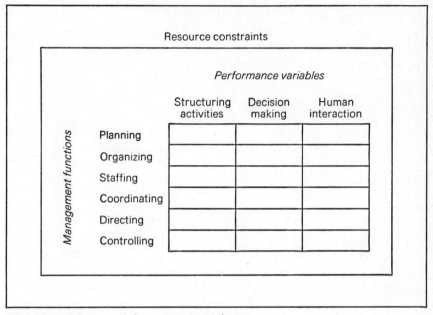

Figure 5-1 A framework for management theory.

This chapter explores human interactions, organizational forms, and planning and control. Chapter 6 is devoted to decision making in organizations.

ORGANIZATIONAL STRUCTURE—THE BASIC MODEL

The organizational structure is the arrangement of its subsystems with authority and responsibility relations. There are a few basic structures in common use. The circumstances under which each structure appears to be advantageous provide bases for changing organizational structure in response to changing conditions such as improved information processing and improved decision systems.

Hierarchical Structure

The basic organizational structure (Figure 5-2) is a hierarchical structure with the top management at the top of the chart, middle management in the middle, and lower management at the bottom. The chart is shaped like a pyramid because top management is small in numbers relative to lower-level management. The organization in Figure 5-2 is arranged

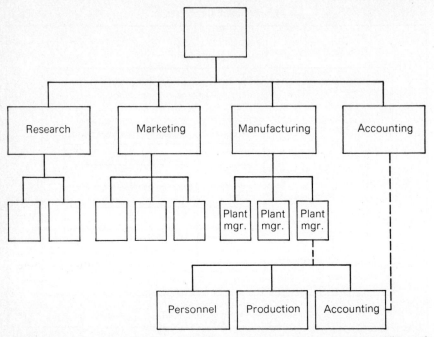

Figure 5-2 Basic hierarchical organization with functional specialization and line and staff relations.

functionally; i.e., the major subsystems under the president are functions of the organization such as manufacturing, marketing, and accounting.

Specialization

The organization divides work into specialized tasks and thus provides specialization. The accountant in the accounting function specializes in accounting. The marketing personnel specialize in marketing. The specialization may continue so that within a function there are specialists for smaller areas—taxation, market research, etc.

Line and Staff Relations

The line (solid lines) describes direct command authority for the functions of the organization. The marketing manager is reported to by sales managers. They have sales representatives reporting to them. Authority goes from top to bottom. Staff positions (broken lines) are concerned with support activities such as analysis and consultation. They have no authority of command over the operating personnel. If the marketing research specialist formulates a new marketing strategy, the specialist cannot implement it by telling the sales representatives to use it. The marketing manager must be convinced and must give the orders for use to the sales manager, who instructs the sales representatives.

Authority and Responsibility

must have auth if responsible for something

Authority is the right to command (leadership). If someone has the responsibility for an activity, that person should have the authority. Authority is evidenced by control over resources, rewards, and functions, and authorization to make decisions regarding them.

Span of Control

The span of control describes the number of subordinates that a superior is to supervise (i.e., the number reporting to the superior). The number is not defined by traditional management theory, but rules of thumb are that it should be small (say, three to seven). Recent research indicates that the effective span of control is dependent on the amount of communication required between the superior and the superior's subordinates. In effect, the information processing limits of the human are the limiting variable.

depends on ability to communicate

ORGANIZATIONAL STRUCTURE—VARIATIONS

The basic model (traditional management theory) emphasizes lines of authority, unity of command (each subordinate has only one superior), a narrow span of control, and use of staff support for the line organization. Authority and responsibility are identical in scope. The line executive is accountable for the performance of all subordinates. This basic model works well in some cases, but many organizations have found alternative structures more effective.

Three major variations on the basic organizational model are common: organization by product or service, use of lateral relations in a functional organization, and project organization.

Organization by Self-contained Product or Service

IBM Corp with divisions

Instead of being organized by functions such as manufacturing or marketing, the organization may be structured first by product (or service). Each product or service group will have its own functions for manufacturing, marketing, accounting, etc. Figure 5-3 illustrates this type of organization. Examples would be a business organization with product groups such as household supplies, appliances, and industrial solvents. A service or governmental organization might have service groupings. For example, a computer software firm might be organized by custom software, package software, and computer time sales.

The organization by product or service results in an organization

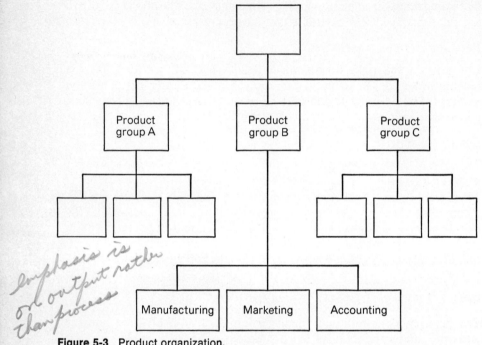

emphasis is on output rather than process

Figure 5-3 Product organization.

directed at the output rather than the processes. It seeks to bring under a unified command all decisions affecting the group of outputs.

Lateral Relations

A functional organization may be partially combined with a product or service organization by the use of lateral relations. The functional organization can be thought of as being a downward flow of activities. Products or services are thought of as flowing through the functional organization. Lateral relations are means for coordinating the activities of

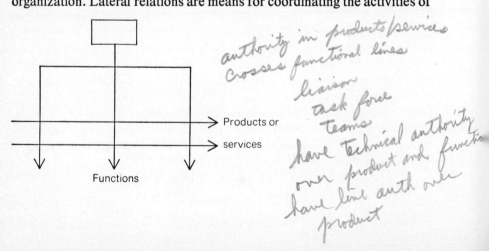

authority in products/services crosses functional lines

liaison
task force
teams
have technical authority over product and functi...
have line auth over product

different departments or functions as they operate to produce goods or services. Some methods for lateral relations are:

1 *Direct contact among managers.* Managers initiate contacts with other managers to resolve conflicts.
2 *Liaison roles.* Responsibility for coordinating lateral flow of a product or service is assigned to an individual. ~~appediter~~
3 *Task force.* A formal group with representation from each department or function is established to resolve conflicts.
4 *Teams.* Teams are formed around frequently occurring problems. For example, a team could be formed to handle certain groups of clients, regions, functions, or products.
5 *Integrating personnel.* Examples are product manager, project manager, and brand manager. They do not supervise actual work, but are responsible for the integration of the independent subunits.
6 *Matrix organization.* See discussion below.

The matrix organization illustrates a substantial use of integrating, lateral relations. For each product or service grouping there is a separate integrating department which has lateral relations with each level of the functional organization. Each level of the organization affected has a vertical authority relation for the function such as manufacturing and a lateral authority relation with the corresponding level of the integrating product or service department such as consumer products. This is illustrated in Figure 5-4. It can be described by a matrix with the rows being integration departments and the columns the functional departments.

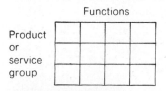

Functions

Product
or
service
group

needs special org. structure

project is temporary

MIS resources often assigned to projects this way. Have project leaders

Project Organization

In project organization, resources are assigned projects headed by a project director (Figure 5-5). A construction company might be organized in this way. Aerospace concerns have used the method for research and development projects. Information systems departments often use the project organization for management of the work of systems analysts and programmers. One might view a project organization as a dynamic form of the organization by product or service. The temporary nature of the projects necessitates special organizational responses to make, coordinate, and reassign resources among different projects. The project

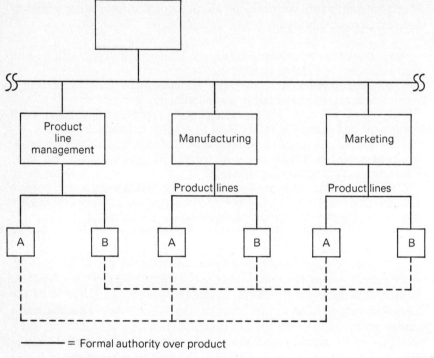

= Formal authority over product

---- = Technical authority over product

Figure 5-4 Matrix organization.

managers have considerable authority over the project and essentially "buy" resources from inside and outside the organization.

INFORMATION PROCESSING MODEL
FOR EXPLAINING ORGANIZATIONAL STRUCTURE

what form is best for an organization?

Several organizational patterns have been presented. A relevant question is how to determine the form that is most effective for a particular situation. A very useful approach to this question is based on the information processing and communication requirements that various situations impose on the organization.[2] The basic premise is that variations in organizational forms are explained by variations in the need for information processing and the differences in the ability of the various organizational forms to process and communicate information.

depends on how much info is required by organization for

[2]The information processing model is developed by Jay R. Galbraith in *Organizational Design: An Information Processing View*, Addison-Wesley Publishing Company, Reading, Mass., 1973. This section reflects many of the ideas in this study.

manual processing (not computer)

Amount of Information Processing

The need for an organization to process information (i.e., the amount of information) is a function of the following factors:

Factor	Comments
Task uncertainty	The greater the task uncertainty, the greater the amount of information that must be processed to ensure effective performance. This is consistent with information concepts presented in Chapter 2. If an activity is well understood, it can be preplanned; if it is not well understood, there will be many changes during task performance.
Number of elements relevant for decision making	The number of elements is related to number of departments, products, clients, etc. An increase in number of elements increases the need for information.
Interdependence of organizational units	If the organizational units are not interdependent or interrelated, the amount of communication for conflict resolution will be small; if they are highly interrelated, the information processing required to handle the coordination will be large.

more uncertainty, more info needed

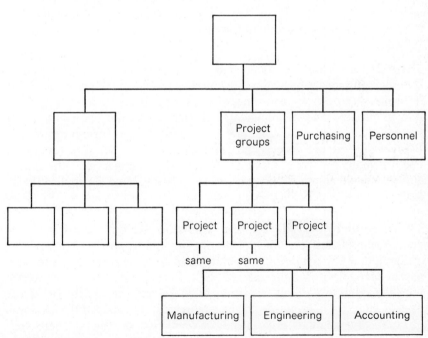

Figure 5-5 Project organization.

Organizational Responses to
Information Processing Requirements

Given that the amount of information processing required by an organization is a function of task uncertainty, number of elements relevant for decision making, and interdependence, the next step is to identify the organizational responses that allow it to handle the information processing load. These are:

(handwritten note in margin: these permit the organization to handle the info processing load.)

1 Operating procedures and
   decision rules

2 Hierarchy of authority
3 Self-organizing subsystems

                                coordinating
                                mechanisms

4 Slack resources

                                reduce need for
                         information processing

5 Self-contained structures
6 Vertical information systems

                                increase capacity for
                         information processing

7 Lateral organizational forms

These responses are not independent—several or even all may be used by the same organization. Some resources act to reduce the need for information processing and others increase the capacity of the organization to process and communicate information in the organization. Of special relevance to the computer-based information system designer is the fact that the use of a computer to process information faster is only one of many possible ways to handle the problem of information processing and communication in an organization. Note the application of system concepts described in Chapter 4.

(handwritten note in margin: Checking Credit limits etc)

Operating Procedures and Decision Rules   Coordination is greatly simplified if organizational behavior can be specified in advance (programmed) by operating procedures and decision rules. This provides partial decoupling of organizational units. Different parts of the organization can operate without communication because the behavior of the parts is known. This solution can be applied to a large part of the activities of some organizations, but to only a small part of others. There will, however, always be many situations that cannot be covered by operating procedures or decision rules.

Hierarchy of Authority   A hierarchy of authority is used for handling unusual situations that are not covered by decision rules and operating procedures. Exceptions are passed up to higher levels in the organization. Conflict involving two organizational units is moved up to the executive who has responsibility over both. For example, a conflict involving inventory at two plants, if not resolved by the plant managers, is referred to the vice-president for manufacturing to whom both plants report. The information processing load imposed on an executive by these and other activities is the major element controlling the span of control that an executive can effectively exercise.

Self-organizing Subsystems   Uncertainty of organizational tasks limits the use of decision rules and operating procedures. It also limits the use of a hierarchy of authority because of the processing load imposed by the number of responses required of executives. One organizational response to these conditions is to define various parts of the organization as self-organizing subsystems. In other words, the organizational unit is given goals plus output and interface specifications and then allowed to exercise discretion as to resource use in meeting the goals. This is also termed *local rationality.*

Slack Resources   The interdependencies that cause organizational communication and information processing can be reduced by relaxing the specifications under which each organizational unit operates or by providing more resources. Each unit operates under time, resource (budget, manpower, etc.), and product specification constraints. Relaxing one or more of these constraints provides slack resources and tends to reduce the necessity for coordination because one of the major needs for interaction is to attempt to resolve conflicts caused by the inability of subunits to perform within the constraints.

Self-contained Structures   Product group organization is an example of self-contained structures. Segments of the organization are furnished with the resources needed to stand alone for decision making. Each product group is provided with its own facilities for manufacturing, marketing, accounting, and other functions. This reduces the number of levels through which decisions must pass that affect two functions such as manufacturing and marketing. However, this occurs at the expense of duplication in facilities and loss of economies of scale and specialization.

Vertical Information Systems The ability of the organization to provide direction under conditions of uncertainty is limited by the time and resources that are required for planning and replanning. The use of self-organizing subsystems is also limited by the amount of planning and replanning to reconcile the changing goals of the subsystems.

The planning and replanning time cycle may be reduced by adding staff (assistants), scheduling staffs, using computer processing, and providing better access to data bases for planning.

Computers also strengthen the use of operating procedures and decision rules because more complex decision rules may be handled with the use of the computer.

Lateral Organizational Forms The lateral organizational forms reviewed earlier in the chapter are means for increasing the communication/information processing capacity of the organization. These are:

1 Direct contact
2 Liaison
3 Task force
4 Teams
5 Integrating personnel
6 Matrix organization

lateral relations is when product group manager wants to know and direct mfg, sale, financing of his own product area

They are listed in approximate order as to their use in situations of task uncertainty. An organization with very uncertain tasks will tend to use more and more of the methods, whereas an organization with less uncertainty may use only the first two methods.

The use of computer data bases may have an effect on lateral communications. If it is possible for an interfacing unit to interrogate a data base to learn about factors generated by another subunit which affect its performance, the need for lateral relations may be reduced or efficiency of lateral relations improved.

HUMAN INTERACTION IN ORGANIZATIONS

Early management theory was somewhat mechanistic in its view of human interaction. The goals of the members of an organization were assumed to be consistent with the organization goals (or at least sublimated to the organization goals). Employees were assumed to respond positively to authority and to be motivated by monetary rewards. The human relations movement which began with the famous Hawthorne studies between 1927 and 1932 established the concept of the organization as a social system. Motivation was found to be based on more than economic reward. Work groups, coworkers, etc., were found to be important. Leadership styles were suggested which would increase the satisfaction of workers with the organization. The behavioral research results have not led to a single set of proved principles, but the main thrust of the research suggests the need to consider human needs in designing organizations.

define → Motivation is the reason for a person to carry out certain activities. *person's* This is usually explained in terms of the person's drives or needs. The *needs* needs of a person are not fixed; they change over time with the stage of *change* his career, and as certain needs receive more satisfaction. A useful *over* classification of general human needs is a hierarchy developed by *time* Abraham Maslow.[3] It cites five basic needs, but the higher needs become activated only to the extent that lower needs have been somewhat satisfied.

The Maslow hierarchy is useful because it points up an important dimension of human need. A starving man concentrates on physiological needs, but when his hunger is satisfied, he becomes concerned about safety and perhaps love and esteem. As needs for safety, love, and esteem are met, the need for self-actualization becomes important. This suggests that organizations cannot depend only on satisfactory pay and safe working conditions to motivate personnel.

Whereas the Maslow hierarchy is of general applicability, a classification more directly related to work situations was developed by Frederick Herzberg.[4] Two clusters of factors relate to job satisfaction. One group comprises environmental factors (called hygiene factors) which do

Level	Need	Explanation
Lowest	Physiological	The physical needs such as satisfaction of hunger or thirst, and activity need.
	Safety	Protection against danger, threat, deprivation.
	Love	Satisfactory associations with others, belonging to groups, giving and receiving friendship and affection.
	Esteem	Self-respect and respect of others.
Highest	Self-actualization	Self-fulfillment. Achieving one's potential. Creativity. Self-development. Self-expression.

[3]A. H. Maslow, "A Theory of Human Motivation," *Psychological Review*, July 1943, pp. 370–396.

[4]Frederick Herzberg, *Work and the Nature of Man*, The World Publishing Company, Cleveland, 1966.

not motivate satisfaction, but their absence will cause dissatisfaction. These are company policy and administration, supervision, salary, interpersonal relations, and working conditions. The other group of factors are termed "motivators" because they are determinants of job satisfaction (which is assumed to lead to superior performance). These are achievement, recognition, interesting and challenging work, responsibility, and advancement.

It should be noted that there is controversy over the validity of the two-factor theory of Herzberg and to a lesser extent to the need theory of Maslow.[5] However, even though there may be oversimplifications, they do provide useful descriptive categories and insight into the motivation of organizational personnel.

Group Dynamics

Within an organization, an individual normally belongs to one or more small groups. They may be formal organizational groups such as a production work team or they may be based on common interests such as ethnic background, profession, recreational pursuits (the bowling club), or car pools. There is much evidence which suggests that small groups are important factors influencing the relations between the individual and the organization.

Leadership Styles

Leadership is interpersonal influence which persuades or motivates a group toward the attainment of a specified goal or goals. This section reviews alternate views of how an organization should be managed and describes theories about leadership.

The way a manager views his or her task may be conditioned by the manager's view of man. McGregor[6] has characterized the two extremes as "Theory X" and "Theory Y."

Theory X[7]   The Theory X view of man, as summarized below, is supportive of an authoritarian leadership style:

1   Management is responsible for organizing the elements of

[5]For summary of research on these theories, see Alan C. Filley and Robert J. House, *Managerial Process and Organizational Behavior*, Scott, Foresman and Company, Glenview, Ill., 1969, pp. 368–387.

[6]Douglas M. McGregor, *The Human Side of Enterprise*, McGraw-Hill Book Company, New York, 1960.

[7]Douglas M. McGregor, "The Human Side of Enterprise," *Management Review*, November 1957, pp. 23, 88–89.

productive enterprise—money, materials, equipment, people—in the interest of economic ends.

2 With respect to people, this is a process of directing their efforts, motivating them, controlling their actions, and modifying their behavior to fit the needs of the organization.

3 Without this active intervention by management, people would be passive—even resistant—to organizational needs. They must therefore be persuaded, rewarded, punished, controlled—their activities must be directed. This is management's task. We often sum it up by saying that management consists of getting things done through other people.

Theory Y The Theory Y view of man is, in contrast to Theory X, supportive of a more democratic and participative leadership style:

1 Management is responsible for organizing the elements of productive enterprise—money, materials, equipment, people—in the interest of economic ends.

2 People are not by nature passive or resistant to organizational needs. They have become so as a result of experience in organizations.

3 The motivation, the potential for development, the capacity for assuming responsibility, the readiness to direct behavior toward organizational goals are all present in people. Management does not put them there. It is the responsibility of management to make it possible for people to recognize and develop these human characteristics for themselves.

4 The essential task of management is to arrange organizational conditions and methods of operation so that people can achieve their own goals best by directing their own efforts toward organizational objectives.

Organizational behavior based on Theory X is widespread and is clearly operational. However, those who prefer the assumptions of Theory Y claim that Theory X has a human cost in the frustration and lack of human development from its application. The trend in behavioral research suggests benefits from organization and leadership based on Theory Y assumptions. One such approach is termed System Four by Likert[8] (the other three being authoritative, benevolent authoritative, and consultative). System Four is characterized by a supportive relation by manager and by group decision making and supervision.

Behavioral researchers have identified several types of leadership styles. The two most important are autocratic and supportive:

[8]Rensis Likert, *The Human Organization*, McGraw-Hill Book Company, New York, 1967.

leadership style

Type	Explanation
Autocratic	The leader determines policy and directs the activities required to carry it out. He or she seldom gives reasons for orders. The leader's commands are enforced by the power to reward or punish.
Supportive	This type is called participative, consultative, or democratic leadership. The leader solicits suggestions and consults with his subordinates about decisions affecting them or decisions they will have to carry out. Supervision is general, and subordinates are encouraged to use initiative.

Other styles are laissez faire, in which the leader provides little direction or regulation, and bureaucratic, in which leadership is based on a set of rules or procedures (a form of autocracy). Some researchers have suggested that the most effective style of leadership is dependent on the personality of the leader; the tasks to be performed; the attitudes, needs, and expectations of the subordinates; and the organizational and physical environment. This is termed *situational theory*.

The evidence to date suggests that a supportive leadership style leads to higher satisfaction, but not necessarily to higher production. One important consideration is the extent to which the manager carries out the management functions (planning, organizing, etc.). Carrying out these functions (also termed *instrumental leadership behavior*) provides the structure which is important to productivity. When highly supportive leadership is combined with effective instrumental leadership behavior, the results have indicated both high satisfaction and high productivity.

An autocratic, nonparticipative leadership style is apparently most effective[9] (especially if benevolent) when decisions are routine, there are standard procedures and rules, and subordinates do not feel a need to participate. Supportive, participative leadership is apparently most effective when decisions are not routine, information and rules for decision making are not standardized, there is sufficient time to involve subordinates, and subordinates feel the need for independence and feel their participation is legitimate.

Implications for Information Systems Design

Designers of computer-based information/decision systems are frequently guilty of the mechanistic view of the human in the system. For example, a proposed online system designed for the loan officers of a bank intended to automate a large number of functions formerly per-

[9]Based on Filley and House, *op. cit.*, pp. 405 and 406.

info system must leave some variety for interesting job environment.

formed manually. The system appeared feasible and very advantageous. However, when the job content which the designers proposed for the loan officer was examined, it was found to have insufficient variety to make an interesting job environment. The system was restructured to enrich the job of the loan officer at a small reduction in some of the automated functions.

If an autocratic, nonparticipative style of leadership and a mechanistic, economic motivation are assumed, the decision system design is clearly less complicated. Functions can be allocated between man and machine on the basis of relative efficiency. Computer-based decision rules provide instant decisions with little participation. However, the following factors suggest difficulties in pursuing this view for all systems.

Problem	Comments
Not all managers have the same leadership style.	This may mean that a system designed for a non-participative leader will not suit a participative leadership style.
Computerizing some activities may reduce task variety and make a job less interesting.	Computers do not need variety; humans do. Computers make possible assembly line style pacing for many clerical and managerial activities, but if the job is reduced in variety, it may cause boredom.
Not all work groups have the same need for participation.	For example, where decisions must be made quickly, there will be little demand for participation. But where the technical ability of subordinates is equal to or even greater than the leader (such as in a research group), participation is likely to be important.

The importance of the structuring activities of the manager (instrumental behavior) suggests that information/decision systems should not overlook the use of the system as a method for helping the manager to initiate structure by planning, organizing, etc. For example, planning forms assist the manager to do the planning activities. In much the same way, man/machine routines can aid the manager's instrumental behavior.

The information system designer may find the area of organizational interaction difficult because the rules and principles are not well defined. However, there are some central tendencies that can be relied upon. Man is clearly quite adaptable and operates successfully in a wide range of systems, so that a system designer need not strive for precision in these matters, but should not overlook the behavioral implications of design alternatives.

PLANNING AND CONTROL

A plan is a predetermined course of action. It represents organizational goals and the activities necessary to achieve the goals. This section surveys the problem of goal setting in organizations and the characteristics of different levels of planning.

Setting of Goals

It is customary to talk of the goals of an organization as if the organization existed apart from its members. As Cyert and March point out,[10] people have goals; collections of people do not. The goals of an organization represent, in effect, a series of constraints imposed on the organization by its participants. If the organization is viewed as a coalition of individuals, each of which has goals, the goals arrived at for the coalition represent bargaining among the members. The goals change in response to changes in the coalition membership and to changes in the goals of the participants.

The bargaining is in general very constrained by the existing structure. Through mechanisms such as operating procedures, decision rules, and budgets, coalition agreements are made semipermanent. The individuals in an organization have limited time to devote to the bargaining process, so that bargaining tends to start not fresh each time but from the current state of affairs. Attention is not focused on all matters at once, but in general in a sequential fashion as the demand arises. Goals in an organization tend to have inherent contradictions, but devices such as organizational slack are used to "absorb" the inconsistency.

The goals of business firms are generally stated in terms of goals for profit, market share, sales, inventory, and production. These must be expressed in operational terms. If the goal cannot be stated quantitatively, substitute goals may be used for this program. The goal "to be a pleasant place to work" is nonoperational. "To reduce turnover to 4 percent" is more meaningful in operational terms.

When objectives are clearly and operationally stated, they form the basis for a plan to achieve goals. When each manager assists in setting goals and means for achieving them and then is measured by how well he or she achieves them, the firm is using what is termed *management by objectives*.

Hierarchy of Planning

A hierarchy of different levels of planning can be identified on the basis of the planning horizon for each level. Three levels frequently referred to in

[10]Richard M. Cyert and James G. March, *A Behavioral Theory of the Firm*, Prentice-Hall, Inc., Englewood Cliffs, N.J., 1963, pp. 26–45.

the literature are strategic planning, tactical planning, and operational planning.[11] They correspond roughly to long-term, middle-term, and short-term planning.

Strategic planning deals with long-range considerations. The decisions to be made relate to business the firm should be in, the market it should sell to, the product mix, etc.

Tactical planning (also identified as management control) is concerned with a medium-term planning horizon. It includes the way resources should be acquired and organized, work structured, and personnel acquired and trained. It is reflected in the capital expenditure budget, the three-year staffing plan, etc.

Operational planning is related to short-term decisions for current operations. Pricing, production levels, inventory levels, etc., are reflected in an operational plan such as a yearly budget.

Control

Control is the activity which measures deviations from planned performance and initiates corrective action. The basic elements of control are:

1   A standard specifying expected performance. This can be a budget, an operating procedure, a decision algorithm, etc.

2   A measurement of actual performance.

3   A comparison of expected and actual performance.

4   A report of deviations to a control unit such as a manager.

5   A set of actions the control unit (manager) can take to change future performance if currently unfavorable. A set of decision rules for selecting appropriate responses.

6   In the event of failure of control unit actions to bring actual unfavorable performance into close harmony with expected performance, a method for a higher planning/control level to change one or more conditions such as new control unit (manager), or revised performance standard.

This sounds in part like the description of a feedback loop in Chapter 4, and in fact the control process is just that. The manager or control unit need be concerned only with deviations outside allowable control limits. This reduces the information processing requirements of the manager and focuses his attention on the items needing investigation or corrective

---

[11]An identical and very common classification using different terminology is Anthony's strategic planning, management control, and operational control. R. N. Anthony, *Planning and Control Systems: A Framework for Analysis*, Harvard University Press, Cambridge, Mass., 1965.

action. This is management by exception and the basis for all variance reporting.

Control activities are subject to the law of diminishing returns. A process can be overcontrolled in the sense that the incremental cost of the controls is greater than the incremental benefit. One sees in every organization examples of controls costing many dollars which have at best a value of a few cents. Or the resources for control are misallocated. For example, a medium-size manufacturing concern had a three-person forms control unit to handle the design, production, and control of forms in use by the company. While a very useful activity, the company had no planning staff and no staff to investigate recurrent inventory problems which finally resulted in a multimillion dollar loss. The gross misallocation of control resources is apparent.

Implications for Information Systems Design

The limitations on the human as an information processor puts a fairly low limit on the amount of manual planning. The processing cost and time to prepare planning variations for consideration is high. A computer-assisted planning procedure removes these constraints.

The control feedback loop is basic to systems design. The computer can improve the control process in several ways:

1 The standard can be more complex. Computational simplifications are not necessary. (But people will generally object to being evaluated by a standard they are unable to compute easily.)
2 The computation of deviation and identification of cause can be more sophisticated.
3 The reporting with computers can use irregular time intervals which is very difficult with manual processing.

SUMMARY

It is vital that the designer of management information systems understands organization and management theory because the systems being designed affect both the organization and its management.

The management functions of planning, organizing, and others involve structuring activities, decision making, and human interactions. The structuring activities consist of formulating the problems to be solved, putting priorities on various activities, defining the limits for solutions to be worked on, etc. Both manual and computer-based procedures can be used to assist the manager to provide structure by suggesting possible structures.

The organizing function involves the formulating of an organization structure and assignment of responsibility and authority. There are a few "principles" which traditionally have been used to decide on the organizational form. However, the organization best suited for a task depends on many factors, one of the most important being the requirements placed on the organization for communication and information processing (by individuals, not computers).

Human interaction is a vital ingredient in an organization. The production effect of different patterns of leadership seems to depend on several factors, but the satisfaction of employees is generally higher with participative, supportive management.

Goal setting is an important element of management. One theory is that such goals are a result of bargaining among the individuals in the group, each one having his individual goals. Planning is carried on at all levels of an organization. It can be classified into three types of planning: strategic, tactical, and operational. Control is exercised through a feedback mechanism and requires elements such as a measurable standard of performance against which to measure actual performance.

EXERCISES

1 What are the functions of management? Why does not everyone agree on the same list?
2 Describe the basic organizational model. What are the principles underlying this model?
3 Explain how each of the different organizational variations differ in form from the basic model.
4 Using the information processing model, explain why each of the organizational forms is used. Define the conditions which suggest the use of each model.
5 Explain the Maslow hierarchy of needs. How is it relevant to organization and management?
6 Explain Theory X and Theory Y and how they are related to management.
7 Identify leadership styles. If leadership style does not affect production (evidence not clear), what difference does it make?
8 What are the implications of the human interaction element to the design of information/decision systems?
9 How does the managerial performance of structuring activities affect performance by subordinates?
10 Evaluate the argument of Cyert and March that only individuals can have goals. Does their theory mean that there are no organizational goals that can be identified?
11 What are the elements of control? Using the budget as an example, show the way the budget is used for each of the elements of control.

SELECTED REFERENCES

*Anthony, Robert N.: *Planning and Control Systems: A Framework for Analysis*, Harvard Graduate School of Business Administration, Boston, 1965.

Argyris, Chris: "The Individual and Organization: Some Problems of Mutual Adjustment," *Administrative Science Quarterly*, vol. 2, no. 1, 1957, pp. 1–24.

*Cyert, Richard M., and James G. March: *A Behavioral Theory of the Firm*, Prentice-Hall, Inc., Englewood Cliffs, N.J., 1963.

Drucker, Peter F.: *The Practice of Management*, Harper & Row, Publishers, Incorporated, New York, 1954.

Filley, Alan C., and Robert J. House: *Managerial Process and Organizational Behavior*, Scott, Foresman and Company, Glenview, Ill., 1969. Excellent for understanding the evidence which supports management and organizational theory.

*Galbraith, Jay R.: *Organizational Design: An Information Processing View*, Addison-Wesley Publishing Company, Inc., Reading, Mass., 1973.

Herzberg, F.: "One More Time: How Do You Motivate Employees?," *Harvard Business Review*, January-February 1968, pp. 53–62.

*Hofstede, G. H.: *The Game of Budgetary Control*, Royal Van Gorcum, Ltd., Assen, The Netherlands, 1967. An excellent text for understanding the human problems of budgeting.

Koontz, Harold, and Cyril O'Donnell: *Principles of Management*, 4th ed., McGraw-Hill Book Company, New York, 1968. A good survey of management.

*Likert, Rensis: *The Human Organization: Its Management and Value*, McGraw-Hill Book Company, New York, 1967. Describes management system called System Four.

*McGregor, Douglas: *The Human Side of Enterprise*, McGraw-Hill Book Company, New York, 1960. Describes Theory X and Theory Y.

*March, James, and Herbert A. Simon: *Organizations*, John Wiley & Sons, Inc., 1958.

Mee, John F.: "Matrix Organization," *Business Horizons*, Summer, 1964.

Paul, W. J., Jr., K. B. Robertson, and F. Herzberg: "Job Enrichment Pays Off," *Harvard Business Review*, March–April 1969, pp. 61–78.

Pugh, D. S., D. J. Hickson, and C. R. Hinings: *Writers on Organization*, 2d ed., Penguin Books Ltd., Harmondsworth, England, 1971. A brief but useful summary of major writers and researchers.

Starr, Martin K.: *Management: A Modern Approach*, Harcourt Brace Jovanovich, New York, 1971. An unusual management text taking a modeling, management science approach.

*These references are especially relevant to the information systems specialist and should be part of his background knowledge.

Chapter 6

Decision-making Concepts
for Information Systems

How are decisions made? The answer affects the design of computer-based information systems which are intended to support the decision-making process. The purpose of this chapter is to summarize the major concepts of decision making and then to explain the relevance of the theories to design of information systems.

PROCESS OF DECISION MAKING

The useful and well-known model proposed by Herbert A. Simon will be used as the basis for describing the decision-making process. It consists of three major phases:[1]

---

[1]Herbert A. Simon, *The New Science of Management Decision*, Harper & Brothers, New York, 1960, pp. 54 ff.

Phase of decision-making process	Explanation
Intelligence	Searching the environment for conditions calling for decisions. Raw data is obtained, processed, and examined for clues that may identify problems.
Design	Inventing, developing, and analyzing possible courses of action. This involves processes to understand the problem, to generate solutions, and to test solutions for feasibility.
Choice	Selecting a particular course of action from those available. A choice is made and implemented.

[handwritten margin notes: define problem / list strategies / evaluate and select a strategy]

The decision process can thus be conceived of as a flow from intelligence to design and then to choice, but at any phase the result may be a return to a previous phase to start over. The phases are thus elements of a continuous process. For example, the choice may be to reject all the alternatives and to return to the design phase for generation of additional solutions (Figure 6-1).

The force which initiates the decision-making process is either dissatisfaction with the current state or expected rewards from a new state. In the case of dissatisfaction, the initiating force is the discovery of

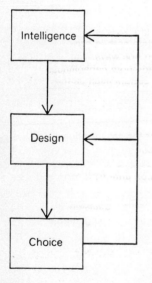

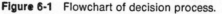

Figure 6-1 Flowchart of decision process.

a problem; in the case of expected rewards, it results from the search for opportunities.

Another way to explain the process of decision making is in terms of a continuous activity motivated by an objective of transforming the system (business, department, family, etc.) from its current state to a desired state. The desired state or goal causes a search for the means to achieve it. This process is often termed a *means-end analysis*.

Some models of decision making place more emphasis on feedback of results of the decision. For example, Rubenstein and Haberstroh proposed the following steps:[2]

1 Recognition of problem or need for decision
2 Analysis and statement of alternatives
3 Choice among the alternatives
4 Communication and implementation of decision
5 Followup and feedback of results of decision

systems approach

use this

The two models are not contradictory. The Simon model essentially says that execution is decision and that another decision is required for followup.

The Simon model is relevant to the design of management information systems. This relevance is summarized for the three phases of the Simon model.

Phase of decision-making process	Relevance to MIS
Intelligence	The search process involves an examination of data both in pre-defined and in ad hoc ways. The MIS should provide both capabilities. The information system itself should scan all data and trigger a request for human examination of situations apparently calling for attention. Either the MIS or the organization should provide communication channels for perceived problems to be moved up the organization until they can be acted upon.
Design	The MIS should contain decision models to process data and generate

[2]A. A. Rubenstein and C. J. Haberstroh (eds.), *Some Theories of Organization*, Richard D. Irwin, Inc., Homewood, Ill., 1965.

Phase of decision-making process	Relevance to MIS
	alternate solutions. The models should assist in analyzing the alternatives.
Choice	A MIS is most effective if the results of design are presented in a decision-impelling format. When the choice is made, the role of the MIS changes to the collection of data for later feedback and assessment.

FRAMEWORKS AND CONCEPTS FOR DECISION MAKING

There are a number of different ways of classifying decision making. An understanding of these frameworks and concepts will be useful in subsequent discussion.

Decision-making Systems

A decision system, i.e., the model of the system by which decisions are made, is either open or closed. A *closed decision system* assumes that the decision is insulated from unknown inputs from the environment. In this system the decision maker is assumed to:

1 Have knowledge of the set of alternatives and the consequences or outcomes of each.
2 Have a method (rule, relation, etc.) which allows him to make a preference ordering of the alternatives.
3 Choose the alternative which maximizes something, such as profit, sales volume, or utility.

The concept of a closed decision system clearly assumes the rational man who logically examines all alternatives, preference-orders the consequences, and selects the alternative which leads to the best (maximizing) consequence. The quantitative models of decision making are typically closed decision system models.

An *open decision system* views the decision as taking place in a complex and partially unknown environment. The decision is influenced by the environment, and the decision process in turn influences the environment. The decision maker is assumed not to be logical and completely rational but rather to display rationality only within limits imposed by background, perception of alternatives, ability to handle a decision model, etc. This is the bounded rationality described in Chapter 3. Whereas the goal of the closed model is well defined, the goal of the open model is similar to an aspiration level in that it may change as the decision maker receives evidence of success or failure. Compared with the three assumptions of the closed model, the open decision model assumes that the decision maker:

1 Does not know all alternatives and all outcomes.
2 Makes a limited search to discover a few satisfactory alternatives.
3 Makes a decision which satisfies his aspiration level.

The open model is dynamic over a sequence of choices because the aspiration level changes in response to the discrepancy between outcome and aspiration level. This is explored further in the description of the behavioral theory of decision making in a later section of this chapter.

Knowledge of Outcomes

An outcome defines what will happen if a decision is made and/or course of action taken. In the analysis of decision making, three types of knowledge with respect to outcomes are usually distinguished:

Outcome state	Explanation
Certainty	Complete and accurate knowledge of the outcome from each choice. There is only one outcome for each choice.
Risk	The possible outcomes can be identified, and a probability of occurrence can be attached to each.
Uncertainty	Several outcomes are possible and can be identified, but there is no knowledge of the probability to be attached to each outcome.

If the outcomes are known and the consequences of the outcomes are certain, the problem of decision making is to compute the optimal action/outcome. However, the computation can be quite large or impractical. Linear programming is an example of a technique for locating an optimal solution under certainty. Without a computer, linear programming problems of any size are computationally infeasible. Even with the computer, some problems are too large for standard computation methods.

The making of rational decisions when only the probabilities of various outcomes are known is similar to certainty, but instead of maximizing the outcome, the general rule is to maximize the expected outcome. For example, faced with a choice between two actions, one offering a probability of 1 percent of a gain of $10,000 and the other a 50 percent chance of a gain of $400, the rational decision maker will choose the second because it has the higher expected value.

Probability	× outcome	=	expected value
.01	× 10,000	=	100
.50	× 400	=	200

There are several difficulties with the rational approach using expected value. Expected value as a criterion is most valid when the decision will be repeated. But if the decision is made only once, there is evidence to suggest that behavioral factors will influence the decision. Also, objective probabilities may not be available, only subjective probabilities. These conditions are explored later in the chapter.

Decisions under uncertainty (outcomes known but not probabilities) present a problem because the maximization criteria cannot be applied. Most suggestions for handling uncertainty are designed to supply the unknown probabilities so that the problem can be treated as a decision problem under risk. For example, one suggestion is to assign equal probabilities. Other decision rules that have been suggested are to minimize regret and to use the maximin and maximax criteria. These are explained in connection with the statistical decision theory.

Decision Response

Decisions can be classed as programmed or nonprogrammed on the basis of the ability of the organization or individual to preplan the process of making the decision. *Programmed decisions* are those decisions that can be prespecified by a set of rules or decision procedures. Programmed decisions can presumably be handled by a computer program since the rules for arriving at a decision are completely defined and only the values of variables must wait for the specific problem. In addition to a computer program, other examples of methods for implementing programmed decisions are rule books, decision tables (say, in a manual procedure), and regulations. These programmed decision methods imply a closed decision model because all outcomes and consequences must be known.

Nonprogrammed decisions are one-time or recurring decisions which change each time they are required. Decisions in an open decision system are nonprogrammed because it is not possible to prespecify all factors. Nonprogrammed decisions may range from one-time decisions relating to one-time crisis such as a civil war in a country where a plant is located to decisions relating to recurring problems that change so much that decision rules cannot be formulated.

Programmed decisions can be delegated to low levels in an organization; nonprogrammed generally cannot. One strategy for increasing the number of programmable decisions is to specify rules for all normal conditions and let the programmed decision rules handle these normal cases. When conditions or actions do not fit the decision rules, the decision becomes nonprogrammed and is given to a higher level of decision making. In a decision table analogy, the decision table has an ELSE rule with the action being "refer to supervisor." The dangers of programmed decision methods are, of course, rigidities and attempts to apply inappropriate rules.

Descriptions of Decision Making

A model of decision making which tells the decision maker how he *should* make a class of decision is *normative* or *prescriptive*. A model which describes how decision makers actually make decisions is *descriptive*. The normative models have generally been developed by economics and management science. Linear programming, game theory, capital budgeting, and statistical decision theory are examples of normative models. The descriptive models attempt to explain actual behavior and therefore have been developed largely by behavioral scientists.

Criteria for Decision Making

The criterion for selecting among alternatives in the normative model is maximization (of profit, utility, expected value, etc.). This goal, when stated in quantitative terms, is referred to as the objective function for a decision. In the classical economic model, rational man was assumed to maximize utility, utility being defined as the pleasure-giving or pain-avoiding properties of the outcome. For a business firm, utility is usually thought of as being profit, but it can also be sales, market share, etc. The traditional view of the criterion for decision making under risk is to maximize expected value. There is evidence that suggests limitations on this criterion. For example, people who fly in airplanes buy flight insurance, yet the expected value of the insurance is well below the cost, the difference being accounted for by the high-cost sales method and the profit to the insurance companies. Phenomena such as this have resulted in the suggestion that individuals choose so as to maximize expected utility rather than expected value. In other words, the utility of a large

Bernoullian utility logs etc (handwritten)

payment (to beneficiary) at unexpected death is greater than the same sum without that condition. People gamble even when the percentage paid back is low. These examples suggest that the utility of a large amount (say, of dollars) has for individuals a greater utility than the sum of very small amounts.

An alternative view of the criterion for decision making is satisficing. This view comes from the descriptive, behavioral model which says that decision makers are not completely informed about alternatives and must therefore search for them. They are not completely rational or thorough in their search. They simplify the factors to be considered and thereby reduce the number to be considered. The assumption of the satisficing concept is therefore bounded rationality rather than complete rationality. Decision makers have limited cognitive ability to perceive alternatives and/or consequences. One result of these constraints is seen when decision makers limit their search and accept the first alternative which *satisfies* all the problem constraints. There is further discussion of this in the next section.

Relevance of Decision Concepts to MIS Design

The computer-based MIS is valuable in both a closed and an open system. In the closed decision model, the computer acts as a computational device to compute the optimal result. In the open model, the computer acts as an adjunct to the human decision maker in computing, storing, retrieving, analyzing, etc., data. The design allows the human decision maker to allocate tasks to himself or to the computer.

The differences in decision making for decisions under the conditions of certainty, risk, and uncertainty suggest the need for several decision models for the MIS. For each model, the data requirements vary, the presentations are different, and the decision inputs from the human decision maker vary.

The limits of human decision makers in organizations plus the relative efficiency of human processing of decisions mean that MIS should program as many decisions as possible. If the decision cannot be fully programmed, it may be partially programmed, in which case predecided rules are used up to a certain point and then remaining decisions are turned over to a human decision maker. The MIS should be designed to monitor programmed decisions and to identify those for which the decision rules do not seem to be applicable or do not seem to produce planned results. Nonprogrammed decisions are generally unstructured. For these, the MIS provides, where possible, a set of tools by which the decision maker can structure the decision-making process. For recurring nonprogrammed problems, the MIS may be designed with partial structuring to speed up the remaining human processing.

The MIS models may use either optimizing or satisficing criteria. It is important to recognize this in the design of the information/decision system. The use of optimizing is generally to be preferred over satisficing. When satisficing is used as the criterion, it should be clearly identified so that the decision maker is not led to believe the decision represents an optimal strategy when it may not.

BEHAVIORAL MODEL OF ORGANIZATIONAL DECISION MAKING

The behavioral theory of the firm has been described most fully by Cyert and March.[3] The ideas of Simon and others have also contributed to the material in this section. The behavioral theory of decision making reflects an open system. The theory is descriptive rather than normative. The four major concepts used by Cyert and March to explain organizational decision making are quasi–resolution of conflict, uncertainty avoidance, problemistic search, and organizational learning.

Quasi–Resolution of Conflict

An organization represents a coalition of members having different goals and different power to influence the organizational objective. The organizational goals change as new participants enter or old participants leave. There are conflicts among the various goals of the organizational members. Even if various personal goals are ignored, the goals of subunits such as production (level production of standard items), sales (responding to what customer wants and high inventories), and inventory control (low inventory) are contradictory. Such conflicts are resolved by three methods:

Method of conflict resolution	Explanation
Local rationality	Subsystems are allowed to set their own goals. This was described in Chapter 5 as a self-organizing subsystem.
Acceptable-level decision rules	Within certain limits, subsystems are allowed to make own decisions using agreed-upon decision rules and decision procedures.
Sequential attention to goals	The organization responds first to one goal, then to another, so that each conflicting goal has a chance to influence organizational behavior. Giving sequential attention to conflicting goals means also that certain conflicts are never resolved because the conflicting goals are never handled at the same time.

[3]Richard M. Cyert and James G. March, *A Behavioral Theory of the Firm*, Prentice-Hall, Inc., Englewood Cliffs, N.J., 1963.

Uncertainty Avoidance

Organizations live in uncertain environments. The behavior of the market, suppliers, shareholders, government, etc., is uncertain. The decision models under risk assume that the decision maker will maximize expected value (or expected utility). The behavioral theory of organizational decision making is that the organization will seek to avoid risk and uncertainty at the expense of expected value. In general, a decision maker will be willing to accept a reduction in expected value of an outcome in exchange for an increase in the certainty of outcome. A person, for example, is more likely to choose a 90 percent chance of obtaining $10 than a 12 percent chance of obtaining $100 even though the expected value of the latter is higher. In some cases of collusion by sellers (such as the assigning of markets) the profits of the conspirators do not appear to have been substantially increased. The major benefit received was apparently a reduction in uncertainty. Some legal methods used to reduce or avoid uncertainty are the following:

Methods for avoiding uncertainty	Explanation
Short-run feedback and reaction cycle	A short feedback cycle allows frequent new decisions and thus reduces the need to be concerned about future uncertainty.
Negotiated environment	The organization seeks to control its environment by industry-wide conventional practices (sometimes just as restrictive as collusive behavior), by long-term supply or sales contracts, etc.

Problemistic Search

Search is problem-stimulated and is directed at finding a solution to the problem. Regular, planned search is relatively unimportant compared with problem-stimulated search.

The behavioral theory postulates that search is based on rather simple rules:

1 Search locally either close to the present symptom or close to the present solution. For example, a failure in achieving the sales goal will cause the search to start with the sales department and the sales program.

2 If local search fails, expand the search first to organizationally vulnerable areas before moving to other areas. Vulnerable areas are areas with slack resources or with goals difficult to calculate (such as research).

Organizational Learning

Organizations exhibit adaptive behavior over time. They change their goals and revise their procedures for search on the basis of their experience. The aspiration level goals are assumed to change in response to the result experienced. In the steady state, aspiration levels are a little above achievement; when there is increasing achievement, the aspiration level will lag behind achievements, and where there is a decreasing level of achievement, aspiration levels will decrease but remain above achievement levels.

Application of the Behavioral Model of Decision Making to MIS

The behavioral theory is a descriptive model of organizational decision making. It emphasizes satisficing, uncertainty avoidance to control the environment, the existence of inconsistent goals based on the current members of the organizational coalition, problem-stimulated search, and organizational adaptive behavior over time. The search for problem solutions is assumed to be restricted to local search unless a solution cannot be found in that region. Only when a satisfactory solution is not found is the search process expanded.

The main value of the behavioral mode to MIS design is to alert the designer to behavioral considerations. The MIS designer may be interested in rationality, but the decision maker may stress uncertainty avoidance. The behavioral theory defines the methods for uncertainty avoidance which may need to be supported by MIS information. The MIS design should recognize the practical, behavioral problems of organization-wide optimization models because these models assume consistent organization goals, whereas the behavioral theory emphasizes the existence of inconsistent goals. Recognition of the problem-stimulated local search will provide guidance in designing information/decision models that provide an adequate search space and assist the decision maker to recognize the value of expanded search if such value appears to exist. Organizational learning and adaptive behavior is important in the design of information procedures for planning and control systems because of the need to recognize changing goals and aspirations.

IMPACT OF COGNITIVE STYLE ON DECISION MAKING BY INDIVIDUALS

The strategy by which an individual operates to reach a decision or solve a problem is termed *cognitive style*. There is evidence that individuals differ in their cognitive styles. One researcher[4] characterizes individuals by their communication mode (how they acquire data) and by their appraisal manner. The communication mode ranges from preceptive (uses data to generalize about the environment) to receptive (builds image of environment from specifics within the environment). The appraisal manner ranges from systematic to intuitive. Individuals can be classified by combinations of these two dimensions of cognitive style.

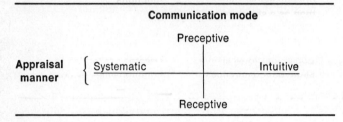

The two extremes of cognitive-style decision approaches have also been termed "analytic" and "heuristic." The analytic or systematic individual relies upon organized information and planned, organized approaches to decision making; the heuristic or intuitive individual relies upon analogies and lets the situation guide the decision making. Individuals are not necessarily at the extreme in terms of this classification but may tend toward one or the other. The following is a summary by Barrett of the two approaches.[5]

Description of Cognitive-Style Decision Approaches

Problem-solving dimension	Heuristic	Analytic
Approach to learning	Learns more by acting than by analyzing the situation and places more emphasis on feedback	Employs a planned sequential approach to problem solving; learns more by analyzing the situation than by acting and places less emphasis on feedback
Search	Uses trial and error and spontaneous action	Uses formal rational analysis

[4]McKenney and others at Harvard have been conducting research on cognitive style. See James L. McKenney, "Human Information Processing Systems," working paper 72–4, Harvard Graduate School of Business Administration, Boston.

[5]Michael Barrett et al., "Information Processing Types and Simulated Production Decision Making," working paper 73–2, The Management Information Systems Research Center, University of Minnesota, Minneapolis.

Problem-solving dimension	Heuristic	Analytic
Approach to analysis	Uses common sense, intuition, and feelings	Develops explicit, often quantitative, models of the situation
Scope of analysis	Views the totality of the situation as an organic whole rather than as a structure constructed from specific parts	Reduces the problem situation to a set of underlying causal functions
Basis for inferences	Looks for highly visible situational differences which vary with time	Locates similarities or commonalities by comparing objects

The research on cognitive styles is directly relevant to the design of management information systems. Computer-based systems tend to be designed by analytic/systematic individuals who perceive the nature of decision making as analytic/systematic. Analytic/systematic managers are generally willing to use such systems because they adhere to their decision style. But the systems designed for the analytic/systematic manager will not be utilized by the heuristic/intuitive decision maker. This situation suggests that information systems to support decision making should be designed so that both types of individuals will be willing to use them. A likely means to this end is a system that allows the user to explore a wide set of alternatives but also provides a predetermined sequence of analysis for the individual who desires it. In other words, the decision model is available to structure the decision, but the manager may depart from the model to explore alternative approaches. Such a system may also teach the intuitive user to utilize the systematic approach by allowing for an intuitive learning process.

METHODS FOR DECIDING AMONG ALTERNATIVES

The methods for selecting among alternatives generally assume that all alternatives are known. But for many decisions, the search process stops well before all reasonable or feasible alternatives have been examined. Keeping in mind this practical limitation to the decision process, this section reviews the methods for deciding among alternatives. An objective (profit, sales, reduced loss, increased safety, etc.) is assumed, and, furthermore, is assumed to be quantifiable as an objective function. The classes of methods to be reviewed are optimization techniques, payoff matrices, decision trees, game theory, and statistical inference. Methods for handling a problem when it is difficult to estimate probability are also discussed. The explanations provide an idea of the range of methods but are not detailed.

Optimization Techniques under Certainty

The techniques for optimization assume a closed decision system in which all alternatives and their outcomes are known. The computational problem is to compute which alternative is optimal for a given objective function. Some of the techniques are listed below to illustrate the variety of techniques used, but an explanation of how to use these techniques is beyond the scope of this text:

    Systems of equations
    Linear programming
    Integer programming
    Dynamic programming
    Queueing models
    Inventory models
    Capital budgeting analysis
    Breakeven analysis

problem is great # of feasible solutions

Payoff Matrix in Statistical Decision Theory

The term *statistical decision theory* is used to refer to techniques for evaluating potential outcomes from alternative actions in a given decision situation. It is a closed decision system model, so that all alternatives and outcomes are assumed to be known. The decision maker has an objective such as maximization of profit. The methods of presenting the data in decision theory are a payoff matrix or a decision tree. The payoff matrix will also be used in Chapter 7 in computing the value of information.

    The payoff matrix consists of rows for the alternatives or strategies available to the decision maker and columns for the conditions (states of nature is decision theory terminology) that affect the outcomes of the strategies. Figure 6-2 shows the general model. It is possible (and many authors do so) to make the rows stand for states, events, or conditions and columns for alternatives. Each cell (intersection of a strategy and a state of nature) contains the payoff (the consequences, say, in dollars) if that strategy is chosen and that state of nature occurs. If certain as to which condition or state of nature will prevail, the decision maker need only select the strategy that provides the highest payoff.

    The payoff matrix is best explained by an example. Assume the data in Figure 6-3. An entrepreneur is deciding among three alternatives for a fast-service restaurant that she owns: (1) leave as is, (2) remodel it to

Strategies	States of nature			
	n_1	n_2	n_3	n_4
S_1				
S_2				
S_3				

Contains conse-
quences (payoff)
if strategy S_1
is chosen and state
n_2 occurs

Figure 6-2 General payoff matrix.

improve the layout, or (3) rebuild completely to add capacity and improve layout. There are three significant, independent conditions, one of which may occur, that affect the possible profit (payoff) from each of the alternative strategies. These conditions are: (1) a competitor may open on a nearby property, (2) a proposed highway rerouting will change traffic passing by, or (3) conditions will stay approximately as they are. The entry in each cell of the matrix indicates the profit (or loss) from the combination of a strategy and a condition. The decision to refurbish will yield a profit of \$4,000 under a continuation of existing conditions, a profit of \$3,000 with a new competition, and a loss of \$3,000 if there is a highway change. Assuming it is known that conditions will stay the same, then rebuilding is the best alternative. But assume that probabilities are assigned to each possible state of nature—the same conditions given a probability of .50, a new competitor a probability of .20, and a highway rerouting a probability of .30. The expected value of each strategy is

Strategies	Conditions or events (states of nature) with probability of occurrence		
	Same .50	New competitor .20	Highway rerouting .30
Do nothing	2	0	−1
Refurbish	4	3	−3
Rebuild	7	2	−10

Figure 6-3 Payoff matrix for owner of quick service restaurant (payoff in 1,000s of dollars).

computed by multiplying each payoff by the probability for the column and summing across the row. The results are:

Strategy	Arithmetic	Expected value
Do nothing	(.50) (2) + (.20) (0) + (.30) (−1) = .70	.70 or $ 700
Refurbish	(.50) (4) + (.20) (3) + (.30) (−3) = 1.70	1.70 or $1,700
Rebuild	(.50) (7) + (.20) (2) + (.30) (−10) = .90	.90 or $ 900

The maximum expected value is to refurbish, and this should be chosen under the criterion of maximizing expected value.

The probabilities of various conditions or states of nature are assumed to be known with reasonable exactness in the above analysis, but what if the decision maker is very uncertain about the probabilities of the various conditions which may occur? Some rules for deciding are minimize regret, maximin, and maximax. The way they would be applied in the case of the payoff shown in Figure 6-3 is summarized below:

Decision rule	Explanation
Minimize regret	The rule is to select the action or strategy which minimizes the sum of the regrets for the strategy. The regrets are the differences between the best payoff for a state of nature and the other outcomes. To compute a matrix of regret, subtract the value in each entry in the column from the highest value in the column. Sum the rows to compute the regret for each action. (If the payoff matrix has columns for actions and rows to show states, the instructions would be reversed.) The regret matrix based on Figure 6-3 is the following:

Max Regret
5
(3)
9

Regret Matrix

Do nothing	5	3	0	= 8
Refurbish	3	0	2	= 5
Rebuild	0	1	9	= 10

The action which minimizes regret is therefore the action to refurbish. The above assumes equal probabilities for outcomes. An expected regret for each strategy can also be computed by multiplying each regret by its probability. *(X)*

| Maximin rule | Select the strategy which will have the highest utility payoff (max) if the worst state of nature (min) occurs. Stated differently, identify the worst payoff for each strategy and choose the strategy with the least unfavorable payoff. Essentially a pessimistic view, this would result in choosing to do nothing |

best of worst

Decision rule	Explanation
	because the worst case for that strategy is −1, while the other strategies have worst case results that are more unfavorable.
Maximax rule	Select the strategy alternative which provides greatest (max) utility payoff if the most favorable state of nature (max) occurs. An optimistic view, this rule would result in the strategy of rebuilding because the payoff of 7 is the best.

Each of these decision rules has been criticized as having some disadvantages when applied as a general decision rule.[6]

Utility and Indifference Curves

The examples of decisions in the statistical decision theory have used monetary value (dollars) or expected monetary value. The case of dollars, sales, or other such measures works reasonably well for a narrow range of values, but not at the extreme values. Also it is often desirable to weigh nonmonetary considerations.

For these reasons, a measure called "utility" is frequently used in place of monetary or other value. The units are called "utiles." Figure 6-4 shows a possible utility function for money. If this function is true, it may explain some behavior such as attitudes toward insurance and gambling. The shape of the curve says that the relation is linear ($1 = 1$ utile, $2 = 2$ utiles, etc.) over a certain range but then rises rapidly. This means that the

[6]W. Edwards, "The Theory of Decision Making," *Psychological Review*, vol. 51, no. 1, 1954, pp. 380–417.

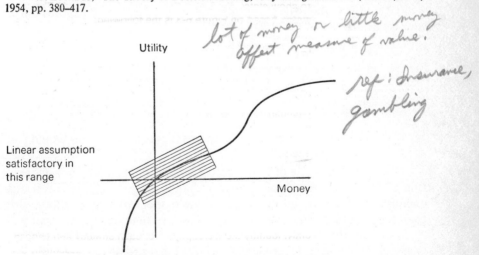

Figure 6-4 Estimated utility function for money.

utility of getting a fairly large sum is larger than the sum of a smaller utility relation. In other words, $1 = 1 utile, but $100,000 in one payment is larger than 100,000 utiles. This helps to explain attitudes toward insurance, and it may partially explain gambling (but is certainly not a complete explanation). After rising steeply, the curve flatens out. This means that after a certain point (which varies with each individual), the utility of substantially more money is not great. $2 million has not much greater utility for the average individual than $1 million.

The loss side of the curve has a different behavior than the gain side. A large loss has a significantly greater negative utility than merely the sum of disutilities for smaller losses. The loss of $10,000 is greater than the quantity: (1,000 × the disutility of losing $10). This phenomenon is relevant to insurance. Assume an insurance problem with the following payoff matrix:

	Fire .003	No fire .997
Insurance	−240	−240
No insurance	−50,000	0

Insurance costs $240—potential loss is $50,000, and expected value of the insurance policy is $150 (.003 probability of loss by $50,000 loss). Therefore, the insurance is uneconomic. However, assume a utility function as shown in Figure 6-4 and that a loss of 50,000 will have −150,000 utiles while the insurance has −240 utiles. The payoff matrix with utiles instead of dollars is now:

	Fire	No fire	
Insurance	−240	−240	= −240 expected value
No insurance	−150,000	0	= −450 expected value

For the utilities in this example, it appears the decision maker would pay up to $450 for insurance.

The above example of utility used only one valued property—money. But in many cases, there is more than one property, and various combinations of the properties may yield the same total utility. For example, a person may be interested in leisure time and money and will trade off one for the other. This tradeoff can be represented by indifference curves for each level of total utility (Figure 6-5).

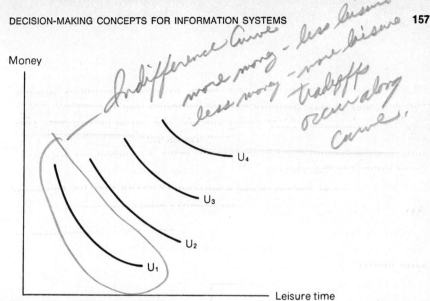

Figure 6-5 Utility indifference curves.

Decision Trees

When the decision maker must make a sequence of decisions, a decision tree is a useful method for presenting the analysis. The analysis is named a "decision tree" (or "game tree") because the different actions and decisions form branches from an initial decision point. The analogy with a tree suggests that the initial decision should be at the bottom of the page and the branches stretch upward to the top. However, it is more common to arrange the presentation from left to right.

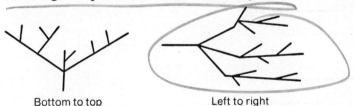

Bottom to top   Left to right

The decision tree is best explained by an example. A hotel chain with hotels in major cities around the world is analyzing the decisions in building a hotel in a newly independent, developing country. The decisions are whether to build or lease and whether to have local shareholders. Figure 6-6 shows the decision tree. The states of nature (events) are government decisions to either have free enterprise or expropriate

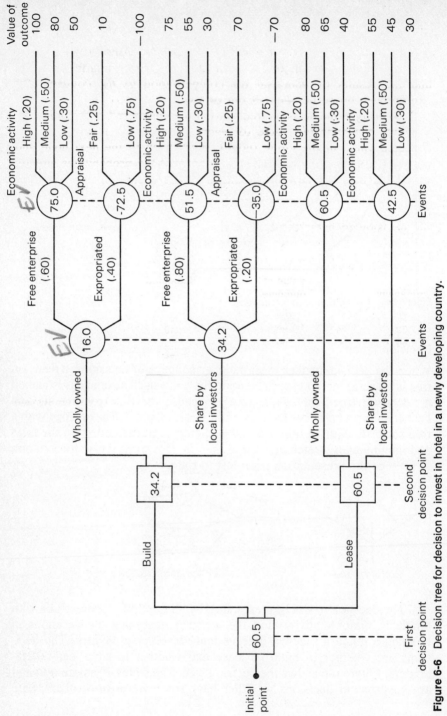

Figure 6-6 Decision tree for decision to invest in hotel in a newly developing country.

foreign-owned properties (but not locally owned properties), economic activity which is the major determinant of occupancy and thus income, and the results of appraisal for compensation to the company for expropriated properties—either fair or low.

To analyze the decision tree, start at the tips or end of the branches. Compute the expected value for each set of branches and write the expected value in the circle (node). Work back to the next node and compute the probabilities, taking into account the probabilities already calculated plus the new probabilities. At the decision point, write the highest expected value coming into the decision point in the rectangle. In Figure 6-6, the value resulting from this process is the expected value of the decision to enter the hotel business in the country. For example, starting at the top right, we compute the first node as:

Probability		Value of outcome		Expected value
.20	×	100	=	20
.50	×	80	=	40
.30	×	50	=	15
				75

Moving down the tree to the second set of branches from the second node, we calculate as follows: $(.25 \times 10) + (.75 \times -100) = 72.5$. These two nodes are the data to calculate the expected value from which they stem:

75 × .60 (probability of free enterprise)	45.0
−72.5 × .40 (probability of expropriation)	−29.0
Expected value of decision to build a wholly owned hotel	16.0

The decision point to build or lease shows an expected profit of 34.2 if the build policy is coupled with a "share by local investors" policy, etc. The expected profit of 60.5 from a lease policy is coupled with a policy of having a wholly owned hotel.

The use of both payoff matrices and decision trees requires the use of probability estimates. Objective probabilities based on measurement of like situations are not generally available, and so the probabilities used are subjective. The advantage of the technique is that it requires the explicit use of the subjective probabilities rather than using them without making them explicit.

Game Theory

Game theory is a means of analyzing decision where there is a competitive situation such that when one decision unit (player) gains, the other loses. In a two-person zero-sum game, there is equality of gains and losses; what one person gains, the other loses. Game theory is useful in understanding conflict bargaining situations, but appears to have limited utility in organizational decision making.

Classical Statistical Inference

Statistical inference is termed "classical" or "objectivist" as opposed to the Bayesian approach using subjective probabilities. The techniques of classical statistics can be very useful in preparing information for decision making. Some techniques are listed to remind the reader of the variety of tools available.

Statistical technique	Comment
Sampling	A small portion of the population is sampled in order to estimate parameters—mean, variance, etc.
Probability distributions	There are a number of distributions (e.g., normal, Poisson, exponential, Weibull). If the data approximates one of these distributions, the theoretical distribution can be used for decision purposes. The chi-square goodness-of-fit test is one of the most common methods for determining how well a theoretical distribution approximates the real data.
Regression and correlation analysis	The relation between a dependent variable and one or more independent variables is determined by correlation analysis. The correlation coefficient is a summary measure to explain the degree to which changes in the dependent variables are explained by changes in the independent variables.
Testing of hypotheses	Hypotheses can be tested to judge whether true or false.

Relevance of Decision Methods to MIS Design

The set of methods for deciding among alternatives should be part of the information/decision system. For some problems, the appropriate technique should be provided automatically; for others, two or more alternatives may be provided. The information system should be supportive of the decision maker in his search for the best technique.

Where probabilities and other estimates must be provided, a man/machine dialog is often helpful. For example, a decision process may require a best estimate of the sales for a new product. The decision maker may be asked to provide greater than/less than estimates of finer and finer limits until he or she indicates an inability to continue. The result is converted to probability statements which are used in the decision process. Various checks for consistency are used to assist the decision maker in arriving at the final estimate.

SUMMARY

The process of decision making can be described as consisting of three major phases: (1) *intelligence* to search out problems, (2) *design* to analyze problems and generate feasible solutions, and (3) *choice* to select among alternatives and implement the choice. The decision-making systems may be closed with all factors known or open, allowing for new factors to influence the decision. The decision making may be based on outcomes that are known with certainty, outcomes with known probabilities of occurrence (risk), or outcomes with unknown or very uncertain probabilities (uncertainty). The decision response may consist of preprogrammed application of decision rules and procedures or may be a nonprogrammed procedure to look for a solution.

The descriptions of decision making that indicate how decisions should be made are termed *normative* or *prescriptive*; the descriptions that explain actual behavior are termed *descriptive*. A behavioral model of decision making is descriptive. It explains organizational decision making in terms of quasi–resolution of conflict, avoidance of uncertainty, problemistic search, and organizational learning.

The methods for deciding among alternatives were listed, and some were explained briefly with some focus on payoff matrices and decision trees.

The orientation of MIS to both information and decision means that the MIS analyst/designer needs to be well versed in decision theory and decision techniques. The MIS should be designed to provide decision support in the form of various techniques and approaches.

EXERCISES

1 Identify, for the following decisions, the activities which may have preceded the choice. Classify each activity as either intelligence or design:
   a Market a new product.
   b Hire Bill Smith as controller.
   c Cancel development of a new product.
   d Enter into licensing agreement with a firm holding a patent.
   e Lower prices on widget from $1.15 to $1.
2 Explain how the Rubenstein and Haberstroh model can be described by the

Simon model. Illustrate with an example of the problem of a production process that is high cost (but apparently can be reduced in cost by new machinery).

3 Identify each of the following as being in general more closely identified with (a) closed decision model or (b) open decision model:

(1) Optimizing.
(2) Descriptive.
(3) Bounded rationality.
(4) Quantitative.
(5) Nonprogrammed.
(6) Limited search.
(7) Normative.
(8) Behavioral.
(9) Rational man.
(10) Satisficing.
(11) All outcomes known.
(12) Programmed.

4 Define the following with respect to decision making:
a Certainty.
b Risk.
c Uncertainty.

5 Identify the following techniques as being *most* relevant to decisions under (a) certainty, (b) risk, or (c) uncertainty:
(1) Linear programming.
(2) Payoff matrix.
(3) Capital budgeting.
(4) Integer programming.
(5) Game theory.
(6) Set of simultaneous equations.

6 What is the difference between maximizing expected value and maximizing expected utility?

7 Using the concept of expected value, show why it is not rational to buy insurance. Using the concept of maximizing utility, explain why insurance is purchased.

8 Gambling cannot be explained by use of expected value concepts. It is explainable with utility concepts. Can the utility concept include nonmonetary satisfaction associated with taking risks?

9 Organizations (and presumably individuals) are said to avoid risk, yet gambling persists. How is this explained by use of the utility theory?

10 Define programmed and nonprogrammed decisions. Identify each of the following with the type of decision to which it is *most* likely to apply:
a Computer program.
b Ad hoc decision.
c ELSE rule in decision table.
d Decision table.
e Lower levels in organization.
f Judgment.
g Rule book.
h Regulations.

11 Define *normative* and *descriptive* as they apply to decision making. Identify each of the following with the one to which it is *most* applicable:
a Management science.
b Game theory.

    c Microeconomic theory.
    d Behavioral science.
    e Scientific management.
    f Risk avoidance concept.
    g Operations research.
    h Satisficing concept.
12 What is the objective function for a decision? State an objective function for each of the following decisions:
    a To introduce new product.
    b To increase advertising.
    c To replace unsafe machine.
    d To buy a new automobile for personal use.
    e To drop a course in which a failing grade is probable.
13 Explain the difference in decision making procedures if the criteria are satisficing versus optimizing. Explain the use of the two criteria for the following decisions:
    a Purchase new automobile for personal use.
    b Decide on quantity of inventory to order.
    c Decide on new plant site.
    d Decide on feed mix formulation.
14 Explain the implications to organizational behavior of the following pairs of assumptions:
    a Single organizational goal versus a coalition of members with different goals.
    b Uncertainty avoidance versus risk taking.
    c Restricted search versus unrestricted search for solutions.
    d Cognitive limits on decision maker versus no limits.
    e Single aspiration level versus adoptive, changing aspiration level.
15 A decision problem involves three alternative strategies called Alpha, Beta, and Gamma. There are four possible events or states of nature. The following is the payoff matrix:

Strategies	W	X	Y	Z
	.10	.25	.35	.30
Alpha	0	15	30	10
Beta	25	10	10	20
Gamma	45	10	25	−10

Make the decision and indicate payoff using each of the following decision rules:
    a Maximax.
    b Expected value with equal probabilities.
    c Maximin.
    d Minimize regret (equal probabilities).

e Expected value.

f Minimize expected regret.

16 Draw indifference curves for money and prestige as two alternative forms of compensation using the following data (P = prestige, $ = money):

	P	$	P	$	P	$
Curve 1	2	6	4	3	6	2
Curve 2	4	6	6	3	8	2
Curve 3	6	6	8	4	10	3

17 Draw a decision tree and prepare an analysis for the following problem. A company must make a decision whether to market a new product. The success of the venture depends on the success of a competitor in bringing out a competing product (.60 probability) and the relationship of the competitor's price to the firm's price. Because the firm expects to be able to differentiate its product somewhat, there will be sales even if the competitor's price is lower. Traditional pricing in the industry suggests 0.99, 1.29, and 1.59 as the prices that are at issue. The table contains the conditional profit for each set of prices by the company and its competitor.

| Company's | Competitor's price | | | Profit if |
price	.99	1.29	1.59	no competitor
.99	30	40	45	50
1.29	21	42	45	70
1.59	10	30	53	90

The probability of the competitor's price being one of these three is influenced by the company's price which must be set first because its product will be out first. If the company's price is specified, the probability of a competitor's price is shown below:

| If company | Competitor's price will be | | |
sets price of	.99	1.29	1.59
.99	.80	.15	.05
1.29	.20	.70	.10
1.59	.05	.35	.60

Probabilities of given competitor price if company sets a stated price

SELECTED REFERENCES

Alexis, Marcus, and Charles Z. Wilson: *Organizational Decision Making,* Prentice-Hall, Inc., Englewood Cliffs, N.J., 1967.

Archer, Stephen H.: "The Structure of Management Decision Theory," *Academy of Management Journal,* December 1964, pp. 269–287.

Bierman, Harold, Jr., Charles P. Bonini, and Warren H. Hausman: *Quantitative Analysis for Business Decisions,* 3d ed., Richard D. Irwin, Inc., Homewood, Ill., 1969.

Chernoff, Herman, and Lincoln E. Moses: *Elementary Decision Theory,* John Wiley & Sons, Inc., New York, 1959.

Cyert, R. M., and J. G. March: *A Behavioral Theory of the Firm,* Prentice-Hall, Inc., Englewood Cliffs, N.J., 1963.

Edwards, W.: "The Theory of Decision Making," *Psychological Bulletin,* vol. 51, no. 1, 1954, pp. 380–417.

Fishburn, P. C.: "Methods of Estimating Additive Utilities," *Management Science,* March 1967.

Hammond, John S., III: "Better Decisions with Preference Theory," *Harvard Business Review,* November-December 1967, pp. 123–141.

Luce, R. D., and H. Raiffa: *Games and Decision,* John Wiley & Sons, Inc., New York, 1957.

Magee, John F.: "Decision Trees for Decision Making," *Harvard Business Review,* July-August 1964, pp. 126–138.

Schlaifer, Robert: *Probability and Statistics for Business Decisions,* McGraw-Hill Book Company, New York, 1959.

Simon, Herbert A.: *The New Science of Management Decisions,* Harper & Brothers, New York, 1960.

Chapter 7

Value of Information for Decision Making

Chapter 2 introduced the concept that a message (report, etc.) has information only if it is relevant to some current or future decision to be made by the receiver. Information systems are very costly, and a frequently repeated question is the value of the information systems. There is no simple answer. This chapter presents some methods based on decision theory as described in Chapter 6.

Decision theory provides approaches for making decisions under certainty, risk, and uncertainty. The decision under certainty assumes perfect information as to outcomes; risk assumes information as to the probability of each outcome but not which outcome will occur in any given case; and uncertainty assumes a knowledge of possible outcomes but no information as to probabilities. A value of information can be computed for decisions which fit these frameworks of analysis.

In general, the value of information is the value of the change in decision behavior caused by the information less the cost of the information.[1] In other words, given a set of possible decisions, a decision maker will select one on the basis of the information at hand. If new information causes a different decision to be made, the value of the new information is the difference in value between the outcome of the old decision and that of the new decision, less the cost of obtaining the information.

The first part of the chapter, dealing with the value of perfect information using payoff matrices, is quite simple to understand and requires no special knowledge of statistics. The section on the value of information with continuous distribution of outcomes is somewhat more complex and assumes some knowledge of statistics. However, the idea of that section is not to explain the mechanics of the computations in detail; it is to communicate the concept of the value of information with a continuous, normal distribution of outcomes. A student with little background in statistics may therefore read the section with the objective of obtaining some general understanding rather than developing computational proficiency.

VALUE OF PERFECT INFORMATION

Single Condition or State of Nature

A very simple example will illustrate the value of perfect information in a decision with only one future condition or state of nature. Assume there are only three alternatives called A, B, and C. The decision maker, on the basis of prior knowledge (imperfect knowledge), estimates that the outcome (payoff) from choosing A will be $20, of B $30, and of C $15, and is therefore ready to choose B. Perfect information is then provided which establishes that the payoff of C is $30 and the payoff from B is only $22. The information causes the decision maker to select C instead of B, thereby increasing the payoff from $22 to $30. The value of the perfect information is therefore $8.

Payoff Matrix #1   **Payoff Matrix #2**

A	20
B	30
C	15

theoretical

Decision = B

A	20
B	22
C	30

actual

Decision = C

The value of perfect information is computed as the difference between the optimal policy without perfect information and the optimal

---

[1]For a rather complete exposition of this concept, see James C. Emery, *Organizational Planning and Control Systems*, The Macmillan Company, New York, 1969, chap. 4.

policy with perfect information. The value of perfect information in this example involves only one state of nature, so that once an alternative is chosen, the choice is the one that has the highest outcome. The only uncertainty is the value of each outcome.

More than One Condition or State of Nature

In the preceding example, there is no uncertainty as to the possible payoff because there is only one condition or state of nature. Suppose that there are two conditions or states of nature, x_1 and x_2 [say, corresponding to government contract obtained (x_1) and government contract not obtained (x_2)]. Each of these has a probability attached to it by the decision maker. Assume .60 for x_1 and .40 for x_2. The payoff matrix might then look like the following:

Payoff Matrix

	x_1	x_2	
	Probabilities		
Strategies	.60	.40	Expected value
A	20	18	A = $19.20
B	30	0	B = $18.00
C	15	8	C = $12.20

If actually .0   1.0

then

A = 18
B = 0   perfect info
C = 8.4   useless here but

if actually 1.0   0
A = 20
B = 30
C = 15

value = 30 − 20 = 10

This says that if A is chosen and x_1 (contract received) occurs, the payoff will be $20; if A is chosen and x_2 occurs, the payoff is $18. The expected value or average payoff is the sum of the payoff for each decision times the probabilities for each outcome. The expected value for decision strategy A is .60 (20) + .40 (18) = $19.20.

The value of information for more than one condition is the difference between the maximum expected value in the absence of additional information and the maximum expected value with additional information. Note that the expected value can change by a change either in the probabilities for the conditions x_1 and x_2 or in the payoffs associated with them.

The payoff matrix presented in Chapter 6 for the decision to rebuild, refurbish, or do nothing to a roadside restaurant will be used to further illustrate the concept of perfect information with more than one condition (Figure 7-1). The optimal policy is to refurbish the restaurant because that policy has the highest expected value. In other words, if the investor had many investments with exactly the same decisions to be made, the average result of always choosing refurbish" would be $1,700 per

Strategies	Conditions or events (states of nature) with probability of occurrence		
	Same .50	New competitor .20	Highway rerouting .30
Do nothing	2	0	− 1
Refurbish	4	3	− 3
Rebuild	7	2	−10

Figure 7-1 Payoff matrix for owner of quick-service restaurant (payoffs in thousands of dollars) (same as Figure 6-3).

decision. Not knowing which event will occur, the policy of choosing "refurbish" provides the highest result on the average.

Policy	Computation of expected value	Expected value
Do nothing	$2(.50) + 0(.20) + -1\ (.30)\ =$	.70 ($700)
Refurbish	$4(.50) + 3(.20) + -3\ (.30)\ =$	1.70 ($1,700)
Rebuild	$7(.50) + 2(.20) + -10(.30)\ =$	.90 ($900)

perfect predictability

   If information could be obtained on the actual event to occur in each case, the investor would not choose "refurbish" in every case, but would choose the optimal decision for the event that is certain to happen. Since the different states of nature or events occur with the frequency of .50, .20, and .30, the average result when the condition is known and all decisions are optimal is as follows:

P(outcome) won't change but we know outcome ahead of time.

Condition	PERFECT INFO Optimal strategy	MAX Payoff	Percentage of occurrences	Average payoff from optimal decision
Same traffic and competition	Rebuild	$7,000	.50 *WON'T CHANGE*	$3,500
New competitor	Refurbish	3,000	.20	600
Highway rerouting	Do nothing	−1,000	.30	− 300
Expected payoff with perfect information				$3,800

Strategies	Condition, event, or state		
	Same	New competitor	Highway rerouting
Do nothing	5	3*	0
Refurbish	3	0	2
Rebuild	0	1	9

*For a new competitor event, a do nothing strategy is 3 worse than the optimal strategy of refurbish.

Figure 7-2 Matrix of opportunity losses (in thousands of dollars) (based on Figure 7-1).

The average or expected payoff per decision with perfect information as to each condition is $3,800 whereas the maximum expected value without the knowledge of the future condition other than its probability is $1,700. The difference of $2,100 (3,800 − 1,700) is the expected value of perfect information. In other words, a decision maker could pay up to $2,100 for information which identified with perfect foresight the event or condition affecting this decision.

The value of perfect information may also be defined as the expected value of opportunity losses. In other words, there is a difference between the optimal, perfect-foresight policy and the other strategies for a given event. The difference is the opportunity loss for not taking the optimal decision. The matrix of opportunity losses is given by Figure 7-2. Note that this is the same as the regret matrix presented in Chapter 6. The expected value of any strategy is the difference between the optimal set of decisions under certainty and the expected opportunity losses. As presented in Chapter 6, the opportunity loss is the difference between the best decision and the decision being evaluated. The opportunity loss for "refurbish" for the "same" future condition is the difference of 3 between the highest payoff of 7 for rebuild and the payoff of 4 for refurbish. The expected opportunity loss for refurbish is thus (.50) (.3) + (.20) (0) + (.30) (.2) = $2,100, which is the same as the value of perfect information. By use of these figures, the expected value of the optimal policy under risk is obtained as follows:

Expected value under certainty	$3,800
Expected opportunity loss (same as value of information)	−2,100
Expected value of optimal policy under risk	$1,700

This is another way of indentifying the fact that a decision maker can afford to pay up to $2,100 for perfect information.

SAMPLE INFORMATION AND BAYSIAN ANALYSIS   *A PRIORI*

There is usually uncertainty about the probabilities assigned to conditions or states of nature. The probabilities (referred to as "prior probabilities") are the best estimates at the beginning of the decision-making process but are subject to modification on the basis of more information. The revised probabilities are termed "posterior probabilities." The additional information may come from sampling and is therefore imperfect information. *A POSTERIORI* *Sampling can give prob estimates of conditions*

The method for incorporating the sample information to compute posterior probabilities utilizes Bayes's theorem. The details of the Baysian analysis will not be presented here (see selected references). The approach is applicable to discrete prior distributions where a quantity will be observed or measured. For example, the basic variable may be the parameter of a Bernoulli process or a Poisson process. Problems to which this analysis is applicable are quality control, estimation of defective products, estimating if a sample is part of a given population, etc. The expected value of information from various sample sizes may be computed and an optimal sample size selected.

When the conditions or states of nature represent continuous prior distributions, Bayes's theorem cannot be strictly applied. An alternative approach to evaluating sample information is available if the distribution can be considered normal. This approach is applicable to a range of business problems and is therefore surveyed in the next section.

VALUE OF INFORMATION
WITH NORMAL DISTRIBUTION OF OUTCOMES

Value of Perfect Information

In many decisions, point estimates (single value such as 600) are used when the data suggests that the estimate should be a probability distribution (such as 600 with a standard deviation of 125). For example, the sales estimate for a new product may be stated as 40,000 units at $1 or $40,000. If there is a fixed cost of $25,000 to introduce the product and a variable cost of $0.25 for each unit sold, the relation may be shown in the breakeven chart (Figure 7-3). The following are the estimates for decision making:

	Units	$
Estimated sales	40,000	$40,000
Fixed costs (F)		24,000
Unit variable cost (C) 25¢		
Unit variable profit (V) 75¢		
Breakeven point (no profit or loss)	32,000	32,000
$BE = \dfrac{F}{V}$		
Profit at 40,000 units		6,000

$$BEP = \frac{\$24\,000}{.75} = 32,000$$

$$\text{Profit} = S_{\$} - F - C \cdot S_{u}$$

where $S_{\$}$ = sales in dollars
$\quad\;\; S_{u}$ = sales in units
$\quad\;\; C$ = unit variable cost
$\quad\;\; F$ = fixed cost

The decision maker will choose to introduce the product because it yields a profit (ignore any alternative investments). The decision will not result in a loss unless sales turn out to be less than the breakeven volume of 32,000 units.

The sales estimate is probably not a single point estimate, but the

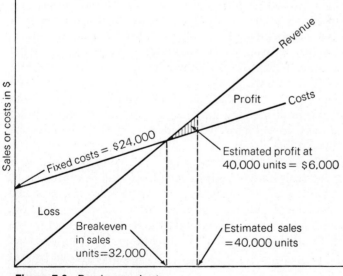

Figure 7-3 Breakeven chart.

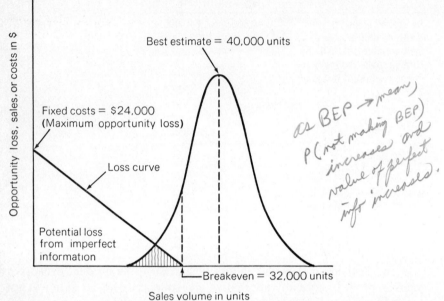

Figure 7-4 Sales volume estimate as normal distribution around best estimate.

estimate is the mean value of a distribution of estimates. Assuming that the sales estimate distribution took the shape of a normal probability distribution, it might look like Figure 7-4. The estimate need not be a normal curve, but computationally it is convenient to use a normal distribution and in most cases is probably a reasonable assumption. A line drawn on the curve in Figure 7-4 from the fixed costs to the breakeven point represents the loss curve. The loss at zero sales is equal to the fixed costs, and the loss decreases at the rate of 75 cents for each unit sold (because the variable profit per unit is 75 cents) until the breakeven point is reached. The loss curve may be stated as .75 times (breakeven sales − actual sales).

Information has no value unless it causes a change in the decision. If we assume that the decision will be to proceed with the new product as long as there is a profit, perfect information that actual sales will be 38,000 has no information value because it does not change the decision. Perfect information has value if it says that the sales will be below the breakeven point. The distribution of sales estimates indicates only a small probability of the sales being in the loss category, but this is what perfect information would prevent. Therefore, the value of perfect information in this case is the expected value of potential loss if the wrong decision is made (i.e., sales turn out below breakeven, and therefore the decision to proceed was not the right one).

The estimated area of the sales estimate curve representing a loss may be computed if the standard deviation for the sales estimate curve is known (or estimated). For example, in this case, the standard deviation is estimated to be 6,000 units. This means that the decision maker believes that if the decision were to be repeated many times, the mean sales would be 40,000 units, and 67 percent of the sales figures would be between 34,000 and 46,000 units (40,000 ± 6,000). Given the estimated standard deviation (σ) of 6,000, the estimated value of perfect information is computed as follows:

Estimated value of perfect information = expected loss
from imperfect
information
= variable loss per
unit x number of
units in distribution of
sales that are less
than breakeven
= $k\sigma_x G(D)$

Loss per unit (k) = slope of loss curve = $0.75 per unit
Number of units in loss proportion
of normal probability distribution = $\sigma_x G(D)$

$$D = \frac{|B - \overline{X}|}{\sigma_x}$$

where B = breakeven point   (32,000)
$\overline{X}$ = mean   (40,000)
σ_x = standard deviation   (6,000)

$$D = \frac{32,000 - 40,000}{6,000}$$ In other words, D is the number of standard deviation from the mean to the breakeven point.

$D = 1.33$

G(D) is a unit normal loss integral which will be read from a table.[2]
The value for G(1.33) is .04270.
The estimated value of perfect information = .75 × 6,000 × .04270
= 192.15

---

[2]Use unit normal loss integral table such as table IV in Robert Schlaifer, *Probability and Statistics for Business Decisions*, McGraw-Hill Book Company, New York, 1959, pp. 706–707 (reprinted at end of this chapter).

The result of 192.15 is the value per decision of the perfect information that would allow the decision maker to avoid the cases when a loss would occur.

The expected profit for this decision was stated as $6,000. This consists of an expected gross profit of $6,192 per decision and an expected loss of $192 per decision to yield a net expected profit of $6,000. The two components of the expected profit are often not analyzed, with a resulting loss of understanding about the nature of the expected profit.

An assumption was that the decision maker is satisfied with profit greater than zero. The change in assumption to a minimum profit can be made by adding the minimum profit to the fixed cost. The breakeven point will change but not the slope of the line. For example, assume a minimum profit of $3,000 in the preceding case:

Fixed cost = ($24,000 + $3,000) = $27,000
Breakeven = $36,000

$$D = \frac{|36,000 - 40,000|}{6,000} = .66$$

G(D) = G(.66) = .1528   from unit normal loss integral table
                           (Table 7-1 reprinted at end of chapter)
Value of perfect information = .75 × $6,000 × .1528
                            = $687.60 per decision

When the breakeven point is moved closer to the mean, the value of perfect information is increased from $192.15 to $687.60 because there is greater probability that a given outcome will show a result less than breakeven.

The effect of increased variance is to increase the possible loss and therefore to increase the value of perfect information. For example, assume a variance of 15,000 instead of 6,000 (Figure 7-5 shows this graphically). This means that there is greater uncertainty than before about the actual value that sales might take. The computations are as follows:

Fixed cost = same = $24,000
Breakeven = same = $32,000

$$D = \frac{|32,000 - 40,000|}{15,000} = .53$$

G(D) = G(.53) = .1887   from Table 7-1

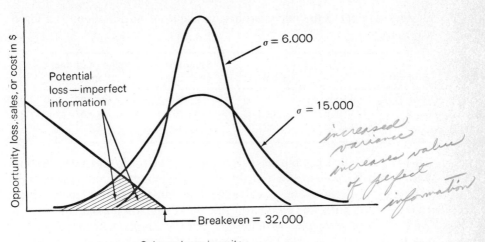

Figure 7-5 Effect of greater variance in sales distribution.

Value of perfect information = .75 × $15,000 × .1887
= $2,123

When the variance is high relative to the mean, the expected gross profit is large, but the expected loss is also large. For example, in this case, the expected profit of $6,000 consists of an expected gross profit of $8,123 and an expected loss of $2,123. The high value of information is a reflection of the risk attached to the decision. The example also illustrates the value of computing the expected loss in assessing decision alternatives.

Value of Imperfect Information

The value of perfect information is that it allows the decision maker to select the optimal decision in each case rather than the decision that "on the average" will be optimal and to avoid those events that will result in a loss. But perfect information may not be available. In such cases, prior estimates of outcomes may be influenced by additional information even though the information does not provide certainty. The imperfect information is essentially information from sampling. It is imperfect because it provides an estimate with an associated variance rather than providing a figure with certainty.

In the previous example, a distribution of outcomes was postulated, and it was found that changing the breakeven point or the standard deviation affected the expected loss or value of information. The three cases were:

Example	Mean	Breakeven	Standard deviation	Value of perfect information
1	40,000	$32,000	6,000	$ 192
2	40,000	36,000	6,000	687
3	40,000	32,000	15,000	2,123

This suggests that if a business decision is to be made and a distribution and standard deviation of outcomes are postulated (a subjective prior estimate), it is possible to calculate the value of information which reduces (but does not eliminate) the possibility of making the wrong decision. For example, assume the third example with a subjective estimated mean of 40,000, breakeven of 32,000, standard deviation 15,000, and value of perfect information of $2,123. A sample or market survey of 100 customers is proposed in order to obtain more information. The estimated standard deviation of the sample means is 8,000; the estimated sample mean is 42,000. The estimated information value of the proposed sample can be computed by replacing σ with σ_r in the prior formula for information value, σ_r being defined as the amount of revision in the variance from presample to postsample distribution.

$$\sigma_r = \sqrt{\sigma^2 \frac{\sigma^2}{\sigma^2 + \sigma_s^2}}$$

where σ_s^2 = variance of sample means

$$\sigma_r = \sqrt{15,000^2 \frac{15,000^2}{15,000^2 + 8,000^2}} = 13,200$$

Expected value of sample information = $k\sigma_r N(D_r)$

$$D_r = \frac{|B - X_r|}{\sigma_r} = \frac{|32,000 - 42,000|}{13,200} = .76$$

$N(D_r) = N(.76) = .1289$ from Table 7-1

Expected value of sample information = .75 × $13,200 × .1289
$$= \$1,276$$

The meaning of this result is that if the proposed sample turns out as expected, it will reduce the uncertainty of $2,123 by $1,276. The estimated value of the sample is the estimated value of the information it can provide. Up to $1,276 could be spent on the sample. If the sample were going to cost $2,000, it would not be worth it.

The expected value of sample information is influenced by the two factors of the expected standard deviation and the expected mean. If the expected sample mean were to remain 42,000 and the standard deviation 2,000 (indicating less uncertainty about the sample mean), the expected value of information would be:

$$\sigma_r = \sqrt{15,000^2 \frac{15,000^2}{15,000^2 + 2,000^2}}$$

$$\sigma_r = 14,870$$

$$D_r = \frac{|32,000 - 42,000|}{15,000} = .66$$

$N(D_r) = N(.66) = .1528$ from Table 7-1

Expected value of sample information $= .75 \times \$14,870 \times .1528$
$$= \$1,704$$

As anticipated, a sample that is expected to have the same mean but a smaller standard deviation has a greater expected information value than the sample with a larger standard deviation (1,704 versus 1,276).

These computations address the question of whether it is worthwhile to obtain sample information. The sample itself will turn out more or less different than estimated. The actual sample results will provide the basis for revising prior probabilities for decision making.

The concept of imperfect information applies in many situations where sampling or market surveys may obtain imperfect information to apply to the decision analysis. The steps in the decision process are:

1   Determine the best action based on prior probabilities.
2   Determine whether it will be worthwhile to obtain sample information.
3   Determine optimal sample size.
4   Sample.
5   Revise prior probabilities based on the sample data.

EVALUATION OF DECISION THEORY APPROACH TO VALUE OF INFORMATION

There is a tendency to always seek more information. The decision theory approach focuses attention not only on the value of information in a decision but also on the fact that the cost of obtaining more information may not be worthwhile. An understanding of the decision theory approach to value of information should assist the designer of information systems to keep the concept of cost/value in mind as a design consideration.

The value of information is the value of the change in decision behavior because of the information (less the cost of the information). An interesting aspect of this concept is that information has value only to those who have the background knowledge to use it in a decision. The most qualified person generally uses information most effectively but may need less information since experience (frame of reference) has already reduced uncertainty when compared with the less-experienced decision maker.

The quantitative approach to information value can be useful in two ways:

1 In system design
2 In decision approaches

The information/decision system designer will encounter situations in which the decision algorithm is to be developed. The cost/value analysis may be used to decide how to build an algorithm to use existing data, to obtain more data, to use less data, etc. The cost/value of information methods may also be built into decision models. For example, the decision maker may be assisted in making payoff matrices. The computer assists by evaluating the matrix, providing data on the value of more information. The approach may be extended to cases where imperfect information is all that can be obtained. The decision maker may be asked to provide prior subjective estimates of the mean and standard deviation for the population and for a sample. The decision model can calculate the expected value of the information to be provided by the sample, etc. This can be applied, for example, in marketing research problems.

The value of information approach can be applied in only part of the decisions. The theory is difficult to apply in many complex, ill-structured situations, but the theory is still useful for insight into these decisions.

SUMMARY

This chapter has provided an overview of quantitative approaches to the measurement of the value of information for decision making. When payoff matrices are available, the expected value of perfect information is relatively simple to compute. When the payoff is stated in terms of a distribution such as the normal one, the value of perfect information can be calculated by use of more complex concepts and computational methods. If the distribution is estimated and only imperfect information can be obtained, the same formulas used for the normal distribution of outcomes may be used to calculate the value of the imperfect information obtainable from sampling, market research, etc.

The methods in the chapter may, in many cases, be impossible to apply, but the underlying concepts are useful in providing insight for system design. In other instances, the methods may be used in the system design or built into the decision algorithms.

EXERCISES

1   A decision maker has four alternatives with payoffs and estimates as follows. Additional information changes the estimated payoffs. What is the value of the information?

Alternative	Payoff	Revised payoff
S	7	18
T	19	19
R	12	15
N	13	16

none

no change in value of decision

2   A decision maker has the following prior probabilities and payoffs:

Action	Probability of success	Payoff if successful
Z	.30	$100
Y	.10	350
X	.20	200
W	.40	150

E V

30
35
40
60

The decision rule followed by the decision maker is to choose the action with the highest expected value. The decision maker receives a message revising the probabilities or payoffs. What is the information content of each of the following messages?

   a   Z = .50; Y = .10; X = .15; W = .25; payoff the same.
   b   Payoff Z = 200; Y = 150; X = 200; W = 80; probabilities the same as problem.
   c   Payoff Z = 150; Y = 525; X = 300; W = 225; probabilities the same as problem.

3   A decision maker has four alternatives which have varying payoffs based on different conditions that may occur.

	Conditions			
	1	2	3	4
	Probabilities			
Alternatives	.10	.30	.25	.35
B	15	8	− 3	5
L	10	10	− 5	6
M	12	5	−10	7
P	6	7	− 1	5

a Calculate expected value.

b Calculate value of perfect information.

c Show that the expected value is equal to the expected value with perfect information less the opportunities loss.

4 Assume that an investor has a choice of (1) a highly rated bond (income certain) yielding 6 percent per year or (2) a more risky investment with an expected yield of 9 percent but having a normal probability curve of possible outcomes with standard deviation of 3 percent. Calculate the value of perfect information (for one year) for selecting between the two investments. (Hint: Use the 6 percent as a breakeven and then apply the formula in the text.) Use $1,000, which is the value of the bond, as in the formula.

5 Repeat Problem 4 with the alternative investment being 8 percent instead of 6 percent. Explain the difference in answers.

6 A company proposes to buy and sell 100,000 units of government surplus property during a period of one year. After the year, the value of unsold goods is nil. The investment is $100,000. The net selling price (after selling costs) for each unit is $2. The company feels the most likely sales will be 60,000 units (but they have to buy the entire lot). They are, however, uncertain and feel the standard deviation of estimated sales is 10,000.

a Calculate breakeven. (Hint: The cost of the lot is fixed; the net selling price is a variable profit.)

b Calculate the loss curve.

c Calculate the value of perfect information.

7 Repeat Problem 6 changing the breakeven point by adding a minimum profit of $10,000.

8 Repeat Problem 7 changing the standard deviation of sales to 5,000.

9 If the results of a sample or market survey do not change the decision, what is the value of the imperfect information?

10 In production equality control, a lot is sampled for quality. If the number of rejects exceeds a certain amount, the lot is rejected. If the rejects are less than or equal to this number, the lot is accepted. The sample represents imperfect information. By use of the value of information concepts, what is the value of an increased sample size?

11 A new product is proposed. The market manager follows a computer-assisted decision procedure:

  a   Estimate subjectively the sales and the standard deviation for the sales.

  b   Estimate costs—fixed and variable.

  c   Estimate the market research required to provide better but imperfect information.

  d   Estimate the mean and standard deviations for the results obtained by the research.

The computer calculates the breakeven, the costs of perfect information, and the cost value of the market research. For the following data, do the computations and evaluate the results:

Sales: 100,000 units at $1.00: σ = 20,000 units.

Fixed cost: $25,000.

Variable costs: $0.50 unit.

Minimum profit: $20,000.

Cost of market survey: $5,000.

Estimated mean of market survey: 100,000 units; σ = 10,000 units.

Table 7-1 Unit Normal Loss Integral

$G(u) = P_N'(u) - u\, P_N(\bar{u} > u)$

u	.00	.01	.02	.03	.04	.05	.06	.07	.08	.09
.0	.3989	.3940	.3890	.3841	.3793	.3744	.3697	.3649	.3602	.3556
.1	.3509	.3464	.3418	.3373	.3328	.3284	.3240	.3197	.3154	.3111
.2	.3069	.3027	.2986	.2944	.2904	.2863	.2824	.2784	.2745	.2706
.3	.2668	.2630	.2592	.2555	.2518	.2481	.2445	.2409	.2374	.2339
.4	.2304	.2270	.2236	.2203	.2169	.2137	.2104	.2072	.2040	.2009
.5	.1978	.1947	.1917	.1887	.1857	.1828	.1799	.1771	.1742	.1714
.6	.1687	.1659	.1633	.1606	.1580	.1554	.1528	.1503	.1478	.1453
.7	.1429	.1405	.1381	.1358	.1334	.1312	.1289	.1267	.1245	.1223
.8	.1202	.1181	.1160	.1140	.1120	.1100	.1080	.1061	.1042	.1023
.9	.1004	.09860	.09680	.09503	.09328	.09156	.08986	.08819	.08654	.08491
1.0	.08332	.08174	.08019	.07866	.07716	.07568	.07422	.07279	.07138	.06999
1.1	.06862	.06727	.06595	.06465	.06336	.06210	.06086	.05964	.05844	.05726
1.2	.05610	.05496	.05384	.05274	.05165	.05059	.04954	.04851	.04750	.04650
1.3	.04553	.04457	.04363	.04270	.04179	.04090	.04002	.03916	.03831	.03748
1.4	.03667	.03587	.03508	.03431	.03356	.03281	.03208	.03137	.03067	.02998
1.5	.02931	.02865	.02800	.02736	.02674	.02612	.02552	.02494	.02436	.02380
1.6	.02324	.02270	.02217	.02165	.02114	.02064	.02015	.01967	.01920	.01874
1.7	.01829	.01785	.01742	.01699	.01658	.01617	.01578	.01539	.01501	.01464
1.8	.01428	.01392	.01357	.01323	.01290	.01257	.01226	.01195	.01164	.01134
1.9	.01105	.01077	.01049	.01022	$.0^{2}9957$	$.0^{2}9698$	$.0^{2}9445$	$.0^{2}9198$	$.0^{2}8957$	$.0^{2}8721$
2.0	$.0^{2}8491$	$.0^{2}8266$	$.0^{2}8046$	$.0^{2}7832$	$.0^{2}7623$	$.0^{2}7418$	$.0^{2}7219$	$.0^{2}7024$	$.0^{2}6835$	$.0^{2}6649$
2.1	$.0^{2}6468$	$.0^{2}6292$	$.0^{2}6120$	$.0^{2}5952$	$.0^{2}5788$	$.0^{2}5628$	$.0^{2}5472$	$.0^{2}5320$	$.0^{2}5172$	$.0^{2}5028$
2.2	$.0^{2}4887$	$.0^{2}4750$	$.0^{2}4616$	$.0^{2}4486$	$.0^{2}4358$	$.0^{2}4235$	$.0^{2}4114$	$.0^{2}3996$	$.0^{2}3882$	$.0^{2}3770$
2.3	$.0^{2}3662$	$.0^{2}3556$	$.0^{2}3453$	$.0^{2}3352$	$.0^{2}3255$	$.0^{2}3159$	$.0^{2}3067$	$.0^{2}2977$	$.0^{2}2889$	$.0^{2}2804$
2.4	$.0^{2}2720$	$.0^{2}2640$	$.0^{2}2561$	$.0^{2}2484$	$.0^{2}2410$	$.0^{2}2337$	$.0^{2}2267$	$.0^{2}2199$	$.0^{2}2132$	$.0^{2}2067$

u	.00	.01	.02	.03	.04	.05	.06	.07	.08	.09
2.5	$.0^{2}2004$	$.0^{2}1943$	$.0^{2}1883$	$.0^{2}1826$	$.0^{2}1769$	$.0^{2}1715$	$.0^{2}1662$	$.0^{2}1610$	$.0^{2}1560$	$.0^{2}1511$
2.6	$.0^{2}1464$	$.0^{2}1418$	$.0^{2}1373$	$.0^{2}1330$	$.0^{2}1288$	$.0^{2}1247$	$.0^{2}1207$	$.0^{2}1169$	$.0^{2}1132$	$.0^{2}1095$
2.7	$.0^{2}1060$	$.0^{2}1026$	$.0^{3}9928$	$.0^{3}9607$	$.0^{3}9295$	$.0^{3}8992$	$.0^{3}8699$	$.0^{3}8414$	$.0^{3}8138$	$.0^{3}7870$
2.8	$.0^{3}7611$	$.0^{3}7359$	$.0^{3}7115$	$.0^{3}6879$	$.0^{3}6650$	$.0^{3}6428$	$.0^{3}6213$	$.0^{3}6004$	$.0^{3}5802$	$.0^{3}5606$
2.9	$.0^{3}5417$	$.0^{3}5233$	$.0^{3}5055$	$.0^{3}4883$	$.0^{3}4716$	$.0^{3}4555$	$.0^{3}4398$	$.0^{3}4247$	$.0^{3}4101$	$.0^{3}3959$
3.0	$.0^{3}3822$	$.0^{3}3689$	$.0^{3}3560$	$.0^{3}3436$	$.0^{3}3316$	$.0^{3}3199$	$.0^{3}3087$	$.0^{3}2978$	$.0^{3}2873$	$.0^{3}2771$
3.1	$.0^{3}2673$	$.0^{3}2577$	$.0^{3}2485$	$.0^{3}2396$	$.0^{3}2311$	$.0^{3}2227$	$.0^{3}2147$	$.0^{3}2070$	$.0^{3}1995$	$.0^{3}1922$
3.2	$.0^{3}1852$	$.0^{3}1785$	$.0^{3}1720$	$.0^{3}1657$	$.0^{3}1596$	$.0^{3}1537$	$.0^{3}1480$	$.0^{3}1426$	$.0^{3}1373$	$.0^{3}1322$
3.3	$.0^{3}1273$	$.0^{3}1225$	$.0^{3}1179$	$.0^{3}1135$	$.0^{3}1093$	$.0^{3}1051$	$.0^{3}1012$	$.0^{4}9734$	$.0^{4}9365$	$.0^{4}9009$
3.4	$.0^{4}8666$	$.0^{4}8335$	$.0^{4}8016$	$.0^{4}7709$	$.0^{4}7413$	$.0^{4}7127$	$.0^{4}6852$	$.0^{4}6587$	$.0^{4}6331$	$.0^{4}6085$
3.5	$.0^{4}5848$	$.0^{4}5620$	$.0^{4}5400$	$.0^{4}5188$	$.0^{4}4984$	$.0^{4}4788$	$.0^{4}4599$	$.0^{4}4417$	$.0^{4}4242$	$.0^{4}4073$
3.6	$.0^{4}3911$	$.0^{4}3755$	$.0^{4}3605$	$.0^{4}3460$	$.0^{4}3321$	$.0^{4}3188$	$.0^{4}3059$	$.0^{4}2935$	$.0^{4}2816$	$.0^{4}2702$
3.7	$.0^{4}2592$	$.0^{4}2486$	$.0^{4}2385$	$.0^{4}2287$	$.0^{4}2193$	$.0^{4}2103$	$.0^{4}2016$	$.0^{4}1933$	$.0^{4}1853$	$.0^{4}1776$
3.8	$.0^{4}1702$	$.0^{4}1632$	$.0^{4}1563$	$.0^{4}1498$	$.0^{4}1435$	$.0^{4}1375$	$.0^{4}1317$	$.0^{4}1262$	$.0^{4}1208$	$.0^{4}1157$
3.9	$.0^{4}1108$	$.0^{4}1061$	$.0^{4}1016$	$.0^{5}9723$	$.0^{5}9307$	$.0^{5}8908$	$.0^{5}8525$	$.0^{5}8158$	$.0^{5}7806$	$.0^{5}7469$
4.0	$.0^{5}7145$	$.0^{5}6835$	$.0^{5}6538$	$.0^{5}6253$	$.0^{5}5980$	$.0^{5}5718$	$.0^{5}5468$	$.0^{5}5227$	$.0^{5}4997$	$.0^{5}4777$
4.1	$.0^{5}4566$	$.0^{5}4364$	$.0^{5}4170$	$.0^{5}3985$	$.0^{5}3807$	$.0^{5}3637$	$.0^{5}3475$	$.0^{5}3319$	$.0^{5}3170$	$.0^{5}3027$
4.2	$.0^{5}2891$	$.0^{5}2760$	$.0^{5}2635$	$.0^{5}2516$	$.0^{5}2402$	$.0^{5}2292$	$.0^{5}2188$	$.0^{5}2088$	$.0^{5}1992$	$.0^{5}1901$
4.3	$.0^{5}1814$	$.0^{5}1730$	$.0^{5}1650$	$.0^{5}1574$	$.0^{5}1501$	$.0^{5}1431$	$.0^{5}1365$	$.0^{5}1301$	$.0^{5}1241$	$.0^{5}1183$
4.4	$.0^{5}1127$	$.0^{5}1074$	$.0^{5}1024$	$.0^{6}9756$	$.0^{6}9296$	$.0^{6}8857$	$.0^{6}8437$	$.0^{6}8037$	$.0^{6}7655$	$.0^{6}7290$
4.5	$.0^{6}6942$	$.0^{6}6610$	$.0^{6}6294$	$.0^{6}5992$	$.0^{6}5704$	$.0^{6}5429$	$.0^{6}5167$	$.0^{6}4917$	$.0^{6}4679$	$.0^{6}4452$
4.6	$.0^{6}4236$	$.0^{6}4029$	$.0^{6}3833$	$.0^{6}3645$	$.0^{6}3467$	$.0^{6}3297$	$.0^{6}3135$	$.0^{6}2981$	$.0^{6}2834$	$.0^{6}2694$
4.7	$.0^{6}2560$	$.0^{6}2433$	$.0^{6}2313$	$.0^{6}2197$	$.0^{6}2088$	$.0^{6}1984$	$.0^{6}1884$	$.0^{6}1790$	$.0^{6}1700$	$.0^{6}1615$
4.8	$.0^{6}1533$	$.0^{6}1456$	$.0^{6}1382$	$.0^{6}1312$	$.0^{6}1246$	$.0^{6}1182$	$.0^{6}1122$	$.0^{6}1065$	$.0^{6}1011$	$.0^{7}9588$
4.9	$.0^{7}9096$	$.0^{7}8629$	$.0^{7}8185$	$.0^{7}7763$	$.0^{7}7362$	$.0^{7}6982$	$.0^{7}6620$	$.0^{7}6276$	$.0^{7}5950$	$.0^{7}5640$

$$G(-u) = u + G(u)$$

Examples: $G(3.57) = .0^{4}4417 = .00004417$

$G(-3.57) = 3.57004417$

Source: These tables of Unit Normal Loss Function appear in *Probability and Statistics for Business Decisions*, pp. 706–707, by Robert Schlaifer, published by the McGraw-Hill Book Company in 1959. They are reproduced here by specific permission of the copyright holder, the President and Fellows of Harvard College.

SELECTED REFERENCES

Bierman, Harold, Jr., Charles P. Bonini, Lawrence E. Fouraker, and Robert K. Jaedicke: *Quantitative Analysis for Business Decisions*, Richard D. Irwin, Inc., Homewood, Ill., 1965.

Emery, James C.: *Organizational Planning and Control Systems*, The Macmillan Company, New York, 1969.

Schlaifer, Robert: *Probability and Statistics for Business Decisions*, McGraw-Hill Book Company, New York, 1959.

Willis, Raymond, and Norman Chervany: *Statistics and Modeling for Decision Making*, Wadsworth Publishing Company, Inc., Belmont, Calif., 1974.

Chapter number and title	Notes on content
8 Structure of a Management Information System	Defines the structure of a management information system—on the basis of physical components, management activity, or organizational functions. Describes some issues of MIS structure.
9 The Hardware, Software, and Control Environment for Information Processing Systems	Surveys the hardware and software for a management information system. Describes the hierarchy of controls that influence quality of the information processing.
10 The Transaction Processing System	Outlines the procedures for transaction processing in both periodic batch and online immediate processing modes.
11 The Data Base Subsystem	Explains how data is stored in files for use by the information system and defines the use of a data base management system.
12 Information System Support for Decision Making	Describes the type of software to be included in the MIS for support of the decision-making activities of intelligence, design, and choice.
13 Information System Support for Planning and Control	Explains the information system software to aid in planning and control activities.

Section Two

Structure of a Management Information System

A management information system is more than a set of ideas or concepts; it is an operational system performing a variety of functions to produce outputs which are useful to the operations personnel and management of an organization. MIS structure is based on what the system is to accomplish, yet its design is constrained by its need to be not only workable but valuable. This section begins by defining the structure of a management information system and then explores its significant subsystems. The table on the facing page contains notes on the contents of each chapter that will illustrate the nature of this section.

189

Chapter 8

Structure
of a Management
Information System

What does a management information system look like? What are its elements? What is the conceptual structure? What is the physical structure? This chapter describes the structure of a management information system and discusses answers to the above questions. There is no standard, agreed-upon framework for describing management information systems, but the chapter does reflect the central tendency of thought in this area. The chapter emphasizes the scope of the MIS concept and thus reflects an "ideal" toward which an organization may move as it designs or redesigns its information processing system.

The approach used is to describe first the operating elements plus some basic structural concepts and then the MIS structure in two ways, on the basis of:

1 Management activity, and
2 Organizational function.

The structural concepts and the two approaches are then synthesized into an MIS structure which is defined both conceptually and physically.

OPERATING ELEMENTS
OF AN INFORMATION SYSTEM

If one asks to see the information system of an organization, he will probably be shown the physical components. An inquiry as to what these physical components do may be answered in terms of processing functions or perhaps in terms of the outputs from the system. These elements are important in understanding an information system and so they will be surveyed before the framework or structure to which they belong is described.

Physical Components

If a management information system were purchased in the same way as an automobile or other equipment item, the components that would be delivered to furnish an operational system would be hardware, software, procedures, operating personnel, and files (data base). These elements, shown below and in Figure 8-1, are described in further detail in Chapters 9, 11, and 13.

System Component	Comments
Hardware	The hardware for an information system consists of the computer (central processor, input/output units, file storage units, etc.), data preparation equipment, and input/output terminals.
Software	The software can be divided into three major types: 1 Generalized system software, such as operating system and data management system, that makes the computer system operate 2 Generalized applications software such as analysis and decision models 3 Application software consisting of programs written specifically for individual applications
Files (data base)	The files containing programs and data are evidenced by the physical storage media (computer tapes, disk packs, etc.) kept in the file library. The files also include printed output and other records on paper, microfilm, etc.
Procedures	Procedures are physical components because they are provided in a physical form such as manuals and instruction booklet. Three major types of procedures are required: 1 User instructions 2 Instructions for preparation of input 3 Operating instructions for the computer center personnel
Operating personnel	Computer operators, system analysts, programmers, data preparation personnel (keypunch operators, keydisk operators, etc.), information systems management.

Hardware

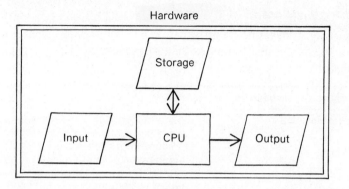

Files

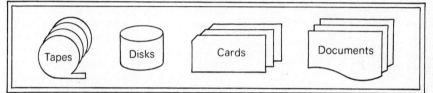

Software

General operating software	General application software	Specialized application software

Procedures

User procedures	Input procedures	Operating procedures

Personnel

Management	Analysis and programming personnel	Operating personnel

Figure 8-1 Physical components of an information system.

An information system can be described as consisting of physical components, but these components do not explain the system, just as a description of a hardware configuration does not explain why it was configured in that way.

Processing Functions

Another way to describe an information system is to tell what it does in terms of the processing functions that are performed. The major processing functions are the following (Figure 8-2):

Processing function	Comments
Process transactions	A transaction is an activity such as making a purchase or a sale or manufacturing a product. Performance of a transaction by an organization generally requires a document to (1) direct a transaction to take place, (2) record its performance, or (3) report, confirm, or explain its performance.
Maintain history files	Many processing activities require creation and maintenance of history (master) files. For example, payroll processing to prepare an employee's paycheck requires that the employee's rate of pay, deductions, etc., be known. This type of permanent information is carried in the payroll master files, which are also used to hold accumulated data. The master files must therefore be updated to reflect the most current information.
Produce reports and other output	Outputs are the usable product of the information system. The major outputs are scheduled reports, but an information system should be able to respond promptly to inquiries and requests for ad hoc reports. The processing cycle often requires special outputs. For example, a detected error results in a message requesting a correction.
Interact with human user	The trend is to applications designed as man-machine systems. The computer does the processing using a planning model, a decision model, etc.; the user provides responses to iterate to a satisfactory solution.

Outputs for Users

From a user's standpoint, the computer-based information system is somewhat of a black box. The user provides inputs and receives outputs. The user's assessment of the information system is therefore dependent on the output the user sees. The outputs thus form one description of an information system and can be classified as being of five major types:

1   Transaction documents
2   Preplanned reports
3   Preplanned inquiry responses

Process transactions

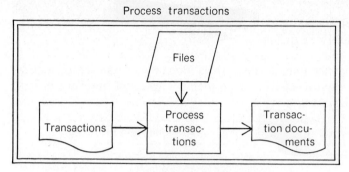

Maintain history files

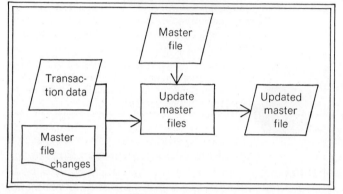

Produce outputs

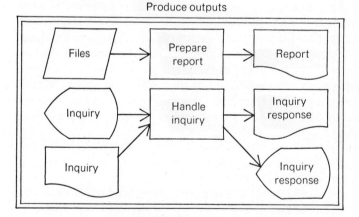

Interact with human user

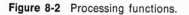

Figure 8-2 Processing functions.

4 Ad hoc reports and inquiry responses
5 Man/machine dialog

Transaction documents (or activity documents) are items such as sales invoices, payroll checks, customer billings, and purchase orders; they are generally of two types:

Transaction document type	Explanation and examples
Informational	Describes or confirms that action will be taken or has been taken. Examples are a sales order confirmation verifying receipt of an order from a customer and a report describing receipt of goods previously ordered. The informational transaction documents confirming actions are feedback to persons connected in some way with the action.
Action	Requests for action or instructions as to action. A purchase order initiates a purchase, a check instructs the bank to pay, a production order instructs production actions.

A single document or different copies of it may serve both transaction purposes. For example, one copy of the sales order confirmation may be sent to the customer to confirm the order; a second copy may be used as an action document to initiate filling of the order. Transaction documents may also be used for managerial information or control scanning, as when a purchasing manager scans all purchase orders. In general, however, managerial information purposes are better met by reports or analyses which summarize individual transactions. (Recall the research on raw versus summarized data described in Chapter 3.)

Preplanned reports are preplanned as to content and format. Examples are sales, inventory, and cash flow reports. Prepared at a given time, they reflect one of two conditions with respect to the time period they cover:

1 They describe status or condition at a point in time (such as inventory status at January 31, 1974), or
2 They summarize what has occurred during a period such as a week, month, or year (e.g., purchases during month of March 1974).

Preplanned inquiries are generally associated with limited output, usually with respect to a small number of items, and result in such output as inventory on hand of part #37518, pay rate of employee #518238142, or balance due from customer XYZ Industries. The inquiries can be handled either online or offline. In online operation, the inquiry and response are processed via a terminal. Since the inquiry has been preplanned, the coding of the inquiry is generally quite simple, and therefore the terminal may be under the direct control of user personnel.

Ad hoc reports and inquiry responses occur at irregular intervals and require data or analysis that has not been preplanned. If the data is not available, a data collection procedure must be planned and implemented. If the data is already in the system, the ad hoc request may be handled in two ways:

1 The user may be provided with a means for preparing and processing the user's own request. The inquiry may, for example, be coded by use of an inquiry language via offline forms or an online terminal.

2 An information service may be provided to process ad hoc requests. Staffed with specialists, the information service analyzes requests and then arranges the retrieval and processing that is necessary to provide the requested data or analysis.

Man/machine dialog differs from reports or inquiries. It is essentially a way in which a user can interact with a model to arrive at a satisfactory solution. Man/machine interaction requires a terminal such as a CRT or typewriter for the user and a model such as an analysis, planning, or decision model for the computer to process. Examples are site planning models, capital investment analysis models, and portfolio management models.

BASIC STRUCTURAL CONCEPTS

It will be useful to describe a few concepts relating to the structure of information systems before describing the frameworks to be used. The concept of a formal and informal system is significant in understanding the increased formalization under the MIS approaches. The idea of an information network will aid in understanding the interrelations of the information system and will provide the basis for defining information subsystems. Information requirements can be stated in terms of either management function or operational function. Both approaches will be introduced and then described in more detail in subsequent sections. Modularity is a key design concept which will again be emphasized.

Formal and Informal Information Systems

The information system for an organization consists of a formal, structured system and an informal or unstructured system (Figure 8-3). The formal, structured system operated by the organization is available to anyone who is authorized to obtain the information. In other words, it is a

The organizational information system

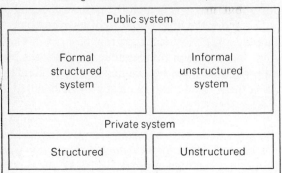

Effect of MIS on relative sizes of information
system components

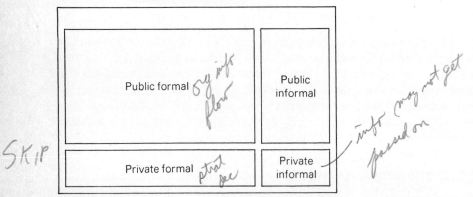

Figure 8-3 Components of an information system.

public system in which access to data is dependent only upon having the proper organizational authority. There is an informal, unstructured system which is also public in the sense that it serves all persons in the organization who might happen to connect with it. The informal information flow consists of telephone calls, conversations at the water cooler, notes on the bulletin board, articles clipped from the newspaper and sent around the office, telephone calls from sales representatives, etc.

In addition to these formal and informal public systems, many private information systems tend to exist among personnel in organizations. Some of these are quite highly structured. For example, an executive may maintain a little black book of data for use in decision making. The executive may maintain reference material in the office which is available essentially only to the executive. This information system might be termed a "formal private system." It is based not upon the function or the job title but upon the person who occupies the position. Many individuals also have their own private information systems which operate in a nonstructured way. By personal contact they are able to maintain a flow of information that depends upon the individual who occupies the position rather than proceeding freely to whomever has the responsibility.

As shown in Figure 8-3, the public information system tends to be larger than the private system, but the latter is a significant part of information flow in an organization. On the other hand, the effect of a comprehensive information system of the type described in this chapter is to increase the scope of the formal, public system. This increase reduces the need for private, formal systems and probably reduces the need for informal, public systems as well as informal, private systems. The difficulty with an informal information system is that the individual who should have information may not be part of the system. A person who has been in a position for some time and has developed an informal system may find that it serves him or her very well, but a new person coming into that position will often not have the information available. The private, formal system has similar difficulties. There is no guarantee that the information will be passed on to the next individual who occupies the position.

This discussion does not imply that informal information systems should be abolished; some are desirable because the formal system would become overly complicated if it had to provide for every individual variation in information requirements. A formal system which attempted to encompass all such requirements would be large, costly, and unwieldy. On the other hand, the private systems and the public, informal segments have generally been too large compared with the formal, public systems. They tend to have information which might better be processed in the formal system. In a survey by Adams[1] of 75 managers, the middle managers indicated 20 to 35 percent of the information they use comes from informal sources. The comparable figure for top managers is 45 to 60 percent.

The management information system described in this chapter is the formal, public system of an organization. "Public" does not mean that everyone inside or outside the organization has access to it; it means that it is run by the organization rather than being a private affair run by a single individual. In analysis of information system requirements, it is

[1]Carl R. Adams, "Attitudes of Top Management Users toward Information Systems and Computers," working paper 73-07, The Management Information Systems Research Center, University of Minnesota, Minneapolis.

important to recognize the opportunity for an improvement in information availability through bringing into the formal system some of the data being provided outside it.

Information Network

The concept of the information system as a network (an approach adapted from Blumenthal[2]) is based on industrial dynamics.[3] The organization is described at the lowest level as consisting of actions or activities which change the level or state of the system. These activities take place in an activity center which is under the direction of a first-line manager. A manager plus the decision procedures for directing an activity is termed a *decision center.* In other words, the smallest component in the organization is an activity center which is directed by a decision center. This combination of activity center plus decision center is termed a *functional unit* because it performs a function. The decision center associated with a functional unit requires information about the variables upon which it operates (level or state of the system) and information about decisions by other decision centers (Figure 8-4). An organization is described as consisting of a number of functional units connected by a network of information flows.

This concept of an organization is useful in designing information systems because it provides an approach for designing the necessary subsystems. As pointed out in Chapter 4, a tightly coupled system with many interconnections becomes unwieldy, and the coordination requirements virtually impossible to handle. Several methods were described for reducing the interaction among systems. One method was to connect systems into clusters and interconnect the clusters. Other methods were use of buffers, slack resources, and standards. An information system that was designed solely at the level of the functional units would be very complex because of the communication among these units. To reduce this complexity, the various functional units may be clustered into groups of related activities which are then placed under the direction of a higher-level decision center (Figure 8-5). The interaction among the functional units in a cluster may be high, but interaction with other clusters or operational functions is simplified. The cluster of related activities might

[2]Sherman C. Blumenthal, *Management Information Systems: A Framework for Planning and Development*, Prentice-Hall, Inc., Englewood Cliffs, N.J., 1969.

[3]Jay W. Forrester, *Industrial Dynamics*, The M.I.T. Press, Cambridge, Mass., 1961. In the industrial dynamics approach, an organization is described as a set of networks, each network consisting of (1) a level (inventory such as materials inventory, money, customer service orders, personnel hours, etc.) or the state of a variable, (2) an activity which utilizes the inventory or changes a state, and (3) decision functions which determine how information is transformed into decisions to cause activity to take place. There is a flow of information not only within each network but also among networks.

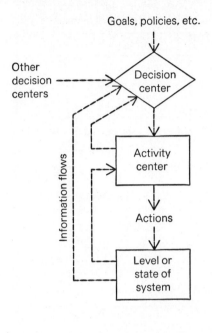

Goals, policies, etc.

Figure 8-4 Flow of information in a functional unit. *(Adapted from Sherman C. Blumenthal, Management Information Systems: A Framework for Planning and Development, Prentice-Hall, Inc., Englewood Cliffs, N.J., 1969.)*

be termed an "operational function." While a functional unit might be writing purchase orders, the operational function would be purchasing, which would include several functional units. The clustering of the functional units into operational functions also results in a hierarchy of decision making and control (Figure 8-6). It is useful to think of two levels of control, first being operational control which directs the day-to-day operations of the functional units and the second being management control (including tactical planning) for each operational function. Budgetary control generally fits in at this level. Overall management control and strategic planning activity encompass all operational functions.

The use of files also acts to simplify information flow. The files essentially serve as an inventory of information. One function may prepare data and store it; another may access the data, operating on a different (but compatible) cycle.

The implications of this network view of the organization for information systems are:

1 The information system is designed to provide information to each functional unit.
2 The information systems for related functional units can be clustered into an information subsystem serving the cluster (operational function).

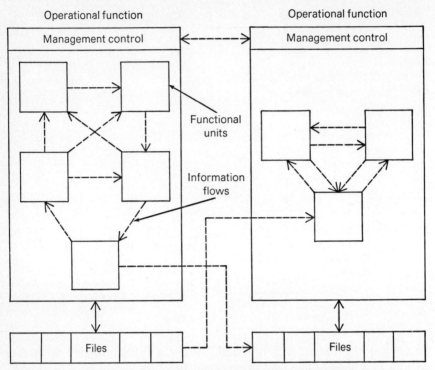

Figure 8-5 Clustering of functional units into operational functions.

3 Interfaces among functional units can be simplified by using information interfaces among clusters in place of individual functional unit interfaces and by using files as buffers.

The design of information systems on the basis of related activities does not necessarily yield functional groups that are identical with organizational functions. Organizations are frequently set up along functional lines (marketing, finance, production, etc.), but organizational responsibility assignments are often based on the capabilities of the current executives. Under such conditions, change in executives may cause a realignment of responsibilities. The information system based on related activities will therefore be similar but not identical to the organization chart functions.

Since functional groupings vary among organizations, it is impossible to provide a single model based on functional groups. As an example of a common functional breakdown, the following are the major functions in a manufacturing organization:

Function	Examples of activities
Marketing	Marketing research, advertising and promotion, sales
Production	Product engineering, production
Logistics	Purchasing, inventory, distribution
Personnel	Personnel, payroll
Finance and accounting	Financing, financial accounting, cost accounting

Another classification (by Blumenthal, op. cit.) illustrates the fact that most functional groupings are similar. Note that the classification is divided into major types of operations—physical and administrative.

Physical operations
    Logistics
        Raw material
        Production
        Saleable product
    Physical assets
        Property and equipment
        Capital projects
Administrative operations
    Financial
        Accounting
        Treasury
    Manpower
        Payroll
        Benefits
        Personnel administration

Information Requirements Depend On Operational Function

info requirements by function vary.

The preceding discussion explained the network of functional units and how they can be combined into operational functions. These operational functions have different information requirements, which is one reason for the proposal that the information system be designed as a set of functional subsystems. The subsystems interface directly in some cases; in other cases the information interface is through the data base.

The information requirements vary with operational functions in two ways:

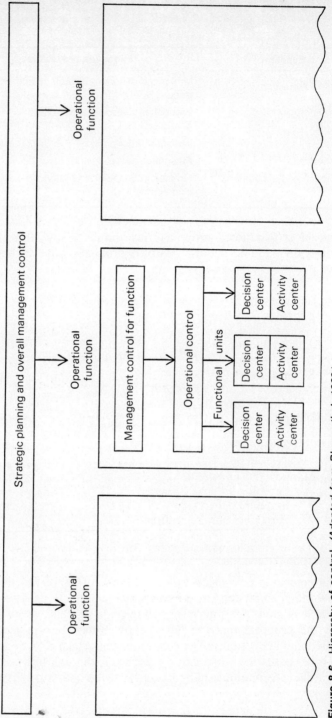

204

Figure 8-6 Hierarchy of control. *(Adapted from Blumenthal, 1969.)*

1 Content
2 Information characteristics

Variations in content are due to the different activities involved. The marketing function needs data on customers, sales, etc., whereas the personnel function needs data on employees, such as on their skills and retirement benefits accrued. Some data will be associated with only a single function; other data is required by more than one function. The characteristics of current and desired information have been found to vary with business functions. A study of 39 middle managers from 10 major corporations disclosed the variations in information characteristics with changes in managerial functions shown by Table 8-1. The results of the study are similar to what one might expect. Financial and accounting information tends to be more accurate, precise, numerical, repetitive, summarized, and from inside sources. Marketing tends to be the opposite. Personnel and operations fall between the extremes defined by marketing and finance.

Table 8-1 Variation in Information Characteristics with Changes in Managerial Functions

Accuracy or precision (less to more accurate or precise)	Age of data (younger to older)	Repetitiveness (less to more repetitive)	Summarization (less to more summary)	Descriptive content (less to more descriptive)	Source (less to more outside)
Marketing	Personnel	Personnel	Production	Personnel	Finance
Personnel	Production	Production	Personnel	Production	Personnel
Production	Marketing	Marketing	Marketing	Finance	Production
Finance	Finance	Finance	Finance	Marketing	Marketing

Source: Carl R. Adams and Roger G. Schroeder, "Current and Desired Characteristics of Information Used by Middle Managers: A Survey," working paper 72–01, The Management Information Systems Research Center, University of Minnesota, Minneapolis.

**Information Requirements Depend On
Level of Management Activity**

Whereas the operational function view of a management information system is to group all activities and information processing in an organization by function, the management activity approach is to group activities and information system support by level of management activities. The different levels (also described in Chapter 5) in the management planning and control hierarchy are:

Level	Comments
Strategic planning	Setting of organizational objectives. Defining of goals, policies, general guidelines charting course for organization. Type of business to be in.
Management control (and tactical planning)	Acquisition of resources. Acquisition tactics, plant location, new products. Use of budgets, variance reports.
Operational planning and control	Effective use of existing facilities and resources to carry out activities.

A manager at the operational level (supervisor or foreman/forewoman) will spend most of his or her time on operational planning and control. A top manager will devote, by comparison, more time to strategic planning. A study by Adams and Schroeder gives the following percentage of middle-manager time devoted to three types of activities:[4]

Type of activity	Percentage of time
Planning	10
Budgeting and control	40
Operations	50

Depending on level of mgt, info will have different characteristics

The level of management activity influences the characteristics required of the data used by that level. Strategic planning requires more outside information, less accuracy, and more summarization than tactical planning. Management control tends to require more accurate, precise, current, and repetitive data than strategic planning. Operations activities tend to use data in less summarized form than management control. There is a marked contrast between the information characteristics for strategic planning and those for the operational level, with the management control/tactical planning being somewhat in the middle. Table 8-2 shows the differences for seven characteristics. Given these differences, the information system for strategic planning is not identical with the information system for operational control. These differences are explored in further detail later in this chapter and in subsequent chapters.

[4]Carl R. Adams and Roger G. Schroeder, "Current and Desired Characteristics of Information Used by Middle Managers: A Survey," working paper 72-01, The Management Information Systems Research Center, University of Minnesota, Minneapolis, p. 10.

Table 8-2   Information Requirements by Decision Category

Characteristics of information	Operational control	Management control	Strategic planning
Source	Largely internal ——————————→ External		
Scope	Well-defined, narrow ——————→ Very wide		
Level of aggregation	Detailed ————————————→ Aggregate		
Time horizon	Historical ————————————→ Future		
Currency	Highly current ——————————→ Quite old		
Required accuracy	High ——————————————→ Low		
Frequency of use	Very frequent ————————→ Infrequent		

Source: G. A. Gorry and M. S. Scott Morton, "Framework for Management Information Systems," *Sloan Management Review*, Fall 1971, p. 59.

Information Requirements Depend On Type of Decision Making

In Chapter 6, two types of decisions were identified: programmed and nonprogrammed. The information system requirements differ for these decisions. A programmed decision can be expressed as a set of decision tables, a formula, or a flowchart. In other words, the decision is prespecified. This allows management to turn over such decisions to lower-level personnel. In fact, the decision may be completely automated, although human review is generally considered desirable. Examples of programmed decisions are inventory reorder rules and credit-granting algorithms. The information system requirements are well-defined input and quality assurance over the input, the processing of the decision logic, and output of the decision. A human review of the decision requires an output that will assist the reviewer in assessing the reasonableness of the decision.

Some programmed decisions define the normal situations but do not attempt to enumerate all possible conditions. If the conditions do not fit into the rules, there may be an ELSE rule to transmit these unusual situations to a human decision maker or a higher decision level. This output from unusual situations must be in a format which assists the decision maker to assess the applicability of the decision rules and to apply one of the rules or alternative rules when appropriate.

The nonprogrammed decision has no preestablished decision procedure, either because the decision is too infrequent to justify a rule or because the decision is too changeable to allow a stable decision procedure. The information system requirements are for data access that cannot be known exactly in advance and analysis and decision procedures to be applied in the solution of the problem. This suggests the need for data retrieval systems and a model bank of analysis and decision programs that can be used as needed.

Modularity—A Key Design Concept   *(good)* ✓ ✓

Modularity is the design of an information system as a number of small modules. Some modules are used only once in a single application; others are used in a large number of applications. The use of modules even in cases where each has a single purpose is desirable because it allows improved project control. The modules can be written and tested separately, allowing more efficient maintenance by identification of the boundaries of the system being changed. The use of modules is thus an application of system principles.

The use of common modules not only reduces the total programming and design effort but probably results in improved programs because of the increased effort that can be applied to the common module. A program using modules will essentially consist of a small control section which does initialization and then calls the program modules in the proper order (Figure 8-7). Since modules may be used by programs which are part of diverse applications, there is a need for planning to arrive at a framework under which the common modules may be identified and designed.

MANAGEMENT INFORMATION SYSTEM STRUCTURE BASED ON MANAGEMENT ACTIVITY

Can also be based on org function

This section uses the Anthony categories (see Chapter 5) of three levels of management planning and control activities: strategic planning, management control, and operational control. Each level is described in terms of its operational characteristics and information needs.

Operational Control   *activities carried out*

Operational control is the process of ensuring that operational activities are carried out effectively and efficiently. Operational control makes use of preestablished procedures and decision rules. A large percentage of the decisions can be programmed. The procedures to follow are generally quite stable. The operating decisions and resulting actions generally cover short time periods. Individual transactions are often important, so that the

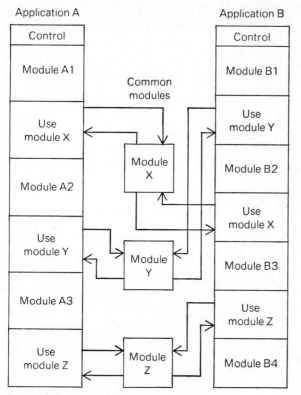

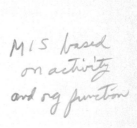

Figure 8-7 The use of common modules.

operational system must be able to respond to both individual transactions and summaries of transactions.

The processing support for operational control consists of (Figure 8-8):

1 Transaction processing
2 Report processing
3 Inquiry processing

These three types of processing contain various decision-making modules which implement agreed-upon decision rules or provide an output describing the decision that will be taken unless the human operator wishes to override the programmed decision rules. Some examples will illustrate the type of decision support that can be designed into operational modules.

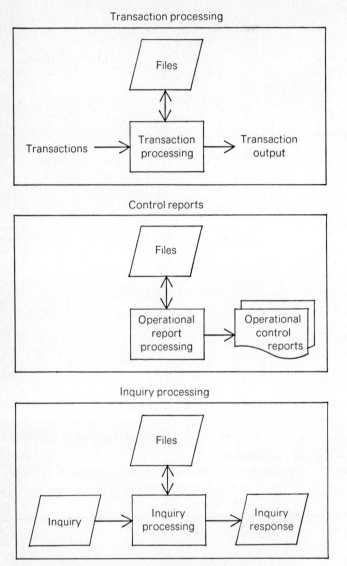

Figure 8-8 Processing to support operational control.

• An inventory withdrawal transaction produces a transaction document. The transaction processing can also examine the balance on hand, etc., and decides (using preestablished criteria) if a replenishment order should be placed. If so, the order quantity is calculated by use of an order quantity algorithm, and an action document is produced which specifies the need for an order plus the order quantity. The human recipient (say, inventory analyst) may accept the order as it is or may choose to override the computer program.

 • An inquiry to a personnel file describes the requirements for a position. The computer search of the employee file uses preprogrammed rules to select and rank candidates.

 • An employee taking an order inserts the order online using a CRT. The processing sequence uses programmed decision rules to instruct the telephone order taker to inquire whether the customer wishes related items (the list also being provided).

 • Routine reports are produced periodically as a matter of course, but a programmed decision rule in a report processing procedure may cause issuance of special reports to provide information in a problem area. An example might be an analysis of orders still outstanding after 30 days.

The data base for operational planning is built on internal data generated from transactions. The sequence of processing is often significant; for example, the additions to inventory should be processed before withdrawals in order to avoid the appearance of being out of stock when new stock has been received.

Management Control

Management control information is required by managers of departments, profit centers, etc., to measure performance, decide on control actions, formulate new decision rules to be applied by operational personnel, and allocate resources. There is a need for summary information—processed so that trends may be observed, reasons for performance variances may be understood, and solutions suggested. The control process requires the following types of information:

1 Planned performance (standard, expected, budgeted, etc.)
2 Variances from planned performance
3 Reasons for variances
4 Analysis of possible decisions or courses of action

The data base for management control consists of two major elements: (1) the data base provided by operations, and (2) the plans, standards, budgets, etc., which define management expectations about performance. There may be some outside data such as industry comparisons and cost indices (Figure 8-9).

The processing requirements to support the management control activities are the following:

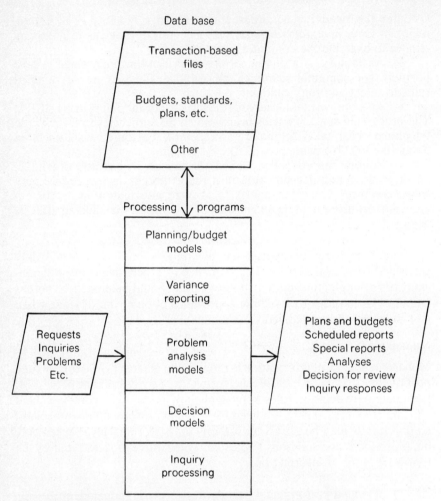

Figure 8-9 Management control data base and processing support.

1 Planning/budget models to assist managers in preparing and revising plans and budgets

2 Variance reporting programs to process scheduled reports showing variances from planned performance

3 Problem analysis modules to analyze data to provide input for decision making

4 Decision models to analyze a problem situation and provide a optimal (or satisficing) solution for management approval

5 Inquiry modules to assist in responding to inquiries

The outputs from the management control information system are plans and budgets, scheduled reports, special reports, analyses of problem situations, decisions for review, and inquiry responses.

Strategic Planning

Strategic planning develops the strategy with which an organization will attempt to achieve its objectives. The time horizon for strategic planning tends to be fairly long, so that fundamental shifts in the organization may be made. For example:

- A department store chain may decide to diversify into the mail order business.
- A department store chain with downtown stores may decide to change to a discount type of operation in the suburbs.
- A company manufacturing industrial products may decide to diversify into consumer lines.

Strategic planning activities do not have to occur on a periodic, regular cycle as do management control activities. They can be somewhat irregular, although some strategic planning may be scheduled into the yearly planning and budgeting cycle. The data requirements for strategic planning are generally for processed, summary data from a variety of sources. There is considerable external data. Some examples of the types of data that are useful in strategic planning illustrate the nature of the data: *uses a lot of external, summary data*

1 Outlook for the economy in the company's current and prospective areas of activity
2 Current and prospective political environment
3 Current capabilities and performance of the organization by market, country, or other category
4 Projection of future capabilities and future performance by market, country, etc. (based on current policies)
5 Prospects for the industry in each country
6 Capabilities of competitors and their market shares
7 Opportunities for new ventures based on current or expected developments
8 Alternative strategies
9 Projections of resource requirements for the alternative strategies

This data contains some "hard" facts, but much is based on judgment. Much of the data cannot be collected on a regular basis. In fact, the data needed is difficult to specify completely in advance. For this reason, some have argued that it is impossible (or certainly impractical) to have a management information system for strategic planning activities. They point out the difficult of efficiently coding, storing, and retrieving the multitude of rumors, facts, hunches, etc., that enter into an assessment of prospects for an industry, a market, or an economy.

The information system support cannot be as complete for strategic planning as it is for management control and operational control. However, the management information system can provide substantial aid to the process of strategic planning. For example:

• The evaluation of current capabilities is based on internal data generated by operational processing requirements, but it may need to be summarized in a special way for planning use.
• The projections of future capability can be developed by analysis of past data and projected into the future. This first approximation is adjusted by management on the basis of their judgment.
• Data on the industry and competitors is fundamental market data that can probably be profitably kept in the computer data base.

MANAGEMENT INFORMATION SYSTEM STRUCTURE BASED ON ORGANIZATIONAL FUNCTION

The management information system can be viewed as a federation of subsystems based on functions performed in an organization. As explained previously, the functional subsystems should be grouped in a logical fashion rather than being based on organizational structure. But in general, the functional groupings will be compatible with the organizational groupings. In the federation of functional subsystems, each subsystem has facilities to perform all processing related to the function, although this may involve calling upon a common data base, a common model base, and common programs when necessary. There will be applications for transaction processing, operational control, managerial control, and strategic planning (Figure 8-10). There is no standard functional grouping, but major functions found in most organizations are marketing, production, logistics, personnel, and finance and accounting. Information processing may also be defined as a function, and top management can be defined as a function separate from the organizational functions of marketing. Each of these will be described in terms of the information subsystem to support operational control, management control, and strategic planning.

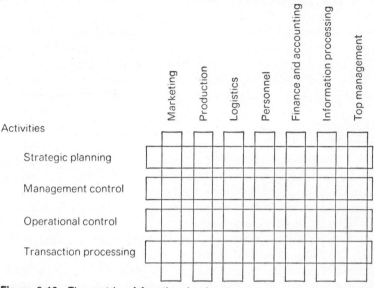

Figure 8-10 The matrix of functional subsystems and management activities.

Marketing Subsystem

The sales or marketing function generally includes all activities related to the promotion and sales of products or services. The transactions are sales orders, promotion orders, etc. The operational control activities include the hiring and training of the sales force, the day-to-day scheduling of sales and promotion efforts, and day-to-day status of deliveries (because these affect customer satisfaction). Managerial control is based on a marketing plan. Information for managerial control may include data on customers, competitors, competitor products, and sales force requirements. Strategic planning for the marketing function involves new markets and new marketing strategies. The information requirements for the strategic planning include customer analyses, competitor analyses, trends, consumer survey information, income projection, demographic projections, and technology projections.

Production Subsystem

The production or manufacturing function responsibilities include product engineering, planning of production facilities, scheduling and operation of production facilities, employment and training of production personnel, and quality control and inspection. Typical transactions to be processed are production orders (based on an explosion of the sales orders and inventory requirements into component parts), assembly orders, finished parts tickets, scrap tickets, and time-keeping tickets. The management control requires summary reports which compare planned or standard performance to actual performance for such items as cost per unit and manpower used. Strategic planning for manufacturing includes alternative manufacturing approaches and alternative approaches to automation.

Logistics Subsystem

The logistics function encompasses such activities as purchasing, receiving, inventory, and distribution. The transactions to be processed include purchase requisitions, purchase orders, manufacturing orders, receiving reports, tickets for inventory, shipping orders, and bills of lading. The operational control function uses information contained in listings and reports such as past-due purchases, past-due shipments to customers, out-of-stock items, overstocked items, inventory turnover reports, vendor performance summaries, and shipper performance analyses. Managerial control information for logistics consists of comparisons between planned and actual for inventory levels, costs for purchased items, stockouts, turnover, etc. Strategic planning involves the analysis of new distribution strategies, new policies with regard to vendors, and make or buy strategies. Information on new technology, distribution alternatives, etc., is required.

Personnel Subsystem

The personnel subsystem includes the hiring, training, record keeping, payment, and termination of personnel. The transactions result in documents describing employment requisitions, job descriptions, training specifications, personnel data (background, skills, experience), pay rate changes, hours worked, paychecks, benefits, and termination notices. Operational control for personnel requires decision procedures for actions such as hiring, training, termination, changing pay rates, and issuing benefits. Management control of the personnel function is supported by reports and analyses showing the variances resulting from differences between planned and actual performance for such items as number of employees hired, cost of recruiting, composition of skills inventory, cost of training (by employee, by program), salary paid, distribution of wage rates, and competitive wage rates. The strategic planning for personnel is involved with evaluating alternative strategies for recruiting, salary, training, and benefits that will ensure the organization of the necessary personnel to achieve its objectives. The strategic data involves analysis of shifting patterns of employment, education, wage rates by area of country (or world). Examples of internal personnel data useful for strategic planning are the shifting internal patterns of employment, skills, training, correlation between job performance and university major, and performance by geographical area.

Finance and Accounting Subsystem

Finance and accounting are somewhat separate functions but are sufficiently related to be described together. Finance is responsible for ensuring adequate organizational financing at as low a cost as possible (in a manner consistent with other objectives). This function covers granting of credit to customers, collection processes, cash management, and financing arrangement (loans, sales of stock, leasing). Accounting covers the classifying of financial transactions and summarizing them into the standard financial reports (income statement and balance sheet), the preparing of budgets, and classifying and analyzing of cost data. The budget and cost data are input for managerial control reports, which means that managerial accounting is part of the information processing system supporting managerial control for all functions. Among the transactions associated with finance and accounting are credit applications, sales, billings, collection documents (statements), payment vouchers, checks, journal vouchers, ledgers, and stock transfers. The operating control over the function itself uses daily error and exception reports, records of processing delays, reports of unprocessed transactions, etc. The managerial control level for accounting and finance utilizes information on budgeted versus actual for cost of financial resources, cost of processing accounting data, and error rates. The strategic planning level for accounting and finance involves a long-run strategy to ensure adequate financing, a long-range tax accounting policy to minimize the impact of taxes, and related goals.

Other Functional Subsystems

The listing of functions has not been exhaustive, and a specific listing must be prepared for each organization. Two functions have not been included because they are not normally defined in such a list— information processing and top management.

Information processing may, in some companies, be considered as part of the accounting function; in other organizations, the computer-based information system may be defined as a separate function. Typical transactions for information processing are requests for processing, requests for program corrections or changes, project proposals, and control counts. Operational control requires information on the daily schedule, jobs delayed, error rates, equipment uptime, and other matters.

Managerial control over information processing requires data on planned and actual utilization, error rates, cost, performance (such as lines coded by programmer), and project progress for each project. The strategic planning for information systems involves the type of information system, the organization of the function (such as centralized or decentralized), and the general shape of the hardware and software environment to be available.

The top-management function (president plus staff) operates separately from the functional areas, but the top-management function also includes the functional vice-presidents acting in a top-management capacity such as in management committees. The transactions processed by top management are primarily inquiries for information and for decisions. The transaction documents, therefore, tend to be letters and memoranda. Responding to the inquiries and making decisions requires either access to the data base and decision models of the organization or the transmittal of the requests to other parts of the organization. The information for operational control in the top-management function includes meeting schedules, correspondence control files, and contact files. This was recognized by one proposal[5] for top-management use of computers which involved, for example, the establishing of computer files for calendars of all executives and a list of professional contacts. The managerial control by top management uses information which summarizes the management control being exercised by other functions to evaluate whether they are performing as planned. This requires access to the plans and actual performance of all the functions. The strategic planning activities relate to matters such as direction of the company (which business it should be in) and designs for obtaining resources. The top-management strategy sets the framework for functional strategic planning and also coordinates planning to remove major inconsistencies. The strategic planning at the top management level requires a wide variety of external and internal data. The information system support for strategic planning may include ad hoc retrieval of data, ad hoc analysis, and computer planning models.

SYNTHESIS OF MANAGEMENT INFORMATION SYSTEM STRUCTURE

The MIS structure has been described in two ways—on the bases of management activity and organizational function. These two approaches plus the structural concepts will now be synthesized into a management

---

[5]Proposed by Richard E. Sprague as a personalized data system. "Personalized Data Systems," *Business Automation*, October 1969, pp. 43–51.

information system structure. This is essentially a conceptual framework which allows one to describe and plan the information system. There is also a physical structure which defines the way an MIS is implemented.

Conceptual Structure

[handwritten annotation: each functional subsystem broken into transaction, oper control, mgt control, strat planning]

The conceptual structure of an MIS is a synthesis of the ideas already presented. The MIS is defined as a federation of functional subsystems, each of which is divided into four major information processing sections: transaction processing, operations information system support, managerial control information system support, and strategic planning information system support. Each of the functional subsystems of the information system has unique data files which are used only by that subsystem. In fact, some individual applications within the subsystems have unique data files not required by any other applications in that or other subsystems. There are also files which need to be accessed by more than one application and need to be available for general retrieval. These files are organized into a general data base which requires special software (the data base management system).

[handwritten margin note: each has its own data file & common data base]

A further amplification of the structure is the introduction of common software. The subsystems contain application programs written especially for the subsystems, but there are common applications which serve many functions. Each subsystem has linkages (or calls) to these common applications. There are also many analytical and decision models (regression programs, linear programming routines, capital budgeting models, planning models) that can be used by many applications. These form the model base for the information system.[6]

This structure is diagrammed for a functional subsystem in Figure 8-11. The subsystem has unique programs for each activity and unique files. It shares the use of common applications software, a model base, a data base, and the data base management system. The latter controls all common files in the common data base, but it may (depending on the application) also be used for storage and retrieval from the unique files. When all subsystems are combined, they form the computer-based information system for the organization. This is diagrammed in Figure 8-12.

These diagrams differ from the pyramid diagram frequently used to describe MIS. The triangle can be derived from the structure already developed. The different activities for functions do not have identical information processing support requirements. For example, transaction processing is substantially more significant in terms of processing time

---

[6]For amplification of the model base concept, see Hart J. Will, "MIS—Mirage or Mirror Image?," *Journal of Systems Management*, September 1973, pp. 24–31.

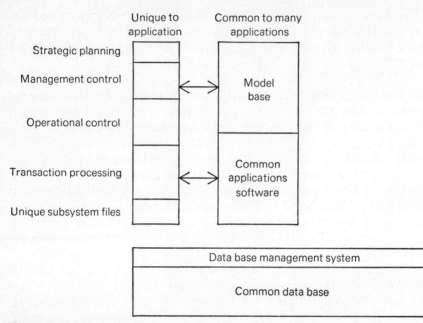

Figure 8-11 The information subsystem for a function (such as marketing or production).

used, files used, etc., than strategic planning. The transaction processing provides the base for all other information support. This concept of the large transaction processing base and a fairly small strategic planning component can be visualized as a pyramid (Figure 8-13). The lower part of the pyramid describes structured, well-defined procedures, while the top part of the pyramid involves more ad hoc, unstructured processes. The bottom levels of the pyramid are of more use to clerical personnel and lower-level managers, while the higher levels apply primarily to top management. The decision processes at the lower level tend to be programmed, top-level decisions to be nonprogrammed.

Physical Structure

The conceptual structure of an MIS is for separate functional subsystems plus a common data base, some common applications, and a model base of common analysis and decision models. The physical structure would be identical if all applications consisted of completely separate programs, but this is frequently not the case. There are substantial economies from:

1   Integrated processing
2   Use of common modules

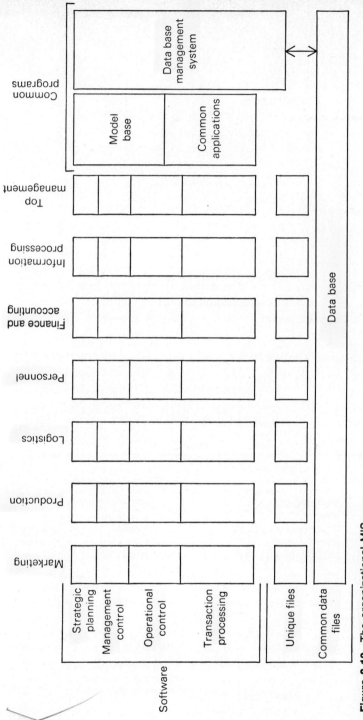

Figure 8-12 The organizational MIS.

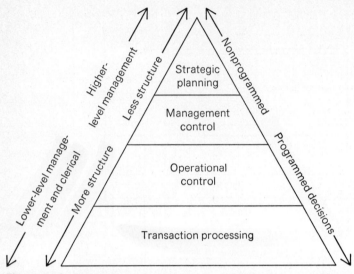

Figure 8-13   The management information system as a pyramid.

Integrated processing is achieved by designing several related applications as a single system in order to simplify the interfaces and reduce the duplication of input. A good example is an order entry system. The recording of an order initiates a sequence of processing, each step using new data but also much of the data from prior processing. The major steps in a typical sequence are:

Step	New data entered	Documents produced
Order entry	Sales representative identification Customer identification Items ordered Quantity of each item	Order acknowledgment Credit exception notice Order register Picking document Items out of stock Items to be ordered
Shipping	Actual quantity shipped	Shipping document
Invoicing	Freight cost	Invoice register Sales journal Back-order register
Collection	Amounts received Returns and allowances	Statements Credit memos Returns and allowances register Cash receipts journal

Step	New data entered	Documents produced
		Accounts receivable aging
Analysis		Sales by sales representative, district, customer, or other category

Note that a large number of documents and reports are prepared from the entry of the order plus actual quantity shipped, freight, amounts received on account, and returns and allowances. The assumption is made that the customer name, address, and credit status, plus price of each item, are contained in customer and billing files. These documents and reports belong to the marketing, logistics, and accounting and finance functions. In other words, an integrated order entry system crosses functional boundaries (Figure 8-14).

The physical structure is also affected by the use of common modules for many processing operations. For example, a common input edit routine may be used for all applications. If an application consists of input, input edit and error control, processing, and output, the use of a common module for input edit and error control means that no application is complete without using this module (Figure 8-15).

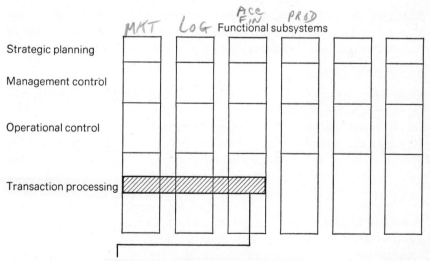

Application such as order entry crossing functional boundaries

Figure 8-14 Applications crossing functional boundaries.

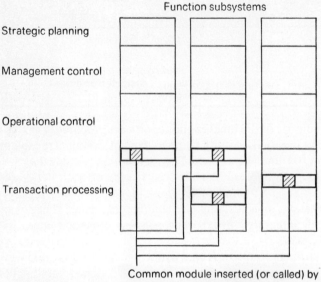

Function subsystems

Strategic planning

Management control

Operational control

Transaction processing

Common module inserted (or called) by
all programs needing the function

Figure 8-15 Use of common modules in physical structure of MIS.

SOME ISSUES OF MIS STRUCTURE

There are several issues in the structure of an MIS. Among them are the extent of processing integration and file integration, the extent of man/machine interaction, and generalized versus individualized MIS.

Extent of Integration

Some advocates of "total systems" have argued for complete integration of all processing. The experience to date suggests that such a tightly coupled system is impractical. There are too many factors to consider all at once, and maintenance is difficult. For this reason, the system is decoupled into major modules with integration only where required (as in the order entry system). Inconsistencies among subsystems are reduced by the use of standards and the common data base.

The file integration is accomplished by a single file which serves a number of applications that might otherwise have separate files and by the use of a common data base. This does not mean that there should be no separate files. Some files are of significant interest to one application only and therefore may be designed for and maintained by that application.

The data requirements for different levels of activity also suggest the need for more than one data base rather than complete integration. For example, the data collected and stored for strategic planning is so different from data for operational control that some separation may be desirable.

Extent of Man/Machine Interaction

The MIS structure does not specify online man/machine interaction; it indicates only that there is an information system to support various operational and management activities. Online processing of transactions is often desirable because it allows for the transaction to be completed immediately. Inquiries at all levels are generally more effective if online response is available. The use of analysis, planning, and decision models is frequently enhanced if the analyst, planner, or decision maker can interact online with the computer program. In some cases, the interaction is vital.

The computer system that supports online transaction processing may not be able to support interactive models. But setting up an MIS does not mean that a single computer system must be used. An organization may use its in-house computer for transaction processing, but rent time-sharing for interactive models.

Generalized versus Individualized MIS

The MIS for each user should suit the decision needs of the position. But do these needs change with the person who occupies the position? The alternatives might be defined as follows:

MIS based on position

| Organization-defined decision models for decisions assigned to the position | + | information system support for decisions | = MIS |

MIS based on user occupying the position

| User-defined decision models for his decisions | + | information system support for user | = MIS |

The information system support for a decision area might range from simple data base retrieval support to automated decision making. A decision maker with a variety of different decisions might have a variety of decision support structures. Since managers differ in their decision styles and in their use of information, it would appear desirable to individualize the information system to suit the manager. The counter arguments center on the use of training and the cost of individualized systems.

Some differences in the use of information resources may be due to inherent differences in humans, but these differences can be reduced by training in the use of these resources. The desirability of uniformity through training may depend somewhat on the level of the position. Lower-level positions benefit more from this uniformity than do the higher-level positions, which suggests that individualized systems are most appropriate at higher levels.

The cost of an MIS is substantial, but it can be reduced if generalized software can be used and if the system remains the same in spite of changes in user personnel. A compromise possibility is the use of generalized software with a variety of options by which a user may customize his information system support.

SUMMARY

The chapter has defined the structure of an MIS. This is an ideal structure, and an actual MIS will differ from this model because the cost/effectiveness of certain elements is not sufficiently high to justify their inclusion and because the implementation is performed slowly rather than all at once.

The MIS may be described in terms of its operating elements. Its physical components are hardware, software, files, procedures, and personnel. Its processing functions are to process transactions, maintain history files, produce outputs, and interact with human users. The outputs for users are transaction documents, preplanned reports, preplanned inquiry responses, ad hoc reports and responses, and man/machine dialog.

Some basic structural concepts are surveyed. There are an informal and a formal information system, each of which can be divided into a public portion available to all authorized personnel and a private, individually operated, system. An organization consists of functional units, each unit being composed of an activity center directed by a decision center. The functional units are connected by a network of information flows. Functional units are clustered into operational functions which form the basis for information system subsystems. Information requirements vary for the different operational functions. They depend on level of management activity (strategic planning, management control, and operational control). The requirements also depend on type of decision making—programmed or nonprogrammed. Another key concept is modularity, which is the design and operation of the information system as a number of small modules.

The logical structure of an MIS consists of a federation of information subsystems for different functions. Each subsystem provides support for transaction processing, operational control, management control, and strategic planning. Some typical subsystems might be marketing, production, logistics, personnel, and finance and accounting. Information systems and top management may also be defined as subsystems. The logical structure includes some unique files for subsystems plus a common data base. There is unique software for each subsystem and there is common software used by or available to all subsystems—a data management system, common software routines, and a model base of analysis, planning, and decision models. The physical structure of an MIS consists of individual applications, integrated applications, and common modules.

Some issues of MIS structure discussed in the chapter are the extent of integration of processing and files, extent of man/machine interaction, and generalized versus individualized structure.

EXERCISES

1 Describe the physical evidence of the existence of an MIS in an organization.
2 What does an MIS do (what are its processing functions)?
3 Describe the outputs from an information system.
4 Explain the variety of transaction documents.
5 Describe the informal information system.
6 Evaluate cost/value of the private information system.
7 Explain the logic of combining functional units into organizational functions. What determines the combination?
8 What is the relation of activity center, decision center, and functional unit?
9 How are information requirements influenced by:
 a Operational function?
 b Level of management activity?
 c Type of decision?
10 Why is modularity such a key concept?
11 Define the processing requirements for:
 a Transaction processing
 b Operational control
 c Management control
 d Strategic planning
12 Discuss the extent to which a formal information system can support strategic planning.
13 Describe the strategic planning by each function.

14 Explain how the physical structure of an MIS differs from the logical structure.

15 Describe and discuss issues of MIS structure. (You may add to the list in the text.)

16 Write a reply to John Deardon's article, "MIS Is a Mirage," *Harvard Business Review*, January–February 1972, pp. 90–99. (Hint: Also read the letters to the editor about the article in the March–April issue.)

17 Make a comparison between Head's description of MIS and the structure in this chapter. (See the Head references at the end of the chapter.)

18 How might a small company with a small computer provide analytical, planning, and decision models for interactive use?

19 Why is order entry such an important integrated application?

20 Why might an organization not achieve a "complete" MIS?

SELECTED REFERENCES

Ackoff, R. L.: "Management Misinformation Systems," *Management Science*, December 1967, pp. B147–B156.

Aron, J. D.: "Information Systems in Perspective," *Computing Surveys*, December 1969, pp. 213–236.

Blumenthal, Sherman: *Management Information Systems: A Framework for Planning and Development*, Prentice-Hall, Inc., Englewood Cliffs, N.J., 1969.

Brady, Rodney H.: "Computers in Top-Level Decision Making," *Harvard Business Review*, July-August 1967, pp. 67–69.

Churchill, Neil C., John H. Kempster, and Myron Uretsky: *Computer-based Information Systems for Management: A Survey*, National Association of Accountants, New York, 1969.

Cox, Donald F., and Robert E. Good: "How to Build a Marketing Information System," *Harvard Business Review*, May-June 1967, pp. 145–154.

Dean, Neal J.: "The Computer Comes of Age," *Harvard Business Review*, January-February 1968, pp. 83–91.

Dearden, John: "Can Management Information Be Automated?," *Harvard Business Review*, March-April 1964, pp. 128–135.

———: "Computers: No Impact on Divisional Control," *Harvard Business Review*, January-February 1967, pp. 99–104.

———: "MIS Is a Mirage," *Harvard Business Review*, January-February 1972, pp. 90–99.

———: "Myth of a Real-Time Management Information," *Harvard Business Review*, May-June 1966, pp. 123–132.

———, and Warren McFarlan: *Management Information Systems: Text and Cases*, Richard D. Irwin, Inc., Homewood, Ill., 1966.

Dickson, Gary W.: "Management Information Decision Systems," *Business Horizons*, December 1968, pp. 17–26.

Diebold, John: "Bad Decisions on Computing Use," *Harvard Business Review*, February 1969.

Drucker, Peter F.: "What the Computers Will Be Telling You," *Nation's Business*, August 1966, pp. 84–90.

Forrester, Jay W.: *Industrial Dynamics*, M.I.T. Press, Cambridge, Mass., 1961.

Garrity, John T.: "Top Management and Computer Profits," *Harvard Business Review*, July–August 1963.

Gorry, G. A., and M. S. Scott Morton: "A Framework for Management Information Systems," *Sloan Management Review*, Fall 1971.

Head, Robert V.: "The Elusive MIS," *Datamation*, September 1, 1970, pp. 22–27.

———: "Management Information Systems: A Critical Appraisal," *Datamation*, May 1967, pp. 22–27.

Hodges, Bartow, and Robert N. Hodgson: *Management and the Computer in Information and the Control Systems*, McGraw-Hill Book Company, New York, 1969.

Hung, Pearson: "Fallacy of the One Big Brain," *Harvard Business Review*, August 1966, pp. 84–90.

Kelly, Joseph F.: *Computerized Management Information Systems*, The Macmillan Company, New York, 1970.

Krauss, Leonard I.: *Computer Based Management Information Systems*, American Management Association, Inc., New York, 1970.

Kriebel, Charles H.: "MIS Technology—A View of the Future," *Proceedings of the Spring Joint Computer Conference*, 1972, pp. 1173–1180.

Massey, L. Daniel: *Management Information Systems*, D. H. Mark Publishing Company, Braintree, Mass., 1969.

Smith, Robert D. (ed.): *Management Information Systems for the 1970's*, Center for Business and Economic Research, Kent State University, Kent, Ohio, 1972.

"What's the Status of MIS," *EDP Analyzer*, October 1969.

Will, Hart J.: "MIS—Mirage or Mirror Image?" *Journal of Systems Management*, September 1973, pp. 24–31.

Withington, Frederic G.: *The Real Computer: Its Influence, Uses, and Effects*, Addison-Wesley Publishing Company, Inc., Reading, Mass., 1969.

Zaney, William M.: "Blueprint for MIS," *Harvard Business Review*, November-December 1970, pp. 95–100.

Zannetos, Zenon S.: "Toward Intelligent Management Information Systems," *Industrial Management Review*, vol. 9, no. 3, 1968, pp. 21–37.

Chapter 9

The Hardware, Software, and Control Environment for Information Processing Systems

The text assumes a familiarity with the basic hardware, software, and controls required for computer-based data processing. This chapter does, however, provide a review of this environment. As an organization moves toward implementation of a comprehensive, advanced information system, the hardware and software environment becomes more complex. This chapter, therefore surveys system elements especially applicable to advanced organizational information systems.

REVIEW OF A BASIC COMPUTER
DATA PROCESSING SYSTEM

There are five basic elements in the data processing system: hardware, software (system software and application software), files, procedures, and personnel. Elements to be reviewed in this chapter are hardware, software, and control procedures. The files are described in Chapter 11; personnel and procedures are explained in Chapters 14 and 15. This first section is a review of the basic hardware and software for data processing; subsequent sections describe additional hardware and software to support a comprehensive MIS.

Hardware

Hardware for computer data processing consists of equipment which performs the following functions:

  1 Data preparation
  2 Input to the computer
  3 Computation, control, and primary storage (central processing unit or CPU)
  4 Secondary storage
  5 Output from the computer

Equipment connected directly to the computer is termed "online," whereas equipment used separately and not connected is called "offline." The relation of these equipment functions in a computer system is shown in Figure 9-1.

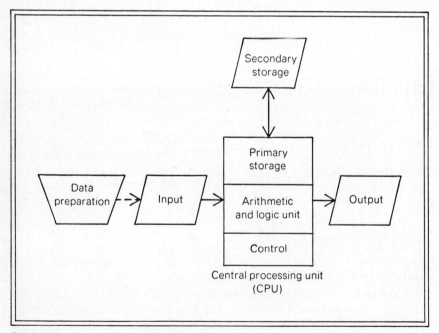

Figure 9-1 Basic functions in a computer system.

Data preparation equipment includes card punches, verifiers, keydisk systems, data collection terminals, and CRTs. Typical input devices are punched card readers, optical scanners, and magnetic ink character readers. The most common output device is the printer, but output can be put on a CRT display device, a typewriter terminal, graph plotter, computer output microfilm, or other devices. The CPU for a computer system typically consists of the control unit, the arithmetic unit for performing arithmetic and logic operations, and storage (often called "primary storage" to differentiate it from the "secondary storage"). Secondary or auxiliary storage is supplementary to the primary storage contained in the CPU. It has large capacity relative to the primary storage and is used to hold data files plus programs not currently in use. The most common secondary storage media are magnetic tape and magnetic disks.

Software

Software consists of computer programs and routines which direct or facilitate the operation of the computer and can be divided into two major categories:

1 System software
2 Application programs

System software consists of computer programs which facilitate the use of application programs. Examples are the operating system which directs and assists the execution of application programs, utility programs to do common tasks such as sorting, compilers to translate programs coded by the programmer into machine-level instructions, and data management systems to manage storage and access into the data base.

Application programs are computer programs written for an individual application such as payroll processing. They generally require system software in their execution. For example, the application program may specify the reading of a card from the card reader; the operating system provides the instructions to manage the actual execution of the physical reading of the card.

CONTROL ENVIRONMENT FOR COMPUTER PROCESSING

Quality control over computer data processing is achieved by two sets of controls—a hierarchy of organizational controls, within which information processing is conducted, and the specific controls for an application (Figure 9-2). There are also control procedures to protect the information resources from destruction and theft.

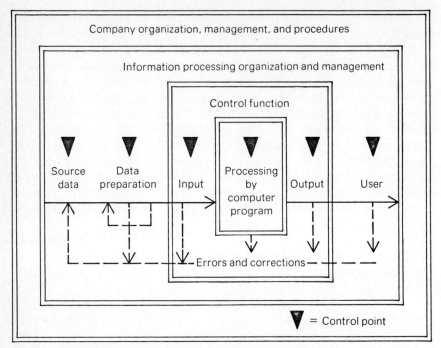

Figure 9-2 The control framework for computer-based information processing.

The organizational structure which establishes and oversees the control of computer data processing consists of a three-level hierarchy:

Organizational element	Control description
Top management	Establishes and monitors overall organizational controls for information processing
Information processing management	Establishes and monitors operating controls for computer processing
Control function	Administers the controls associated with information processing jobs

Top-Management Control

Top management has the overall responsibility for the information processing system. This responsibility is reflected in activities such as the following:

Authorization of major systems additions or changes

Postinstallation review of actual cost and effectiveness of systems projects

Review of organization and control practices of the information processing function

Monitoring of performance

Top-management responsibility for authorizing major systems work means that each such major addition or change must be presented to management in the form of a proposal to be evaluated in terms of cost and benefits. A new or improved data processing system is similar to a large expenditure for an addition to the plant or equipment and should be carefully scrutinized before resources are committed to it. Also, since data processing systems will affect both the data handling requirements of other departments and the information available to them, top-management understanding of a proposed addition or change and top-management approval are necessary for adequate control. Requiring top-management approval also enforces adequate preplanning by information processing management. The top-management role receives further discussion in Chapter 14.

Information System Management Control

The information system management has responsibility for the control practices associated with the operation of the information system. The following are some examples of activities associated with this management responsibility:

Maintenance of qualified staff (selection, training, and evaluation)

Scheduling and control over work of processing staff

Control over program resources of the installation (documentation, program change controls, etc.)

Control over computer files (a program and file library, file retention plan, and file reconstruction plan)

Control over development life cycle for new applications

Control over maintenance (correction and revisions) of existing applications

The information processing management should also ensure that all applications to be run by the department are adequately documented, adhere to standards for design and maintainability, have an adequate processing trail, and include adequate application controls. For applications designed and programmed by the internal staff, this review may be included in the regular review of an application design and of programming. For purchased software, there must be a prior specific investigation and review. Systems are frequently designed with controls that are very good but that are never made operational nor applied consistently or correctly. A continuing data processing management responsibility is therefore to review the staff's adherence to the controls.

Control Function

The plan of organization and the operating procedures should provide for a control function, which can be divided into two types: (1) Processing control internal to information processing, as in Figure 9-2, and (2) independent outside checks. The internal processing control, a function of the data processing department, is concerned with monitoring accuracy of processing and ensuring that no data is lost or mishandled within the department during processing. For example, if the payments-on-account file is processed with the current accounts receivable file to produce an updated accounts receivable file, the sum of the payments-on-account transaction file and the accounts receivable file records before updating should equal the total of the records on the updated accounts receivable file. The person charged with the processing control function is responsible for making, or reviewing the results of, such a comparison. The activities of the data administrator in exercising control over the data base can also be thought of as part of the control function. This administrator is described in Chapter 11.

The activities of the control staff arc specified in the systems and procedures manual and in the description of control activities for each computer application. The control function will include duties such as the following:

Logging (making a journal or log) of input data and recording of control information

Recording progress of work through the processing department

Reconciling computer controls with other control information

Supervising distribution of output

Scrutiny of computer console logs and other control information entries in accordance with control instructions

Liaison with users regarding errors, logging of correction requests, and recording corrections made

Scrutiny of error listings and maintenance of error log or error report

Independent, outside checks can take several forms, but they are basically concerned with an independent check of the functioning of the data processing department. This check may be performed by a user department. If the general ledger, for instance, is maintained on the computer, the accounting department may keep a control total of all debits and credits to be posted by the computer. This control can be compared against the debits and credits from the computer run. Another possibility is an independent quality control evaluation group in a user department where the volume of data to be controlled is large. As an example, a large corporation has a payroll processing control group responsible for evaluating the payroll data produced by the computer. Independent review of the data processing function may also be carried out by a review staff such as the internal auditors.

Application Controls

Controls are applied to an application in two different ways—in its development and in its operation. The application development controls are described in Chapter 15; the operational controls to detect errors in processing are surveyed in this section. Additional discussion of controls in connection with the explanation of processing methods appears in Chapter 10.

There is a fairly standard flow of processing activities for most applications. Controls should be operable at each stage in the processing flow. The following are indicative of the control points:

Offline data entry
    Data recording
    Data transmitted to processing
    Data preparation for processing (keypunching, verifying, etc.)
Online data entry
Input to processing
Processing
Access to files and programs
Distribution of output
Use of output

The error control for an application begins with the recording of the data. Good design of forms and understandable instructions are essential at this point. There may also be visual review and coding of account numbers. Documents are transmitted to data processing input preparation, where they are logged on a transmittal record that keeps track of data entering the system. The data records are converted to machine-readable form and verified. Upon input to computer processing, data records are analyzed for errors. Erroneous records are rejected and returned for correction and resubmission. The processing programs have various controls to detect errors in the data, the processing, and the files being used. The distribution of output follows an approved distribution list. Early in the processing cycle, controls are activated for batches of data, and these controls follow the batch through the entire processing cycle. The batch may also be used as part of the processing or audit trail which allows the processing of an item to be traced from input document to output report or from output back to input. There are also regular procedures for correcting errors and resubmitting the corrected data.

Security and Protection Provisions

The equipment in a computer installation devoted to organizational information processing has a value ranging from, say, $100,000 to several million dollars. The equipment is concentrated in a small area and is easily damaged. In a civil commotion or riot, the computer facility is a likely target for destruction. The magnetic tapes and magnetic disk packs have a modest intrinsic value, but when they contain data files, they have a high value to the organization. In many cases, the data on the tapes and disks has a value to outsiders—for example, prospect lists, employee lists, and mailing lists.

Because of the risk of damage from unauthorized access and the potential loss from theft or destruction of data files, programs, proce-dures, etc., access to the computer facility is generally controlled. Organization controls for security and protection include division of duties (so that a single person does not have complete control over the processing for an application), internal and external audit review, restrict-ed access by operators to program documentation, and restricted access to data files and program files. This latter control is exercised through the use of a file librarian who keeps track of the files and checks them out to authorized personnel only.

The procedures for operations generally call for both external and internal file labels to inhibit incorrect use of a file. Among the safeguards used by a computer installation to prevent destruction of processing capabilities are:

Fire protection including fireproof vaults
Off-premises storage of backup files and programs
Advance arrangements for backup processing capabilities

These safeguards emphasize the capability to recover from a disaster. The procedures should be supplemented by insurance against loss of equipment, software, and data. Fidelity insurance should be used to protect against employee dishonesty.

TRANSACTION INPUT
HARDWARE AND SOFTWARE

Almost all early computer-based processing applications used punched card input. The traditional data preparation activites with punched cards consist of the writing of input data on documents, the assembling of the documents into batches, the keypunching of the data into cards, and the verification of the keypunching. Any keypunching errors detected by verification are then corrected. The punched, verified batch of cards is read by a computer application (run) which performs input editing. Errors detected by the input checking are returned to users for correction and resubmission (Figure 9-3).

The data preparation process tends to be error-prone, and the fairly long cycle of punched card data preparation results in significant delays in correcting errors. Newer systems are being designed to improve the speed of data preparation for transaction processing and to reduce the time for error correction. This is being accomplished for both offline and online input. The emphasis is on recording the data and checking it for errors as near the point of transaction as possible and on improved feedback to assist the person recording the transaction in performing error detection and correction.

Offline Transaction Input

One method for compressing the preparation time for input data is the keydisk system. The data is keyed from documents much as in card punching but then is sent to a minicomputer in the keydisk system. The minicomputer stores temporarily, edits, and validates the data in a way similar to the computer edit and validation run, and writes validated batches of data onto magnetic tape. This process simplifies the data preparation and provides "cleaner" data to processing (Figure 9-4). Many errors can be detected and corrected earlier than with card punching.

Another offline possibility is the use of offline intelligent terminals which accept input, edit it for errors, and record onto magnetic disk or magnetic tape storage for subsequent input to processing. The intelligent terminals can also perform simple data processing tasks.

Online Transaction Input

The direct entry of transactions online to a computer is a clear trend in advanced systems. The advantages are immediate capture of data in machine-readable form, immediate editing, immediate feedback for error correction, and immediate correction. The direct entry of data may be

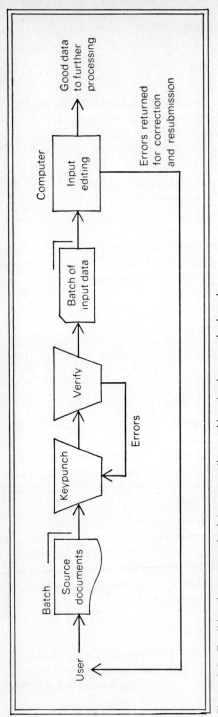

Figure 9-3 Traditional sequence in data preparation and input using punched cards.

Typical operation flow for keydisk system

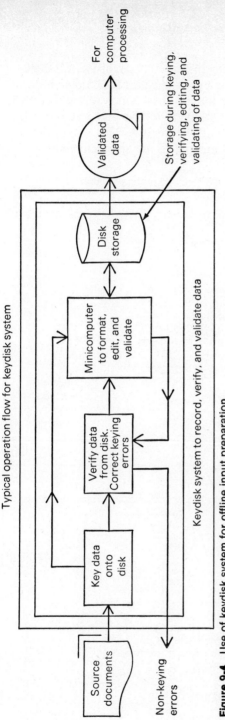

Figure 9-4 Use of keydisk system for offline input preparation.

241

combined with immediate processing of transactions, or the transactions may be immediately tested for errors but batched for subsequent processing (Figure 9-5). In both cases, the input transaction is tested for errors and compared with the file against which it will be processed to detect transactions without a corresponding file record. The reason for the delayed transaction processing alternative is the simplicity inherent in

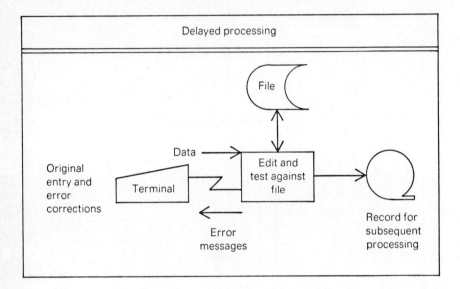

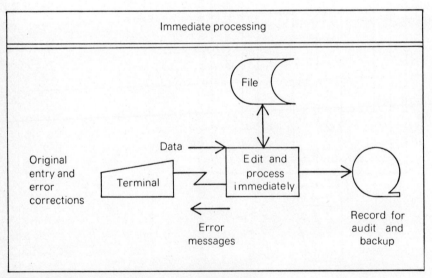

Figure 9-5 Two alternatives for online direct entry.

batch processing. Therefore, unless immediate processing is required, batching transactions before processing may be a more suitable alternative.

The online, direct input may use a variety of terminal devices. Among them are:

1 *Programmable terminal.* This type of terminal contains the logic to perform data validation. It has storage for transactions, formats, error messages, etc. The terminal can operate offline with subsequent transmission to the computer.

2 *Logic terminals.* These terminals contain logic for input validation but no storage. Therefore, they must transmit immediately to the computer; they cannot support offline operation.

3 *Visual display terminals (CRTs).* These usually have neither logical capability nor storage capacity. They merely send and receive; all processing is performed by the computer to which they are connected.

The variety of entry devices is large; the major point of this discussion is the trend toward direct entry of data through terminals, direct and immediate error feedback, and immediate correction of erroneous data. The terminals are also used for sending data to personnel, such as instructions relating to the transaction and responses to inquiries.

COMMUNICATIONS HARDWARE AND SOFTWARE

Remote input/output devices may be wired directly to the central computer if the distances between the computer and the devices are short. However, in most cases data is transmitted over communication lines. Communications hardware is required in order to manage input/output over the lines between the central processor and the remote input/output devices. The user terminal is connected to the communication lines by means of a modem (also called a "data set"), which converts the digital symbols of the data processing equipment to the analog symbols to be transmitted. The communications network then handles the transmission and performs automatically all necessary error control over the data between the data set at the terminal and the modem at the computer site.

Communication Facilities

Almost all data communication is over a network maintained by a communications company. The largest is operated by American Telephone and Telegraph (AT&T), but there are companies which have specialized data communications facilities. The services available from the communications carriers include leased lines and public switch lines

("lines" refers to all types of communication facilities even though they may use nonwire methods such a microwave). Leased lines provide the user with a specific communication path, dedicated to its use only, that can be conditioned to allow higher transmission rates. The switched or dialup line provides access to the communications network. The switching path through the network can vary from use to use because the automatic switching equipment in the network selects one path from those available. The leased line is therefore more expensive, but its quality is known.

There are three modes of operation for communication facilities— simplex, half-duplex, and full-duplex:

> *Simplex.* Communication is in only one direction at a time. This is used, for example, for a remote device which receives but does not send.
> *Half-duplex.* Communication is in both directions, but only one direction at a time.
> *Full-duplex.* Communication is in both directions at the same time.

Remote terminals for direct entry generally require either half-duplex or full-duplex transmission. The advantage of full-duplex is that the input data is sent to the computer which transmits back the data it received for display on the terminal typewriter or CRT. This is an additional check on the quality of transmission.

The speed of transmission is important because a device may be able to operate faster than it can receive data, and this may slow down its use. The service offered by the common carriers can be divided into three classes based on the band width. Band width determines the maximum transmission speed because the width of the band affects the frequency range that can be accommodated. A high frequency state provides faster communication. There are three common band widths:

> *Narrow band.* Communication facilities capable of transmitting data in a range of up to 300 bits per second. Used for teletype transmission.
> *Voice band.* Used for transmitting voice signals. Maximum speed range of 2,400 bits per second on a normal line and up to four times this rate on a special line. This is the most common band for direct-entry terminals.
> *Broad band.* Very high rates of transmission.

User Hardware for Communications

A user may not wish to tie up the processing capabilities of the central computer in order to manage the receipt or transmission of data between the computer and remote devices. If so, the servicing of the communications (message formatting, communication line control, etc.) is placed in a separate minicomputer termed a "frontend computer." It receives all data communication and edits and assembles blocks of data, which are then sent to the main computer for processing. When the main computer has data to send, the block is turned over to the frontend processor for transmission. The frontend computer has storage for data, so a major advantage of this approach is that transmission of data between user terminal and the frontend computer may proceed even if the main computer is not functioning.

The transmission of data between the remote devices and the central computer frequently occurs at a fairly slow rate, which means that several devices can share a single transmission line. This sharing is performed by a device called a "multiplexor." It either divides the transmission capacity into tiny time slices, each of which is provided to a different device (time division multiplexing), or divides the frequency into several subbands (frequency division multiplexing).

User Software for Communications

When online, remote terminals or divices are used, special software is required to manage the communications between the terminals and the computer. This software is often termed a "teleprocessing monitor." These systems are available from both the manufacturers of computers and independent software vendors. The teleprocessing monitor provides for messages to operators, error recovery procedures, usage reports, etc. This software may be used by a frontend computer, or it may be used by the main computer, depending on which one manages communications.

CENTRAL PROCESSOR FACILITIES

The hardware and software in the central processor provide one of the technological environments for advanced information systems. The complexity of management of the computer has resulted in hardware and software to assist in that task.

Hardware/Software for Advanced Information Systems

The hardware to support advanced information systems will generally need the following characteristics:

   1 Data communications capabilities. The hardware for this was discussed in the previous section.

2   Channel capacity and interfaces for a variety of high-speed and low-speed input/output devices.
3   Capabilities for online operation (such as handling of interrupts).
4   Large primary (internal) storage.
5   Very large online secondary storage.

In other words, the central processor in most advanced systems must have the hardware capability (perhaps supplemented or complemented by software) to support online operation involving a variety of devices and some data communications (Figure 9-6).

The primary storage required for advanced systems is generally fairly large. For example, some large systems have a million bytes of primary or internal storage. The capabilities for virtual storage provide a significant additional storage support to advanced systems. In virtual storage, the programmer can ignore almost all limitations on the size of primary storage. The hardware and software for virtual storage segment the program, store it in segments on direct access storage (usually disk storage), and bring each segment into storage as needed. The online secondary storage generally consists of disk units. Several billion characters of online secondary storage are not unusual.

The software to support advanced information systems includes the following:

1   Communication monitor
2   Operating system
3   Data base management system

The communications monitor was explained earlier in the chapter; the data base management system is explained in Chapter 11. A specialized operating system will generally be required to support realtime processing and multiprogramming. *Realtime processing* is defined as immediate, fast-response processing. Examples are online transaction processing and online inquiries. Multiprogramming means that more than one program will be in execution state at the same time, but certain programs will be given priority. The priority programs take precedence over other programs, generally because they are the fast-response realtime applications. The nonpriority programs share the rest of the processing time. The number of programs that can be executed concurrently depends on the storage size and the software system. Each program occupies a partition in memory. In simple operating systems, the partitions are fixed in size, and a small number (say, three or four) are allowed. The more sophisticat-

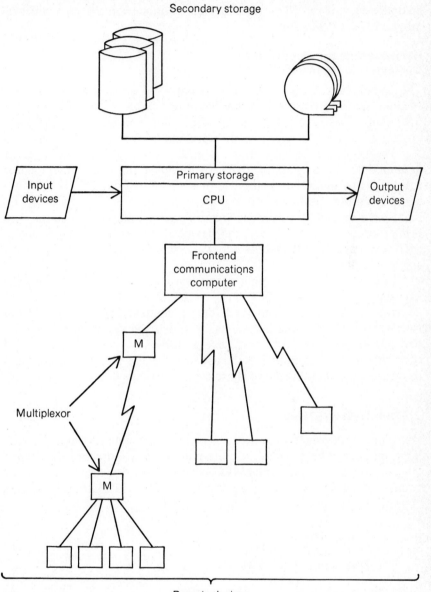

Remote devices

Figure 9-6 Advanced computer system hardware configuration.

ed operating systems allow variable-size partitions and a large number of programs (say, 15 to 20).

Hardware/Software for Computer Operation Management

The complexity of the computer hardware and software for advanced systems suggests the need for hardware and software to aid in efficient operations. Two examples will illustrate this part of the information system environment—spooling software and performance monitors.

The processing speed of the central processor is generally much greater than the output speed for hard-copy output. One method for resolving this difference is the use of spooling software. This software accepts output from application programs, stores it temporarily on high-speed secondary storage such as a disk, and manages the output to a printer or other device when the device becomes available. Spooling software is available from both hardware manufacturers and independent software vendors.

In early-generation computers, measurement of computer utilization was simply elapsed time. If a job started at 8:09 and finished at 8:49, the computer was said to be utilized for 40 minutes. This approach is not satisfactory for advanced systems in which the channels operate independently of the CPU and several programs are being executed concurrently. An alternative is the use of hardware or software monitors to measure actual utilization. These will be explained in Chapter 16.

DISTRIBUTED SYSTEMS

One trend in information systems is toward large central computers with large mass storage capacity; an alternative trend is toward distributed systems. In such systems, there is a decentralization of activity within the framework of a network with system-wide rules. The distributed system consists of the following physical elements:[1]

1 Distributed processing
2 Distributed communications
3 Distributed data bases

Distributed Processing

In distributed processing, a hierarchy of processors (Figure 9-7) allows much of the processing logic and storage to be placed at or near the

---

[1]"In Your Future: Distributed Systems?," *EDP Analyzer*, vol. 11, no. 8, August 1973.

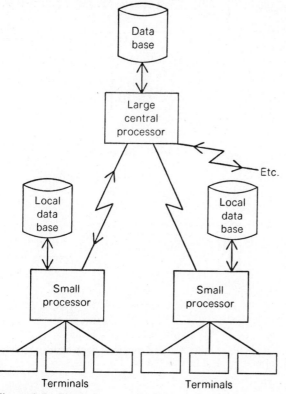

Figure 9-7 Distributed processing.

transactions while maintaining some of the advantages of large, centralized computers. The first or lowest level of processors is small or minicomputers which have some local data storage and perform local processing. Tasks too large at this level or requiring data not available in the local data base are transmitted to a higher-level regional or centralized computer. The highest level in the hierarchy of processors has the capacity to handle large-scale problems.

Distributed Communications

Distributed communication uses a network structure—each node consists of a minicomputer which manages communication in both directions (Figure 9-8). This means that a communication between two nodes in the network can travel at least two alternative paths. The minicomputer assembles bits into larger blocks, adds error detection bits, disassembles data blocks, checks for errors, and sends back messages indicating either

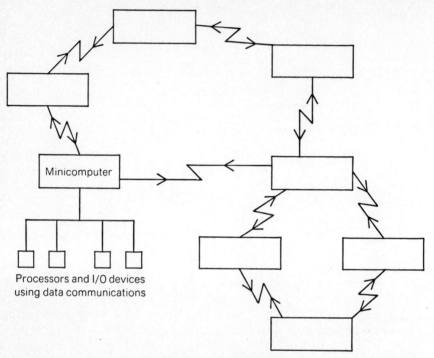

Figure 9-8 Distributed communications using minicomputers at each node to handle activities such as receiving, formatting, and forwarding of data.

error-free receipt or need for retransmission. Each node processor may manage communications for a number of devices at the node. An organization may have its own distributed network, or it may use a facility operated by a distributed-network vendor.

Distributed Data Bases

In the distributed system, data bases can be located near the major use. This may involve some duplication of organizational data for efficiency of operation, but since the system is interconnected by the distributed communications network, a data base at any node is available to the processor at any other node.

TIME SHARING AND THE MIS

It is difficult for many organizations to provide transaction processing and management control reports, and also provide the interactive model building and analysis that is useful for tactical and strategic planning. For example, many computers do not have either the storage or the software to support such activity. Time sharing is one method by which interactive analysis and modeling may be provided.

Time sharing is the concurrent use of a single computer system by many independent users, each expecting fast response and each operating without an awareness of the use of the facility by others. The users share the facility, each obtaining a small but frequently repeated slice of the computer time. The user is normally provided with a terminal (Teletype, typewriter, CRT) connected to the computer over the dialup telephone network. The user may define his or her own computational procedures by coding in a high-level language or may utilize programs furnished by the time-sharing supplier. The response is usually fast (within a few seconds) so that a user can interact with the program during execution (inserting new data, etc.).

One advantage from the use of time sharing to supplement inhouse processing is the range of software that is supplied by most time-sharing vendors in order to assist the analyst or decision maker. Analysis routines and planning languages are examples. Another advantage is the ability of analysts throughout an organization to access the same planning data. Many organizations have also found that time sharing provides a learning environment for managers who are experimenting with the use of computer-based modeling.

The disadvantages of this use of time sharing are the cost, the storing of confidential planning data at outside locations, and the necessity to work with an outside system. But on balance, it appears that time sharing is a useful supplement to an inhouse installation, especially in specialized areas of interactive analysis and model building.

SUMMARY

The hardware, software, and control procedures available to support an information system are constraints on the system design and operation. The basic elements were surveyed in the chapter. There are hardware and software capabilities (beyond the basic computer system) that are generally found in advanced information systems. The chapter described some of the more significant of these capabilities.

The control environment for computer data processing consists of the organizational controls and the application controls. The organizational controls consist of a hierarchy of supervision and review; the application controls consist of program steps and procedures to detect errors in processing. Security provisions are also necessary to safeguard the data assets of an organization and to provide for reconstruction in case of loss.

Transaction processing is changing to provide for reductions in the data preparation cycle. One approach is the use of editing and checking at the point of data conversion to machine-readable form as in keydisk systems. Another approach is direct entry to a computer. This may be performed offline using intelligent terminals or online to the computer.

Communications hardware and software are necessary to support remote access to the computer. The facilities of the communications carrier (usually voice band and half-duplex or full-duplex service) are supplemented by a frontend communications processor and a teleprocessing monitor.

The central processor site facilities for advanced information systems include hardware capabilities for online operation involving data communication; software such as a teleprocessing monitor, operating system, and data base management system; and various hardware and software aids to operations.

Distributed systems are an alternative trend in the hardware/ software environment. These involve distributed processing with a hierarchy of computers (beginning with a small processor close to the transaction), distributed communications with a network of communications processors, and distributed data bases with data bases kept close to the point of major activity but accessible to the entire distributed system.

Time sharing may be a method of providing the analysis and model building capability needed for tactical and strategic planning, especially in cases where interactive processing is preferred.

EXERCISES

1 Explain the control framework for computer data processing.
2 A computer processing installation burns down suddenly; nothing is saved. What prior provisions, if made, should allow the organization to recover from the disaster?
3 Identify the advantages of keydisk systems compared with keypunching of cards.
4 Identify the advantages and disadvantages of direct entry of data with:
   a Immediate processing of each transaction
   b Testing for errors immediately, but delayed, batch processing
5 Identify the advantages and disadvantages of a frontend processor for data communications.
6 Define the following terms:

a Teleprocessing monitor
b Voice band
c Full duplex
d Spooling
7 Explain the use of both a hardware and a software monitor.
8 Explain the elements of a distributed system.
9 How can time sharing be used in MIS applications to supplement an inhouse MIS?
10 Compare the hardware/software in a computer system used for offline, batch processing of transactions with the hardware/software to support an advanced management information system.

SELECTED REFERENCES

Bauch, James H.: "Cut Input Costs with Key-to-Tape Devices," *Computer Decisions*, May 1971, pp. 36–39.

Bayless, Donald, and David Shuman: "Protect Your Data Base," *Computer Decisions*, October 1973, pp. 14–16.

Data Communications Primer, International Business Machines Corporation, order no. c20-1668, White Plains, N.Y.

"Distributed Intelligence in Data Communications," *EDP Analyzer*, vol. 11, no. 2, February 1973.

"In Your Future: Distributed Systems?," *EDP Analyzer*, vol. 11, no. 8, August 1973.

Martin, James: *Design of Real-Time Systems*, Prentice-Hall, Inc., Englewood Cliffs, N.J., 1967.

Reagan, Fonnie H., Jr.: "A Manager's Guide to Telephone and Data Services," *Computer Decisions*, October 1971, pp. 20–23.

"The Emerging Computer Networks," *EDP Analyzer*, vol. 11, no. 1, January 1973.

Chapter 10

The Transaction Processing System

The transaction processing system is vital to the operations of organizations. Without it, bills would not be paid, sales orders would not be filled, manufacturing parts would not be ordered, etc. Transaction processing was performed manually or with machines prior to computers; computer-based data processing has altered the speed of transaction processing but not the basic function. However, computer-based transaction processing can also be more complex than prior systems. The transaction processing system is one of the building blocks of a management information system because transaction processing furnishes the data base with much of the data required for decision making, planning, and control.

TRANSACTION PROCESSING CYCLE

The transaction processing cycle begins with a transaction which is recorded in some way. Some examples of transaction data capture tools are handwritten paper documents, machine-readable documents (such as optically read document), and input devices (such as CRT or typewriter). Recording of the transaction generally is the trigger for processing data to produce a transaction document (Figure 10-1). Data about the transaction is frequently required for the updating of master files; this updating may be performed concurrently with the processing of transaction documents or by a subsequent computer run. The type of storage and the processing mode (periodic or immediate) will influence the processing cycle, but the elements of transaction recording and data preparation, input editing, sorting, transaction output, and master file updating will generally be found.

Transaction Recording and Data Preparation

The capturing of data is a necessary first step in processing the transaction. The transaction recording may consist, for instance, of a handwritten form, a typed document, or an online input via a typewriter or CRT. Some examples will illustrate this step:

Transaction	Initial data capture method	Comments
A sales order from a customer	Manual	A sales order form is prepared by the salesman.
Purchase order	Manual	A purchase order is prepared manually and then typed for use.
Savings deposit (where online system is in use)	Manual/terminal	Customer makes out deposit slip manually. Teller records transaction via online terminal.
Completion of job (where transaction recorder is in use)	Terminal	Employee inserts badge plus job identification and job performance data into a transaction recorder.

The initial recording of the transaction is critical—errors which occur at this point are difficult to detect. The design of the initial recording procedure has a substantial impact on speed and accuracy of recording. Some examples will illustrate this fact.

• A form designed for typewriter use can eliminate positioning time, backspacing, and tabbing.
• A form designed for manual recording can assist accuracy and legibility by use of boxes, guidelines, etc.
• A form can reduce input requirements by use of preprinted alternative responses and boxes to check correct response.
• Templates on input keyboards can reduce errors by specifying the use to which keys are put. For example, a terminal on which a 1 is used to

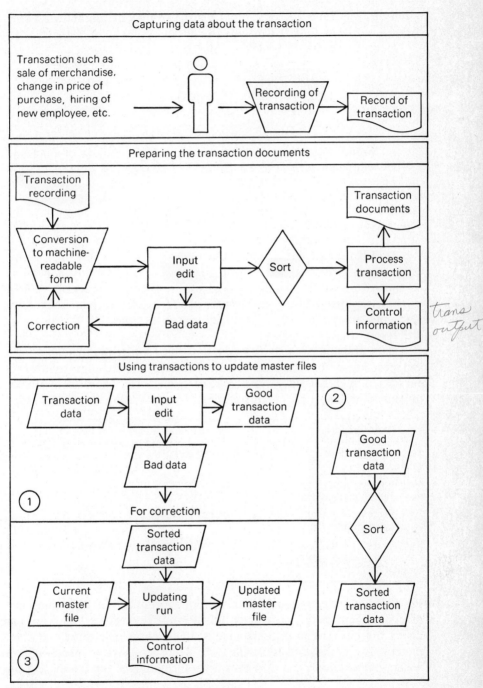

Figure 10-1 The transaction processing cycle.

specify a "yes" and 0 a "no" reply, the 1 key may be marked with both "yes" and "1" and the 0 key marked with both "no" and "0."

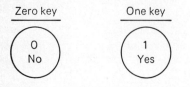

Zero key   One key

0   1
No   Yes

• Multiple forms can eliminate duplicate recording of data and thereby eliminate transcription errors. For example, a three-part form may be used to collect employment data. The first copy is filed with the employment office, the second copy is given to data processing in order to establish a record on the payroll file, and the third copy is given to the department employing the person.

The transaction data capture may result in a handwritten or typewritten document which is filed either temporarily or permanently, depending on the nature of the document and the transaction it records. Where computer-controlled input devices are used for entry of data, a record of the input is retained for reference purposes (part of the audit or processing trail).

Data preparation activities take data in non–machine-readable form and prepare it for computer input. This type of data preparation is eliminated by direct entry in machine-readable form. There are a number of ways that data is prepared for computer input. Some examples are:

Data preparation	Machine-readable result
Keypunching and key verification	Punched card
Keydisk or keytape transcription and verification	Data on magnetic tape
Typing with optical font and visual verification	Documents readable by optical reader
Marking documents to be read optically and visual (sight) verification	Documents readable by optical reader

The data preparation activities offer opportunities for detecting some errors and introducing new ones. It is generally considered necessary to check the conversion into machine-readable form. The most important method for doing this is verification which consists of performing a separate operation such as either rekeying the data and comparing the result with the prior recording or sight proofreading. Check digits can also be used to verify account numbers when the data is converted to machine-readable form. A check digit is a redundant digit derived by computations on the account number which is made part of the account number. During data preparation, the check-digit derivation procedure is repeated. If the procedure results in a different check digit, there has been an error in recording or transmitting the account number.

A problem in data preparation is to make sure that all transactions have been converted to machine-readable form but that no transactions have been recorded twice. Techniques for error control at this point are logs or registers which identify the data received and log-out batches of data which have been converted and verified. Open items are in process (or have been lost). When batches of data are transmitted from an originating department to data processing, a return receipt may be used to acknowledge receipt of the batch. Documents that have been converted to machine-readable form are frequently canceled by rubber stamps or cancellation machines to avoid duplicate conversion.

Processing the Transaction Data

In some cases, the initial data capture for a transaction completes the processing requirements, but in most cases the data capture provides input data for the performance of processing related to the transaction. The processing may involve a variety of activities. Some examples are:

- Printing documents for initiating other transactions. An example is a sales order which initiates a picking ticket or a shipping document.
- Making computations and formatting a document recording the performance of the transaction. An example is a sales slip with only quantities issued and unit prices that is processed to add such items as extensions, subtotals, sales tax, discounts, or final totals.
- Adding data from relevant files. Many transactions cannot be completed without data from master files. For example, a sales transaction to be billed may use product codes and a customer code in the sales order document. In processing the sale, a look-up is made to a product file to obtain the product description for each item and to a name-and-address file to obtain the customer name and address.

Updating Master Files

The master files are the permanent files of the organization and are updated both from normal transaction data and specific file change and file correction data. Examples of master files and updating transactions are:

Master file	Updating transactions
Accounts receivable file	Credit sales
Payroll file	Wage and salary payments
Personnel file	Hiring of employees, employee terminations, transfers, rate changes

Control totals

The procedure for updating of the master file depends on the file organization and processing methods. These are described later in the chapter. In general, the record on the master file to be updated is read, updated, and then written onto an updated file. Control information is accumulated in order to detect errors or omissions in updating the files.

Output of Transaction Data

Output of transaction data is in a form suitable for human use. The output may take a variety of forms:

- Paper documents on preprinted forms
- Paper documents with computer-generated form
- Punched cards
- Computer output microfilm
- Transaction terminal—hard-copy output (say, typewriter)
- Transaction terminal—visual display only

Transaction data output can be classified as to its purpose. There are four major reasons for transaction documents or other transaction output.

1 For action
2 For confirmation or advise of proposed or completed action
3 For background information to recipient
4 For reference use

Action documents include shipping orders, purchase orders, manufacturing orders, and customer statements. These documents instruct someone to do something. Several copies may be required. By the use of preprinted forms having special carbon areas and no-carbon areas, a single printing can produce documents having different information on them, or the computer may run the different documents separately.

When action is taken, the completed action (or lack of completion) must be reported back to the organizational unit initiating the action. Lists of checks not paid by bank represent a confirmation of completed action (if not on list, checks have been paid) and lack of completed action (by being listed as unpaid). A copy of the action document is often used for this purpose. A document designed for return and use in processing the completion of the transaction is known as a "turnaround document." Examples are punched cards or optically readable documents sent with customer billings with the request they be returned with the payment (Figure 10-2). The turnaround document assists in positive identification and improves feedback because the document for feedback is already prepared.

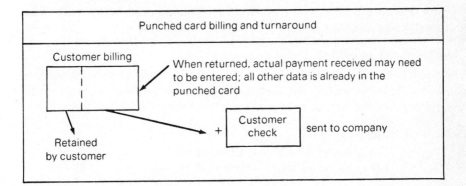

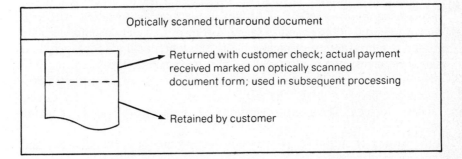

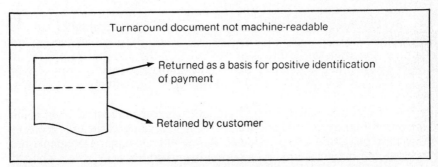

Figure 10-2 Turnaround documents as used in customer billing applications.

Some transaction data is distributed to provide background information for the recipient in the event he or she needs to respond to inquiries. For example, copies of purchase orders over a certain amount may be sent to the sales manager, who will thereby be kept informed of the company's purchases. This information may, for example, be valuable in making a sale to the same company.

Some transaction documents are issued for reference purposes. For example, a copy of the purchase order in the purchasing department does not require action; it is both confirmation that the order was placed and a reference document, should questions arise or inquiries be made.

Importance of Sorting

Sorting is an important data processing activity requiring a significant part of the data processing time. Transactions are sorted for three reasons, all related to efficiency of processing or use of data.

1 Efficiency in processing
2 Efficiency in distribution of output
3 Efficiency in subsequent retrieval

Transactions may need to be sorted for ease of processing if the processing involves reference to files or involves file updating. Although never required in the absolute sense, sorting of transactions into the same order as the reference or master file is for all practical purposes required for files accessed serially (such as files on magnetic tape). Sorting into the file sequence is sometimes required and often done for improved processing efficiency when the reference or master files are on direct-access devices. These considerations are explored further later in the chapter.

Sorting of output for distribution is important both for efficiency and control in distribution. Some examples illustrate this need:

- Paychecks are processed in order by employee number but are distributed to each department for issuance. Before the checks are printed, the transaction file is sorted so that the checks are printed in order by department. Control totals and employee counts for control over payroll check distribution are based on departmental employee counts, etc.
- Customer statements of amounts due are prepared from a file organized by customer account number. The mailing of the bills requires that they be sorted into zip codes. Before the customer statements are printed, the output file must be sorted by zip codes.
- Copies of customer statements are filed for reference purposes on computer output microfilm. Depending on the requirements, this refer-

ence output may need to be in customer number order or alphabetical order.

An explanation of sorting methods in computer data processing is beyond the scope of this chapter. Most installations use standard software packages for this purpose rather than write their own sorting algorithms. *sort strings*

Audit Trail

The *audit trail* (more properly called a *processing reference trail*) is the trail of references (document numbers, batch numbers, transaction references, etc.) which allows an investigator to trace a transaction from the time it is recorded through to the reports in which it is aggregated with other transactions, or to perform the reverse procedure, in which a total (such as an expense total) is traced back to individual source documents. The processing trail is required for internal processing and management use because of the frequent need to examine the details behind a total. It is also needed by the auditor and is required by certain tax regulations for tax-related records.

A good processing trail should always be present. The form of the trail may change in response to computer technology, but two major requirements should be met:

1 Any transaction can be traced from the source document through the processing to the totals in which it is aggregated. For example, a purchase of goods for inventory can be traced to its inclusion in the inventory totals.

2 Any total can be traced back to the transactions or other elements which were summed to arrive at the total. For example, the total amount owed by a customer can be traced to the sales and payments that were used to arrive at the balance due.

INPUT OF TRANSACTION DATA

Input is one of the major continuing problems in computer data processing. The preparation of data for input is a large cost factor and a major point where errors must be detected if the output is to be kept within acceptable limits as to error rates. There are three approaches to the timing of input for processing: input at periodic batch processing, direct entry for later processing, and online input for immediate processing. In each of these approaches, editing of the transaction to detect errors is required, and so this procedure will be described before explaining the input procedures.

Input Editing

Input editing is the examination and testing of the input data to detect missing or erroneous data. The data that passes the test is assumed to be correct; data that fails is presumed to be in error and is sent to error correction procedures.

The examination and testing of input data takes place at computer input or as soon as practical thereafter. Some editing can take place manually before input, and in many cases this is desirable. For example, a clerk can check input documents for completeness, reasonableness, and inconsistencies. The explanation in this section will concentrate on the computer input editing procedure which follows any manual editing and any data preparation activities.

The process of input editing by the computer uses a set of programmed checks to test each field of the input records. Some examples of possible input editing tests are:

Input editing test	Explanation
Valid identification code	A check-digit procedure is generally most effective.
Valid transaction code	Not all transaction codes are valid. The code being read may be checked to see if it is one that is valid.
Valid character	If only certain characters are allowed in a data item, the computer can test for invalid characters.
Valid field length, sign, and composition	If a data item should be a specified size, this can be tested. If the sign should always be negative (or positive), this can be checked by program statements.
Valid transaction	Typically, only a relatively small number of transactions are valid. These can be tested.
Missing data check	The data items that should be present for a valid transaction can be tested.
Sequence test	If data is processed in batches, it must usually be in a certain sequence. This can be checked (if data is sorted before editing). The sequence check can also be used to account for all documents, if these are numbered sequentially.
Limit, range, or reasonableness test	Input data should usually fall within certain limits. For example, hours worked should not be less than zero and should not be more than, say, 50. The limits or ranges are established by the experience of the particular organization. This is a basic test for accuracy, and all data should be checked in this way, if possible.

Input editing test	Explanation
	Some examples follow. A purchase order for more than two times the established economic order quantity for the item might be subject to question. A receiving report showing a receipt much larger than the purchase order quantity should be questioned. In utility billing, consumption is compared with prior periods to detect possible errors.

The input editing is performed as early as possible in the input process (Figure 10-3). The point at which it is performed will vary, however, depending on the circumstances. Some common methods are:

Point at which input editing occurs	Explanation
Prior to sorting (periodic batch processing)	At the first input, such as card to tape, the input editing is performed.
Subsequent to sorting (periodic batch processing)	The input editing is delayed until after sorting to detect duplicate transactions or to check sequence.
At input (online, immediate processing)	Transaction is tested before any processing is performed.
Prior to input (using intelligent terminals or keydisk systems)	Editing is performed with a minicomputer prior to input into main computer.

Input editing may be written separately for each application, or alternatively the installation may use a single input editing module for all applications (Figure 10-4). The advantage of a generalized module is ease of establishing and enforcing standard procedures for performing editing, reporting errors, introducing corrections, etc. The single generalized module can be very complete and be driven by parameters established for each application.

When errors are detected by the input editing procedure, it is considered good practice to log the errors, remove them from the processing stream, and send a notice back to the originating department requesting a correction (or confirmation of correctness of a doubtful transaction). When the correction is received, an entry is made in the error log. If corrections are not received in a reasonable time, the error log provides a basis for followup.

Input at Periodic Batch Processing

Periodic batch processing involves the accumulation of transactions until a sufficient number have been assembled to make processing efficient or

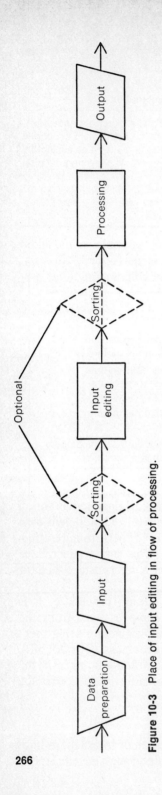

Figure 10-3 Place of input editing in flow of processing.

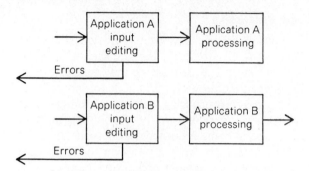

Separate input editing program for each application

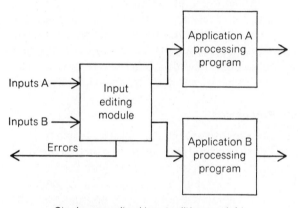

Single generalized input editing module

Figure 10-4   Separate versus generalized input editing.

until other considerations, such as a report cycle, require the processing. The processing of the batches can be daily, weekly, monthly, etc., depending on the volume of transactions and other considerations. The flow of input in periodic batch processing is tied to the batch. The input editing is performed on individual transactions, but there are additional controls based on the batch.

The batch processing of input is efficient because economies of scale can be applied to conversion of data, processing of transactions, and other activities. Control is enhanced by the use of batch controls to be described later. Disadvantages are the delay in detecting errors. For example, if a transaction is coded with a valid, but nonexistent, customer number, it will not be detected until processing is attempted against the customer file.

Direct Entry for Subsequent Processing

When transactions are recorded by use of an entry device such as a typewriter or CRT connected to a computer, the transaction may be entered directly into the computer. The processing may be performed immediately or at a subsequent time as with periodic batch processing. The direct entry with subsequent processing has an advantage over regular periodic batch processing in that most of the editing may be performed while the transaction is being recorded. Many types of errors can be identified and reported back to the entry device for immediate correction. In the direct entry with subsequent processing approach, the computer uses the direct connection to edit but not to process. The edited transactions are stored for periodic batch processing.

The advantage of delayed processing is more control over the processing, especially processing against a master file. Online, immediate updating presents backup and file protection problems that do not appear with the delayed batch processing. The disadvantage compared with immediate processing is the absence of an up-to-date master file.

Direct Entry for Immediate Processing

In direct entry with immediate processing, the entry devices such as CRT or typewriter are connected to the computer, and the transaction is edited and processed when received. Either a return response with the result of processing or a confirmation of completion of processing is generally provided to the input terminal. The advantages of this approach are the same as direct entry with subsequent processing (i.e., immediate editing with opportunity for immediate corrections by the person doing the input) plus the additional advantage of immediate processing with immediate results. The immediate processing means that files are always up to date and any problems in processing that do not show up in the editing are immediately known and can be referred to the person doing the input. The difficulties of immediate processing are primarily the higher cost of online processing versus periodic batch processing and the extra procedures required to maintain an audit trail and to safeguard the files against accidental or deliberate destruction during online updating.

PERIODIC PROCESSING
OF BATCHED TRANSACTIONS

Periodic processing of batched transactions is generally referred to as "batch processing" and is contrasted with immediate online processing. The basic concept is that the transactions are accumulated into batches before processing. The frequency of processing for the accumulated batch may be hourly, daily, weekly, monthly, etc., depending on the application and the cost/benefits involved. Batch processing tends to be less expensive than immediate, online processing because a substantial part of the cost of data processing is the cost of setup—getting the program into storage, loading the file, and loading output forms (if there are special forms). If batches are large, the cost of setup is spread over many units; if small, the cost is divided among few units. Batch processing allows better control over processing accuracy and better protection against file destruction. The primary disadvantage in batch processing is the delay that users experience before receiving the result of processing and the fact that the master files are out of date. As explained in Chapter 2, processing delay is a significant element in the concept of the age of information. The way batch processing is implemented depends somewhat on the access and organization of the storage. Some storage devices provide locations that are accessed serially (such as magnetic tape); other devices such as disk storage provide locations that can be accessed directly (randomly). This leads to two basic approaches to batch processing—with files organized sequentially and with files organized nonsequentially. This is not simply a distinction between a file on magnetic tape and a file on a magnetic disk or other direct access device because files on a direct access device may still be organized sequentially. File organization is explained further in Chapter 11.

Sequential Batch Processing

A sequential file consists of records organized sequentially by a record key. Examples of a record key are a name and an identification number. The sequence may be in ascending or descending order. The identification or key field identifies the record, not the position on the file medium. For example, the first record may have a key of 1761, the second record in the second storage location a key of 1783, and the third a key of 1785.

If a file is accessed serially, as with a magnetic tape, a record is located for batch processing by reading the file serially from the beginning until the record is located. As each record of the file being processed is read, its key is compared with the key for the record being sought. There are three possibilities from the comparison of the two keys.

1 The record keys are the same. This means the record being sought has been located.

2 The record key of the record from the file being processed is smaller than the record key being sought. This indicates the desired record is further in the file—keep reading.

3 The record key of the record from the file being searched is larger than the record key to be located. This is an error condition indicating that either no such record exists in the file or the file is out of sequence.

The serial access approach is used with magnetic tape, punched cards, etc. It is also used with sequential files on direct access files such as magnetic disk files. However, disk files provide alternative methods that are sometimes used. These are explained in connection with the discussion on processing of inquiries.

The logic of sequential batch processing is illustrated by the updating of a master file using a file of transactions which affect the file. An example of a master file is an accounts receivable file containing the amounts due from customers. This file is updated by transactions which show, for example, payments made by customers, new charges, and credits.

The updating of a master file which is organized sequentially and accessed serially requires the transaction file records to be in the same order as the master file records. This generally requires sorting of the transaction file before processing. For example, with punched card input for transactions and magnetic tape files, a file update run is probably the third of three computer runs (Figure 10-5). The logic of updating requires the entire master file to be passed through the computer. If a master record is not to be updated, it is copied onto the new master file; if there is a transaction affecting the master record, the master record is updated in the computer, and the updated record is written on the updated file. This logic is shown in Figure 10-6. Since reading the current file does not erase it, at the completion of the updating run there is the current (old) master file still unchanged plus the new master file. The existence of the old file will prove valuable in the protection and reconstruction procedures. The sorting sequences not only the records but also the transaction types on the basis of the transaction codes. For example, a new record should be added to the file before transactions for the record are processing.

A substantial fixed time is involved in the sequential batch updating procedure since every record is read and copied or read and updated. Therefore, batch updating is most efficient when the activity rate (percentage of master records to be updated by transactions) is high. The rates tend to be fairly low in any case. A 10 percent activity rate in a file updating would represent a high level of activity.

Nonsequential Batch Processing

There are essentially two reasons for using nonsequential batch processing instead of sequential batch processing to update a master file.

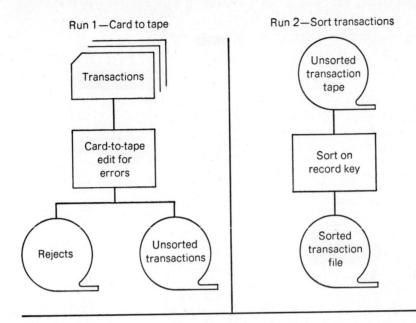

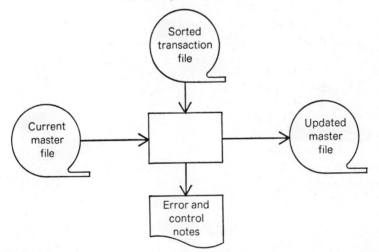

Figure 10-5 Runs to update a master file on magnetic tape using transactions on punched cards.

In both instances, the assumption is made that the individual master records can be accessed directly (as with files on magnetic disk storage).

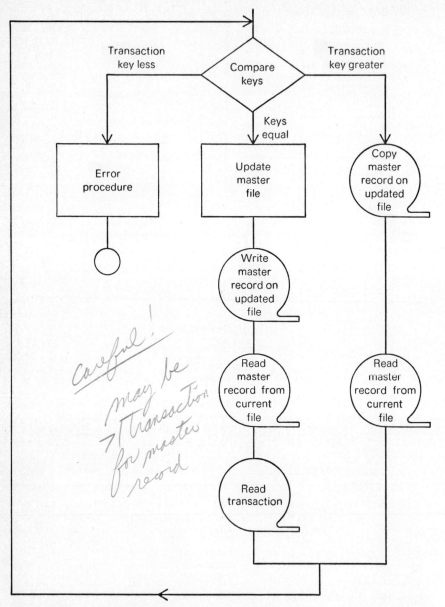

Figure 10-6 Logic in serial updating of sequential master file. Assumes only one transaction per master record.

1 The master file is organized sequentially but it is not cost/effective to sort the transactions and access the sequential file serially from beginning to end.

2 The master file is not organized sequentially.

The main problems in nonsequential updating of a master file are (1) locating the record, and (2) handling transactions in the proper order, such as when there are additions, deletions, and updating transactions in the same period. *Deposits B4 checks for today*

The problem of transactions in illogical sequence can be handled by the use of flags and suspense records. For example, a transaction to update a record which does not yet exist may be processed by creating a dummy or temporary record with a reference to indicate that a transaction is being held for processing against the record. When the record-building transaction arrives for processing, it replaces the dummy or temporary record, and by use of the reference in the dummy record the updating transaction is processed. A list of suspense items is maintained so that any "uncleared" items may be investigated at the completion of the processing run.

The locating of the master record when there is nonsequential processing is a significant problem in data processing. The record keys do not normally correspond to storage addresses, which means that there must be some other way to decide where to store a new record so that it can be retrieved and to identify the storage site, if its record key is given. The methods used in information retrieval applications are complex. For most data processing applications, one of these two methods is used:

1 Randomizing — *synonym's, packing*
2 Indexing

The two procedures are described in more detail in Chapter 11.

In randomizing, the record key is manipulated mathematically to produce a random number which can be used as a disk address. For example, dividing the record key by a prime number and using the six middle digits of the remainder is a method of obtaining a disk address from the record key. The use of the randomizing procedure means that the file is not organized sequentially and there is no advantage in sequencing the updating transactions. In the index method, there is an index in storage which allows the program to identify the disk address for any record key. There are various methods for implementing the index.

Batch Processing Controls

A fundamental control procedure in batch processing is the accumulation and checking of control totals. In the flow of controls, input editing applies to individual items; control totals apply to the batch. The purpose of the control counts is to ensure completeness of processing by detecting lost or unprocessed data. The control totals can be record counts, financial totals such as dollar amounts, or hash totals which add up figures (such as hours worked) that are not normally added. The size of the input batch is related to the problems of error detection. If a control count error is detected in a batch, the entire batch is generally rejected and must be examined for the cause of the discrepancy. If batches are too large, the search for the discrepancy is difficult; if too small, the number of batches and batch totals may become excessive. Given these considerations, installations use batches of, say, 50 to 200 transaction documents. The control total is generally developed prior to input by a separate process, such as counting the number of transactions or taking an adding machine tape of financial amounts. The control total is input along with the batch and is the figure against which the computer-generated control figure is tested. If the batch is out of balance, it must be rejected and the discrepancy located. If an individual transaction is rejected in the input edit run, it is diverted to a reject file for correction, and the batch total is adjusted so that the batch may continue being processed. The computer program generally makes a comparison of preestablished control totals and computed control totals. A comparison is also made (or computer comparison is reviewed) by a control clerk or other member of the control staff (Figure 10-7).

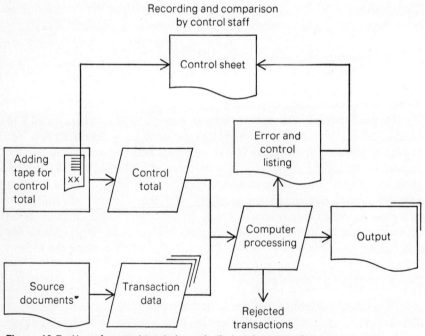

Figure 10-7 Use of control totals in periodic batch processing.

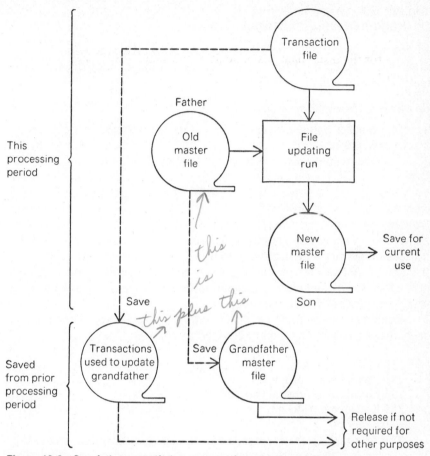

Figure 10-8 Son-father-grandfather concept for retention of files.

File backup and reconstruction are provided in batch processing by the use of the "son-father-grandfather files." When a file on magnetic tape or punched cards is updated, a new updated file (son) is created. The old file (father) plus the transactions is retained for file reconstruction purposes (Figure 10-8). If an error is discovered later or the current file is accidentally destroyed, the file may be recreated from the father tape plus the transactions. A further safeguard is obtained by retaining the grandfather tape. When disk files are updated sequentially, the file is copied prior to the updating and this copy is used for backup and reconstruction.

ONLINE IMMEDIATE PROCESSING
OF INDIVIDUAL TRANSACTIONS

In contrast to the delay inherent in periodic, batch processing, online, immediate processing provides immediate response, immediate results, and immediate updating of files.

Handling a Transaction Online

Transactions for online processing are entered into a terminal device such as a typewriter or CRT. These devices may be connected directly to the computer via cables (hardwired) or via communication lines. An alternative method is to have a minicomputer (frontend) handle the receipt of the transactions and do some preprocessing before the transaction is turned over to the central processing unit. In all cases, the computer (either frontend or central processor) must accept the transaction when it is sent. Either the transmission interrupts the processor or the processor polls the devices to identify a device ready to transmit. The transaction is stored in the central memory for processing and is generally copied onto a file on a secondary storage medium (magnetic tape or disk) in order to keep a log of all transactions for control purposes.

Each transaction must have a code to indicate its type. For example, sales order transactions might be coded as follows:

251 Place sales order
252 Cancel sales order
253 Modify existing sales order
254 Retrieve but do not modify existing sales order

The first task after acceptance of a transaction for online processing is to examine the code to determine the type of transaction. The transaction code essentially identifies the program modules to be used. If not already in the processor memory, these modules are read. The transaction is edited to detect errors, and, if required, error messages are sent to the initiator of the input. The erroneous transaction is put into a suspense file area in storage or otherwise flagged until the corrections are received and processed. After passing the input editing, the transaction is processed and transaction documents or other output are produced.

Some of the problems of online transaction processing are listed below:

Problem	Comments
Computer time required to manage input/output from	Special software is required. As explained in Chapter 9, heavy involve-

Problem	Comments
terminals	ment of CPU may be reduced by the use of a frontend minicomputer.
Overhead time to bring in program modules for editing and processing	Modular design and permanent main storage of most-used modules reduce this overhead.
Complexity of operating system	The operating system is much more complex than for batch processing.
Control over errors	See discussion later in this section.

These problems point up the fact that the advantages of online processing of individual transactions are obtained at the price of increased complexity and increased processing cost.

Updating a File with a Transaction

After a transaction has been edited and has entered processing, referencing master files is generally necessary in order to process the transaction. Processing also frequently involves updating one or more master files. Referencing master files presents no problems except finding the proper record to reference. Updating online involves reading (copying) the master record from secondary storage into main storage, updating it with any changes, and writing the altered record back into the same location (Figure 10-9). The old record is no longer available since it is replaced by

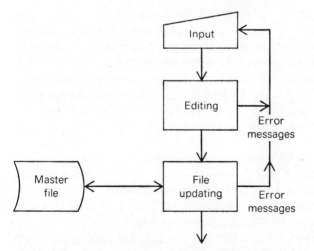

Figure 10-9 Online updating of master file records.

the updated record. The next transaction to access the master file record will find the updated version.

Online Processing Controls

Compared with batch processing, immediate, online updating has additional error and control problems. The file changes continuously, and therefore any error can disrupt the file and create additional errors as subsequent transactions are processed. The straightforward batch control totals cannot be used to check batches before processing. Some of the problems and examples of controls will illustrate how this problem is handled.

Problem	Possible control procedure
Transaction is lost—never gets processed	Feedback to terminal to verify processing.
Computer system goes down when transactions need to be processed	Backup computer attached to same storage. Procedures to manually process and introduce transactions into computer when system is again working. Restart procedures tell input personnel which transactions were lost and must be reintroduced.
Errors in file updating may not be detected until later, making file correction difficult	A copy of the file is used for online updating. A separate backup copy is available for reconstruction. A log of all incoming transactions is used for reconstruction and error tracing.

A basic thrust of these online control procedures is the preservation of an adequate processing trail and reconstruction capability. Backup copies and transaction logs are vital. There are, however, many possible control procedures. For example, the file in use during the day may be a work file only. The transactions may be accumulated and again processed, say, at night, to produce a daily updated file. In other words, the work file is used temporarily during the day for updated reference, but the processing at night produces the necessary file control and reconstruction.

Control totals may be used in online processing in a different way than batch processing. Control totals may be developed for logical batches during a processing period. These logical batch totals may be compared after the fact to ledger totals, totals developed at terminals, etc. The log of transactions is frequently sorted into logical batches (by terminal, by input person, by type of transaction) and printed to provide a review and audit trail (Figure 10-10).

During period such as day

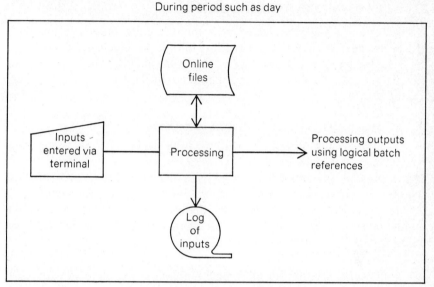

At end of each period

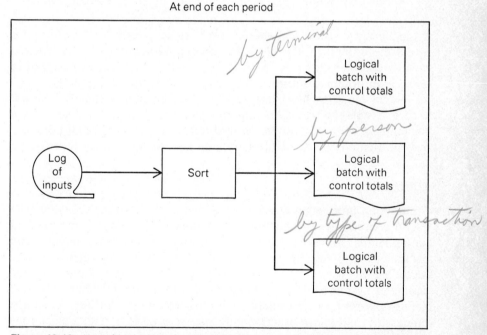

Figure 10-10 Use of logical batches in processing or audit trail in online processing.

PROCESSING INQUIRY TRANSACTIONS

A sales order, a pay rate change, a payment to be recorded are generally processed against only one record in each file to which the transaction applies. Inquiry transactions may be fairly simple involving a request to view a record, the record being identified by key or other identifier. Examples are:

- Display the record of employee 5183289
- Display the record of customer John Brent

These present few processing problems because the record retrieval required for processing transactions is easily adapted for this use.

In the case of complex inquiries, the problem of processing depends on the file structure and processing approach. Examples of complex inquiries are:

- Display records for all female employees age 30 to 40 with more than five years' experience
- Display number and amount of sales by specified categories

If the file is processed sequentially, each record is tested to determine if it meets the criteria. If the file is not processed sequentially, the desired records can be located by the use of special data structures designed to assist in information retrieval. These are described in Chapter 11.

Some inquiries need immediate response; others can be delayed. Where a delay is feasible, inquiries may be grouped and processed sequentially in batch mode. If immediate response is required, a retrieval-oriented data structure is usually needed for efficient processing.

SUMMARY

Transaction processing is vital to the operation of an organization. The use of computers has made the processing faster and more complex, but the essential functions must be performed under both manual and computer-based systems. The processing of transactions begins with the recording of data about a transaction. This triggers input into the computer system and the preparation of transaction documents. Permanent or master files are usually required as references for the transaction processing, and the transaction may also be used to update a master file record. The output from processing may be printed documents or terminal display. Sorting is frequently used for efficiency of processing and efficiency of output distribution. An audit trail must be maintained for processing reference.

The input of transaction may take many forms. Input may be prepared by offline data preparation procedures such as keypunching, keytape, and keydisk. The data js presented for input as a batch. Direct entry may be used for input by means of terminal devices such as typewriters and CRTs. The direct entry may be edited and then stored for subsequent batch processing or edited and passed on for immediate processing. A common requirement in all the input procedures is input editing to detect errors.

Periodic processing of batched transactions may use either sequential or nonsequential processing, depending on the file organization and processing requirements. Control totals are a fundamental method in batch processing for detecting missing or unprocessed items.

Online, immediate processing involves special hardware for data communication and for handling the identification of terminals transmitting transactions. Special software is used to prepare transactions for processing. The transaction may involve file updating, and this presents special concerns with respect to file safeguards. Logical batch totals, feedback mechanisms, and reconstruction provisions are examples of control procedures in online processing.

Inquiries present no special processing problems if processing is periodic and proceeds sequentially through the file. However, if response is to be immediate, the use of fairly complex data structures which allow rapid retrieval is necessary.

EXERCISES

1 Define the following terms:
  a Audit trail
  b Input editing
  c Batch processing
  d Online processing
  e Transaction
  f Turnaround document
2 Explain the difference between the following:
  a Direct entry and offline data preparation
  b Sequential batch and nonsequential batch
  c Batch and online processing.
3 Explain the difference between the backup provisions in batch processing and backup provisions in online processing.
4 Explain why sorting is performed in the following instances:
  a Prior to printing output report

    b Prior to input editing
    c Subsequent to input editing
5 Explain the difference between the audit trail in a typical batch processing situation and a typical online processing organization.
6 Explain the advantages and disadvantages of direct entry.
7 Explain the difference in data processing controls for batch processing and online processing.
8 Explain input editing. How might the following errors be detected by adequate input editing:
    a Payroll hours field blank?
    b Customer order for 15 gross instead of 15 units?
    c Customer account number incorrect?
    d Price for item of $0.99 instead of $9190?
    e Incorrect spelling of customer name in new record being added?
    f Zip code field is AA114 instead of 55114?
9 How is an inquiry satisfied (a) when processing is done sequentially in batch mode, and (b) when processing is done online?
10 Explain the difference between updating a file in batch processing and updating a file in online processing.

SELECTED REFERENCES

Davis, Gordon B.: *Computer Data Processing*, 2d ed., McGraw-Hill Book Company, New York, 1973, chaps. 13 and 16.

Gildersleeve, T. R.: *Design of Sequential File Systems*, John Wiley & Sons, Inc., New York, 1971.

Jancura, Elise G., and Arnold H. Berger (eds.): *Computers—Auditing and Control*, Auerbach Publishers, Inc., Philadelphia, 1973.

Laden, H. N., and T. R. Gildersleeve: *System Design for Computer Applications*, John Wiley & Sons, Inc., New York, 1963.

Maloney, Robert F.: "New Generation EDP Control Considerations," *Management Services*, March-April, 1968.

Chapter 11

The Data Base Subsystem

Data has value to the extent that it can be retrieved, processed, and presented to the person needing it within the time allowed for the decision or action to which it applies. Data that cannot be located or processed in time has no value.

A management information system envisions the availability of a fairly comprehensive set of stored data in order to provide information to support operations, management, and decision making in an organization. The set of logically related data files maintained for the MIS is termed a *data base.* There are a number of data bases in an organization. The software required to effectively manage and use the data base is a *data base management system.* The entire system composed of data base, data base software, data base administrator, and data base procedures constitutes the *data base subsystem* of the management information system. This chapter is a comprehensive survey of data concepts, data organization, file storage methods, file organization, and list organization. These topics provide a background for understanding the data base subsystem.

DATA CONCEPTS AND DATA ORGANIZATION

Data must be organized in order for processing to be feasible and efficient. There are four major levels of data organization: item, record, file, and data base. This section describes item, record, and file; the data base concept is explained later in the chapter.

Data Items

A *data item* describes some attribute of an object of data processing. For example, if the object of data processing is an employee, a data item may describe the attribute "name." Another data item may describe the attribute "age," a third may describe the attribute "social security number." Data items may form a hierarchical relation among themselves. For example, the attribute date is composed of three subitems: year, month, and day. These are termed "elementary items" because they have no subitems into which they can be divided.

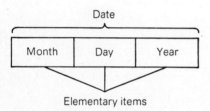

An item is sometimes termed a "field," but a field is the storage space on the physical data processing file medium, whereas the data item is what is stored there. This is most easily seen on a punched card. Sets of columns are defined as fields in which specified data items are punched.

Data items are of either fixed or variable length. For example, names and addresses vary considerably in the number of characters required, but two numeric digits will handle the age of any employee.

Records

Data items which relate to an object of data processing are combined into a record for that object. If the object of processing is a customer, items such as customer number, name, address, balance due, and credit rating form the record for the customer. Other examples are an employee record for payroll processing, a sales order record for sales order processing, and a parts record for parts inventory processing. Each record in the file is identified by a record identifier or record key. An employee account number, employee identification number, and a part number are examples of identifiers that could be record keys.

Each data item for a record occupies a field on the storage medium. The sum of the storage required by the various record fields is the storage required by the record. Records of a given type may be all the same length (fixed length) or may differ in length (variable length). There are two reasons that records might differ in length (Figure 11-1).

1 The size of the fields required differs because the length of the data items varies for different records. For example, names differ in length.
2 Some fields will not be present on all records, thereby reducing the size of the record.

In general, it is simpler to program for and to process fixed-length records, but the potential savings in storage space may offset the difficulties of variable-length records.

Where variable-length records are employed, there must be a method for specifying the length of variable-length fields (if used) and the variable length of the record. Two methods may be used:

1 A length field is used. For example, a length field may be set as the first item on the variable-length record to specify the length (say, in characters) of the record.
2 A special symbol may be inserted as the last character in a data field or the last character in the record. The computer program reads the field or record until the termination character is sensed, thereby defining the end of the field.

Some records may be divided into two parts—a master portion containing relatively permanent data and detail or trailer portions. For example, an accounts receivable system which keeps track of individual invoices might have a master record portion containing fairly permanent customer data, such as name, address, and credit rating, plus several trailer records or repeating records, each containing data on an unpaid invoice.

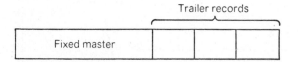

Trailer records

| Fixed master | | | |

Files

A collection of related records is called a *file* (also called a *data set*). Examples are a payroll file containing all employee records related to

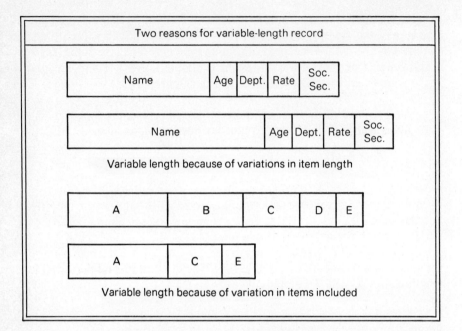

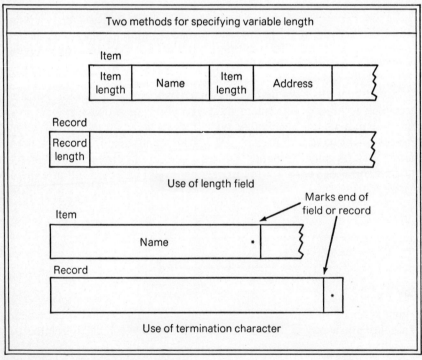

Figure 11-1 Variable-length records.

payroll and an accounts receivable file containing all customer records related to accounts receivable processing, etc. Files are created when the need for a particular collection of records is recognized. This may necessitate obtaining new data from source documents, or it may involve a selection of records from existing files and restructuring them into a new file. The creation and maintenance of files is a major factor in the workload of a computer information processing system. Files are kept for a variety of purposes. Four main types are usually identified.

File type	Purpose	Examples
Master file	Relatively permanent records containing statistical, identification, and historical information. Used as a source of reference and for retrieval.	Accounts receivable file, personnel file, inventory file
Transaction file (also called "detail file")	Collection of records describing transactions by the organization. Developed as a result of processing the transactions and preparing transaction documents. Used to update a master file.	Sales invoice file, purchase order file, pay rate change file
Report file	Records extracted from data in master files in order to prepare a report.	Report file for taxes withheld, report file for delinquent customer accounts, report file for analysis of employee skills
Sort file	A working file of records to be sequenced. This may be the original or a copy of the transaction file, master file, or report file.	

The record key is used as the basis for sequencing and searching of files. The record key for this purpose can be numeric such as social security number or alphabetic such as a name. More than one identification field can be used as a key, and therefore the same record may be sequenced on one key for one file and on another key in a second file. For example, a customer file for a department store might be sequenced on account number for processing of sales and customer payments, but another lookup file used by accounting personnel responding to customer inquiries might be sequenced by customer name.

Blocks

A *block* is the group of characters that are read or written with each read or write operation on the storage medium. For example, a single punched card is read or written with each operation, so the punched card is a block.

The block on magnetic tape is the amount of the magnetic tape that is read with each read operation or written with each write operation. For disk storage, the block may be part of a track or an entire track, depending on the disk device used. Blocks are, in other words, the smallest unit of data moved from or to a physical file device.

Although blocks may be of variable length, it is usually convenient to have them of fixed length because the core area into which a block is read has to allow for the largest-size block that is going to be read by the application. Some installations establish a standard size block for use on the disk; others allow each application designer to define the disk block size.

Information Structures

An information structure defines the relation that data has for the user. For example, the user defines a person's last and first names as having an important relation to each other and the person's address as being related to his or her name. Information structures can be classified as hierarchic or associative (Figure 11-2). The *hierarchic relation* is one in which there is an inferior-superior relation. For example, the invoices in an accounts receivable file belong to a customer (the customer is the owner of the invoices), so the invoice records bear an inferior relation to the record of the customer who is to pay them. Each invoice may have line items which reflect merchandise the customer ordered and received. These line items are in an inferior (belong to) relation to the invoice. This hierarchic relation exists in many parts of the file. On the other hand, the term *associative relation* defines records as related if they have the same value for variables. Examples are records for employees in the same department which have an associative relation because they all have the same department number or records for employees which are related because the employees are all women.

In contrast to information structures, the file organization or file structure is the logical formatting of the file for storage purposes. This may be a sequential, random, indexed, indexed sequential, etc., organization.

The distinction between physical storage relation and the logical relation among data records is important. The physical storage depends upon the storage medium that is used and the physical relationships that will make processing most efficient. The logical relations exist in the minds of the users and are not necessarily the same as the physical storage. For example, a file of customers for a department store may be physically stored in sequential order by customer account number. But a large number of logical relations can exist among the records in the file. The credit manager may think of the file as consisting of two associative

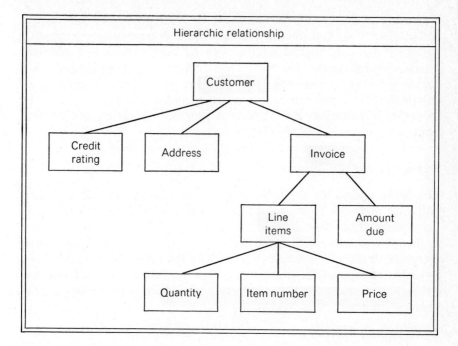

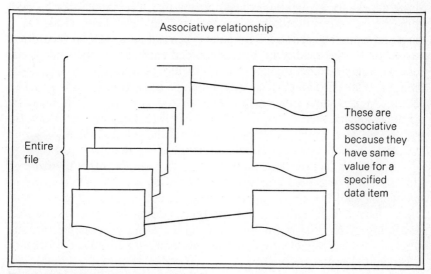

Figure 11-2 Information structures.

groups: nondelinquent and delinquent customers. A marketing manager
may visualize the data in terms of zip code areas where people live

(especially if the store uses direct mail or other promotion that can be identified with zip code areas). The task of file organization is to create a file such that any logical relation can be converted into a physical relationship for output. The task of data management systems and other similar software is to assist not only in creating and maintaining the file so that logical relations can be converted to physical output, but also in extracting, formatting, etc., data with specified characteristics or relations.

FILE STORAGE DEVICES

The most commonly used file storage media are magnetic tape and magnetic disk. There is still some use of punched cards, but this is decreasing. Other storage media such as large-capacity core magnetic drum and laser storage are used much less frequently. File organizations are influenced by the properties (especially the access to records) of the available storage media and devices. This section reviews serial access devices (as characterized by magnetic tape) and direct access devices (as characterized by disk storage).

Serial Access Devices

Serial access (or sequential access) means that a record cannot be read until the records preceding it on the storage have been read. On a magnetic tape, the second record cannot be read until the first record has passed under the read/write head. Punched cards are in the same serial access category except that they have a further characteristic which limits their usefulness: There is no possibility of backspacing with punched cards. Once a card has passed through the card reader, it must be manually redeposited in the input hopper before it can be read again. By way of contrast, a magnetic tape can be backspaced (and sometimes read in reverse direction) under command of the computer.

The major fact of serial access for system design is that the average time required to access a record at random from a tape file is approximately one-half the time required to read the entire file on magnetic tape. Once located, the read time for the record being sought is very small. Accessing of records in random order is therefore very inefficient, and because of this, magnetic tape files are normally organized and processed in sequential order.

There are no addresses on a magnetic tape to identify the location of stored data. The data is stored in blocks on the tape (Figure 11-3), each block being separated from the next by an interblock gap (of, say, 0.6 in.). The gap allows the magnetic tape unit to accelerate to reading speed before sensing the data and to sense the end of the data and decelerate. The start and stop times mean that reading time is significantly shortened

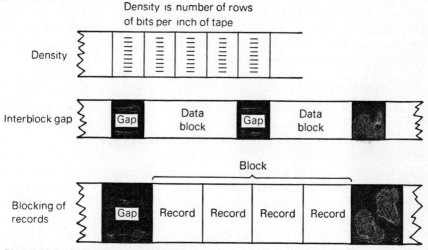

Figure 11-3 Magnetic tape characteristics.

by having large blocks between the interblock gaps. The limit on the block size is the amount of core memory available for the block when it is read into main storage. The block may contain more than one record. Each record on the tape has a record key which identifies it. In order to determine if the record just read is the one being sought, its record key is compared with the key of the record to be located.

The technical details of magnetic tape operation and of programming the use of magnetic tape are beyond the scope of this chapter. The data transfer rate for magnetic tape is based on:

1 Tape density (characters per inch)
2 Tape speed (inches per second)
3 Size of interblock gap (sometimes called an "interrecord gap")

The capacity of a magnetic tape is based on tape density, interrecord gap, and the length of the reel (normally 2,400 ft). Some concept of the range of performance is given below for third-generation nine-track tape:

	Performance		
	Low	Medium	High
Tape density (bits per inch)	800	1,600	6,250
Tape speed (inches per second)	75	125	200
Size of interblock gap (inches)	0.6	0.6	0.3
Transfer rate (thousand characters per second)	60	200	1,250

The storage capacity and effective transfer rate are very dependent on block size. Figure 11-4 shows graphically the effect of block size and illustrates why block size is an important processing consideration when using magnetic tape. A similar graph would show the importance of block size on transfer rates.

Direct Access Devices

A direct access device (DASD), such as a disk storage device, can access any storage location without first accessing any other. The read/write arm moves directly to the location desired. The disk drives have been called "random access devices," but this term is not completely accurate because the time required to access a storage location is somewhat dependent upon the current location of the read/write head. If the record immediately next to the one desired has just been read, the read/write head is positioned over the record to be read. But if the last record was on a different track, the arm may be required to move to obtain the next record. This is in contrast to magnetic core or semiconductor memories where there is no difference in read time.

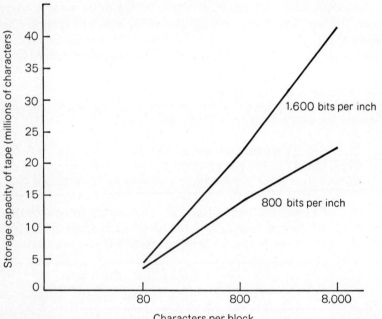

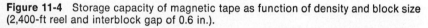

Figure 11-4   Storage capacity of magnetic tape as function of density and block size (2,400-ft reel and interblock gap of 0.6 in.).

Most disk units use removable packs containing from 1 to 11 individual disks. A separate read/write arm accesses each pair of disk surfaces so that movement of the arm is in and out (but not up and down). Some disks use head-per-track arms which do not move at all. The disk revolves at high speed underneath the read/write arm. For disks with movable arms, the arms generally all move in and out at the same time so that the arms are at any one time positioned over a cylinder (Figure 11-5). The time to read any location on the disk is composed of two elements:

1 The seek time to position the read/write arm
2 The time for the disk to revolve so that the address to be read moves under the read/write head (rotational delay)

There are various methods for organizing records on the disk to minimize the seek time and, to a lesser extent, minimize the rotational delay (which is small compared with seek time). Disk files are addressed by disk face, track on the disk face, and perhaps a sector on the track (Figure 11-5). Both fixed and variable block lengths may be used, depending on the disk and accompanying software. Since each record stored on a disk file is stored in some addressable location, a problem in data processing is the determination of the storage location for a record if all that is known is the record key. Methods of coping with this problem are discussed in the next section.

The technical specifications for disk files are beyond the scope of this overview. However, some concept of disk performance is given by the following data:

Characteristics	Common performance range		
	Low	Medium	High
Average access time (in milliseconds)	87.5	72.5	38.4
Data transfer rates (thousand bytes per second)	156	312	806
Storage capacity per pack (million bytes)	7.25	29	200
Storage capacity for subsystem (million bytes)	58	233	1,600

FILE ORGANIZATION FOR DATA PROCESSING

The objectives of a file organization are:

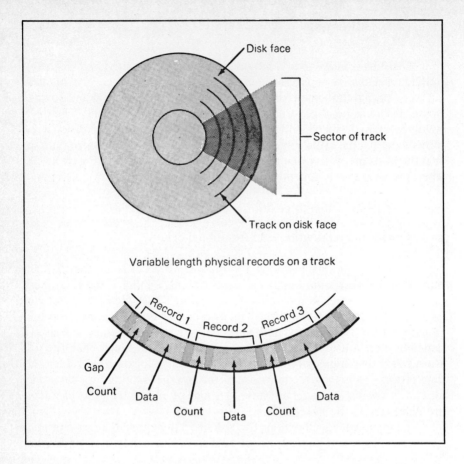

Disk face

Sector of track

Track on disk face

Variable length physical records on a track

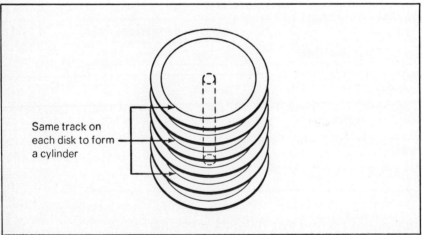

Gap

Count

Data

Record 1

Count

Data

Record 2

Count

Data

Record 3

Data

Same track on
each disk to form
a cylinder

Figure 11-5 Disk file addressing.

1 To provide a means for locating records for processing, selection, or extraction
2 To facilitate file creation and maintenance

In attempting to achieve its objectives, the file organization should be designed to take advantage of the characteristics of the equipment and the data processing system. Some key considerations in file design are the following:

Considerations	Comments
The file access method	Serial access or direct access
File size	Affected by number of records, record size, block size, and the method of storing the data on the file medium
Item design	Fixed or variable
Cost of file media	Cost highest for direct fast access devices such as drum and disk, lowest for slow access storage media such as magnetic tape
File maintenance processing and inquiry requirements	Frequent online updating and retrieval versus periodic processing
Need for a data base	Data base expands record sizes and increases complexity of file management
File privacy	Security provisions to restrict access and to restrict the making of changes to the file

The file organizations are divided, for the sake of explanation, into organizations used primarily in data processing applications and the list organizations especially applicable for information retrieval. The data processing organizations are sequential, random, indexed random, and indexed sequential.

Sequential File Organization

No! this is serial file can be "succeeding"

In sequential file organization the records are stored physically in order by the record key. If, for example, the records are for employees and the key is employee payroll number, employee 475 will precede employee 476 on the physical file storage. Sequential file organization is very common because it makes effective use of the least expensive file medium—magnetic tape—and because sequential processing at periodic intervals using a batch of transactions is very efficient. For small data processing systems using punched cards, sequential organization is always used because of the difficulty of alternatives. A disk storage device can be used much like a magnetic tape. The data records are stored sequentially

this is correct!

starting at some location so that the first storage location has the first record, the second storage location has the second, etc. If the first location is known, all subsequent locations are filled with data records very much like a magnetic tape. Sequential organization on a disk is often termed SAM for "sequential access method."

When a file is organized sequentially by record key and is accessed serially, there is no need to know specifically where any record is stored, only that it is in order by the sequencing key. Locating any particular record is performed merely by starting at the beginning of the file, reading each record, and comparing its key to the record which is being sought. Efficiency of processing thus requires that all transactions to be processed against a file should be organized in the same order as the file so that the first record on the file to be sought will be found first and the transaction which needs that record will be processed first, the second transaction will find its corresponding record next, etc. In this type of sequential processing using a serial access file, the entire master file is passed through the computer for any type of processing run involving transactions to be processed against the file. This is one reason it is desirable to hold transactions until a reasonable sized batch can be processed. Sequential processing organization is therefore oriented toward periodic batch processing.

The efficiency of sequential organization in locating data required by inquiries depends on the type of inquiry. If the inquiry is for a specific record identified by its key, a serial file such as magnetic tape is searched from the beginning until the record is found. A disk file using sequential organization may search for a specific record by a binary search procedure. This is performed by going to the middle record in the file and comparing the key of that record with the key of the desired record. If the desired record is on the second half of the file, the search continues using only that half. The middle record of the half is examined, and the search then continues with the upper or lower half of that segment. This halving and comparison processing continue until the desired record is located. The binary search is quite efficient. For example, to locate a record with a given key out of 2,000 records requires that only 11 records be accessed and compared. All requests involving selection criteria (such as customers living in Falcon Heights having incomes between $10,000 and $15,000) are processed by reading the entire file and checking each record to see if it matches the criteria. Because of the need to pass the entire sequential file to obtain a subset for processing, secondary files are sometimes maintained. The difficulty in using secondary files is in the extra work in updating them.

$2 \text{ power} = 2048$

In evaluation of the sequential file organization, both the updating process and the inquiry from the file need to be considered. If there is sufficient level of activity and transactions can be batched, the sequential design is excellent for master file updating. The advantages and disadvantages of sequential organization when updating master files are the following:

Advantages	Disadvantages
File design is simple—locating a record requires only a sequence key.	Entire file must be processed no matter how low the activity rate.
If activity rate is high the simplicity of the key as the method for accessing makes for efficient processing.	Transactions must be sorted in the same order as the file.
Low-cost file media (magnetic tape) can be used.	File is always out of date to the extent that a batch has not been processed.

Random File Organization

The advantage of a direct access storage device is that any location can be read without reading the locations preceding it. This means that data stored on the direct access file can be obtained directly if the address of the record is known. The problem of file organization for data processing using direct access storage is therefore how to store the data records so that, given a record key, its storage location can be found.

It would be ideal for direct random access if the record keys could be the same as the identification number for the disk storage locations, but this is almost never the case, and therefore other means must usually be found. Stated another way, the task is to take a set of record keys and map them into a set of disk storage location identifiers If the record keys ran sequentially with no gaps, this might be a fairly simple matter, but this condition almost never exists. In addition to gaps, many identification codes are not sequential because they are designed to be significant, such as showing territory or product line.

Because of the infeasibility of making a simple transformation, other methods must be used. The most common arithmetic procedure to transform the record key into a storage address is termed "randomizing" because transformation of the nonsequential numbers to a range of storage addresses is based on the uniform distribution of random digits. If, for example, 100,000 storage locations are to be assigned and the occurrences of the digits 0 to 9 in each position of the storage addresses are tallied, there will be 10,000 1s, 10,000 2s, etc. Therefore, a procedure which takes part of or all the record identification number or record key and produces a random number will generate storage addresses falling somewhat uniformly in the range of the assigned storage identifiers.

The best-known and most frequently used technique for producing addresses by randomizing is division of the key by a positive integer, usually a prime number. The remainder obtained from the division becomes the address locator. The prime-number divisor is usually chosen to be approximately equal to the number of available addresses. There are additional methods but all attempt to do the same thing—to generate a uniformly distributed set of addresses which will map the keys into the storage area as uniformly as possible.

A major difficulty with the randomizing procedure is that some addresses will never be generated while two or more record keys may produce identical disk addresses (synonyms). In that event, one of the records is stored at the generated location with the synonym being stored in an overflow location. The overflow can be handled in one of several ways. _packing factor_

1 The overflow record can be stored in the first available location following the location where it should be found. On any retrieval for which the desired record is not in the location specified, the procedure is to search succeeding locations until it is found.

2 A special field in each record points to (identifies) the address of the first overflow record for which the same address was generated. If a third synonym was produced, the overflow address linkage for it is put in the second record, etc. When retrieving a record, the program examines the program at the key-generated address. If it does not have the same key, the program looks at the pointer field and goes to the overflow location for the record.

3 Special overflow areas are used. If the record is not found at the generated address, the program goes to the overflow area which is searched sequentially until the record is found.

The advantages of the random storage approach arise primarily in situations where the records need to be located quickly such as in online inquiry and online updating. There is no necessity for sequencing transactions which are to be processed against the file. If a random organization file is to be processed sequentially, it would generally need to be copied onto another file and sorted into sequential order. The random aproach is often termed "direct access method" or BDAM ("basic direct access method").

A difficulty with the random organization is that overflow becomes a severe problem if most of the storage locations are used. If, say, 50

> # of synonyms, overflow causes excessive record access time

percent of the locations are used, overflow is generally not a problem; but if 80 percent of the locations are used, overflow will usually become quite large, and this can increase substantially the average number of accesses to locate a record. In this and other disk addressing methods, it is frequently desirable to have the basic method of obtaining an address refer to a bucket instead of a single record location. A group of records is stored in the bucket, which is then searched sequentially to find the appropriate record. The use of buckets increases storage utilization, and the sequential search of a block or bucket is not typically a substantial hindrance to processing efficiency when compared with the increased use of storage, and reduction in overflow records.

Indexed Random File Organization

file still random but address stored in index

Instead of attempting to locate addresses by randomizing, separate indexes may be maintained in which the address of the record being sought is found. Indexes are frequently in order by record key, thereby allowing the index to be searched either sequentially or by a binary search process to locate the address of a record. In some cases, a sequential index is not desirable, and an indexed organization may be created using a tree index.

A tree index consists of the key of a record, a left branch address, and a right branch address. When the file is created, the first record is placed in the first position in each index. The key of the second record to be stored is compared with the first record key. If its key is greater, the right branch of the first record points to the second index address. If it is less, the left branch index address of the first record is set to point to the second address. When the third record is added, it is referenced as being one part of the tree (see Figure 11-6). The result looks much like a tree and is therefore called a "tree structure."

Master Cyl ind Track ind

When searching for a record using the tree index, the searcher starts at the beginning of the file index and by means of a comparison branch through the tree goes to either the left branch or right branch. The resulting tree search can be reasonably efficient. The storage is efficient since there is a high packing density.

Indexed Sequential Organization

Indexed sequential organization is essentially a compromise between sequential access and random access methods. It is often referred to as ISAM for "indexed sequential access method." The records are stored on the disk sequentially by record key so that sequential processing may be performed, but indexes are also maintained to allow direct retrieval based on a key value.

List of records to be stored (in order of storage)		Tree index		
Key	Index address	Key	Left (Less than) pointer	Right (Greater than) pointer
475	1	475	2	5
396	2	396	4	3
419	3	419	––	7
129	4	129	––	8
617	5	617	6	10
615	6	615	––	––
420	7	420	––	––
319	8	319	––	9
327	9	327	––	––
618	10	618	––	––
491	11	491		(–– = End of branch)

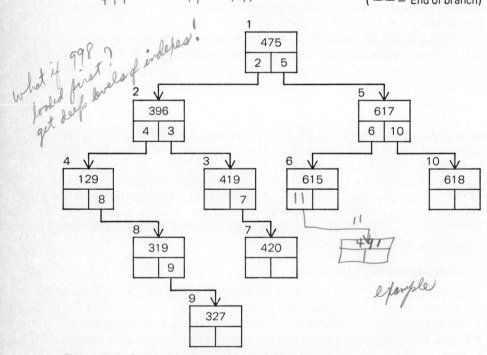

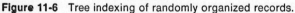

Figure 11-6 Tree indexing of randomly organized records.

In

To order to directly access a particular record with ISAM, the index is searched and the key is located which then provides the address for access. Note that even though the file is sequential, it can be updated with transactions in random order because the index may be used for directly locating a record for updating. If the file is to be processed sequentially, the index need not be used. In updating the file, the records to be updated are read, updated, and written back in the same location. If a new record is to be inserted in the sequence, it is inconvenient to completely reorder the file. The record to be inserted is placed in a special overflow area and a special indicator is placed in the record occupying the location immediately preceding the location where the record will be inserted to indicate the address of the missing record in the sequence. A record that is deleted leaves an empty space. Periodically the file is reorganized to eliminate the overflow addressing and the empty locations.   *IBM*

The indexed sequential organization may be modified slightly to assist in sequential ordering, yet allow for easy insertions into the file without frequent reorganization. A common method is to arrange records in blocks or buckets with the index referencing the block number. This reduces the size of the index but means that once the block is located the block must be searched sequentially. Since the block is usually small, this is not a serious processing impediment. Blocks are organized with extra locations so that the records may be added or deleted from the block without reorganizing the rest of the file. It is usually desirable to use special index sequential software to build the file and indexes and to update and reorganize. Such software is available from both the hardware manufacturers and independent software vendors.   *CDC*

Indexed sequential organization is very popular for direct access storage files because it combines the best features of sequential organization with features of direct access by means of the index. Disadvantages are the extra storage requirements caused by the need to allow for insertions to the file, the extra storage for the indexes, the extra processing required in using indexes, and the need to periodically reorder the file. On balance, however, index sequential is a powerful combination and has received substantial use in computer data processing.

LIST ORGANIZATIONS
FOR INFORMATION RETRIEVAL

The problems of access are most severe in information retrieval applications, and an alternative to sequential or random organization is to use some form of list organization. In a list organization, relations among records are established by pointers so that there need be no special physical organization of the file. The use of pointers allows different logic organizations to be established without regard to the actual physical arrangement. A pointer in a record consists of a data item (occupying a field) which gives the address of another record. If the file is on a disk, the pointer to a record is the disk address of that record. There may be many pointers in a record because many different relations may need to be established. List organizations are methods for building structures with the pointers. The most common are simple lists, inverted lists, and ring organizations.

Simple-List Organization

In a simple list an entry in an index points to the first record. The first record in the list points to the second logical record, the second logical record points to the third, etc. The last record in the logical sequence contains a special symbol in the pointer field (Figure 11-7). This is also termed a "threaded list." The sequence of the physical records is not important because the pointers are specifying the logical relation. For example, in order to establish a logical file involving all employees by department, an index is established with the different department numbers and a corresponding entry into the first employee in the file belonging

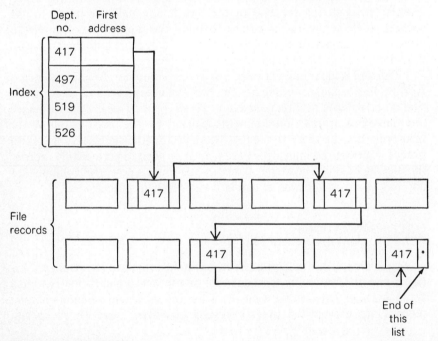

Figure 11-7 Simple list.

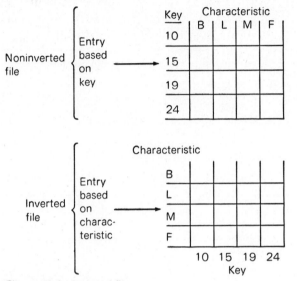

Figure 11-8 Inverted file.

to that department. If the employees in department 417 are to be read, the search begins with entry for 417 in the department index which has a pointer to the first employee in the department. The first record for department 417 will point to the next record which contains an employee working in department 417, etc. A record can be a part of several logical files because there can be many pointers in the same record.

The updating of a list by inserting a record requires that the pointer of the preceding logical record be changed. If a record has multiple pointers, deletion of the record requires that all pointers be revised. If there are only single, forward pointers, there is no method for going backward in the list to revise the prior pointers. Merely by inserting backward pointers which point to the preceding record, it is possible to insert or delete records easily. This also allows the list to be searched in either direction.

Inverted-List Organization

The list concept of the simple list may be extended. For example, a fairly comprehensive list of characteristics may be established as an index with a pointer to the first record in the file which has that characteristic and with pointers from each such record to the next record having the characteristic. Whereas a sequential file can be thought of as being accessed only through the record key, a full set of characteristics would allow the file to be accessed through any characteristic. The file is then said to be "inverted." In other words, all indexing is by content rather than by record key (Figure 11-8).

File sequenced by name

Disk address	Name	Age	Code for occupation	Code for salary range
224	ANDERSON L.	32	1	2
225	FLINT C.	23	7	4
226	THOMAS H.	42	3	3
227	PORTER N.	39	7	4

Content indexing for inverted file

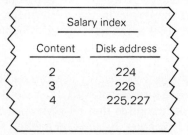

Age index

23	225
32	224
39	227
42	226

Occupation index

Content	Disk address
1	224
3	226
7	225,227

Salary index

Content	Disk address
2	224
3	226
4	225,227

Figure 11-9 Use of content indexes for inverted files.

The index in an inverted list may be expanded to include a list of all records having a specified characteristic. The pointers are then dropped from the records because the index has the complete list (Figure 11-9). In other words, in a file of personnel at a university all the people born in 1930 will be listed by record identifier following the characteristic "born 1930." This allows searching of the index for the content which is to be found in the file, rather than having to search the file itself. Since the fully inverted file makes every data item available as a basis for search and retrieval, it is excellent for information retrieval applications, especially where the retrieval requirements cannot be specified in advance. The disadvantage is that the index for a fully inverted file will be quite large, and a somewhat modified form is usually the most practical approach for day-to-day use.

A problem in an inverted list is how to efficiently store the list or directory of records containing each characteristic. There is generally no way to determine the length of the list prior to its creation, and the length of the list can change as the data changes. For example, if an attribute in the index is sex—say, male—a company with all male employees would list every single employee record as belonging to this list.

One approach to handling the content indexes, especially for characteristics having two values, is the bit index. In this approach, a string of bits is assigned for each record in the file with each bit identifying whether a characteristic exists. If there are 1,000 records in the file, there will be 1,000 separate indexes. The first bit in the index record relates to the first characteristic, the second bit to the second characteristic, etc. If the record has the attribute, the bit is made equal to 1; if not, it is made equal to zero (Figure 11-10). The binary index is very efficient where a large number of records have the attribute, but for a large number of index entries it can become prohibitively large. It also is very efficient for performing logical operations such as finding records which have attribute A AND attribute B OR attribute C, etc.

Ring Organization

A ring organization is a list which has pointers going both forward and backward. The first record is an index record which specifies the nature of the ring, and the last record in the list points to the first. This allows retrieval to proceed from any record, either backward or forward, until the entire list has been examined.

This is a very useful organization because it provides a facility to retrieve and process all the records in any one ring while branching off at any or each of the records to retrieve and process other records which are logically related. For example, a retrieval request may involve injured employees. When one is found, the next question is, "Who does he work with?" This question is answered by taking the pointer for department number and following the list through all employees who are part of that same list until the ring brings the list back to the originating record (Figure 11-11).

DATA BASE CONCEPTS

A data base is a set of logically related files organized in such a way that access to the data is improved and redundancy is minimized. There can be

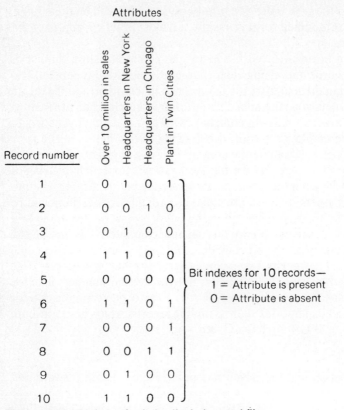

Attributes

Record number	Over 10 million in sales	Headquarters in New York	Headquarters in Chicago	Plant in Twin Cities	
1	0	1	0	1	
2	0	0	1	0	
3	0	1	0	0	
4	1	1	0	0	
5	0	0	0	0	Bit indexes for 10 records—
6	1	1	0	1	1 = Attribute is present
7	0	0	0	1	0 = Attribute is absent
8	0	0	1	1	
9	0	1	0	0	
10	1	1	0	0	

Figure 11-10 Bit index for index list in inverted file.

several data bases to reflect several logical groupings of files. The data base concept is made operational by a data base management system, a software system which performs the functions of creating and updating files, retrieving data, and generating reports. All data in the set of files can be accessed by any program having the right to use the data base. In general a data base needs to be on direct access storage in order to implement the concept. Because many different user programs may access the data base, it is controlled by a separate authority established for this purpose. The data base concept can result in efficiency of storage and efficiency in processing. The efficiency of storage stems from the elimination of redundant files. If each application has its own file, there will be many applications that will be essentially duplicating files. The efficiency of processing arises not only because of the reduction in file storage but also because logically related data which might otherwise be maintained in separate files is now found in a single file and the processing can take advantage of this fact. A single updating will update an item for all processing applications which use that item. This reduces the inconsistencies and errors which often occur among separate files. It reduces the necessity for sorting, comparison, and merging which are often required if separate files are maintained and then merged for interrelated processing (Figure 11-12). The data base improves efficiency for retrieval of information because all the files are found logically related in a single place. Two major concepts connected with data base are the schema/subschema and the data base administrator.

Schema and Subschema

The *schema* is the information that describes the data base. Essentially one can think of the schema as a dictionary which describes all the data items in terms of entry type, length, name, etc. The schema is similar to the data division of a COBOL program in that it defines all data items in the data base. The schema is written in a data definition language which describes the data and logical relations between data entities. The schema is thus a comprehensive directory of all data items in the file.

In a large data base the schema can include a substantial number of

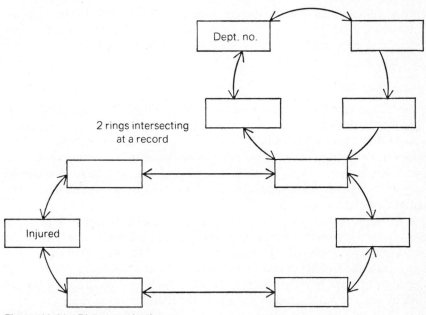

Figure 11-11   Ring organization.

items. Any application program will, however, use only a small subset of the items on the data base. The subschema is essentially a description of the items that are to be used by an application program. The *data manipulation language* (DML) is a language which the programmer uses to transfer data between his program and the data base (also called a "data base command language"). The DML is usually controlled through a higher level language such as COBOL. In other words, the entire data base is structured by means of a data description language statement. This description forms the data base schema. A programmer writing an application program describes the data which he or she needs by a subschema. The subschema must be compatible with the schema, but it need not be concerned with the physical storage. For example, a schema may have a large record with many fields for each employee. A program requiring only two of the items, say, pay rate and age, defines a subschema for only these two items. The binding of the subschema to the schema is done by the software system and need not concern the application programmer. A DML statement will be a mixture of a host language such as COBOL and special data base instructions. The consequence of this concept of data base management is to remove the data base from the control of the individual programmer. All uses of the data base must be handled through the data base management software. This allows the integrity and security of the data base to be under better control than if all programs were allowed to operate directly. Also the individual programmer no longer need be concerned with the physical records. The programmer works with only logical records defined by his or her subschema.

Data Base Administrator

The concept of the data base which is independent from the application programs and is not available to the application programmers except on a controlled basis means that someone must exercise this control. This person is known as a "data base administrator." In other words, a function is required to manage and control the data base in order to preserve its integrity, maintain the data base definition, and prevent unauthorized usage or change.

One of the major problems of a data base is security. When, for example, there were separate files for different programs, security could be maintained merely by physical security over the files. A program not needing a file would not call for it. In the data base approach, a substantial amount of data is collected for use by a variety of programs, some of which are not authorized to access all the data.

The data base administrator has responsibility for the data base. This means he or she has responsibility for the schema and exercises validity and access authority for subschemas. The administrator's activities include defining and organizing the data base, providing for protection of the data base, and preparing documentation of the data base.

Users and Suppliers of the Data Base

The persons who are affected by the data base are its users and suppliers. The users are those who program applications utilizing the data base for persons in the organization who desire information. The suppliers are those who must provide input for storage into the data base.

The supplier of the data for the data base will find that there is greater emphasis upon integrity of the input data than when only individual applications were involved. The effects of an error can now affect much of the organization, whereas individual files could often be in error without affecting the rest of the organization. For example, the personnel file could be in error without affecting the payroll processing. The measures for data integrity will therefore be measurably strengthened when a data base is used and a data base administrator enforces the data quality standards.

Individual parts of the organization have maintained data files, and the amount of control exercised over the quality of the data was connected with the use to which it was put by the organization and the current management attitude. However, with the data base and data base administrator the level of integrity must be established to suit organization-wide objectives rather than the individual organizational element. In other words, there is a tradeoff between, on the one hand, the decentralized data collection and individual files which produced varying levels of quality plus redundant and inconsistent data and, on the other hand, the centralized demands of the data base which has much higher quality of data and much easier access to organizational data. The centralization of data demands a well-conceived plan governing the development and use of the data base.

Some users may notice the need for formal security codes and formal procedures for establishing the right to access data. The users of the data will find that the directory issued by the data base administrator provides substantially greater knowledge of the data resources in the organization than previously existed. The ability to ask questions will be considerably enhanced because there will be a knowledge of data availability. The user will find much easier access to data because of the retrieval capabilities and report generation capabilities. The programmer will find that having these capabilities available will make it easier to respond to requests.

The programmer, in using the data base, will find that many of the tasks formerly done need not be performed. The data administrator will arrange for such matters as security, backup, and data integrity. All the physical problems of the storage will be separated from the programmer. At the same time, the programmer will be left with fewer responsibilities for the data file and more constraint in what can be done to the data. The programmer can extract any data for which his or her program has valid security access but cannot implement programs to alter fields in the data without permission from the data administrator.

DATA MANAGEMENT SYSTEMS

A data management system enables a user to create and update files; to select, retrieve, and sort data; and to generate reports. Data management systems are an extension of prior concepts in software. In first-generation computers, the programmer was required to write in machine-oriented code, and all functions had to be written for each program. It was soon found that many functions could be generalized and used by all programmers. This was especially true of input/output functions, and so macro instructions were added to assembly languages so that the individual programmer did not have to write the input/output code. Other functions soon became generalized, such as sorting and report generation, and this software is found as part of the generalized software support for a data processing installation. The data management system is an extension of these ideas to the management of the files of an organization. There are two types of data management systems—file management systems and data base management systems. The difference between the two is in their scope. The file management system handles individual files, whereas the data base management system has the capability for managing an entire data base as well as an individual data file.

Two different approaches are used in data base management systems. One is the self-contained system; the other is the host language system. Early systems were usually of the self-contained variety, while later systems favored the host language design in which the data management system has an interface with programs written in higher-level language such as COBOL.

A data management system provides efficiency in coding through the use of cataloged file definitions and file management. In a COBOL program, for example, the file must be described in detail. A very large file might require a number of pages of coding to describe the data. Each program using the file would require the same file description. COBOL provides a copy verb which allows a file definition to be cataloged and then brought into use by a program merely by the use of the verb COPY. The same concept has been extended into the data management system. All file definitions are contained within this system, and it is not necessary for the programmer to describe the file at all.

The operation of the data management system is through a data management language which the programmer or other user writes to specify what he wishes to have done. The data management system takes the language specification and produces a program to accomplish the task.

Whereas the language of programming has generally been procedure-oriented, as COBOL or FORTRAN, in which the programmer describes the process and procedures by a series of statements, the data management systems use a specification language which describes what is to happen rather than the steps necessary for it to occur. Since they focus on the result, specification languages are generally easier to use than procedure-oriented languages, which must specify all steps to achieve a result. Specification languages are limited, and so even where they are used in a data management system, it is generally desirable to have a procedural language capability as well.

A method for providing generalized code and still allow for differences in applications is "event processing." In event processing the data management system provides the logic flow for various types of processing but allows the programmer to specify the unique functions that the program is to perform. In other words the data management system combines the generalized logic with the specific logic furnished by the programmer. The advantages are that the generalized logic is done in a standard way, and the programmer need not be concerned with it.

Once the specifications and procedures have been written for an application, the data management system prepares an executable program by one of the standard methods—load and go using linked subroutines or generation of code which is then compiled and executed.

A number of data management systems are available. Each computer manufacturer offers one (generally as extra-cost software); in addition, a number of data management systems are provided by software vendors. Some names are listed below, but substantial changes and new additions to data management software are expected during the next few years.

Name	Vendor	Comments
IMS (Information Management System)	International Business Machines Corp.	IBM's principal data base management system
Mark IV	Informatics, Inc.	A powerful file processing system that has many users, but has less capabilities than generally associated with data base management systems
TOTAL	Sincom Systems, Inc.	A data base system quite widely used
System 2000	MRI Systems Corp.	A comprehensive data base system

Substantial reductions in the time required to program file maintenance and report functions have been reported by installations using data management systems. Many of the systems provide convenient user inquiry language. The newer data management systems continue to improve in generality, flexibility, and modularity. There appears to be a trend toward greater data independence, simpler and more powerful languages, and improved operating performance.

SUMMARY

The data base subsystem is a vital part of the management information system. As an introduction to the data base subsystem the chapter provides a review survey of data concepts (such as data, record, files, blocks, and information structures), serial access devices, and direct access devices. There is an examination of file organizations useful in data processing applications and list organizations designed for information retrieval.

A data base is a set of logically related files organized in such a way that access is improved and redundancy is minimized. The data base is maintained independently of the application programs. It is described by a schema. The application programs describe their data needs with a subschema. A data base administrator controls the data base and the procedures for access.

The software which manages the data base resource is the data management system. It provides special capabilities for creating and updating files; selecting, retrieving, and sorting data; and generating reports. The data management system is required to effectively implement the data base subsystem.

EXERCISES

1 Define the following terms:
   a Data item
   b Record
   c File
   d Block
   e Data base
   f Information structure
   g Elementary item
   h Field
2 Explain and contrast the following pairs of terms:
   a Logical files and physical files
   b Serial access and direct access
   c Fixed length and variable length

    d Hierarchic and associative data relationships

3 Define the following acronyms:

    a DASD

    b ISAM

    c BDAM

    d SAM

    e IMS

4 Explain the methods for defining variable-length fields and records. Explain advantages and disadvantages of using variable-length records.

5 Explain the way a record is located on:

    a Magnetic tape file

    b Disk file

6 Compute the number of 80-column punched card records that can be stored on a magnetic tape that is 2,400 ft long and uses gaps between blocks as follows:

    a One record per block:

        (1) 200 bytes-per-inch density ($^3/_4$-in. gap)

        (2) 1,600 bytes-per-inch density (0.6-in. gap)

    b Ten records per block:

        (1) 200 bytes-per-inch density ($^3/_4$-in. gap)

        (2) 1,600 bytes-per-inch density (0.6-in. gap)

7 Figure 11-4 is based on nine-channel third-generation equipment. Prepare data on older equipment with a 0.75-in. gap and densities as follows:

	Block size		
Density	80	800	8,000
200			
556			

8 Complete the table of effective transfer rates in characters (bytes per second) for the following (assuming tape speed of 125 inches per second):

Block size in characters (bytes)	Density (bytes per inch) and inter-block gap (in inches)		
	800/0.6	1,600/0.6	6,250/0.3
80			
800			
8,000			

The basic formula is:

$$\text{Transfer rate (in bytes per second)} = \text{bytes per inch} \times \text{tape speed (in inches per second)}$$

But the effective transfer rate must take into account the gap which requires time to read but has no data. Calculate an effective total of bytes per inch to use in the above formula as follows:

$$\text{Effective bytes per inch} = \frac{\text{block size in bytes}}{(\text{block size/bytes per inch}) + \text{gap (in inches)}}$$

9 Explain the organization of a sequential file. Explain how it is used in:
  a Updating run
  b Retrieval request
  c Preparing report arranged in different sequence
10 Explain the random file organization
  a How is a record located?
  b How is overflow handled?
11 Explain a tree index. What are the advantages and disadvantages?
12 Prepare a tree index like the one in Figure 11-6 for the following record keys received in the order given:

976 811 894
419 444 519
821 318 709
845 518 240
917 320 200

13 Explain indexed sequential organization. How are blocks used to reduce index size and reorganization needs?
14 Explain what a pointer is and how it is stored in a record.
15 Explain a simple list. Why might it be called a "threaded list" or "knotted list"? Why are forward and backward pointers sometimes used?
16 Explain an inverted file. Why might it be called a content-indexed file? Why are pointers not used in the records?
17 Explain the use of a binary index or bit index to store the indexes of an inverted file. Construct a bit index for inverted file use for a three-record file with data as follows:

Record key	Salary class	Sex	Education code
180	1	Male	4
190	2	Male	7
200	1	Female	6

18 Explain a ring organization. How is it used in information retrieval?
19 Explain the difference between the schema and subschema.
20 What are the characteristics of a data base?
21 What are the duties of a data base administrator?
22 Explain and contrast file management systems and data base management systems.
23 Explain the difference between a host language system and a self-contained data management system.

24 Explain the need for the data base subsystem in a management information system.
25 Explain why some direct access storage is needed for an effective data base subsystem.

SELECTED REFERENCES

Byrnes, Carolyne J., and Donald B. Steig: "File Management Systems, A Current Summary," *Datamation*, November 1960.

CODASYL COBOL Committee Data Base Task Group: "COBOL Extensions to Handle Data Bases," special joint issue of ACM SIGPLAN Notices and ACM SIGBDP Bulletin, Association for Computing Machinery, New York, Summer 1968.

"CODASYL Data Base Task Group, April, 1971 Report," available from Association for Computing Machinery, New York.

CODASYL Systems Committee: "Feature Analysis of Generalized Data Base Management Systems," May 1971, available from Association for Computing Machinery, New York.

Dodd, George G.: "Elements of Data Management Systems," *Computing Surveys*, vol. 1, no. 2, June 1969.

Everest, G. C., and E. H. Sibley: "Critique of the Guide-Share DBMS Requirements," Proceedings of the 1971 ACM-SIGIFDET Workshop, "Data Description, Access and Control," November 1971, pp. 93–113, available from Association for Computing Machinery, New York.

Gildersleeve, Thomas R.: *Design of Sequential File Systems*, Wiley-Interscience, a division of John Wiley & Sons, Inc., New York, 1971.

Joint Guide-Share Data Base Requirements Group: "Data Base Management System Requirements," SHARE Inc., New York, November 1970.

Lefkovitz, David: *File Structures for On-Line Systems*, Spartan Books, New York, 1969.

"Organizing the Corporate Data Base," *EDP Analyzer*, vol. 8, no. 3, March 1970.

"Processing the Corporate Data Base," *EDP Analyzer*, vol. 8, no. 4, April 1970.

Treanor, Richard G: "Data Management, Fact and Fiction," *Data Base*, vol. 3, no. 1, Spring/Summer 1971, pp. 17–24.

Chapter 12

Information System
Support for
Decision Making

The decision support software contained in a management information system is described in terms of the three major phases of the Simon decision-making model explained in Chapter 6: intelligence, design, and choice. The meaning of each phase is summarized below:

1 Intelligence consists of searching the environment for conditions calling for decisions; it is synonymous with problem recognition.

2 Design is inventing, developing, and analyzing possible courses of action.

3 Choice involves selecting a course of action and implementing it.

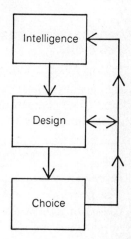

Articles in popular literature frequently state that the computer will make decisions. But decisions are made only by people. A human decision maker must always be part of a choice. A decision algorithm, a decision rule, or a computer program assists by providing the basis for a decision, but the decision choice is made by a human. The statements about computers making decisions are generally based on the face that some decisions may be programmed while others cannot be programmed. This suggests that the programmed/nonprogrammed classification is a significant one for MIS design.

There is some tendency among information system designers to feel that a data base alone will significantly improve decision making. While this may sometimes occur with a data base, this view ignores the fact that there are three elements in decision making:

1 Data
2 Decision model or decision procedure
3 Decision maker

Decision making can therefore be improved through better data, better decision models, or better decision makers (better trained, more experienced).

This chapter surveys the types of data and the types of models that can be provided as part of the decision support contained in a management information system. The decision support software is not as well developed as transaction processing or data management software; however, there is an increasing use of decision support software as organizations implement management information systems.

PROGRAMMED VERSUS NONPROGRAMMED DECISIONS

The distinction between programmed and nonprogrammed decisions is significant because the operational requirements are different for the two types. The characteristics of programmed and nonprogrammed decisions are summarized as follows:

Programmed	Nonprogrammed
Repeated	Occasional
Well-defined	Unique
Decision rules or algorithm for subordinate to use	New analysis for each occurrence

In other words, a programmed decision is one that is well-defined and is repeated often enough that decision rules or decision algorithms may be defined. The rules may be prespecified, and therefore they can generally be coded for computer processing. The use of computers to process programmed decision rules represents a prior choice by a decision maker as to how decisions are to be made in the future. Since decision making is a costly process in terms of a very scarce resource—managerial time and energy—programmed decisions are an efficient method for conserving scarce resources and enhancing the productivity of managers. The nonprogrammed decisions are not repeated frequently or they are so different at each repetition that no general model can be developed as a basis for programming them.

The decision support modules should provide assistance for three types of activities:

1 Establishing a programmed decision
2 Executing a programmed decision
3 Making a nonprogrammed decision

The decision activities for both establishing a programmed decision and making a nonprogrammed decision can follow the decision-making process involving intelligence, design, and choice. The establishing of a programmed decision requires a more general solution than a nonprogrammed decision. The decision rules for a programmed decision must take into account a variety of conditions, whereas the nonprogrammed decision need relate to only a specific situation.

Although the programmed decision represents a conservation of scarce managerial resources, there is a very significant problem in its use in information/decision systems. The problem is the application of the decision rule to a problem situation for which it is not suitable. The lack of applicability may occur in its use on problems for which the rule was not designed, in the existence of conditions not contemplated, or in changes in the characteristics or objectives for the decision. For example, an inventory reorder model for fast-moving items is generally not appropriate for slow-moving items. An inventory model which assumes ready availability of items to be ordered is not suitable if there is scarcity or rationing. A capital investment model to maximize rate of return may not be appropriate for a company faced with minimizing expected losses from nationalization by an unfriendly government. The problem of applying the right decision model to the right problem suggests that MIS decision support modules should be designed to facilitate human review of programmed decision making.

SOFTWARE FOR DECISION INTELLIGENCE

The intelligence phase of the decision-making process is often termed "problem or opportunity recognition." Analysis and choice cannot proceed until the problem has been identified. The intelligence phase, therefore, consists of searching or scanning the environment (internal and external) for conditions which suggest an opportunity or a problem (Figure 12-1). The existence of an opportunity or a problem initiates the subsequent analysis and choice phases of decision making.

Types of Opportunities and Problems

The opportunities or problems to be discovered by the intelligence phase can be classified as follows:

Opportunities	Problems
Profit	Demand for goods or services
Risk reduction	Performance
Societal service	Risk

These types of opportunities and problems are further clarified by examples.

I Opportunities
   A Opportunity for profit by
      1 Expanding services, products, and markets
      2 Expanding market share
      3 Increasing price for goods and services
      4 Reducing costs (manufacturing, materials, distribution and financial costs)
   B Opportunity for risk reduction by
      1 Minimizing impact of competition (as by product differentiation, patents, copyrights, sales agreements, product enhancements)
      2 Diversification (which spreads risk)
      3 Protecting sources of supply (as by vertical integration, long-term agreements)
      4 Influencing governmental regulation (as by lobbying, cooperative endeavors)
      5 Maintaining employee service (benefits such as pensions and seniority)
      6 Insurance or hedging
   C Opportunity for societal service by
      1 Improving quality of product or service (as by improved life or

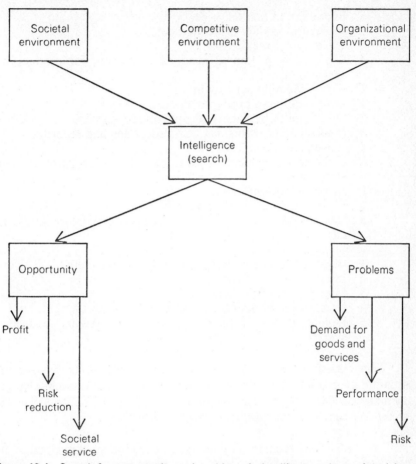

Figure 12-1 Search for opportunity and problems in intelligence phase of decision making.

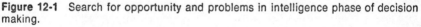

                  service ability of product, reduced danger from product in use)

   2 Improved working environment (such as job enrichment, safety, working conditions)

   3 Reduction in deleterious environmental effects of activities

   4 Improving societal environment (for instance, enhancement of cultural opportunities, educational opportunities)

II Problems

   A Problems affecting demand for goods or services

      1 New or improved competitor products, services, etc.

      2 Increase in competitive behavior (advertising, sales effort, etc.) by rivals in one or more markets

      3   Reduction in market prices
      4   Increased product or service costs
      5   Government regulations
      6   Changes in perceived need by customers for products or services

B   Problems affecting performance
      1   Deterioration in productivity
      2   Deterioration in quality of products or services
      3   Inadequate or erroneous data processing and records
      4   Inadequate cash flow
      5   Incorrect or inadequate decision rules, procedures, and instructions
      6   Increased absenteeism
      7   Deterioration in work environment
      8   Deterioration in quality or timeliness of raw materials, parts, etc.

C   Problems of risk
      1   Interruption in supply of materials, supplies, etc.
      2   Interruption in employee service
      3   Interruption of financing
      4   Interruption in distribution system
      5   Failure of manufacturing, information processing, and other systems

This classification of opportunities and problems emphasizes the situation of organizations set up for profit, but with only slight changes the same concepts can be used in nonprofit organizations. The use of the societal service classification recognizes two factors:

    1   In the long run a profit-making organization must respond to the needs of society or society will not continue to let it operate.
    2   Organizations are run by individuals who generally have an interest in societal service above and beyond that required for survival of the firm. This is consistent with the behavioral theory of decision making which sees an organization as a coalition of individuals with diverse goals.

Risk reduction is an interesting classification since some of the activities are aimed at a reduction in competition. This classification recognizes that even though competition and risk taking are desirable for society, organizations will attempt to reduce them. There are legal and structural limitations on these activities, but within these limits, organizations seem to attempt a reduction in risk and uncertainty.

An information system for the identification of these problems or opportunities requires the following elements:

Data base	1	Data collection and storage
Processing and search	2	Measurement and processing of data related to possible problems and opportunities
	3	Scanning and examination algorithms
Reports	4	Reports to decision makers

Data Base for the Intelligence Phase

The data base for the support of the intelligence phase is very comprehensive. In general, this should cover three environments (Figure 12-2):

Environments	Description
Societal	The economic, social, and legal environment in which the organization operates
Competitive	The characteristics and behavior of the market place in which the organization operates
Internal	The capabilities, strengths, weaknesses, constraints, and other factors affecting the ability of the organization to perform its functions

Organizations generally collect some data on the internal environment, but for organizations to systematically collect and have available societal and competitive data is less common. There may be considerable knowledge of these environments by different individuals, but the lack of a system for recording, classifying, storing, and accessing the data makes such casual systems inefficient for intelligence purposes.

The MIS concept does not require that all the data for intelligence be stored in the computer data base. It does imply, however, that the data is systematically collected and stored and is accessible to any decision maker in the organization. There are advantages to computer storage, but some items of data may be maintained more effectively with manual processing using notebooks, keysort cards, note card files, and other means. The essential requirements are procedures for maintaining the data and providing information to those needing it. The discussion implies computer-based files and processing, but a specific system may use a variety of processing, storage, and access methods.

The data base need not store the actual data. In some cases, the data base can store a pointer to the data such as a reference to a government statistical report. The advantage of the pointer is a reduction in the size of the stored data; the disadvantage is the fact that the actual data is not available in the data base. The pointer is most useful, therefore, for those cases in which the data is not likely to be used often enough to justify

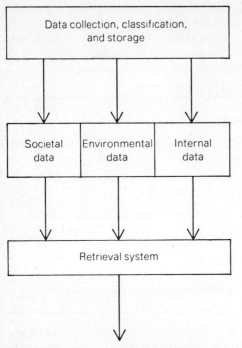

Figure 12-2 Data base for intelligence.

storing and updating it but a need is expected at some time. The stored reference will then indicate how the data can be obtained. This procedure imposes a retrieval delay, but after a referral to the source, the necessary data can be inserted in the decision procedure.

The complete data base (computer and noncomputer) for the intelligence phase will contain data obtained from a variety of sources. Some examples will illustrate the scope and variety of the data.

Examples of types of data	Typical sources
Local, regional, national, and international economy	Published statistics
Forecasts of economy	Public and private forecasts
Historical prices of raw materials	Published statistics
Forecasts of raw material prices	Public and private forecasts
Historical market shares for relevant markets	Public and private statistics and estimates
Yearly calendar with estimated impact of various holidays, etc.	Public calendars, public statistics, private statistics
Internal capabilities (production, storage, financing, and others)	Internal estimates

The complete data base facilities in support of the intelligence phase will include not only the data and the procedures to update and maintain the data base but also means for searching the data and for retrieval of data.

Search for Opportunities and Problems

The search for opportunities and identification of problems is constrained and defined by the organization's environment and markets and its strategic plans. This is the search space to be supported with data and with search procedures.

The search can proceed only if problem and opportunity conditions can be identified. This identification generally requires:

1   Measurement of a variable
2   Comparison of the measurement with a standard, plan, or other yardstick
3   Evaluation of positive or negative difference to determine if a problem or opportunity exists

Two examples will illustrate these concepts: the first is a measurement of direct labor cost, the comparison of this cost with planned cost (standard cost), and an evaluation of the size of an unfavorable variance to determine if there is a problem. A second example is a measurement of a sales trend for a new product in a particular market area, a comparison with the expected sales trend, and an evaluation of a probable sales trend in that market to determine if the marketing followed there has elements which would improve sales elsewhere.

The example of the sales trend illustrates the use of analysis procedures to examining existing and/or forecast conditions or performance. Some examples of this type of analysis are:

• Trend analysis to track changes over time in markets, prices, technology, and costs
• Composition analysis to detect changes in composition of markets, costs, and competition
• Competitor analysis to discover and track behavior of major competitors
• Correlation analysis to discover meaningful relations (which can then be tracked), such as sales/price, price/competitor price, and advertising cost/benefit

The search for problems and opportunities has different characteristics depending on whether the search can be structured and whether it is continuous or ad hoc. These differences are summarized in three types of search (Figure 12-3):

1   Structured continuous search
2   Structured ad hoc search
3   Unstructured ad hoc search

Structured, Continuous Search   The search for many opportunities and problems can be structured and performed regularly. For example, the inventory balances need to be examined frequently in order to identify the need to reorder and the need to dispose of surplus. Product prices relative to competitor prices must be examined often to spot possible need for price adjustments. Because these problem areas are known, the intelligence activity can be structured and a frequency of examination established. The examination or search may be hourly, daily, weekly, monthly, etc., depending upon the expected frequency of the problem, the seriousness when it occurs, and the speed of change in the

Structured continuous search

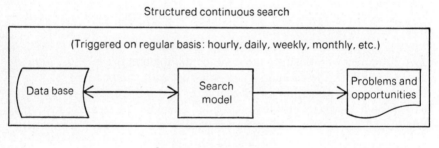

Structured ad hoc search

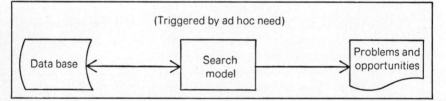

Unstructured search

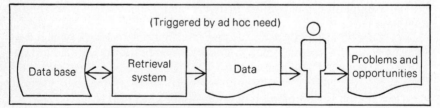

Figure 12-3   Three types of search.

factors involved. Traditional data processing systems have provided some outputs of this type. The trend in computer-base management information systems is to extend the scope, number, and frequency of outputs. Precomputer systems had practical limitations on the frequency of measurement and analysis of data. The use of computers plus programmed algorithms to examine measurements provides a capability for identifying the need for decisions at any time rather than only at a periodic reporting interval. In other words, the MIS intelligence support for recurring problems or opportunities consists of procedures which measure the factors that indicate a need for decisions. The measurement and examination are carried out by computer programs that are applied at frequent intervals (depending on the factors). The practical consequence is a frequent scanning of all known indicators of potential problems or opportunities, with output whenever a potential problem or opportunity is detected. Output may be periodic as well, since periodic reports of a decision area act as an audit of the activities of the period and provide background for individuals involved in the decision-making process.

Structured Ad Hoc Search   Many problems and opportunities do not occur frequently enough to be handled by regular search. However, the search process can be structured. For example, plant location may be a problem for an expanding company, but it may not occur with sufficient frequency to justify a data base and regular scanning for plant location sites. Instead, the intelligence process is structured, but the process is applied only when other indicators suggest the need for it. The MIS structured ad hoc intelligence involves intelligence algorithms and report formats. The data base may be maintained by the organization or may be assembled only when needed. Outside services may be used (such as a plant location service).

Unstructured Search   Structured search depends on knowing how to search. The MIS designer may provide search processes for the conditions that can be thought out in advance, but it is impossible to anticipate all possible conditions or structure all intelligence. In many cases, the search or identification algorithm simply cannot be specified in advance. This suggests the need for a different kind of MIS support for unstructured intelligence, one that takes into account the characteristics of human search. A very significant characteristic that differentiates the human search process from computer algorithms is the ability of the human to approach the task heuristically rather than by logical steps. The human can arrive at conclusions by examining data for which no algorithm for processing exists.

The MIS support for unstructured search is primarily in easy access to the data base. The human needs to be able to perform such functions as retrieval, scanning, analysis, and comparison on data in order to discover new relations and new conclusions that have not previously been defined. The retrieval capabilities of the data base management system are therefore very significant in MIS support at this level. Online terminals greatly enhance the performance of unstructured search; periodic batch processing may be used for unstructured search, but in most cases search performance is significantly reduced by the delay inherent in periodic processing.

Report Output from the Intelligence Phase

The purpose of the intelligence software is to identify problems; output from it can be of three types:

1 Output directly to decision design stage software
2 Output suggesting the decision design and decision choice steps to follow
3 Output suggesting a possible problem or opportunity but with no indicators for future action

The output directly to the decision design stage software is most appropriate for structured, continuous search and situations where a programmed decision procedure is available. The final output from the design stage and choice stage software will be a report suggesting action. An example might be an inventory reorder situation in which the need for a reorder is input to an inventory model for analysis and choice of a suggested reorder quantity.

The output suggesting the decision design and decision choice steps to follow is used where the appropriate process can usually be identified, but not with sufficient certainty to initiate decision analysis without further human review. An example is output from an identification of a labor cost variance which identifies possible reasons for it and possible courses of action.

The output identifying a situation to be examined but without action indicators is generally used for nonprogrammed decisions. A material cost variance may be reported, but no analysis is provided. The human recipient must decide what steps to take for decision design and choice.

SOFTWARE FOR DECISION DESIGN

Following the intelligence stage which results in problem or opportunity recognition, the next step in the decision process is decision design. This process involves inventing, developing, and analyzing possible courses of action. It requires processes to understand the problem, to generate solutions, and to test solutions for feasibility. The decision design may result in several competing alternatives or may yield a single proposal with its competing alternatives being to not do it (the status quo).

Software to Assist in Understanding the Problem

The first step in understanding the problem is to develop a model of the situation. The range of modeling techniques is large. Examples are simple verbal explanation, flowcharts, complex mathematical statements (Figure 12-4), and computer programs. The model base for the MIS may contain a variety of models to use in different situations and for different functions. Some simple, preliminary models will illustrate the modeling approach:

	Verbal	Mathematical
1	An increase in scrap is caused by a deterioration in the accuracy of a milling machine.	$S = f(M)$ where S = scrap and M = machine accuracy performance
2	An increase in scrap is caused by a lack of training of operators.	$S = f(T_o)$ where T_o = training of operators
3	The interest rate being paid by the organization on borrowed funds is a function of capital structure, profitability, cash flow, prime rate, etc.	$I = f(C, P, F, R, \ldots)$

The examples are simple models that are hypotheses and are not proved. They are not precise enough for decision making. To say that scrap is a function of the deterioration in the accuracy of a machine is a useful first approximation, but it must be made more specific as to the cause of the inaccuracy, the amount of change over time, the extent of inaccuracy with different kinds of operations, and other factors. The training hypothesis must be supported by data showing the relation of amount of training with scrap and relating other factors such as prior experience and aptitudes. The interest rate model must have a set of coefficients for each factor in order to develop an estimating model.

These examples illustrate the need for analysis in order to obtain data for the construction of models for clarifying the problem. The MIS software to support this analysis includes a range of statistical and analysis software. Some examples are:

Regression analysis
Simple and multiple correlation
Chi square and other tests of significance

Flowcharts

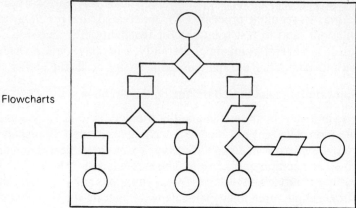

Mathematical equations

$$x_1 = 3.5y_1 + 4.5y_2 + 9y_3$$
$$x_2 = x_1 + y_1^2$$
$$x_3 = 4.5 + \sqrt{y_3}$$

Computer programs   1

```
READ(1,1)X,Y,Z
FORMAT (3F10.0)
IF(X.EQ.Z) 45
ANS = X**2 + 2.0
```

Figure 12-4 Examples of models for understanding problems.

Factor analysis
Sample selection

The MIS software support provides the decision maker (and the decision maker's staff) with the capability for discovering relations that suggest new models or hypotheses and the capability for computing the factors, coefficients, relations, etc., that allow a more precise and more meaningful model of the problem or opportunity to be developed. For example, the result of statistical analysis of the interest rate being charged to an organization might be a model with coefficients for each factor plus a measure of the error to be expected in the estimate. The information system provides programming capabilities for coding models into computer program statements using a high-level programming language such as BASIC, FORTRAN, or PL/I. There are also software systems for modeling in specific areas such as inventory management and financial management.

Software to Assist in Generating Solutions

If the process of understanding the problem has resulted in a model which explains the problem (or opportunity) and also allows some analysis of its characteristics, the generation of possible solutions or courses of action is assisted by two software systems.

    1 *The model itself.* The manipulation of the model frequently provides insight leading to generation of solution ideas.

    2 *The data base retrieval system.* The retrieval capabilities yield data that is useful in generating solution ideas.

    In many cases, the decision model will provide a suggested solution. For example, an inventory reorder model may suggest a solution to the problem of how much to order. This quantity is a suggestion that can be modified, but it represents a feasible solution (and perhaps an optimal solution based on the factors in the model).

    One decision alternative in the case of repeating or continuing problems is to make the decision as was made the prior time a decision was required. The data base of the organization will usually provide data on the past decision and the consequences of this alternative.

    Software support for generating solutions can also consist of a structured approach to the problem (say, a man/machine dialog). In this approach, the computer program leads the decision maker in a rational search strategy for solutions. For example, the solution search procedure might begin with a set of questions relating to common solutions. These questions might be followed by a series of questions which assist the decision maker to consider all alternatives. The advantage of structured approaches is that they assist in systematically exploring the normal decision space, but the disadvantage is the tendency to suppress search outside the normal decision space.

Software to Test Feasibility of Solutions

A solution is tested for feasibility by analyzing it in terms of the environments it affects—problem area, entire organization, competitors, and society. The analysis may be performed judgmentally against broad measures of these environments. This requires retrieval of data for comparison. Another approach is to analyze the proposed solutions using models of the different environments. These models will generally involve computer programs and a data base. The model base in a comprehensive MIS will have a number of such models. The following are examples:

Model	Comment
Overall organization model	This might be a budget model, a comprehensive planning model, or a simple model such as a cash flow model.
Competitor	A model of the market for the goods and services offered by the organization with competitor characteristics and competitive behavior included where feasible.
Society model	Probably not a complete, formal model but essentially a set of societal considerations such as legal, safety, and pollution.

As examples of the use of these models, a problem of increasing scrap might have one solution involving acquisition of a new machine. This would need to be tested against the budget model or cash flow model to determine if the acquisition would be feasible from a cash resources standpoint. This solution might also be evaluated against societal factors relating to pollution standards.

SOFTWARE FOR CHOICE

The software support of the intelligence and design phases assists in providing alternatives that have been evaluated in terms of feasibility, etc. The remaining phase is choice which requires the application of a choice procedure and the implementation of the chosen alternative.

Software cannot make the choice since choice is a human activity. However, software can be used in ranking the alternatives and otherwise applying decision choice procedures to support the choice itself. For example, a decision to acquire a machine from among several alternatives may be structured by one or more criteria such as the following:

Rate of return
Years to payback
Minimum cash outlay
Executive preference
Minimum risk

These criteria can be applied by use of decision software. The choice is then made by a decision maker and communicated to persons who can implement the result. The decision models form part of the model base for the MIS.

An important consideration in evaluating alternatives is the sensitivity of the solutions to changes in the assumptions on which the decision is to be made or in the conditions which are expected to occur. The sensitivity analysis is performed most easily when a quantitative model is available for manipulation.

SUMMARY

The MIS support for decision making in an organization can be described in terms of the three phases of the decision-making process: intelligence, design, and choice. The MIS support will usually involve both computer and noncomputer processing, files, etc.

The intelligence phase is for discovering problems and opportunities. The MIS support requires a data base with societal, competitive, and internal data plus methods for search and discovery. The search may be structured and continuous, structured and ad hoc, or unstructured. The structured search may use predefined search algorithms, whereas the unstructured search requires flexible access to the data base.

The decision design phase is for the generation of alternatives. This involves inventing, developing, and analyzing possible courses of action. The MIS support consists of statistical and analytical software and model-building software. The MIS software to assist in generating solutions consists of structured approaches, model manipulation, and data base retrieval systems. MIS support to test feasibility of solutions consists of various models of the organization and the competitive and societal environment.

The final step in the decision-making process is choice. The MIS support for the choice phase consists of various decision models, sensitivity analysis, and choice procedures.

The MIS support for decision making thus consists of a comprehensive data base, a data base retrieval capability, statistical and analytical software, and a model base containing model-building software, decision models, and decision aids.

EXERCISES

1 Can a computer make decisions? Discuss.
2 Explain the difference between programmed and nonprogrammed decisions.
3 Define the three phases of the decision process and describe the MIS support for each.
4 How can problems and opportunities be identified?
5 Identify the major data bases required for the intelligence phase.
6 Explain the difference in the three types of problem search and the different MIS supports for each.
7 How can unstructured search locate problems and opportunities?

8 What is the difference between heuristic search and algorithmic search?
9 Explain how a model is developed for a problem.
10 What MIS support is needed for (a) model development, and (b) model testing?
11 How can simulation be used in the design phase?
12 How are possible solutions generated?
13 How can a budget model be used to test feasibility of solutions?
14 Explain how decision models are used to support the choice phase of decision making.
15 Summarize the MIS support for decision making.
16 Explain why each of the following statistical packages might be included in the MIS decision support software:
   a Chi-square analysis
   b T test (student distribution)
   c Analysis of variance
   d Mean, median, mode, and standard deviations
   e Factor analyses
   f Correlation (simple and multiple)
17 Explain why each of the following might be included in the MIS software in support of decisions:
   a Linear programming
   b Rate of return analysis
   c Decision tree analysis
18 Explain the use of structured decision approaches in arriving at a choice.
19 Explain the difference in MIS support for
   a Decisions for which an optimal solution may be computed
   b Decisions for which no optimal solution is computable
20 Evaluate the statement: MIS does not mean computer-made decisions; rather it is computer-assisted decision making.

SELECTED REFERENCES

Hinkle, Charles L., and Alfred A. Kuehn: "Heuristic Models: Mapping the Maze for Management," *California Management Review*, Fall 1967, pp. 59–68.

Morris, William T.: "On the Art of Modeling," *Management Sciences*, August 1967, pp. 707–717.

Pounds, William P.: "The Process of Problem Finding," *Industrial Management Review*, Fall 1969.

Rappapart, Alfred: "Sensitivity Analysis in Decision Making," *The Accounting Review*, July 1967, pp. 441–556.

Rowe, Alan J.: "Computer Simulation: A Solution Technique for Management Problems," *Proceedings of the Fall Joint Computer Conference 1965*, Spartan Books, New York, 1966, pp. 259–267.

Sackman, Harold: *Man-Computer Problem Solving*, Auerbach Publishers, Inc., Philadelphia, 1970.

Scott Morton, Michael A.: *Management Decision Systems*, Harvard University Press, Cambridge, Mass., 1971.

Simon, Herbert A.: *The New Science of Management Decisions*, Harper & Row, Publishers, Incorporated, New York, 1960.

Will, Hart J.: "MIS: Mirage or Mirror Image?," *Journal of Systems Management*, September 1973, pp. 24–31.

338

Chapter 13

Information System
Support for
Planning and Control

Management functions were defined in Chapter 5 as planning, organizing, staffing, direction, and control. The information system provides support for all these functions; it is especially relevant for the planning and control functions. Computer-assisted planning and control extend the capabilities of management to perform these important functions.

PLANNING AND CONTROL IN ORGANIZATIONS

A plan is a predetermined course of action. It combines organizational goals and the activities necessary to achieve those goals. The organization plan is not mechanistically determined; it is very dependent on the individuals making up the organization. As explained in Chapter 5, an organization may be viewed as a coalition of individuals, and the organizational goals then represent bargaining among the members. The goals change in response to changes in the coalition membership and in the goals of the participants. The bargaining is, in general, very constrained by the existing structure. Through mechanisms such as operating procedures, decision rules, and budgets, coalition agreements are made semipermanent. Thus, two organizations with the same general structure may arrive at different goals and plans.

Three levels of management activity have been identified—strategic planning, management control, and operational control. Each of these has an associated planning requirement.

Level of management	Reason for planning
Strategic planning	Establishment of organizational goals. Definition of resource constraints.
Management control (tactical planning)	Allocation of resources. How resources shall be acquired, organized, and employed. Examples are capital expenditure budget and the three-year staffing plan.
Operational control	Efficiency of performance. Day-to-day scheduling of activities. Pricing, production levels, inventory levels, etc., are reflected in a yearly budget.

Different types of planning require different rates for adoption of computer-assisted approaches. Operations are characterized by frequent repetition of planning at fairly low levels in the organization, making this area more attractive for computer support than strategic planning, which occurs infrequently.

Project planning, the planning of a specific project, is a special problem that is amenable to computer methods. The project planning aid most commonly used is network scheduling. The network planning approaches are called "critical path scheduling," "PERT," and "CPM." A large number of software packages are used in preparing a network of events. They also calculate expected completion time, the critical path of events for meeting completion time, and slack time available for events not on the critical path.

Resource planning can involve a number of different plans. Some examples are:

- Manpower planning
- Facilities planning
- Raw materials supply planning
- Research planning
- Market planning
- Financial planning

The financial planning tends to be especially significant because it provides a framework for summary planning. Examples of financial planning are the profit plan, the debt/equity plan, and the cash management plan.

The variety of planning requirements suggests that planning is a significant management activity, but the limitations on humans as information processors put a fairly low limit on the amount of manual planning. The high processing time and high cost to manually prepare alternative plans and to manually examine the impact of alternative courses of action severely constrains the feasibility and benefits from planning. A major advantage of the computer-assisted planning to be described in this chapter is that it removes these processing constraints.

Management control is the activity which measures deviations from planned performance and initiates corrective action. The basic elements of control (see Chapter 5) are:

1 A standard specifying expected performance. This can be, for example, a budget, an operating procedure, or a decision algorithm.

2 A measurement of actual performance.

3 A comparison of expected and actual performance.

4 A report of deviations to a control unit such as a manager.

5 A set of actions the control unit (manager) can take to change future performance if currently unfavorable plus a set of decision rules for selecting appropriate responses.

6 A method for a higher planning/control level to change one or more conditions such as new control unit (manager) or revised performance standard in the event the control unit actions fail to bring actual unfavorable performance into a close harmony with expected performance.

The control process uses the concept of a feedback loop. The manager or control unit need be concerned only with deviations which are outside allowable control limits. This reduces the information processing requirements of the manager and focuses the manager's attention on the items needing investigation of corrective action. This is management by exception and the basis for all variance reporting. Control is dependent on planning because the planning process provides the standard against which performance is measured. Improvements in planning can therefore allow improved control.

THE PLANNING PROCESS

The plans of an organization represent expectations about the environment, expectations about the capabilities of the organization, and decisions that have been made on such matters as allocation of resources and direction of effort. The quantified expectations are input variables for models used in planning. One objective of the information system is to assist in the formulation, quantification, classification, and use of these expectations.

Quantification and Classification of Expectations

The analysis to formulate and quantify expectations may use three methods:

Analysis maybe?

1 *Statistical methods.* Trends, projections, correlation analysis, and sampling provide expectations based on statistical analysis of historical data. These methods are surveyed later in the chapter.

2 *Objective analysis of value and priority.* Where quantitative measures of value are available, they can often be applied to alternatives to arrive at priorities for use in planning. Examples are rate of return computation for revenue-producing or expense-saving expenditures and marginal revenue/marginal cost analysis for expenditures such as advertising.

3 *Judgment.* Judgment is used to formulate expectations in cases where there are no statistical or other bases for forecasting. It may also be used to select the proper statistical method when statistical analysis is required.

The reliability of data is important to the planning process. The reader of data symbols must not only interpret their meaning but also evaluate the reliability or trustworthiness of the representation. The reliability of statistical data is measured by the consistency of data resulting from a repetition of the same measurements under identical conditions. According to this concept, planning data would have high reliability if the planning procedure yielded identical results for several different planners, but identical results are impossible because of the uncertainties involved. The reliability of planning data is influenced by such factors as the following:

1 *Source of data.* Data from outside sources will receive different evaluations by different planners because of uncertainty as to its quality, etc.

2 *Influence of plan on outcome.* Some plans, such as an appropriation-type budget, have a strong determining influence on the outcome itself.

3 *Intended accuracy.* Planning estimates do not require a uniform standard of accuracy since certain figures are more critical than others.

For example, an error of 50 percent in the calculation of the cost of office pencils for the budget period is not nearly so serious as a 50 percent error in the cost of raw materials.

4 *Time.* The predictability of future events generally decreases with the prediction time span. When the forecast period is extended, the planning data tends to become less accurate as an expression of what is to be expected. Different planners will tend to have greater variation in their long-term projections than in their short-term estimates.

The classification of expectations is dependent on the type of plan for which they are being classified. Data may be organized in a variety of ways. For example, expenditures in a budget plan may be classified in one or more of the following ways:

Expenditure classification	Example
Object of expenditure	The classes of items being purchased, e.g., salaries, supplies, and travel.
Reason for expenditure	The function might be manufacturing or selling.
Functions Programs	Examples of programs (say, for a government) are health care, sanitation, and protection.
Performance	Performance classification for, say, an appliance manufacturer might be based on end products such as refrigerators and washing machines.
Organizational unit	Departments and other organizational units.
Cost behavior	Classification by variability with changes in activity and by controlability by management.

This brief summary of expenditure classifications illustrates the variety of planning structures. The way data is classified affects the value of the data for analyzing past behavior and generating future expectations. Classifications differ in their objectives; the following examples provide some indication of the variety of their uses:

Classification	Possible purpose
Object of expenditure	Control over what is being purchased
Function	Control over the functions for which expenditures are made
Program	Control over results to be achieved by a level of expenditures
Organizational unit	Control by person making decision to spend
Cost variability	Estimation of planned costs under different levels of activity

Development of Planning Models

A planning model is a method for structuring, manipulating, and communicating future plans. The model describes the process by which plans are developed from input data and from internal calculations. For example, a very simple profit model of a business organization might consist of the following statements:

Sales = input variable
Cost of sales = 0.40 × sales
Gross margin = sales − cost of sales
Operating expenses = input variable
Profit before taxes = gross margin − operating expenses
Taxes = 0.48 × profit before taxes
Net profit = profit before taxes − taxes

The profit model requires two inputs—sales and operating expenses. For example, an input of $100,000 for sales and $52,000 for operating expenses would allow the model to produce the following simplified income plan. A different set of the two input variables would yield a different profit plan.

XYZ Company
Profit Plan for Year Ended 197x

Sales	$100,000
Less: Cost of sales	40,000
Gross profit	$ 60,000
Less: operating expenses	52,000
Profit before taxes	$ 8,000
Less: Taxes	3,840
Net profit	$ 4,160

This simple example illustrates the nature of a planning model. The model provides for the following:

1 A format for presenting the results from processing the model
2 A set of input data
3 A set of processing statements (formulas, logic statements, etc.) to operate on the input data

Model building for a planning model can begin with simple models calling for inputs of major, high-level items. Subsequent model development can expand the details of the model to calculate the high-level items from more basic input. For example, in the simple model just given, the operating expenses were an input variable. An expansion of the model might provide a set of statements such as the following:

Computation of operating expenses:
Selling expenses   = 0.10 × sales
Advertising expense   = 0.05 × sales
Interest expense   = 0.07 × average long-term debt + 0.08 × average short-term loans
Bad-debt expense   = 0.01 × accounts receivable balance at beginning of period
Administrative expense = input variable
Operating expense   = selling + advertising + interest + bad-debt + administrative expenses

Note that the more detailed model for operating expenses requires input data on average long-term debt, average short-term debt, and accounts receivable balance at the beginning of the month. These are from another related model—the balance sheet model. Administrative expenses are still an input item; another level of detail in the model might provide for the calculation of that expense.

In this simple model, the sales estimate is a key variable because so many other variables are computed from it. This is a common pattern in organizational models because expenditures depend to a great extent on the activity which drives the organization. However, sales are not completely under the control of the organization, and estimates of sales must take into account a variety of factors. Examples of such factors are:

Disposable income (available to consumers)
Level of advertising, prior year
Level of advertising, current year
Level of competitive advertising, prior year
Level of competitive advertising, current year
Prior year level of sales
Level of price for product

By the use of such factors, an estimating equation might be developed to yield a sales estimate based on the underlying causal factors for sales. These estimates require estimates of environmental factors such as disposable income.

Certain variables may have a lag relation in which the level of a variable for a prior period will be the estimator for the level of another variable in the current period. For example, the accounts receivable for month n is related to the sales in month n-1 (for 30-day accounts) and to the preceding months for delayed payment plans or slow-paying accounts.

When an estimate for a period such as a year is used to develop estimates for shorter periods such as a month, it is necessary to calculate seasonal patterns. The monthly sales are rarely one-twelfth of the yearly sales. The months vary as percentages of the yearly activity based on seasonal patterns. For example, sales of new automobiles by the manufacturer are nil during the model changeover period in July–August, are high during September, etc. These seasonal patterns tend to persist year after year.

A number of planning models might be developed by an organization—each with a long-term and short-term component.

Profit plan
Financing plan
Staffing plan
Facilities plan
Sources-of-supply plan

These plans are interrelated. The facilities plan, for example, is based on the activity projected by the long-term profit plan. The profit plan is basic to a business organization. It results in planned income (profit and loss) statement, a planned balance sheet, and various supportive schedules showing planned activity. Figure 13-1 shows the interrelated flows among the balance sheet and income statement items.

The planning output should assist the user in understanding the nature of the process being planned and the effect of the variables. Measures such as percentages and ratios are useful and are therefore generally included in the output from planning models. Some examples of financial ratios that might be part of the output from a financial planning model are these:

Current ratio (current assets to current liabilities)
Quick ratio (cash, marketable securities, and current receivables to current liabilities)
Days sales in receivables
Days sales in inventory
Net working capital
Total asset turnover
Interest coverage
Debt to (debt plus equity)
Gross margin percentage [(sales minus cost of sales)/sales]
Earnings as percent of sales

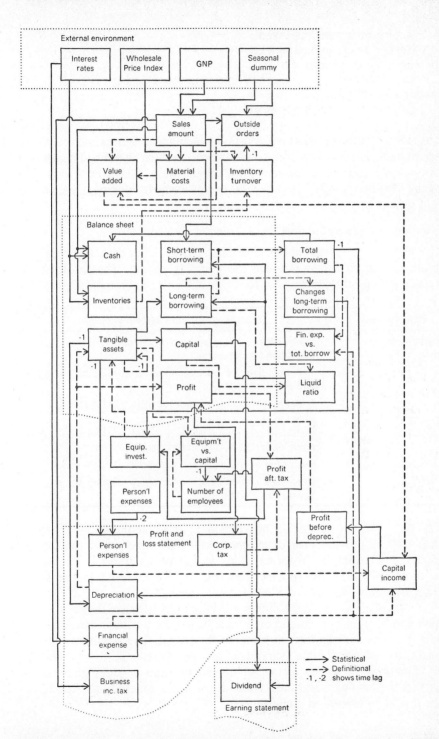

Figure 13-1 A financial forecasting model. (*M. Aiso, "Forecasting Technique,"* IBM Systems Journal, *vol. 12, no. 2, 1973, p. 206. Reprinted by permission from the* IBM Systems Journal. *Copyright 1973 by International Business Machines Corporation.*)

Return on assets employed
Return on common stock equity
Earnings per share
Expected value of a share of common stock (using expected price earnings multiple)
Growth in earnings per share

There is a relation between many individual financial figures and return on investment that is considered to be one of the most significant measures of overall performance for a business organization. It is often referred to as the "Du Pont model" because it received early development and use in that organization; it is shown in Figure 13-2.

Information System Support for Planning

The planning process requires a planning model, input data, and manipulation of the model to produce the planning output. The information system should provide support for each of these requirements.

Requirement	Typical information system support
Planning model	Analytical support in developing the structure and the equations for the model
	Historical data for use in analyses to develop estimating and planning relations
	A planning model generator for writing the model to run on a computer
Input data	Historical data plus analysis and data manipulation to generate input data based on the historical data
Manipulation of the model	Use of the computer to run a computer-based model
	Other data manipulation based on forecasting and extrapolation techniques

The information system provides data and computational capabilities. Data is provided for developing both the model and input to the model. For example, historical sales would be analyzed for seasonal patterns to use in the model; they would also be used in the sales forecasting algorithm to estimate future sales.

The manipulative capabilities are important because they allow the model to be used in a simulation mode. "What if" questions can be posed and the answers obtained by running the model. The sensitivity of the result to different input variables can be examined. A number of combinations of values for variables can be used in judgmental, trial-and-error planning iterations. These capabilities generally depend upon the model being run on a computer.

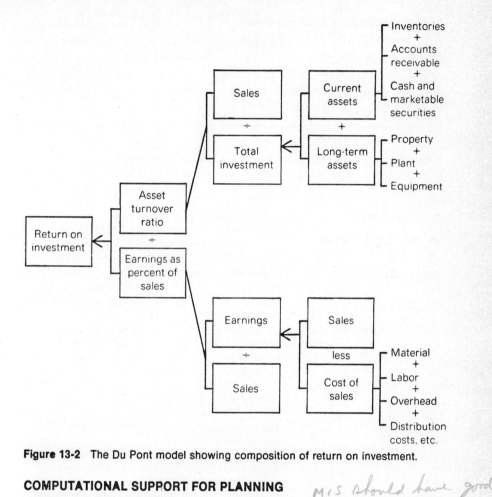

Figure 13-2   The Du Pont model showing composition of return on investment.

COMPUTATIONAL SUPPORT FOR PLANNING

MIS should have good stat package for data analysis

Planning requires the analysis of historical data to discover relations that are expected to continue in the future. By use of relations derived from analysis of historical data or relations postulated by the planner, estimates may be developed for future values of the organizational variables. The information system should provide support for the historical data analysis and the forecasting of future values of data.[1] Financial planning also requires computational support for calculating the various measures related to profitability. This section surveys the techniques that support the analysis of data, forecasting the data, and financial analysis.

[1]For amplification of material in this section, see B. P. Dzielinski, "A Guide to Financial Planning Tools and Techniques," *IBM Systems Journal*, vol. 12, no. 2, 1973, pp. 126–144.

Historical Data Analysis Techniques

Historical data is analyzed to discover patterns or relations that will be useful in projecting the future values of significant variables. Even when quantitative relations are not sufficiently stable to use in forecasting, data analysis is useful for input into the judgmental forecast. The major techniques are summarized below:

Data analysis techniques	Comments
Time trend or growth rate	Computation of rate of change or growth over a specified period. For example, IBM gross income grew at a rate of 19.1 percent during the years 1965 to 1969.
Data smoothing	Raw data generally contains random variations or other irregularities which make seeing the normal level difficult. Moving average techniques are used to smooth the irregularities.
Seasonal analysis	Economic activity varies with the time of year. For example, sales of turkeys are especially high in November and December. Seasonal analysis is used to obtain the seasonal pattern.
Correlation analysis	Correlation analysis is used to measure the relation among variables. For example, the relation of sales expense to sales can be computed using simple correlation. The relation between sales of a building material and such factors as gross national product, housing starts, and interest rates can be obtained from multiple correlation analysis.
Autocorrelation analysis	There are certain variables that have a time delay relation with each other. For example, sales of repair parts in period n is a function of the sales of new units in period n-1. Autocorrelation assists in discovering these relations.
Cross-correlation analysis	The relation between two sets of data is calculated by cross-correlation.
Data description and dispersion analysis	It is useful to understand data in terms of measures such as mean, median, mode, intervals, and standard deviations. For example, the analysis that identifies daily sales as being 100,000 units with a standard deviation of 12,000 units is useful in understanding the nature of the sales activity being planned. Among the techniques to be applied are histogram computation, measures of central tendency (mean, median, mode), and measures of dispersion (standard deviation).

The historical data analysis techniques are primarily statistical. The techniques are useful not only for planning but also for other analyses. The techniques can therefore be part of the general set of analysis software that is available for all uses.

Planning Data Generation Techniques

Historical data describes the past, but planning involves the future. Estimating is generally based on analysis of the past history, with various techniques being used to generate data for planning purposes. Some of the common techniques for developing planning data are:

Data generation techniques	Comments
Extrapolation of time series or growth rate	Time series and growth rates can be extrapolated from historical data analysis. If past growth rate has been 10 percent, the rate.is assumed to continue (unless modified by judgment).
Extrapolation based on regression analysis	Past patterns of activity obtained by regression analysis can be used if they are expected to continue. The patterns may be based on time as in a growth rate or on causal relations among data.
Interpolation	If historical data exists, but not for the values related to planning, the needed value can often be interpolated. If cost is known for 10,000 and 20,000 units, a cost can be interpolated for 13,000 units.
Formula or relation	Many planning figures are derived from computations on other figures. For example, sales returns may be computed as a percentage of gross sales. Sales for the month may be computed from yearly sales multiplied by the seasonal factor for the month.

There are additional techniques in forecasting that will not be described. Other techniques are available but are not often used. For example, it is possible to generate data using the "Monte Carlo" technique of random number generation, but this is a rather specialized technique most applicable to probabilistic models. Since most planning models are deterministic, the technique is not often used.

Financial Planning Computations

Models that involve financial plans need to provide for various computations and analyses commonly required for measuring or evaluating profitability. Examples are the depreciation computation, rate of return analysis, and breakeven analysis.

Depreciation is a significant computation in most financial planning. It affects profit computations because it is considered as an expense, and it affects cash flow indirectly because of its impact on taxes. There are several methods for computing depreciation, all of which should be available to the planner. These methods are straight-line, double-declining-balance, sum-of-the-years'-digits, and production or use basis.

Rate of return analysis is a method for computing the profitability of an investment, taking into account the timing of the investment and the cash flows stemming from the investment. There are several methods for computing rate of return. These should be a part of the information system support for planning.

Breakeven analysis is a fairly simple but very useful computation for determining the volume of activity at which there is no loss or profit. In evaluating alternatives, two situations may have identical expected profit, but the one with a lower breakeven point is to be preferred (all other factors being equal).

PLANNING MODEL GENERATORS
FOR COMPUTER-ASSISTED PLANNING

The preparation and testing of organizational plans can be aided by the use of a computer-based planning model generator. With this approach, it is not necessary to write a new computer program for every new planning situation; the computer programs for computer-assisted planning are generated from planning language statements. This application of technology substantially reduces the cost of using the computer in planning.

Characteristics of Planning Model Generators

The planning model generator system consists of three parts:

1 The planning language for coding the planning model
2 The instructions for using the language to describe a planning situation, for inserting input, and for interpreting the output
3 The computer software to generate the computer programs which perform the processing in developing the plans

The planning model generator approach may be implemented in both periodic batch and interactive online mode. Software is available for both modes of operation. The interactive model will generally use time sharing. There are advantages to interactive processing because it is supportive of the iterative trial-and-error planning processes.

The form of the planning language for describing the planning situation will depend somewhat on the design methodology used. A number of different generators are available from computer manufactures, software vendors, and time-sharing services. There are essentially two different approaches to the language itself.

1 *User codes primarily in a common algebraic programming language such as* FORTRAN, BASIC, *or* PL/I. Special macro instructions and subroutine calls assist the user in specialized tasks such as coding report formats.

2 *User codes in a report-writer format.* Each line is defined by a line number plus a description of the variables which are part of the report line.

A small number of planning model generators have a special planning language which is not part of an algebraic language, but these two methods are the most common.

The output from a computer planning model will generally be a report format showing, for example, the planned results for several periods into the future. The systems also generally provide graphic portrayal of a variable. For example, a financial projection may have planned financial statements for five years into the future; a graphic output might plot actual profit for the past five years and planned profit for the next five years. Illustrative outputs are shown in Figure 13-3.

As an illustration of the capabilities of planning model generators, a description of the capabilities of one of the systems available from IBM is shown in Figure 13-4. Note the list of techniques supported by the system. The illustrated product calls for the user to code the planning model logic in FORTRAN.

Selection and Use of a Planning Model Generator

A fundamental question is whether a planning situation justifies a computer-assisted approach. A manual approach may be satisfactory and more cost/effective. The conditions that suggest the need for a computer modeling approach are:

1 Complex manipulation of data
2 Large volumes of data to be analyzed
3 Several iterations before a plan is accepted
4 Frequent replanning

The ability to ask "what if" questions and quickly see the consequences of changes in planning variables is perhaps the most important advantage of the computer modeling approach. Once the model is available, the cost

```
6
10 SALES (174.6) = 110% * CURRENT COLUMN - 1
15 FIXED ASSETS (500) = 102% * CURRENT COLUMN - 1
20 'COSTS
30   LABOR = IF SALES < 200, THEN 25, ELSE 17%* SALES
40   RAW MATERIALS = 27%*SALES
50   OTHER COSTS = 16%*SALES
55   DEPRECIATION = 4.2% * FIXED ASSETS
60   GENERAL MFG. BURDEN = 2.7% * SALES
70    TOTAL COSTS = SUM LINE 30 THRU LINE 60
80 GROSS PROFIT = SALES - TOTAL COSTS
90 GENERAL ADMIN. EXPENSE = 16.7
110 INTEREST,12.0,10.0,8.2,7.5
120 SELLING EXPENSES = 14.5% * SALES
130 NET PROFIT BEFORE TAXES = LINE 80 - SUM OF LINE 90 THRU LINE 120
140 INCOME TAX = 52% * NET PROFIT BEFORE TAXES, MINIMUM 0
150 NET PROFIT = NET PROFIT BEFORE TAXES - INCOME TAX
160 PER CENT OF SALES = 100 * NET PROFIT / SALES
COLUMN 5 = IF LINE 160, THEN 0, ELSE SUM COLUMN 1 THRU COLUMN 4
COLUMN 6 =  IF LINE 15, THEN 0, ELSE 100 * COLUMN 5 / COLUMN 5 LINE 10
REPORT 1
1
ALL
ALL
```

                          ABC MANUFACTURING COMPANY
                         PROJECTED INCOME STATEMENT
                               (IN MILLIONS)
       &R
                         FIRST   SECOND   THIRD   FOURTH   % OF
                         QUARTER QUARTER QUARTER QUARTER TOTAL   SALES
       &R
       XXXXXXXXXXXXXXXXXXXXXXXXX   XXXX.X   XXXX.X   XXXX.X   XXXX.X   XXXX.X   XXXXXX&R

                          ABC MANUFACTURING COMPANY
                         PROJECTED INCOME STATEMENT
                               (IN MILLIONS)

	FIRST QUARTER	SECOND QUARTER	THIRD QUARTER	FOURTH QUARTER	TOTAL	% OF SALES
SALES	174.6	192.1	211.3	232.4	810.3	100%
FIXED ASSETS	500.0	510.0	520.2	530.6	2060.8	0%
COSTS						
LABOR	25.0	25.0	35.9	39.5	125.4	15%
RAW MATERIALS	47.1	51.9	57.0	62.7	218.8	27%
OTHER COSTS	27.9	30.7	33.8	37.2	129.7	16%
DEPRECIATION	21.0	21.4	21.8	22.3	86.6	11%
GENERAL MFG. BURDEN	4.7	5.2	5.7	6.3	21.9	3%
TOTAL COSTS	125.8	134.2	154.3	168.0	582.3	72%
GROSS PROFIT	48.8	57.9	57.0	64.4	228.0	28%
GENERAL ADMIN. EXPENSE	16.7	16.7	16.7	16.7	66.8	8%
INTEREST	12.0	10.0	8.2	7.5	37.7	5%
SELLING EXPENSES	25.3	27.8	30.6	33.7	117.5	15%
NET PROFIT BEFORE TAXES	-5.2	3.3	1.4	6.5	6.0	1%
INCOME TAX	0.0	1.7	.7	3.4	5.8	1%
NET PROFIT	-5.2	1.6	.7	3.1	.2	0%
PER CENT OF SALES	-3.0	.8	.3	1.3	0.0	0%

Figure 13-3 Sample definition statements and output from computer-generated planning model. [BPL (Business Planning Language) from International Timesharing Corporation.]

of planning iterations is small. Sensitivity analysis to discover how sensitive the results are to changes in the planning variables can be easily performed. Questions can be posed to ascertain what inputs will be required to obtain a specified output; e.g., what level of sales will be required to achieve a profit of $100,000? If there is frequent replanning, the computer model reduces the time required to generate new plans.

The next question is "make or buy," i.e., to design and code a unique

DESCRIPTION OF PLANNING SYSTEM GENERATOR II (PSG II)

Program product from IBM

Mode of operation: batch

Description:

PSG II provides the means to produce and evaluate a variety of financial plans. The user builds financial models within the framework of PSG II. Methods are provided for organizing planning data, for establishing computational logic to be applied to the data, and for generating data displays and reports. The user writes the logic in FORTRAN and, to aid in the development of models, he can use the PSG II library of planning functions to perform certain commonly used calculations. Using the PSG II print specifications, the planner can have input worksheets, single- and double-column reports, and three types of charts produced to display selected data. Transfer of planning data from one model to another and consolidation of the results of detail models into more comprehensive models are additional facilities provided. Financial techniques include:

Simple and compound growth rates
Marginal analysis calculation between the increments of two data lines
Extrapolation using continuation, simple, or yearly growth rate methods
Extrapolation of a previous result given the growth amounts and/or the growth rate for the forecasted periods
Interpolation using linear, sum-of-the-years'-digits, or compound growth rate methods
Depreciation of assets (straight-line, sum-of-the-years'-digits, and double-declining-balance methods)
Average production cost as a function of the volume of production
Discounted cash-flow calculation using the internal rate-of-return methods
Ratios and percentages
Spreading a value into partial amounts by a specific distribution pattern
Year-to-date accumulation
Retirement of assets
Tax carry-forward and carry-back calculation

Figure 13-4 Example of capabilities of a planning model generator—IBM's PSG II (Planning Systems Generator II). *(B. P. Dzielinski, "A Guide to Financial Planning Tools and Techniques," IBM Systems Journal, vol. 12, no. 2, 1973, p. 143.)*

model or purchase access to software for generating a model. Except for unusual situations, both economic and performance considerations suggest the desirability of obtaining a planning model generator instead of trying to "make" a model.

The following are some considerations in selecting a planning model generator to include in the management information system planning subsystem:

1 *Source of the planning model generator.* Software systems are available from computer manufacturers such as IBM, software vendors, planning consultants, and time-sharing services. The time-sharing services generally offer systems in connection with the use of their time-sharing service.

2 *Batch or interactive processing.* As described earlier, there are advantages to each. Both can be supported by software. From the standpoint of the planning process, the interactive system is generally to be preferred.

3 *Scope, level, and frequency of use.* The planning system should be suited to the uses contemplated for it. Simple uses need only a simple system; complex planning chould have a more complex generator. The language should also allow for some growth in complexity of applications.

4 *Ease of use.* A system may be technically elegant but too complex for users, whose support is a consideration. Either the vendor or the in-house staff should be able to provide training in modeling with the system.

The typical steps in using a planning model generator illustrate this element of information system support. The use of the planning model generator is triggered by a management need for planning—a budget, a special analysis, etc. The actual user of the generator system may be the manager, or it may be a planning analyst assigned to the problem. The use of the system might proceed as follows:

1 The output report is defined by use of the language provided.
2 Supporting schedules are defined by use of the language.
3 The variables on the report and the various schedules are defined by statements. The statements can indicate:
  a Variable will be input data.
  b Variable is to be computed, e.g., RETURNS = .015 * SALES.
  c Variable is to be projected from input data, e.g., extend past sales trend.
4 Input data is prepared.
5 The model is run with a base case which is then used as a basis for checking the validity of the model.

6 The model is run, input data changed, and perhaps variable relations changed, until the planners feel a satisfactory plan has been obtained.

The steps in development suggest the possibility of starting with a fairly gross model and refining it as the need arises. This is often accomplished by starting with certain variables as input data or simple formula and later adding supporting schedules to develop them in the model. For example, a first edition of a financial model may define cost of sales as 60 percent of the sales dollars. This is a very gross assumption which is useful only at a very high level modeling effort. However, it allows the model to be completed and run. Later, a supporting schedule can be added to compute cost of sales based on a more complete set of underlying cost factors. In this sense, a model is never complete. The output documentation provided or required by the planning model generator should be sufficient that assumptions are apparent to users of the output.The documentation of the model should be sufficient to allow another analyst who did not built it to modify the model.

ORGANIZATIONAL CONTROL PROCESS

Control consists of activities that cause events and activities to conform to plans. There are requirements for control by each of the functions in an organization. Examples are:

Financial control
Production control
Materials control
Distribution control
Personnel control

Each of these areas utilizes control reports and control activities.

Nature of Control in Organizations

The control process requires measurement of performance and a standard of performance. Measurement is basic to human experience; we think, move, and act in terms of measured amounts of time, distance, and value. Performance is expressed as measured units of input, activity, and output. Management must evaluate performance, but evaluation implies that the planning and control authority knows what is acceptable and what is not. It requires a standard against which an object, activity, or result may be placed to decide whether it is satisfactory. Are oranges at 23 cents per pound expensive? The answer is dependent on having a standard of customary price for oranges. The standard may be vague or precise, written or not written, but for evaluation to take place there must be a standard.

For control purposes, the standard can be a budget or plan that was previously arrived at following due consideration of all the alternatives and surrounding conditions. The planned performance is usually the best to be expected rather than what is desired. A loss may be budgeted by a business. If the actual loss is the same as the budgeted loss, the performance must be evaluated as acceptable. In other words, it is the deviation from the budget or plan that calls for corrective action. Performance is acceptable as long as it does not deviate in an unfavorable direction from the plan, assuming the plan is a correct expression of what should be expected. The information system support for control is therefore based on the comparison of actual performance with the plan and the analysis of reasons for any deviations (Figure 13-5).

The control report issued to management presents a comparison of actual performance with planned performance. The use of the term "control" to refer to such a report does not refer to the performance being reported; the activity presented has already taken place. It is no longer subject to control. An activity can be controlled before it takes place or while it is taking place, but it cannot be controlled after it has been completed. Insofar as a report summarizes past activity it is an evaluation report. Only if the report of past performance is the basis for control of future action may it be considered to be a control report. Interpretive

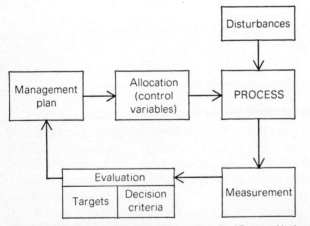

Figure 13-5 The management control cycle. (*Bartow Hodge and Robert N. Hodgson, Management and the Computor in Information and Control Systems, McGraw-Hill Book Company, New York, 1969, p. 116.*)

comments are used by most concerns on their control reports to explain deviations from the planned or budget standard.

The acceptance of an unfavorable variation between planned and actual performance as a basis for corrective action implies that personnel connected with the activity being evaluated regard the standard or plan as being fair. Experiments indicate that individuals reject standards that are too easy or too hard. The acceptance of goals and their use as a motivator (and as a basis for satisfaction, if achieved) are enhanced by their being set within the limits that the individuals involved consider feasible. Therefore it is considered desirable for the individuals themselves to participate in setting the budget or standard by which they may judge themselves and by which they know they will be judged by others.

There are essentially three approaches to the short-term organizational plan (say, the budget or profit plan for the year). Each approach has implications for control.

1   *Single-forecast plan.* The plans are based on a single, estimated level of performance. It is useful for planning, but it is less useful for control unless the forecast can be made with some precision. If the actual activity and expenditures deviate markedly from the forecast, its usefulness as a control guide is impaired.

2   *Appropriation plan.* The various plans for objects of expenditures are in the amount that may be spent for each. It is sometimes used as an authorization to spend up to the stated amount. An appropriation plan budget is indicated where the expenditures are relatively independent of activity and where expenditures are difficult to evaluate in terms of a specific measurement. Examples are found in the advertising and personnel departments.

3   *Flexible-activity plan.* The plan shows relations and is therefore applicable to any performance level. Using the model of relations, expected performance can be computed for the exact activity level being experienced. The control of the plan is enhanced because the plan is easily adapted to changed conditions.

All three approaches may be used in planning. The flexible-activity plan may be used for control during the current period; the single-forecast plan may serve as an overall planning guide for the expected level of performance. The forecast-type budget is used for project budgets or subbudgets in cases when levels of expenditure are not related to changes in activity.

The analysis of differences between what is planned and what is actual is called "variance analysis." There are essentially two types of expense variances that explain the difference between planned and actual performance. Variances can be favorable or unfavorable.

Variance	Explanation of unfavorable variance
Price variance	Resources cost more than planned. Example: Resin cost $1.03 per pound instead of the standard of 99 cents per pound.
Usage variance	More resource was used (per unit of activity) than planned. Example: Material usage was 1.8 pounds of resin instead of 1.7 pounds per unit produced.

The price and usage variances apply to both materials and labor. The overhead variance can be also described as usage (volume) and price (spending), but some accountants use a third type which explains the variance due to the interaction of volume and price.

Information System Support for Control

The information system support for control begins with the planning model. This same model can generally be used to set revised standards of performance which consider the changed level of activity. These revised standards are necessary for control. The computational support for control reports includes variance analysis plus other analyses which might assist in understanding both the reasons for variances and also the courses of action that will correct future performance.

Another use of information system support in control is continuous monitoring of performance rather than just periodic reporting. The monitoring makes use of the planning model plus the concept of control limits to track performance. When the performance falls outside the control limits, a message is provided to the proper control unit. The control limits are set so that random variations do not trigger control actions. The concept may be visualized by a control chart showing one process in control, even though it has random variations, and a second process that has gotten out of control (Figure 13-6).

SUMMARY

Planning sets the course of action an organization will take; control causes events and activities to conform to the plans. The planning process requires future expectations to be quantified and classified. A planning model is prepared as a method of structuring, manipulating, and communicating expectations and plans. Although a budget model can be prepared with manual worksheets, the coding of the model for computer processing expands its usefulness. Computational support for the planning process consists of historical data analysis techniques, planning data generation techniques, and financial planning computations.

The preparation and testing of organizational plans can be aided by

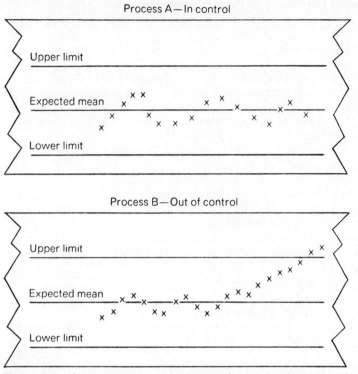

Figure 13-6   Control charts to illustrate use of control limits and continuous monitoring.

the use of a computer-based planning model generator. The generator consists of a language for writing modeling statements and report specifications, instructions for use, and computer software to generate and execute the model. The control process utilizes the planning model to generate the performance standard. Variances are then computed as a basis for understanding why deviations have occurred and what should be done to bring the process back into acceptable limits. An advantage of computer-based information systems is the capability to monitor performance continuously rather than periodically.

EXERCISES

1 Explain why exception reporting is similar to the concept of a feedback loop. See Chapter 4 for discussion of feedback loops.
2 Describe the basic elements of control.

3   What are the factors that influence the reliability of planning data?
4   Explain the reasons why a profit plan might classify expenditures by:
    a   Function.
    b   Organizational unit.
    c   Cost variability.
5   Describe the information system support for planning and control.
6   Explain the usefulness of each of the historical data analysis techniques.
7   Explain the importance of depreciation in financial modeling.
8   Explain the relation of asset turnover to earnings as a percentage of sales.
    (Hint: See the Du Pont model in Figure 13-2.)
9   What are the elements which make up a planning model generator?
10 Evaluate the advantages of interactive planning versus batch planning
    models. What characteristics suggest one or the other?
11 Using the simple model described in this chapter,
    a   Prepare manually a profit for 1975, 1976, 1977, and 1978 with the following
        input variables (all in thousands):

Variable	1975	1976	1977	1978
Sales	110	120	130	150
Average long-term debt	100	100	100	100
Average short-term debt	10	15	10	20
Accounts receivable at beginning of period	30	35	35	40
Administrative expense	40	45	45	55

    b   Program the model on a computer. Run the model for the base case
        computed manually. Then vary factors in the model such as the following:
        Sales of 105, 115, 125, and 135
        Selling expense 15 percent of sales
12 This question is adapted from Paul D. Payollat.[2] Not only does a hospital
    need financial planning for its own financial management, it has federal and
    state requirements for medium-term and short-term budgets. Given the
    following data and relations,
    a   Prepare the financial plan manually.
    b   Prepare and validate a model on a computer.

Revenues	
Daily hospital services	Occupied beds × billing rate
Ancillary	Ancillary procedures × billing rate
Outpatient revenue	Outpatient visits × billing rate
Total revenue	Daily hospital service through outpatient revenue
Deductions	5% of total revenue
Net revenue	Total revenue less deductions

[2]Paul D. Payollat, "HOSPLAN: A Financial Model for Hospitals," *The Arthur Young Journal,* Winter 1972, pp. 1–9.

Expenses	
Salaries	6,000 fixed + .50 × occupied beds
Benefits	12% of salaries
Supplies	200 fixed + 8% of total revenue
Fees	2,150 fixed
Depreciation	1,000 fixed
Total expenses	All the above plus interest
Net income	Net revenue less total expenses

Input data					
	Period 1	Period 2	Period 3	Period 4	Period 5
Beds	360	440	440	440	440
Daily occupancy, %	83	84	82	80	81
Ancillary procedures	300	350	400	450	500
Outpatient visits	8,000	8,000	8,000	8,000	9,000
Daily rate, $	76	77	78	79	80
Ancillary rate, $	31	32	33	34	35
Outpatient rate, $	15	17	19	20	22
Interest	600	550	500	450	400

SELECTED REFERENCES

Ackoff, R. L.: *The Concept of Corporate Planning*, John Wiley & Sons, New York, 1970.

Aiso, M.: "Forecasting Techniques," *IBM Systems Journal*, vol. 12, no. 2, 1973, pp. 187–209.

Argyris, Chris: "Human Problems with Budgets," *Harvard Business Review*, January-February 1953, pp. 97–110.

Benton, William K.: *The Use of the Computer in Planning*, Addison-Wesley Publishing Company, Inc., Reading, Mass., 1971.

Bonini, C. P., R. K. Jaedicke, and H. M. Wagner (eds.): *Management Controls: New Directions in Basic Research*, McGraw-Hill Book Company, New York, 1964.

Boulden, J. B., and E. S. Buffa: "Corporate Models: On-Line, Real-Time Systems," Harvard Business Review, July-August 1970, pp. 65–83.

Comisky, E. E.: "Cost Control by Regression Analysis," *Accounting Review*, April 1966, pp. 235–238.

Dzielinski, B. P.: "A Guide to Financial Planning Tools and Techniques," *IBM Systems Journal*, vol. 12, no. 2, 1973, pp. 126–144.

Emery, James C.: *Organizational Planning and Control Systems*, The Macmillan Company, New York, 1969.

Emshoff, J. R., and R. L. Sisson: *Design and Use of Computer Simulation Models*, The Macmillan Company, 1970.

Gershefski, George W.: "Building a Corporate Financial Model," *Harvard Business Review*, July-August 1969, pp. 61–72.

————: "The Development and Application of a Corporate Financial Model," *Management Science*, February 1970, pp. B303–B312.

Hodge, Bartow, and Robert N. Hodgson: *Management and the Computer in Information and Control Systems*, McGraw-Hill Book Company, New York, 1969.

IBM Systems Journal, International Business Machines Corporation, vol. 12, no. 2, 1973. Entire issue is devoted to computer-based planning models.

Ijiri, Y.: *Management Goals and Accounting for Control*, North-Holland Publishing Company, Amsterdam, 1965.

Jensen, R. E.: "A Multiple Regression Model for Cost Control—Assumptions and Limitations," *Accounting Review*, April 1967, pp. 265–273.

Jones, C. H.: "At Last: Real Computer Power for Decision Makers," *Harvard Business Review*, September-October 1970, pp. 75–89.

Kingston, P. L.: "Concepts of Financial Models," *IBM Systems Journal*, vol. 12, no. 2, 1973, pp. 113–125.

Kotler, Philip: "Corporate Models: Better Marketing Plans," *Harvard Business Review*, July-August 1970.

Lande, H. F.: "Planning Data Systems," *IBM Systems Journal*, vol. 12, no. 2, 1973, pp. 145–160.

Lewin, Kurt, Tamara Dembo, Leon Festinger, and Pauline Snedden Sears: "Levels of Aspiration," in J. McVee Hunt (ed.), *Personality and Behavior Disorders*, The Ronald Press Company, New York, 1944, pp. 333–337.

Malcolm, D. G., and A. J. Rowe: "An Approach to Computer-based Management Control Systems," *California Management Review*, vol. 3, no. 3, 1961, pp. 4–15.

———, ——— (eds.): *Management Control Systems*, John Wiley & Sons, Inc., New York, 1960.

Platt, W. J., and N. R. Maines: "Pretest Your Long-Range Plans," *Harvard Business Review*, January-February 1959.

Sackman, Harold, and Ronald L. Citrenbaum (eds.): *Online Planning*, Prentice-Hall, Inc., Englewood Cliffs, N.J., 1972.

Schrieber, Albert N. (ed.): *Corporate Simulation Models*, University of Washington Press, Seattle, 1972.

Scott Morton, M., and A. M. McCosh: "Terminal Costing for Better Decisions," *Harvard Business Review*, May-June 1968.

Strassman, Paul A.: "Forecasting Considerations in Design of Management Information Systems," *Management Accounting*, February 1965, pp. 27–40.

Tocher, K. D.: *The Art of Simulation*, D. Van Nostrand Company, Inc., Princeton, N.J., 1963.

Chapter number and title	Notes on content
14 Organization and Management of Information Systems	Describes the organizational structure for information systems and explores centralization and decentralization questions. Explains management planning and control of information system development, projects, and costs.
15 The Development of a Management Information System	Explains alternative approaches to both overall planning and to determination of information requirements for an application. Surveys the development life cycle, technology used in development, and human factors in development and design.
16 Evaluation of Information Systems	Describes the various levels of evaluation and the methods and approaches used.
17 Current Issues, Societal Implications, and Future Developments	Surveys current issues and future developments with emphasis on societal implications.

MIS Development and Management

Section 1 explained concepts which underlie information system design; Section 2 described the structure of a management-oriented information system; Section 3 will explain the organization, management, development, and evaluation of information systems. There are various alternatives in organization, management, and development; these will be discussed. The final chapter in this section focuses on the societal implication of information systems and the future developments in the field. The four chapters are listed on the facing page together with a short description of the content of each.

Chapter 14

Organization
and Management
of Information Systems

This chapter surveys the organization and management of information systems with emphasis on organizational issues and the processes by which management exercises controls over information system development, individual projects, and information system costs. Information system organization frequently involves difficult decisions because technological factors related to hardware and software efficiency suggest organizational forms that may be at variance with the organization and its management philosophy. Management of the information system has special problems because of the rapid rate of change in hardware and software technology and because of the need for some technical competence in order to evaluate MIS proposals. The chapter introduces issues related to these organization and management problems and presents approaches that are being used by organizations in handling the issues.

INFORMATION SYSTEMS ORGANIZATION

The development and operation of computer-based information systems involves several functions. The job position for each function will be described briefly. There are alternative approaches to an organizational structure to direct these information systems personnel, and these alternatives are explored. In an organization there are several alternatives with respect to centralization or decentralization of information systems effort. This problem is discussed in the next section.

Position Descriptions for Information Systems

It is customary to identify four major positions in computer-based information system organizations:

Position	Description
Systems analyst	Defines requirements for applications. Designs processing system to meet requirements. Prepares procedures and user instructions.
Programmer	Designs, codes, tests, and debugs computer programs.
Operator	Performs operating functions such as operating equipment.
Data preparation (keypunch personnel)	Prepares data in machine-readable form.

As information systems have grown in size and complexity, these basic functions have been subdivided into further specialities. Some of the major functions which now exist or are beginning to emerge are the following (Figure 14-1):

Position	Description
Information analyst	Works with users to define information requirements. Develops user procedures and instructions. Has understanding of organizations, management, and decision-making functions in an organization. Has an ability to work with people.
System designer	Designs computer-based processing system to provide the information specified by the information analyst. Requires higher technical capability than information analysis. May specialize in area such as data communications.
Systems programmer	Writes specialized software such as

Position	Description
	operating systems and data management systems. Technical proficiency in hardware and software.
Application programmer	Designs, codes, tests, and debugs computer programs for applications. Some installations separate programming into commercial or business applications and scientific applications with separate programming groups for the two types.
Maintenance programmer	Works on the maintenance (changes and corrections) of existing programs.
Data base administrator	Administers and controls the corporate data base.
Computer operator	Operates the computer equipment.
Librarian	Stores and issues the computer files on tapes and disks. Files documentation. Maintains record of usage.
Control clerk (also called input/output control clerk)	Records control information and reviews performance of control procedures.
Information systems planner	Plans the future of the information system.

The division of systems analyst into information analyst and system designer is an emerging one based on an awareness that systems analysis involves two quite separate functions, one being the analysis of information requirements and the other the design of the processing system to achieve the requirements.[1] However, some organizations combine the position of programmer and analyst into a single one of programmer/analyst. The rationale is that this provides more continuity on a job and allows each person to develop both his technical and people-oriented skills. Since many of the problems of application development are with communication, the involvement of the same person in information analysis, system design, and programming reduces these problems.

The diversity of information system functions suggests that the same type of person may not be suitable for all positions. For example, it appears that successful systems analysts have job aptitudes and personality traits different from those of successful programmers. The informa-

---

[1] D. Teichroew (ed.), "Education Related to the Use of Computers in Organizations," *Communications of the ACM*, September 1971, pp. 573–588.

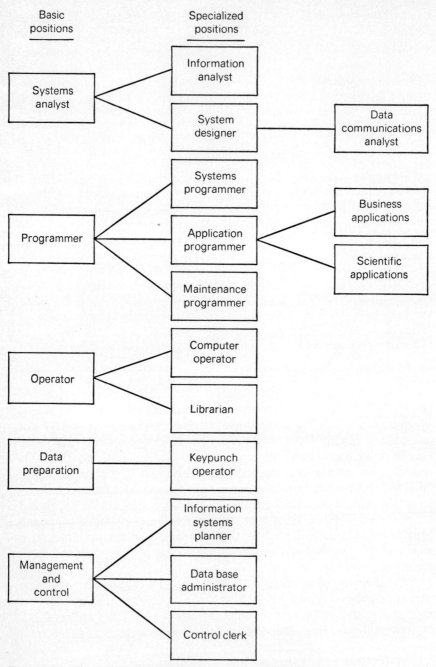

Figure 14-1 Computer-based information processing positions.

tion analysts communicate with users, and they must be able to identify user problems and organizational issues. The successful programmer, on the other hand, must be able to think in terms of the logic of computer procedures and be able to code, test, and document these procedures effectively. One study has characterized the programmer as having a personality which "avoids confrontation, avoids being directed, is willing to do without much social interaction on his job, . . . and has no apparent desire to enter into the aggressive, competitive, confrontation-laden situation associated with line management."[2] In a study of items which provide job satisfaction to data processing personnel, Willoughby[3] found that needs and interests vary for different processing jobs. The differences in aptitudes and factors for job satisfaction for the different information systems personnel suggest the need for different career paths. Some organizations provide two paths—one for employees who become systems analysts and advance through various stages of systems analysis and information analysis and another separate career path for personnel who are more interested in programming. The programming career path begins with applications and advances to systems programming or other specialized programming. Managers can be selected from both of these paths, although it appears that the more people-oriented outlook of systems analysts is more compatible with a management position.

Computer managers who have come through a technical career path tend to be able to supervise technical employees very well but tend to have difficulty in managerial duties such as handling personnel problems and making policy. Computer managers who have come from other disciplines, such as accounting, and have not had considerable technical work tend to be better at the managerial aspects and cost control but to have difficulty in supervising technical personnel.[4]

Organizational Structure

Several organization formats may be used. The most common are the functional organization (Figure 14-2) and the project organization. In the functional organization, the programmers are supervised by a programming manager, and the systems analysts are supervised by a systems analyst manager. Work completed by information systems analysis is

---

[2]Milt Stone, "The Quality of Life," *Datamation*, January 1972, p. 42.

[3]Theodore C. Willoughby, "Needs, Interests, Reinforcer Patterns, and Satisfaction of Data Processing Personnel," unpublished Ph.D. thesis, University of Minnesota, Minneapolis, 1970.

[4]F. Warren McFarland, Richard L. Nolan, and David P. Norton, *Information Systems Administration*, Holt, Rinehart and Winston, Inc., New York, 1973, p. 340.

The functional organization

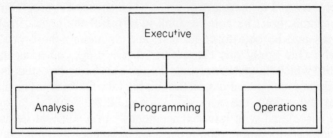

Project organization for new applications

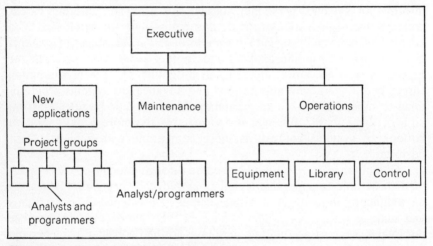

Figure 14-2 The basic organizational patterns.

turned over to the programming group. The advantages are the specialization that can be obtained and the flexibility in training and supervision. In the project organization, each project has a project leader and is provided with analysts and programmers who work together to complete the project. The advantages are the reduction of communication difficulties and the focusing of responsibility on a single group. There can be no shifting of responsibility to another group under a different manager.

The organization charts show an executive over the information system organization. This executive reports to someone else in the company. In a 1967 Booz, Allen & Hamilton study[5] of 108 manufacturing

[5]Neil J. Dean, "Computer Comes of Age," *Harvard Business Review*, January-February, 1968.

companies, 97 companies had established a top computer (information system) executive position. Of these, 35 percent reported to the controller, 19 percent to the vice-president of finance, 12 percent to the president, and 12 percent to the executive or senior vice-president. Stated in another way, 58 percent reported to some financial executive, 24 percent reported to the top executive, and 18 percent reported to the vice-president of a function other than finance or accounting. The top computer executive was not necessarily at the operations level. He may himself not directly supervise a computer. This was the case in half of the companies surveyed. He was likely to also have other activities such as operations research (50 percent of companies have this function reporting to the top computer executive). In a large percentage of the cases he was responsible for standardization, supervision of all computer activities in the organization, and approval of system development plans. There appears to be a trend toward higher-level executive status for the information system executive. This would be consistent with the movement toward a comprehensive MIS.

CENTRALIZATION VERSUS DECENTRALIZATION OF INFORMATION SYSTEMS

The issue of centralization has been active since the beginning of computer use for information processing.[6] In the days of first-generation computers (1955–1960) the power of the computer relative to prior manual processes coupled with the very expensive support requirements prompted many people to suggest that centralization of data processing was desirable. Some companies began to implement centralization, but second-generation computers (1960–1965) were smaller in size, and the result was a tendency to allow divisions or other subdivisions of an organization to have their own computers, each developing its own applications in its own way. The hardware costs decreased over this period so that the prior argument about the need for centralization to achieve hardware economies seemed less relevant. On the other hand, independent development of applications by many different divisions within a company was redundant and costly. Third-generation equipment beginning in 1965 emphasized communications capabilities and the use of remote terminals, remote batch input devices, etc. The centralization issue was then again raised because the hardware capability for centralization was found to be available. Also, economies of scale for a single, large system using standard software were found to be very high. The

---

[6]For a rather complete survey of the centralization issues, see McFarlan, Nolan, and Norton, op. cit., chap. 12, pp. 485–519.

idea of the corporate data base also gave impetus to the centralization issues. There are now hardware trends which are again supportive of decentralization. The issue is therefore a continuing point of discussion.

Alternative Patterns of Centralization/Decentralization

An organization can implement various combinations of centralization and decentralization (Figure 14-3). Five major strategies are identified:

    1 Central control of all electronic data processing (EDP) functions

    2 Central advisory function with all the information processing development and operations remaining in the subunits

    3 Central control of hardware and hardware operations with decentralized system development and programming

    4 Central control of all EDP hardware, operations, and programming, with only systems development being decentralized

    5 Central control of planning, analysis, and programming, with decentralization of hardware

It is possible to have a mixed strategy with both centralized and decentralized facilities. This is "distributed computing" (explored in Chapter 9) in which there is both central and decentralization hardware. The decentralized hardware performs independent processing and also transmits to the central facility for those jobs which are processed centrally.

Criteria for the Centralization/Decentralization Decision

The factors which are supportive of centralization and decentralization are summarized below:

Supportive of centralization	Supportive of decentralization
1 Economies of scale, especially hardware but also personnel	1 Improved service through responsiveness to location conditions (or lack of responsiveness by centralized system)
2 Savings from elimination of duplicate system development	2 Company policy of decentralization in management
3 Advantages from standardization	3 Lack of commonality among organizational units makes standard systems infeasible
4 Advantages from uniform system output	

The major determining factor affecting the centralization/decentral-

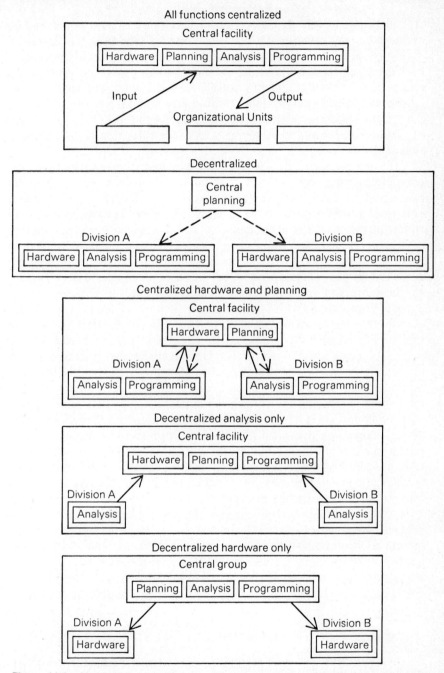

Figure 14-3 Alternative organizations with respect to centralization and decentralization.

ization pattern of information processing is the organizational philosophy of the company in which the system is used. Companies which have a policy of decentralization will tend to have decentralized processing systems, even though there may be diseconomies involved. Companies which have a strong tendency toward centralization will tend to have centralized information systems. Within this context, however, there are a number of alternative strategies. It is therefore useful to consider some of the advantages and disadvantages from centralization or decentralization of the various information system resources.

It was obvious very early in the development of computing that large computers had a cost advantage relative to smaller ones. A relation postulated by Herbert Grosch (now known as Grosch's law) is that a computer system performance in terms of speed is proportional to the square of the cost. Stated another way, the average cost per computation decreases as size increases. Some empirical studies have tended to support this assertion.[7] Not only do large-machine economies mean more computation per dollar expended, but software planning and development can be more sophisticated. There is an opportunity to achieve a large-enough group to provide specialization of various kinds. One study[8] showed that the average cost of all computer personnel decreases as the size of the installation increases. In other words, both hardware and personnel costs may be lower for large installations. The fact that a large-scale system is more cost effective for hardware and personnel than several smaller ones would suggest centralization of computing into one large-scale computing center with the largest machine that would handle computing needs. However, there are some counterarguments to this line of reasoning. The overhead associated with modern operating systems results in a law of diminishing returns with respect to large-scale systems. Communications costs increase as data is transferred from remote locations to a central processing location. In addition, the risk inherent in a single, large-scale facility are such that even if some economies do exist it is often desirable to have more than one computer and even to decentralize some of the hardware to avoid a failure which may disable the entire information processing capability of the organization. Recent hardware trends make the possibility of decentralization based on hardware more feasible than in the past. Minicomputers have become very cost/effective. These small machines make it possible to do many

[7]The studies are summarized in William F. Sharpe, *The Economics of Computers*, Columbia University Press, New York, 1969, pp. 314–322.

[8]Martin Solomon, "Economies of Scale and Computer Personnel," *Datamation*, March 1970, pp. 107–110.

computing jobs without much of the support such as air conditioning required by the large computers. Since many of the computing resources associated with a large computer are not required for many jobs, an organization can use a network of minicomputers for small, uncomplicated processing and transmit large jobs to a central, large-scale machine. This idea of distributed computing was discussed in Chapter 9.

The economies from an overall corporate plan are such that central planning becomes a necessity, no matter what the structure of centralization or decentralization. Such a planning group can, for example, look ahead to hardware requirements, plan for compatibility among the hardware at different locations, and plan various communication interfaces. Where there are decentralized locations, the planning group will presumably include representatives from each decentralized facility. It will have final authority to impose corporate-wide standards, methods, equipment selection procedures, equipment types, etc.

Systems analysis lends itself to decentralization because this is the group that interfaces most closely with the user. Locating the systems analysis personnel within the organizational divisions has the advantage of making the analysts responsive to the needs of the using group. They can design systems and interact with operating personnel much better than systems analysts coming in from outside groups. Managers tend to be more responsive to information processing if they have someone on their staff with whom they can work. Some offsetting disadvantages are the fact that systems analysis personnel who operate in decentralized units tend not to have the amount of cross-fertilization of ideas and the training and the variety of work that occur in a centralized group. Standards are also more difficult to enforce than when a centralized group is being used.

The centralized or decentralized location of programmers is perhaps not as significant to users as systems analysts, so some companies which have systems analysts in the divisions have a central programming group. Where programming is decentralized, company-wide programming standards are preferable to having each programmer or programming group establish a different set of standards.

MANAGEMENT PLANNING AND CONTROL OF INFORMATION SYSTEMS DEVELOPMENT

Management control of information systems development is exercised, typically, by setting of goals, approving specific plans, and measuring performance against budget. This control requires four major activities:

1 Overall planning and direction
2 Project planning and control
3 Cost control
4 Review and audit

Each of these topics is discussed in the chapter. The first, relating to top management responsibility for overall planning, is described in this section.

The value of planning and audit is well understood. For example, in 1968 McKinsey & Company, Inc., management consultants, conducted a study of computer systems in 36 major companies.[9] They assessed the computer-based information systems efforts and divided the companies into two groups: more successful and less successful. The results of this study are summarized below.

	More successful users	Less successful users
Companies that plan EDP activities and audit results against plan	9	3
Companies that plan EDP but do not audit results	7	3
Companies that neither plan EDP nor audit results	2	12

This study corroborates what has been reported by most observers in the field; that is, companies that plan achieve better results than companies that do not. The combination of planning and auditing of results appears to be the best approach. Even with a small sample the contrast between companies that plan and/or audit and companies that do not is striking. The planning activity occurs at the levels of the overall information system and of the project to develop an application. The overall planning activity results in the information system master development plan.

Formulating the Information System Master Development Plan

An information system is complex and therefore needs an overall or master development plan to guide its construction. The plan describes what the information system will consist of and how it is to be developed. Since all projects cannot be developed and implemented concurrently, priorities must be set. Information resources are scarce, as are all

[9]McKinsey & Company, Inc., "Unlocking the Computer's Profit Potential," *The McKinsey Quarterly*, Fall 1968, pp. 17–31.

resources in an organization. In a dynamic organization, there are more opportunities for information processing applications than can be handled at one time, necessitating an allocation process. The master plan, once developed, does not remain constant but must be updated as new developments occur.

A plan of this magnitude requires staff assistance as well as executive involvement. Most well-run companies have a central systems planning group for assisting in the preparation of a long-range plan for information system development. The information system top executive may be in charge of this staff work to develop the plan. The preparation of the master development plan is supervised by an information systems steering committee composed of executives from major functional areas and the information system executive. The committee not only approves the master development plan but also provides a review of progress and overall surveillance of the systems effort. When the information system plan has been completed, it can be presented to the organization top planning committee for review, approval, and integration with other company plans.

The master plan has two components—a long-range plan and a short-range plan. When such a plan is presented to management, it provides information by which to assess information system development and evaluate the impact it will have on overall organization planning. Without such a plan, management has no basis for control. The long-range portion provides the general control, and the short-range portion provides a basis for specific accountability as to operational and financial performance.

Content of the Information System Master Development Plan

The master development plan provides a framework for all detailed information system planning. In general, it contains four major sections (Figure 14-4):

1 Organizational goals and objectives
2 Inventory of current capabilities
3 Forecast of developments affecting the plan
4 The specific plan

Each of these sections of the master development plan is described in more detail in the remainder of this section.

Organizational Goals and Objectives This section of the plan might contain the following parts:

The development of the long-range plan for information systems

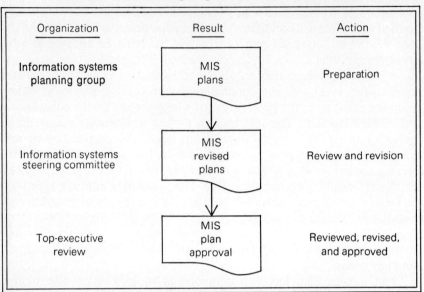

The content of the information system long-range plan

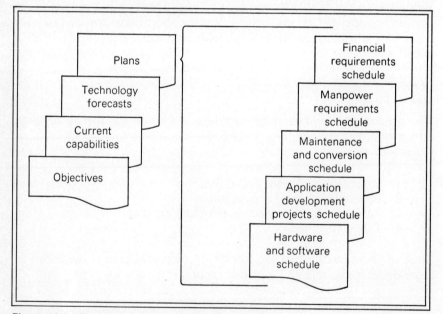

Figure 14-4 The long-range information system plan.

  1 Organizational objectives
  2 External environment
  3 Internal organizational constraints such as management philosophy
  4 Overall objectives for the information system
  5 Overall structure for the information system

Each organization should have a statement of goals and objectives for the guidance of its management and staff. Within the context of these broad organizational goals and the organization-wide plans, there should be goals and objectives for the information system. These can be of two types: general and specific operational goals. The general goals provide guidelines for the direction in which the information system effort should be directed. The operational goals are more specific and should be stated so that performance or nonperformance may be measured. For example, a general goal might be "to provide information resources on a timely basis to all organizational units." An operational goal might be "to provide periodic financial reports no later than 36 hours after the end of the period." The overall structure of the information system provides a framework for the detailed planning. This structure may show the major subsystems which are part of the system.

  Current Capabilities This is a summary of the current status of the information system. It includes such items as the following:

1 Inventory of
  a Equipment
  b Generalized software (system software, data management system, etc.)
  c Application systems
  d Personnel (title, years with firm, etc.)
2 Analysis of
  a Expense
  b Facilities utilization
3 Status of projects in process
4 Assessment of strengths and weaknesses

The inventory of current application systems should identify the status of each. A useful classification is based on the need for additional work on the application.

  1 Applications working reasonably well
  2 Applications which require revised implementation or substantial improvement
  3 Applications which need to be substantially revised or completely replaced by new systems

Forecast of Developments Affecting the Plan   The impact of such developments as low-cost mass storage, minicomputers, intelligent terminals, data management systems, and facilities management need to be part of the long-range plan. It is sometimes difficult to estimate future technology, but most developments are announced one or more years before they become generally available to the user. The broad technological changes can be perceived some years before they are implemented. For example, it was known for several years before intelligent terminals became widely used that this technological development was imminent and that this would have a substantial impact on the design of future systems. The CRT was available for several years before it became widely used. The technological advantages of using the CRTs were such that it was reasonably obvious this would be an important factor in future systems.

The Specific Plan   The plan should cover several years, with the most recent periods (say, the next two years) being reasonably specific. The plan should include:

1   A hardware and purchased software schedule
2   Application development schedule
3   Schedule of software maintenance and conversion effort
4   Personnel resources required
5   Financial resources required

Setting Project Priorities

The information systems planning group has the responsibility for establishing project priorties. As the master plan is developed and subdivided into various modules or subsystems for development, priorities must be assigned. The assignment of priorities will finally have to be set by the information systems steering committee, but each project or subsystem should receive its first evaluation in terms of four factors.

  1 *The expected costs savings or profit improvement resulting from the project.* The savings or profit should be analyzed in terms of rate of return so that projects having different time spans can be compared on a common basis.

  2 *Cost savings or increased profit which cannot easily be quantified.* These are, in other words, judgmental factors which are expected to have a quantitative impact. Examples are improved customer satisfaction for which no specific sales can be estimated or increased employee motivation for which no dollar impact can be preassessed.

  3 *Institutional factors such as the need to have the development*

*proceed in an orderly fashion or the need to have the entire organization
involved in a new information system.* For example, a fairly low payout
project in a department that would not otherwise be involved in an
information system development effort might receive high priority.

4 *System management factors.* Some systems need to be prepared
before others. Certain software packages must be developed so that there
can be suitable interfaces. Personnel may be in short supply, and so they
become a bottleneck which affects the scheduling of jobs.

After these criteria are assigned and made as explicit as possible,
there is still some negotiation of priorities based on the organizational
strength and management dynamics existing in an organization. A manager who has a strong quantitative orientation to management and a
management style which needs a computer-based information system will
tend to push more vigorously for information system projects than a
manager who believes in judgmental management techniques and finds
reports and other access to data not vital to his decision process. Such a
manager may place a lower priority on projects which would enter his or
her domain and in fact may resist their introduction. The planning group
may take the view that this will result in a lower priority, or they may
decide exactly the opposite and place a high priority on a project which
would introduce this manager to the potential advantages of an information system. The information system priority may, in other words, be used
to implement the top management policy on training of managers,
producing changes in decision making and similar matters.

Maintenance of the Master Plan

The master plan has been proposed as a three- to five-year plan which
describes current status and future plans. The plan for the current year is
normally in more detail than those for the succeeding two or four years.
As each year passes, there is a need to update the plan. The current status
is updated with, for example, new equipment and changing personnel
figures. Future plans are affected by changes in technology and experience with systems that have been developed, the changing needs for
systems, and changes which have affected the organization. For example,
an organization may have acquired a new division, and as a result the
necessity for common information processing, common codes, installation of common systems, etc., may affect the entire plan. A new
hardware/software announcement or experience with new development
may also affect future plans. As an example, IBM's introduction of virtual
memory made possible a whole series of changes in operations. After this
development had been assessed, its impact should be put into the revision

of the plan. Another example is the impact of minicomputers on data preparation and direct entry for input. These systems made possible a different approach and may affect a large number of systems or call for changes in the procedures to take advantage of the newer technology. The master plan is also updated to reflect systems installed and system progress. The information system executive and his staff are generally responsible for proposing alterations in the plan, especially as they are affected by changes in the technology or the processing environment, but some changes may come from other sources such as a reduction in planned hardware due to changing financial constraints. A rather complete updating of the master plan once a year would seem to be sufficient.

MANAGEMENT CONTROL OF
INFORMATION SYSTEM PROJECTS

Project control of individual application development projects is most effective if it is performed within the framework of a long-range development plan. It also requires the support of management. Project control systems impose a discipline on both information systems personnel and management. There are requirements for input of estimates, priorities, etc., and reviews of performance.

Project control is accomplished by project management techniques such as the following:

    1   Measurable objectives for the project with definite checkpoints or milestones for assessing progress
    2   Well-defined management responsibility by a project leader
    3   A project management system

Standard milestones based on the life cycle for development (explained further in Chapter 15) assist in project control because there is general understanding of the meaning and significance of each milestone. The project manager must, in general, control the following (Figure 14-5):

    1   Progress on time schedule
    2   Cost performance against budget
    3   Resource utilization (primarily personnel)
    4   Quality of performance

To control these factors, estimates or standards of planned performance are needed.

The status reporting for projects may be of three types: (1) scheduled reporting in which there is report of progress at a scheduled date such as

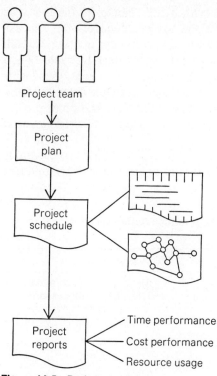

Figure 14-5 Project management.

the end of the month or every two weeks, (2) milestone reporting in which there is a special report as each milestone is passed such as "Completed testing of module one," and (3) exception reporting in which the programmers or systems analysts report progress but also note the exceptions to the plan, with these exceptions being highlighted for review. A project may use control techniques such as Gantt charts to show the scheduling of individual activities over time. If the projects are interrelated so that there are complex precedence relations, network techniques such as PERT or CPM may be used. One advantage of network techniques is that the computations required for keeping them up to date are performed using the computer. Standard software packages are available to provide this processing.

In a research study conducted at the University of Minnesota[10] to

[10]Gary W. Dickson and Richard F. Powers, "MIS Project Management: Myths, Opinion and Reality," working paper 71-01, The Management Information Systems Research Center, University of Minnesota, Minneapolis, May 1971. Also reprinted in McFarlan, Nolan, and Norton, op. cit., pp. 401–412.

determine the correlates of success with MIS projects, 10 factors were found to be significantly related to the project success, the success criteria being time, cost, user satisfaction, and computer operations (lack of difficulty in running the application on the computer). In Table 14-1, a plus sign in the success criterion column indicates that the factor contributed to success; a minus sign means that the factor detracted from success. For example, length of experience in the organization of project personnel was a negative factor in getting the project done on time but was a positive factor in project success.

An interesting conclusion from the study was that having measurable project objectives at the conception of the project bore no significant

Table 14-1   Relation of Project Management Factors to Project Success Criteria

Factor	Time	Cost	User satisfaction	Computer operations
Participation by operating management in design, formal approval of specifications, and continual review of project			+	
Organization level of top computer executive	−			+
Documentation standards used and enforced	+			
Low turnover of project personnel			+	
Source of origination of project (MIS staff or user)			+	
Length of experience in the organization of project personnel	−		+	
High-level programming language used for project	+			
High formal educational level of project personnel	−			+
Separation of analysts and programmers for large projects	+		−	
Overall size of organization systems staff	−	−	+	

relation to success, as measured by any of the four criteria. This suggests that MIS projects should be developed on an evolutionary basis. The project may be initiated on the basis of a set of general objectives, but the project control system should allow a period during which the specific, measurable user requirements evolve rather than being completely specified in advance.

MANAGEMENT CONTROL OF
INFORMATION SYSTEM COSTS

The control of information system costs is based on generally accepted management control principles and practices. These require a financial plan or budget for MIS expenditures, regular reporting against the budgeted amount to determine variances, and followup with analysis and corrective action. The decisions as to the budget amounts to be allowed for information systems are difficult because the value of the system is difficult to measure. Since the user departments are the ones that must finally judge the cost/value of information systems projects, some organizations attempt to establish responsibility by various methods of "charging" departments for the information processing that they use.

Information System Cost Behavior

The costs of the information system are difficult to identify in total because not all are in the data processing budget. A clerk in a functional area engaged in coding documents with budget account numbers before these are processed by computer is part of the data processing cost but not part of the data processing budget. For the purposes of the discussion, the costs of information processing will be specified as those costs which are normally the responsibility of the information processing department.

The breakdown of costs by major functions will depend on the organization, but four major categories based on activity are frequently used—data entry, computer operations, systems analysis and programming, and administration. The rough percentage of total cost devoted to each of these categories is shown in Table 14-2. The information processing department engages in such activities as data entry and operations, but these activities result from expenditures for personnel, equipment, supplies, building, and overhead. The percentages of total cost devoted to each class of objects of expenditure are shown in Table 14-3.

Table 14-2   Expenditure by Cost Center as Percentage of Total

Data entry (keypunching, etc.)	30%
Computer operations (hardware, operations personnel, supplies, etc.)	35
Systems analysis and programming (about one-third for maintenance of old applications)	30
Administration	5
Total	100%

Source: Peter B. Turney, *An Accounting Study of Cost Behavior and Transfer Pricing of Management Information Systems*, unpublished doctoral dissertation, University of Minnesota, Minneapolis, 1972, p. 172; Diebold Research Program, "Management Costs and Controls Studies: Guidelines to the Composition of the ADP Budget," Management Implications Series, M-21, The Diebold Group, Inc., New York, February 1971; and other studies.

It is useful to classify costs as fixed, variable, and semivariable. The definitions generally are applied over the range of volume or activity in which the organization is expected to operate. These three types of cost behavior are diagrammed in Figure 14-6 for both total cost and unit cost. For example, fixed costs do not change in total as volume increases, but the unit costs decrease since there are more units to share the costs. Cost behavior changes depending on the time frame involved. Salaries are fixed for periods of, say, a month, but are variable over longer periods. Equipment costs are fixed over a period of, say, 6 months, but tend to be variable over longer periods.

The cost behavior of major categories of computer-based information processing system costs are summarized at the top of page 391.

Table 14-3   Expenditure by Cost Class as Percentage of Total

Personnel	55%
Equipment (depreciation or rental and maintenance)	30
Supplies	6
Building	4
Overhead	5
Total	100%

Source: Peter B. Turney, *An Accounting Study of Cost Behavior and Transfer Pricing of Management Information Systems*, unpublished doctoral dissertation, University of Minnesota, Minneapolis, 1972, p. 172; Diebold Research Program, "Management Costs and Controls Studies: Guidelines to the Composition of the ADP Budget," Management Implications Series, M-21, The Diebold Group, Inc., New York, February 1971; and other studies.

Cost	Short-run cost behavior
Data entry	
Equipment	Fixed
Personnel	Semivariable
Supplies	Variable
Computer operations	
Hardware	Fixed
Personnel	Semivariable
Supplies	Variable
Systems analysis and programming	Fixed
Administration	Fixed

Information system costs can be divided into capacity costs and marginal costs. Capacity costs represent costs for providing capacity to process information, and the marginal costs are costs of utilizing this capacity.

Type of cost	Examples
Capacity	Equipment and basic maintenance
	System software
	Basic management and supervisory staff
	Building
Usage of capacity	
Development of applications	New projects
Incremental use of applications	Program maintenance
	Supplies and usage-based maintenance

The capacity costs probably represent half or more of total information system costs.

Capacity costs are fixed but increase by increments when usage exceeds the available capacity. When graphed, this cost behavior looks like a series of steps (Figure 14-7). In other words, additional usage may involve little or no extra cost as long as current capacity is not exceeded. The basic dilemma posed by such capacity cost behavior is the fact that some additional usage is without significant extra cost, but as usage is added, there will be a point at which greater capacity will be required. What then does an additional application cost?

MIS development costs represent expenditures to benefit future periods. For financial statements which match costs and revenues, the project costs should be accumulated and amortized over the useful life. This is sometimes not done, and costs are expensed immediately because

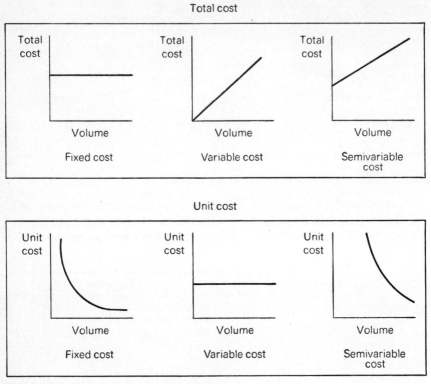

Figure 14-6 Basic patterns of cost behavior.

of the uncertainty as to future benefits. Costs are viewed differently for decision purposes. For decision making, new projects represent variable costs, which are subject to change, whereas old application costs are sunk costs. The programs, procedures, etc., of the existing applications were expected to benefit future periods when the application was developed, but a decision to not use the application system does not recover the costs already expended. In terms of a decision to keep or drop an application, only the future development, maintenance, and operating costs are relevant; all past development costs are not relevant. Care must be taken to analyze the cost figure that is relevant for a specific decision. For example, if an inquiry is made about the cost of an application without specifying more about the decision framework, financial accounting records, which seek to match costs with related revenue (or usage), may provide cost data that is irrelevant to a decision to drop or continue an MIS application.

Budgetary Control over Information Systems

The budget is the financial plan for a period such as a year. It represents authorization from top management to utilize organization resources to operate the existing information system, add new capacity, develop new applications, etc. The budget may be an appropriation-type fixed authorization, a flexible budget, or a combination. There will be summary budgets which are supported by detailed budgets (Figure 14-8).

In the appropriation-type fixed-budget approach, a fixed amount is provided without regard to the level of activity. This approach is appropriate for capacity costs. If a certain capacity for service is decided upon, the hardware, general system software, etc., are fairly well fixed and will not change significantly with usage that is in the range of available capacity.

Variable costs change with activity, and therefore the budget may be expressed in terms of a formula which specifies a budget amount for any

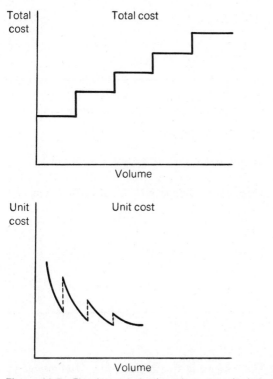

Figure 14-7 Fixed-cost behavior when capacity is increased.

```
                    INFORMATION SYSTEMS
                          BUDGET
                           1974


    Hardware:      Rental           $xx
                   Amortization      xx
                   Maintenance       xx   xx


    Software:      Lease            $xx
                   Purchase          xx   xx


    Personnel:     Development      $xx
                   Maintenance       xx
                   Management        xx
                   Operations        xx   xx


    Supplies                             xx


    Overhead                             xx
                                Total  $xx
```

```
                      PROJECT BUDGET
                           1974


                  Personnel   Supplies   Overhead   Total

  Application projects
    Accounts receivable   xx       xx         xx        xx
    Bidding model         xx       xx         xx        xx
    Etc.
```

Figure 14-8   Information systems summary budgets.

specified level of activity. The budget is flexible because it changes as activity changes. Supplies are an example of a cost that may be controlled by flexible budgeting.

A combination of appropriation and flexible budget may also be used. For example, program maintenance costs represent a combination of fixed and variable costs. A certain amount of program maintenance to keep applications in a usable state will be fixed, but maintenance expenditures will increase with additional usage.

Application development budgets represent appropriations which are contingent upon the projects being worked on. If completed within the budgetary period, the budgeted amount for an application can be used as a control over the total expenditure for the project. However, if the project extends over several budgetary periods, the budgeted expenditures for a period represent the portion of the total to be expended during that period, but was the budgeted progress made? If not, the development project will cost more than planned and corrective action is needed. This is a difficult problem because actual progress must be estimated. This estimate may be based on percentage of completion, phase in life cycle, or specific events completed. Percentage of completion is subject to large estimating bias with the tendency being to overestimate the percentage. The phase in the life cycle is indicative of progress, but still has a wide variance. Tasks or events completed are the most specific and measurable. The planning and reporting of an application in terms of activities in the life cycle are therefore useful in budgeting and managerial control of application development costs.

Control through Pricing

A mechanism is needed for eliminating information processing applications which are no longer cost/effective. The natural tendency is to maintain all applications, even though the user finds them marginally effective or even ineffective. In many organizations it is easier to shelve or throw away a large computer output than to go through the organizational processes to eliminate the application. There are two approaches to controlling the computer resources so that uneconomic applications are eliminated:

    1 *Control at a high level in the organization.* For example, this may be through a cost control committee composed of users. This committee reviews application effectiveness as reported by users and makes recommendations for elimination, change, etc.

    2 *Control at the user level.* This is generally implemented by some method of charging users for the computer resource.

Charging for information services is different than allocating costs. For example, many organizations allocate the cost of computer resources to different profit centers, divisions, etc., within the organization. This allocation is frequently arbitrary and appears as a fixed item over which the user has virtually no control, and therefore it is not meaningful in a managerial control sense. Allocation may have some impact on usage behavior depending on the extent to which the allocation varies with actual usage, but cost control appears to be exercised most effectively when the user has some direct control over the amount charged and can exercise the option to buy, not to buy, or to buy externally instead of internally.

When a chargeout system is used, the monthly statement provided to each user group details the computing resources that were used by them. This report reminds users that information resources do have a cost and informs them how much their group has used. The chargeout system also makes users more responsive to the cost of new applications being requested. When they know that a new application will add a new cost to their data processing bills, they are more likely to ponder the cost/benefit ratio. The chargeout system also makes the users aware of the advantages of those system improvements that reduce cost. They are also reminded of the cost of reruns caused, for instance, by poor input or poor error control.

When a chargeout method is used, there is a problem in deciding how to charge divisions or other organizational units. Table 14-4 shows one proposal. Users pay an allocated share of capacity costs and pay for the development costs and maintenance costs identified directly with their departments. These costs are based on budgeted amounts. Variable usage costs are charged at a standard rate per unit of usage. If the information system costs are different than budgeted, the variance is an item for management attention and is handled for chargeout purposes as a general overhead item.

The transfer or chargeout pricing scheme can also be used to even the workload on the computing resources. For example, jobs that are run on an evening schedule may receive a lower rate than those that are demanded on a high-priority basis. The premiums for high-priority response are identified as congestion costs in Table 14-4.

When happens if users are not charged? The systems which do not charge out computer services treat computing as a free good to users. Since most computing has some marginal benefit, users are motivated to take advantage of the free good and utilize it. One factor inhibiting use for information system applications is the cost before the free good can be used, namely, the system design and programming work required to effectively use it. Where this factor is insufficient, there must be some authority who allocates the available resource. Time-sharing services

Table 14-4   Proposed Transfer Pricing Model*

1 Equipment costs—itemized, some software, operators	Capacity costs		
2 Systems and programming, operations research, some software development	Development costs	Three lump sum charges	Transfer price = revenue for MIS = cost for user
3 Systems and programming, operations research, some software maintenance, conversion	Incremental costs		
4 Supplies, extra-shift rentals, specifically assigned operators, input preparers	Variable costs	Two per- unit charges	
5 Congestion costs	Short-run capacity cost		

*All costs as estimated for the ensuing budget period.
Source: Peter B. Turney, *An Accounting Study of Cost Behavior and Transfer Pricing of Management Information Systems*, unpublished doctoral dissertation, University of Minnesota, Minneapolis, 1972, p. 172.

present special problems. Terminals may be easily utilized for frivolous purposes without significant preparatory expenses. The necessity for control over terminal access in time-sharing applications is therefore greater than data processing applications. Since it is easier to charge for time-sharing use, a chargeout system may be used for it even though data processing applications are not charged. Or a committee or other allocating authority may be used.

INFORMATION SYSTEM AUDIT

A management audit of the EDP or information systems function is desirable at periodic intervals. The audit should evaluate the performance of the function for all activities. The audit team might be composed of a representative from the management committee supervising information systems, the information systems group, the EDP auditing group, and the administrative vice-president or his staff. Some examples of the topics for review are:

1 Adequacy of management.
  a Adequacy of planning.
  b Adequacy of personnel management.
  c Adequacy of supervision.
  d Adequacy of cost control.
2 Performance compared with plans. Projected cost and performance for major projects compared with actual cost and actual performance.
3 Evaluation of performance of existing applications.
4 The adequacy of controls for protection against error and loss.
  a Backup provisions.
  b Application controls.
  c Error-handling procedures.
  d Risk insurance.
  e Auditing.

An information system audit can be very threatening to the information system department and to users who have advocated major applications. The review process needs to recognize not only the potential usefulness of the audit but also the potential harm from a poor or misdirected review.

SUMMARY

The chapter has surveyed topics related to the organization and management of information systems. The trend in information system positions is toward more specialization. The personnel may be organized for management purposes by functions, by projects, or by mixed organization. The most common method is a mixed organization with a project organization for new projects and a functional organization for operations.

The questions of centralization versus decentralization of computer-based information processing equipment, programming and system analysis personnel, and operations has been active since computers were first introduced. Both approaches (or a mixed approach) can be supported technically and organizationally. There are costs and benefits with each approach, but the decision in a particular case is generally more sensitive to overall organizational strategy than to the cost/benefits involved.

Management planning of information system development is generally by means of a planning steering committee and a master development plan. Management control of MIS projects is through project organization and various project management planning and reporting techniques. Management control of costs is by a budget. Control over usage may be through top-level allocation of computer resources or through pricing methods such as transfer pricing. An audit of the information system is also significant to quality control.

EXERCISES

1 Some organizations feel that using combination analyst/programmer positions is superior to separate analyst and programmer positions. Discuss advantages and disadvantages of each.

2 What career paths are available through the information system organization?

3 If the position of information analyst becomes more common, what is likely to be the impact on training, selection, and career paths for persons entering information processing?

4 It is not common to have a project organization extend to the operation of applications. Evaluate advantages and disadvantages of having the same project team do analysis, programming, and operating.

5 Describe and evaluate the economics of computer hardware that influence the desire for centralization.

6 Describe and evaluate centralization/decentralization strategies.

7 Evaluate the advantages and disadvantages of centralization and decentralization from the viewpoint of:
   a Programmer and analyst
   b User of information
   c Operator

8 Explain the function of an MIS planning and steering committee.

9 Explain the purpose and value of an MIS audit.

10 In the Dickson and Powers study (see footnote 10 in this chapter), the use of project management techniques was not influential in determining project success, yet managers agree they need to be used. Why?

11 Identify the following MIS costs as fixed, variable, or semivariable:
   a Communications
   b Data management system on lease
   c Microfilm for computer-output microfilm
   d Extra-shift maintenance
   e On-call maintenance

12 What is the difference between charging out at a standard rate and charging out an allocated share of the actual cost?

13 If a company uses profit centers and charges them for the information processing costs at a standard rate, what happens if the standard rate does not charge out all the costs (or charges out too much)?

14 Does transfer pricing or charging out MIS costs have any real cost control value? Explain.

15 There is some research which suggests that a transfer pricing approach does not reduce usage of information processing resources. Describe some reasons why this may be so.

16 Describe the contents of a master plan for MIS development.

17 Describe the rational criteria for deciding on project priorities. Describe nonrational factors that may influence the priorities.

18 What impact does technology have on the master development plan?

SELECTED REFERENCES

Brown, W. F., R. E. Bibaud, and G. L. Hodgkins: "Planning for the Future Computer Complex," *Computer Decisions*, January 1973, pp. 30–35.

Campise, James A.: "Managing Programming Projects," *Journal of Data Management*, June 1968, pp. 28–36.

Dean, Neal: "The Computer Comes of Age," *Harvard Business Review*, January-February 1968.

Duston, Jack: "Your First Information System Must Be Simple," *Industrial Engineering*, March 1969, pp. 14–27.

Evans, Marshall K., and Lou R. Hague: "Master Plan for Information Systems," *Harvard Business Review*, January-February 1962, pp. 92–103.

Fredericks, Ward A.: "A Case for Centralized EDP," *Business Automation*, January 1972, pp. 21–24.

Garrity, John T., and V. Lee Barnes: "The Payout on Computers: What Management Has Learned about Planning and Control," *Management Review*, vol. 53, no. 12, December 1964, pp. 4–15.

Glaser, George: "The Decentralization-vs-Decentralization Issue," *Data Base*, Fall/Winter 1970.

Gray, Max, and Herberg B. Lassiter: "Project Control for Data Processing," *Datamation*, February 1968, pp. 33–38.

Knight, Kenneth: "Evolving Computing Performance, 1962–1967," *Datamation*, January 1968, pp. 31–35.

Krauss, Leonard I.: *Administering and Controlling the Company Data Processing Function*, Prentice-Hall, Inc., Englewood Cliffs, N.J., 1969.

Lowe, Ronald L.: "The Corporate Data Centers: Getting It All Together," *Computer Decisions*, May 1973, pp. 12–16.

McFarlan, F. Warren, Richard L. Nolan, and David P. Morton: *Information Systems Administration*, Holt, Rinehart and Winston, Inc., New York, 1973.

Middleton, C. J.: "How to Set Up a Project Organization," *Harvard Business Review*, March-April 1967.

Moore, Michael R.: "A Management Audit of the EDP Center," *Management Accounting*, March 1968, pp. 23–32.

Nielson, Norman R.: "The Allocation of Computer Resources—Is Pricing the Answer?," *Communications of the ACM*, August 1970, pp. 4–6.

Reuben, Martin: *Handbook of Data Processing Management*, Brandon Systems Press, New York, 1968.

Schroeder, Walter J.: "If You Can't Plan It, You Can't Do It," *Journal of Systems Management*, April 1969, pp. 8–15.

Schwartz, M. H.: "Computer Project Selection in the Business Enterprise," *Journal of Accountancy*, April 1969.

———: "MIS Planning," *Datamation*, Sept. 1, 1970, pp. 28–30.

Sharpe, William F.: *The Economics of Computers*, Columbia University Press, New York, 1969.

Spett, Milton C.: "Standards for Evaluating Data Processing Management," *Datamation*, December 1969.

Sullivan, Martin B., Jr.: "Economies of Scale and the IBM System/360," *Communications of the ACM*, June 1966, pp. 435–440.

Taylor, James W., and Neal J. Dean: "Managing to Manage the Computer," *Harvard Business Review*, September-October 1966, pp. 98–109.

Wagner, L. G.: "Computers, Decentralization, and Corporate Control," *California Management Review*, Winter 1966.

Withington, Frederic G.: "Crystal Balling: Trends in EDP Management," *Infosystems*, January 1973, pp. 20–21.

Wofsey, Marvin F.: "Managing the Computer Department," *Systems*, November 1963, pp. 13–24.

Chapter 15

The Development of a Management Information System

In the previous chapter, the management of information processing included the preparation of a master plan for information system development. This chapter explains alternative approaches for developing the master plan. The plan is not implemented all at once; development is based on smaller component subsystems or applications. Each of these is designed and implemented by means of a process known as the "information system development life cycle," to be explained in the chapter.

The state of the art in analysis and design of information systems is quite primitive. Manual, quantitative, and automated methods are surveyed in order to introduce the state of the art. The success of information system design, implementation, and operation is directly related to human factors such as resistance to change and man/machine interfaces. These areas are also described in the chapter.

ALTERNATIVE APPROACHES TO THE MIS MASTER DEVELOPMENT PLAN

The MIS master plan explained in Chapter 14 contains the proposed structure of the information system and the schedule of how the individual components will be developed. Although there are similarities in problems involved, the development of the overall master plan has different problems than the development of an individual application. However, the approach taken by the master plan can affect the ease with which individual systems are developed. In terms of system theory explained in Chapter 4, the master plan defines the system, subsystems, and the interfaces. Each subsystem or application is then developed within the framework already defined for it. The development is constrained by the boundaries and interfaces set by the master plan.

Before describing the two most common approaches, it may be useful to describe approaches to master plan development that are generally rejected as being inappropriate in most organizations. The rejected approaches are:

1 *The development of individual applications without regard to the integration that might be possible.* This approach might be justified in situations where there is such a rapid organizational change that the best that can be done is to handle a few systems and plan to redesign when the organizational structure is finally established. The approach is essentially ad hoc and not consistent with the idea of a management information system.

2 *The data base approach.* This method puts great emphasis upon the data base and upon retrieval and manipulation of data from the data base. The rationale put forth for this approach is that it is impossible to really anticipate the decision requirements and strategic planning requirements of management. Therefore the best that can be done is to develop a data base and provide tools for accessing it. The difficulty with such a system is that it places too much burden upon the user, who must pass all his requirements through an ad hoc processing system. Also, the design of the data base and the decision as to content can be improved if there is some indication of the uses for which data will be required, the relation among data items, etc.

3 *An organization chart approach.* In this method, the subsystems are defined by the shape of the organizational chart. If there is a vice-president in charge of marketing, there will be a marketing information system. If there is another vice-president who has responsibility for purchasing, there will be an information system in support of purchasing. The boundaries are automatically defined as the organization chart boxes. The difficulty is that organizations are transitory; the responsibilities held by one vice-president might be altered and shifted to other vice-presidents, making this kind of information system easily obsolete. Perhaps more importantly, the design based on organization responsibility will tend to ignore the possibilities for integration, the need for commonality across different functions, etc.

Two approaches have been advocated by practitioners. Although designated by various terms, they are generally understood as a top-down approach and a bottom-up approach. The master development plan can be prepared using either method. Each approach has its advocates and the reasons it is supposed to be best. Probably both approaches should be used, with the extent each approach is used being based on such factors as organizational maturity and the state of the planning effort.

Evolutionary or Bottom-Up Approach

Since the basic elements of any processing system are the modules for processing transactions and updating files, the evolutionary or bottom-up approach states that the way to develop an overall plan is to start with the operations modules for processing transactions and updating files and then to add planning, control, decision, and other modules as demand develops. In other words, the information system is assumed to grow in response to the needs expressed by management and other personnel in the organization. The master development plan then reflects the orderly implementation and integration of the modules that have been requested. As an illustration of this approach, the evolution might consist of the five stages described by Figure 15-1.

    1 The system plan for the first stage consists of separate applications, each with its own files. The applications are in support of operations—primarily transaction processing, updating of files, and simple reports.

    2 A next step in development might be the integration of related files into data bases and the use of a data base management system to manage the storage and access of the data. This provides added capability for inquiry processing and ad hoc requests for reports.

    3 The next development might be the addition of decision models and various planning models for the support of planning activities involved in management control. The data bases become support modules for this expanded system.

    4 The addition of various models might be followed by an integration of the models into a model base having a wide variety of analysis, decision, and planning models. The data bases are enlarged to include the data necessary for expanded use of the models.

    5 Strategic planning data and strategic planning models are added to the information system. Support for strategic planning involves use of existing models and the addition of new models especially designed for strategic planning. The data requirements for strategic planning involves new environmental data and the support to maintain it in the files.

The advantages of the evolutionary approach are that the information system expands in response to real needs rather than needs which someone thinks ought to be met. It builds on the transaction processing

Step 1 Separate files and applications to support operations

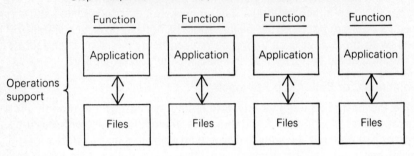

Step 2 Integration of files into data base and introduction of inquiry capabilities

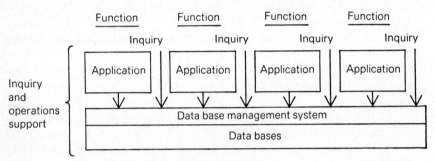

Step 3 Addition of some separate decision and planning models

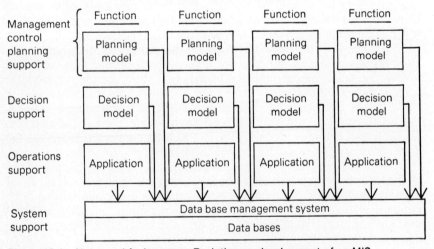

Figure 15-1 Above and facing page: Evolutionary development of an MIS.

Step 4   Integration of models into a model base

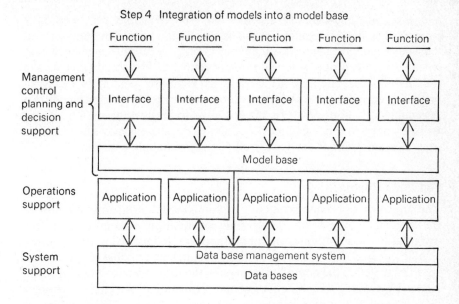

Step 5   Addition of strategic planning data and strategic planning models

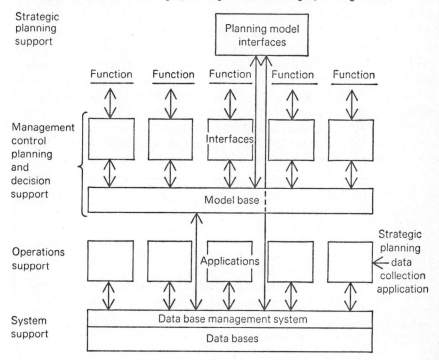

and file updating capabilities that must be available for operations support. The need for each addition or change can be well understood and the cost justified. The risk of having a very large-scale system which cannot operate properly is accordingly reduced. The disadvantages are the inability to integrate as closely as might be desirable. Delay in installing very desirable systems will occur because the management in a particular area does not take the initiative to request the system. There will be a need to redesign many modules as the system grows because the early system was not designed well enough to handle changes.

Top-Down Approach

The top-down approach seeks to develop a model of information flow in the organization and to design the information system to suit this information flow. Modules or subsystems are defined using the information flow model. Integration is planned as much as possible (Figure 15-2). In order to define the overall system plan, the top-down analysis approach begins by defining the objectives of the organization, the kind of business it is in, and the constraints under which it operates. The activities or functions are identified. The crucial strategic and tactical decisions are then defined and the decisions necessary to operate the activities are specified. From the activity or functional analysis and the decisions to be made, the major information requirements are specified in fairly broad terms. Information flow is defined as it travels through the organization. Given this basic structure, the next step is to define subsystems within the overall system. Major modules within the subsystems are defined as the basic unit for development projects. Priorities are then assigned to the modules, taking into account the necessity to develop modules in certain order to take advantage of integration, for the data to be available to support each module, and for similar purposes.

Step 1   Analyze objectives, environment, constraints.
Step 2   Identify activities (functions).
Step 3   Identify decisions and actions.
Step 4   Identify types of information needed for each decision and action.
Step 5   Group decisions and information requirements into subsystems and modules within the subsystems.
Step 6   Establish priorities for developing data base and the subsystems and modules. (When approved, this is the master plan.)

Figure 15-2   Steps in a top-down approach

An advantage of the top-down method is its very logical approach to the development of an overall plan. It focuses on the necessity for integration and careful coordination and planning. A disadvantage is the fact that it is difficult to make such large-scale plans by factoring from the objectives and activities of an organization down to the information processing development modules. The approach does not necessarily yield the order of module development that has the most organizational support or the most potential use. It is more difficult to assign cost and value to the system elements.

Evaluation of the Master Plan Alternatives

Although the two approaches have been presented as alternatives, it is possible to employ a combination of the two. The top-down approach may be employed to define an overall structure, but the logic of the evolutionary approach may be used in setting priorities and in developing and implementing the system slowly, letting the experience of each stage assist in determining the next stage of development. Experience to date suggests the value of this rather careful staging but within a logical framework of development.

ALTERNATIVE APPROACHES TO DETERMINATION OF INFORMATION REQUIREMENTS FOR AN APPLICATION

A first step in the design of an application is a determination of information requirements. Two approaches are examined—decision analysis and data analysis. These correspond roughly to the top-down and bottom-up philosophies explained for the development of the master plan.

Decision Analysis Approach

Decision analysis is a top-down approach to analysis of information requirements for an application. It seeks to derive the information requirements for an application by analysis of the objectives and/or decisions to be made. The flow of information identification activity is:

1 Identify objectives and/or current and potential decisions.
2 Identify or formulate a decision-making model or decision procedure for each decision or a process model for other objectives.
3 Identify the data required for the decision-making model or process model.
4 Test the sensitivity of the model to the availability and accuracy

of input data. Specify accuracy and availability limits for the data needed for the model.

The result of the decision analysis approach is a set of data required for the decision or process and some measure of the importance of each data element and the accuracy needed. The philosophy of this approach is to collect and report only information that is useful in the decision or process model.

Data Analysis Approach

Data analysis is a bottom-up approach to analysis of information requirements for an application. It seeks to derive the information requirements by analysis of the data currently or potentially used. The flow of analysis activity in the data analysis approach is:

1 Collect all documents, reports, files, etc., currently in use and identify data currently being collected and processed.
2 By interviews, examination of similar systems in other organization, etc., identify additional data not currently being collected and processed.
3 By interviews and analysis, seek to eliminate data for which no need can be perceived.

The result of the data analysis approach is an identification of data currently collected and perceived to be needed or not currently collected but perceived to be of value. The philosophy of the data analysis approach is to accept these representations of need unless they are found to be incorrect. There is an assumption that the data requirements may change with time, decision makers, the environment, etc., and so potentially useful information should be part of the system. It is somewhat of a data base approach.

Evaluation of the Decision and Data Analysis Alternatives

The two approaches of decision analysis and data analysis should not be viewed as mutually exclusive approaches for an application. In many cases, a combination of the two approaches may be appropriate. Analysis and design are an iterative process, and data from both approaches may be useful in arriving at information requirements for an application. The utility of the different approaches may also depend on the type of application—a decision-making situation or a transaction processing application.

The identification of the information requirements for a decision-making application is difficult. An analyst does not generally have sufficient background to identify all the information requirements by himself. He will miss some of them if he merely studies what is currently being provided because the current method operates with both formal and informal information systems. For example, the manager may keep significant notes or record important information in his memory. A new information system application which tries to assist in a decision area but does not take into account the informal information processing will not be complete. The manager will in general not be able to identify all information requirements because the manager does not tend to think in these terms and has no structure by which to identify the complete requirements.

The decision analysis approach to information for decision support generally yields a smaller amount of data and results in a decision-orientated or even a decision-impelling output. The data analysis or data base approach generates and stores more data, but the decision support from this approach is more responsive to such factors as change in decision makers, decision-making style, and environmental conditions affecting the decision. A compromise position is often possible in such cases, namely, to define the decision model and process data for it, but to collect at least some potentially useful data which the decision maker can access if he wishes to venture beyond the limits of the current decision model.

A useful approach to identification of decision requirements is an interaction between the manager and the information analyst. The analyst and manager identify the decisions, the decision model or procedure in making the decision, the information requirements, etc. If the analyst has studied the existing system, this promotes interaction. The analyst can inquire as to the reasons for data currently provided that does not fit the decision model being developed.

The data analysis approach of examining data in use or potentially in use is very appropriate for applications involving mechanization of an existing clerical process or changes in an existing transaction processing system. For example, information analysis for an online order entry system will generally benefit from a rather complete analysis of all data currently being used for order entry activities. The advantages of the data analysis approach in the transaction processing and clerical system automation situations is that it quickly provides a list of data items presumed to be useful; these can then be subjected to analysis. It also assists the analyst to be complete and not overlook essential data.

Generalized or Individually Tailored Applications

In deciding upon information decision system design, there is a question as to whether the system should be tailored to suit the management and decision style of an individual manager or whether the individual manager should be required to adapt to the information/decision system. For example, one manager may feel it is important to examine transactions to "get a feel for what is happening" while another wishes to look only at summarized data. One manager may wish to use formal decision models while another may wish to use more intuitive judgment.

The advantage of a tailored approach is that the information system ties directly to the management and decision style of the individual user. There are no reports that the user feels are not useful. The disadvantages are:

1 The system must be redesigned for each new person who becomes a user.

2 There will not be uniformity if more than one user is making the same type of decision.

3 The system may not suit the executive who reviews the user's performance.

4 The system that is tailored to the individual style may reinforce unsuitable approaches to management and decision making.

The advantages of the generalized approach of designing a system are that the system can be designed as a guide to decision making. The user is provided with information processed and presented in such a way that the decision maker is assisted in arriving at a rational decision. The system guides and instructs the decision maker. There can be a uniform system for all similar users, and supervision and review are made easier because of the uniformity. The disadvantages are that the generalized, uniform-system approach depends very heavily on the skill of the analyst/designer in understanding the information needs of the users and in understanding all aspects of the management and decision-making process for that application. The uniform, standard system may also tend to inhibit innovative ideas by an individual manager.

A compromise position in system design is to provide the best generalized system possible and to provide for training in its use. After a user has become familiar with the standard system, he can obtain additional information tailored to his specifications. This additional information may range from lists of transactions to additional complex decision algorithms. There are several problems with this solution:

1 Cost of the added systems tailored to individual users is high.

2   Availability of individualized systems may inhibit users from learning to use the standard system.

3   Eliminating tailored reports is difficult when the individual requesting them moves from the position. The new person in the position may be unwilling to dispense with the report used by a predecessor because it "may be important." The net result is a proliferation of unused reports.

On balance, the standard, generalized system is probably to be preferred but with additional tailored reports allowed. However, the additional reports should be subject to cost/benefit justification and should be rejustified at periodic intervals.

INFORMATION SYSTEM APPLICATION DEVELOPMENT LIFE CYCLE

The basic idea of the development life cycle is that every application needs to go through essentially the same process when the application is conceived, developed, and implemented. Therefore, neglecting any portion of the life cycle activities may have serious consequences for the end result.

Information system development involves considerable creativity; the use of the life cycle is the means for obtaining more disciplined creativity by giving structure to a creative process. The life cycle is important in the planning, management, and control of information system application development. The use of the life cycle concept provides a framework for planning the individual development activities. If an application cannot be planned as activities in the development life cycle, it probably cannot be accomplished at all. In order to manage and control the development effort, it is necessary to know what should have been done, what has been done, and what has yet to be accomplished. The phases in the development life cycle provide a basis for this management and control because they define segments of the flow of work which can be identified for managerial purposes and specify the documents to be produced by each phase.

Overview of the Life Cycle

The steps or phases in the life cycle for information system development are described differently by different writers,[1] but the differences are

[1]See Robert Benjamin, *Control of the Information System Development Cycle*, New York: Wiley-Interscience, a division of John Wiley & Sons, Inc., New York, 1971, p. 29, for a tabular presentation of different categorizations of the information system development life cycle. See also table 1, p. 577, in "Education Related to the Use of Computers in Organizations," *Communications of the ACM*, September 1971.

primarily in amount of detail and manner of categorization. There is general agreement on the flow of development steps and the necessity for control over the development cycle.

The information system development cycle consists of three major stages:

> Definition of the system or application
> Physical design
> Implementation

In other words, there is first the process which defines the requirements for a feasible cost/effective system. The requirements are then translated into a physical system of forms, procedures, programs, etc., by system design, computer programming, and procedure development. The resulting system is tested and put into operation. No system is perfect, so there is always a need for maintenance changes. To complete the cycle, there should be an audit of the system to evaluate how well it performs and how well it meets cost and performance specifications. The three stages of definition, physical design, and implementation can therefore be divided into smaller steps or phases as follows:

Phases in development cycle	Comments
Feasibility assessment	Evaluation of feasibility and cost/benefit of proposed application.
Information analysis	Determination of information needed.
System design	Design of processing system and preparation of program specifications.
Program development	Coding and debugging of computer programs.
Procedure development	Design of procedures and writing of user instructions.
Conversion	Final test and conversion.
Operation and maintenance	Day-to-day operation, modification, and maintenance.
Post audit	How well did it turn out?

The eight phases can be organized in terms of the three major stages of information system development:

Stage	Phase
Definition	Feasibility assessment
	Information analysis
Physical design	System design
	Program development
	Procedure development

Stage	Phase
Implementation	Conversion
	Operation and maintenance
	Post audit

The information system development cycle is not followed in 1,2,3 fashion (Figure 15-3). The process is iterative so that, for example, the review after the system design phase may result in cancellation or continuation, but it may also result in going back to the beginning to prepare a new design.

Each phase in the development cycle results in documentation. The sum of the documentation for the phases is the documentation for the application. The amount of detailed analysis and documentation in each phase will depend on the type of application. For example, a large, integrated application will require considerable analysis and documentation at each phase; a report requested by a manager will require little analysis and documentation, but all phases are still present.

Note that the information system development life cycle does not include the equipment selection and procurement cycle. The reason is that the selection and procurement of equipment (except for some specialized equipment) are generally related to many systems rather than a single application. If an application requires equipment selection, this will generally take place during the physical design development stage.

The following percentages provide a rough idea of the allocation of effort (say, man-hours) in the information system development life cycle from inception until the system is operating properly (i.e., excluding operation and maintenance). These percentages will, of course, vary with each project. The ranges shown are indicative of the variations to be expected.

Stage in life cycle	Phase in life cycle	Rough percentage of effort	Range in percentage of effort
Definition	Feasibility assessment	10	5–15
	Information analysis	15	10–20
Physical design	System design	20	10–30
	Program development	25	20–40
	Procedure development	10	5–15
Implementation	Conversion	15	10–20
	Operation and maintenance	(Not applicable)	
	Post audit	5	2–6
		100	

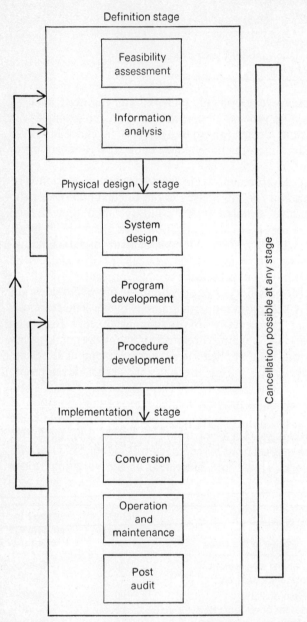

Figure 15-3 The information system development life cycle.

It is instructive to note that upon completion of coding of programs (about half way through program development), the application is probably only about 60 percent complete. For complex systems involving much testing, completion of coding may mark about the halfway point.

Definition Stage

During the definition stage the project is proposed, a preliminary survey is prepared, and the feasibility assessed. If the project is deemed feasible and is approved, the next phase is the preparation of information and information flow requirements. A project may be a module defined by the master development plan, a major maintenance project, or a project allowed but not scheduled in the master plan.

After the project or problem is proposed, the first step is to define the problem. An analyst is assigned to work with the potential users and prepare a report describing:

- The need for the project (a problem, opportunity for savings, improved performance, etc.)
- The expected benefits (in very rough form)
- The outlines of a feasibility study (objective, time required, and resources required)

The proposal report is reviewed by the department proposing the project, the information system executive, and the MIS planning committee. If the project definition is approved, the feasibility study is begun.

One or more analysts conducts the feasibility study which is to assess three types of feasibility:

1 *Technical feasibility.* Is it possible with existing technology?
2 *Economic feasibility.* Will the system provide benefits greater than the cost?
3 *Operational feasibility.* Will it work when installed?

The objectives of the system are amplified from the rough objectives in the feasibility study proposal and the following are prepared:

- Rough outline of the system
- Development work plan
- Schedule of resources required for development
- Schedule of expected benefits
- Project budget

The feasibility report is reviewed by the management of information systems and by the requesting department. If not part of the master plan (and of significant impact), the project will need to be reviewed by the information systems planning committee. If the project is approved, the next phase is information analysis.

One or more information analysts (or systems analyst if no distinction is made between information analysts and system designers) are assigned to the project. The analysts work with users to define the information requirements in detail and to define the information flow. The results of the information analysis phase are:

1 Layouts of the outputs (reports, transaction documents, CRT screens, etc.)

2 Layouts of inputs (transaction input forms, CRT screen input, etc.)

3 Data definitions for required data items

4 Specifications regarding information such as response time, accuracy, frequency of updating, and volume

These specifications complete the definition of what the system is to do; the next step is to design the processing system to produce the results as defined.

Physical Design Stage

The design of the processing system is divided into three phases—system design, program development, and procedure development. Upon completion of this stage of the life cycle, the processing system will be ready for implementation.

The physical design stage begins with the system design. This is the design of the processing system that will produce the reports specified in the information analysis. It designs the equipment usage, the files to be maintained, the processing method, the file access method, and flow of processing. The results of the system design phase are:

1 File design layouts and specifications including access method

2 System flowcharts showing, for example, use of equipment, flow of processing, and processing runs

3 A file-building or file-conversion plan

4 Control flowchart showing controls to be implemented at each stage of processing

5 Backup and security provisions

6 A system test plan

7 A hardware/software selection schedule (if required)

The programming and procedure development phases can proceed concurrently. Programmers will be assigned to do the programming; analysts will normally prepare the procedures. The programming phase uses the system specifications from the information analysis and system design phases to define the programming task. A program plan is prepared which breaks the programs into modules and specifies interfaces among the modules. A test plan is prepared for each module and for the system when all modules are combined. Modules are assigned to programmers who code and test them. The modules are then combined, tested, and debugged as a program system. Documentation is completed and assembled. The result of the programming phase is a set of tested programs that are fully documented.

Procedure development involves the preparation of instructions for the following:

1 Users
2 Clerical personnel providing input
3 Control personnel
4 Operating personnel (computer operator, librarian, data administrator, etc.)

The procedures are written; tested for completeness, clarity, and ease of use; and reproduced for distribution. The procedure development phase can also include the preparation of training material to be used in implementation.

Implementation Stage

When the programs and procedures are prepared, the conversion phase can begin. Data is collected, files built, and the overall system tested. There are various methods of testing. One .is to test the system under simulated conditions; another is to test under actual conditions, operating in parallel with the existing systems and procedures. It is generally considered not good practice to implement a complex system without one of these full system tests.

After all errors and problems that have been detected in the system test are corrected, the system is cut over into actual operation. When it appears to be operating without difficulty, it is turned over to the maintenance group in information processing. Any subsequent errors or minor modifications are handled as maintenance. This is not a trivial activity—about one-third of the analyst/programmer effort is devoted to maintenance of existing programs. Because of the importance of maintenance, it is important that the system be designed and documented for maintainability. Some organizations require the maintenance group to review all new applications for maintainability and allow them to reject systems that do not meet acceptable standards.

The last phase of the implementation stage is a post audit. This is a review by an audit task force (composed, for example, of a user representative, an internal auditor, and a data processing representative). The audit group reviews the objectives and cost/benefit representations made in behalf of the project and compares these to actual performance and actual cost/value. It also reviews the operational characteristics of the system to determine if they are satisfactory. Documentation is reviewed for backup and maintainability considerations. Control and security provisions are examined. The results of the post audit are presented in a report. The recommendations are intended to assist in improved management of future projects, improvements in the application under review, or cancelation of the application if it is not functioning properly.

STATE OF THE ART FOR TECHNIQUES AND TECHNOLOGY USED IN INFORMATION SYSTEM DEVELOPMENT

One might expect that the designers and implementers of computer-based systems would use quantitative techniques and computers very intensively in the development effort. This is not the case; there is little use of quantitative models and computers in the development cycle. This section reviews the current state of the art in terms of the techniques in use. The explanation divides the methods into process- or forms-driven methods, quantitative models, and automated methods. For the student who has an interest in any one technique, there is a special section of references at the end of this chapter.

Process- or Forms-driven Methods

Almost all systematic approaches to information system development consist of a specified process to be followed and forms to be used. Some emphasize the process or set of procedures to follow, while other put more emphasis on the forms which, when filled out, complete a particular phase such as information analysis. There are several well-known and somewhat similar systems for systematically doing analysis and design. Installations following systematic approaches tend to have methods that are very similar to these.

Development system	Comments
SOP (Study Organization Plan)	IBM plan for overall system planning centered on the organization chart. Consists of three phases: 1 Understanding the present system

Development system	Comments
	2 Determining system requirements
	3 Designing the new system
	Forms and report formats are part of the system.
ARDI (Analysis, Requirements Determination, Design and Development, and Implementation and Evaluation)	Developed by Phillips Electric Company, a multinational organization headquartered in the Netherlands. A comprehensive, four-phase approach including processes and forms:
	1 Feasibility study
	2 System analysis and design
	3 System development
	4 System implementation and evaluation
ADS (Accurately Defined Systems)	A set of forms and related processes to define a processing application; developed by The National Cash Register Co.
BISAD (Business Information System Analysis and Design)	A Honeywell product, the system stresses analysis of functions. The steps are:
	1 Background analysis
	2 Functional analysis
	3 System prototype design
	4 Designing the working system
	5 Operational planning
	6 System specification

Quantitative Models

The process approach and the forms-driven methods do not allow for any quantitative analysis or manipulation. There have been some attempts to apply some quantitative models. These have generally been useful for part of the process rather than being comprehensive systems. None is in widespread use. Some illustrative attempts are:

1 Matrix models
2 Systems algebra
3 Industrial dynamics models

The matrix models use matrix algebra to understand and manipulate data and report relations. The matrix in Figure 15-4 shows data items as the rows and first-level transaction documents as the columns. The notation 1 in a matrix cell indicates that a data item appears in that transaction document; 0 indicates it does not appear. A similar matrix can show the use of transaction documents to prepare second-level documents or reports. A third matrix is used to describe how these second-

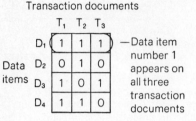

Figure 15-4 Use of matrix to show data item and document relation.

level reports are used to prepare top-level reports. The matrices can be manipulated to calculate the possible redundancy in the system. Additional features can be added, but to date these methods have had more conceptual appeal than real use.

Systems algebra is an application of linear graph theory and matrix arithmetic to some problems in information analysis and system design. It is based primarily on the work of Borje Langefors, a Swedish professor and consultant. The information system is defined as a network of elementary information sets connected by elementary processes. An "elementary information set" is a set of data elements required as input to an elementary process. For example, employee number, hours worked, and rate of pay might be the elementary information set that is input to a gross pay computation process. Once all the elementary information sets and processes have been defined, the information algebra can be applied to grouping of processes (into modules and runs), consolidation of elementary information sets into files, and calculation of data transfer requirements. The computational approaches are beyond the scope of this overview; they utilize matrices showing precedences among information sets and precedences for processes. The information algebra is a significant contribution to quantitative analysis in information systems, but additional development is needed to integrate it into day-to-day system analysis and design.

Industrial dynamics modeling is well known and will therefore only be mentioned as one method for analysis. Industrial dynamics is a simulation modeling technique which is designed to demonstrate the relation between organizational structure, policies, and decision/action time delays. System behavior is described by the change through time of levels of resources (money, inventory, etc.) and their rate of change. Information feedback causes the system to adjust rates of change. The analyst prepares an industrial dynamics model by drawing a flowchart of material flows, levels, and information flows. Equations describing the rates and levels are written. The equations form a model of the system.

The model is manipulated through simulated time by a software package designed to assist the user of industrial dynamics. The results are useful in understanding what information should be available and the consequences of poor or missing information; it is not intended to assist in the design of the physical processing system.

Automated Procedures

The use of automated processes in information system design is still in a development stage. Four systems are surveyed briefly to provide a feel for the methods that have been tried or are being developed. They are:

1 AUTOSATE (Automated Data Systems Analysis Technique)
2 TAG (Time Automated Grid system)
3 ISDOS (Information Systems Design and Optimization System)
4 Hoskyns system for automatic specification programming

All these systems are classed as experimental except the last.

AUTOSATE was developed at Rand Corporation in 1964 and 1965. It is a computer-assisted procedure for analyzing document flows in an organization and is therefore a data analysis approach to analysis of information requirements. AUTOSATE requires the definition of work stations where documents are processed, the events that initiate processing, and the flow of documents or messages among work stations. The analyst fills out specification forms to provide input to AUTOSATE. The output consists of an event-chain report showing the flow of processing caused by each event, a report of forms used for the processing initiated by each event, and a list of the processing stations involved with each document. Inconsistencies and missing links in the processing chains are identified. The AUTOSATE approach is useful in understanding the current system; it does not analyze the information that is needed but not already provided. The software is not well supported.

TAG is a computer-assisted information system study technique developed by IBM in the mid-1960s. Software is available from IBM, but is a class of programs that do not receive continuing support. In other words, a potential user may obtain TAG programs but he cannot look to IBM for training, program corrections, program changes, etc. Using TAG, an analyst defines the required output documents for an application, then works backward to determine the inputs that are necessary to produce the outputs. Documents are assigned to a time interval and to a processing order within a time interval. The outputs from the TAG processor are reports to assist the analyst to spot redundant data items, design files, define sorting requirements, etc. The need for files to preserve data for subsequent processing is shown, and TAG prepares a first approximation of record design. TAG does not define processing logic. The defining of documents and files into time periods was a useful contribution, but the overall cost/effectiveness of the system is in doubt (as evidenced by very little use).

ISDOS is a comprehensive research project (headed by Daniel Teichroew at the University of Michigan) to develop more powerful approaches to the design of information systems. A comprehensive software system is being developed to automate many of the system-building functions. The system is designed to operate with three major components:

1 The problem definer (i.e., the analyst)
2 The problem statement
3 Software to prepare and operate a processing system which meets the requirements of the problem statement

The ISDOS approach begins with the problem definer who defines the information needed, the timing and volume, plus computations and logic to produce output. The requirements are written in a problem statement language (similar to PL/I). The software system analyzes the problem statement, does system design, compiles programs, organizes files, and directs execution of the resulting application system. In other words, information analysis must be performed prior to writing the problem statements. The ISDOS system thus performs tasks associated with system design, programming, implementation, and operation phases of the system development life cycle. It is still in a research stage.

The Hoskyns system approach (see selected references at the end of the chapter) is less ambitious than ISDOS, but is an example of an operational system. The system prepares COBOL programs from specifications and is therefore a step beyond the normal use of procedure-oriented languages. The designer prepares three matrices as specifications:

1 Program/file matrix—defines files required by programs
2 Record/data matrix—defines record types, file organization, access keys, data specifications, etc., for each file
3 Action/condition matrix—defines the logic of processing in decision table form

The three matrices are converted by preprocessors to the divisions of a COBOL program which is then compiled, tested, etc. The system thus transforms specifications in matrix form to COBOL programs without the necessity for hand-coding of COBOL statements.

Evaluation of Systems Analysis and Design Techniques

As evidenced by the preceding discussion, the attempts to use quantitative or automated approaches have not achieved any significant success. However, current research developments suggest the possibility of future improvements over manual methods. It is one of the anomalies of information systems that this field, which is applying technology to information processing at such a rapid rate, has not applied technology to any significant degree to its own analysis and design processes.

Almost all current methods of analysis and design are based on sets of forms or sets of processes, but no single method is used. The tendency is for installations to make use of fairly standard flowcharts, layouts, and decision tables but to be less standardized in the remaining forms and methods. The manual basis of design allows for considerable variety, and so there has been little pressure to standardize the manual approaches. Any change is likely to come because of automation of part of or all the processes.

HUMAN FACTORS IN INFORMATION SYSTEM DEVELOPMENT AND DESIGN

In one organization a well-designed system fails; a similar but poorly designed system in another organization succeeds. The reason can usually be traced to human factors. Employees who dislike and distrust a system can make a well-designed system fail; employees who want a system to succeed can usually make it work, even if the design is somewhat poor. Resistance may arise because of dislike of change, or it may be due to design features which make the system an irritation to the operators or users. Therefore, in design and implementation of a system, attention must be given to human factors.

Overcoming Resistance to New Systems

Resistance to change is a common phenomenon. In some cases, the resistance is very small and the affected persons adjust quickly to the new system. But in extreme cases, the reaction can be subversion or destruction of the new system. The reason for this resistance is generally that change is threatening.[2] Some ways this resistance may be manifested are

[2]Donald H. Sanders, *Computers and Management*, McGraw-Hill Book Company, New York, 1970, pp. 320–334.

the following; these relate directly to the human needs explained in Chapter 5.

Human need	Basis of resistance
Safety	Fear of loss of employment
Social contact	Fear of disruptive change in work groups (which meet social needs)
Competence	Fear of inability to do the job when it is changed
Recognition	Fear of not being needed

These fears are generally based on real or perceived effects that other new systems have had on friends or acquaintances or that have been reported in the literature. The following are examples of changes that have occurred.

• Employees have been terminated (although the effect is generally to reduce new employment rather than resulting in terminations).
• Work groups have been altered to suit the requirements of the new system, affecting both employees' ability to work effectively and the existing social groups. Employees who have had coffee breaks together have received incompatible schedules. Individual interaction with adjacent work stations had been altered.
• Feelings of competence have been challenged. Employees who have learned the routine and rules of a job have found new procedures difficult to learn, especially when quantitative techniques were involved.
• Employee status has been altered. Many employees derive status from the fact that they know how to do their jobs very well and have a wealth of information tucked away in their memories. Other employees at all levels including management come to them for information. Computer systems have changed this status; the long-time employee has become the same as employees of less tenure and understanding. A manager may feel his or her status has been reduced when decisions have been programmed because the manager's judgment has become less valuable.

The reasons for resistance represent fear of what may happen. The actual event is usually less traumatic than thinking about it. In other words, uncertainty is a cause of increased resistance. This suggests that methods, which reduce uncertainty will assist in reducing resistance. Given the theory of information explained in Chapter 2, the way to reduce uncertainty is to increase information.

It is generally agreed that participation and communication are the ways to overcome resistance. Employees will tend to accept systems they have helped to design because they see the need for the design features. They derive satisfaction from designing a good system, even though it may disrupt some established routines. The participation allows the employee some control over the change and thus increases the employee's security. Communication to all interested personnel will generally assist in reducing unfounded fears which add to resistance. These observations suggest the following procedures to be used in information system design and implementation:

1 Encourage initiation of projects by users rather than by the information systems department.
2 Include user personnel in project group where feasible (such as feasibility study and information analysis phases).
3 Establish a user advisory/supervisory channel such as a person or group from user department to assist and guide the project.
4 Hold informational and feedback sessions with employees at each level who will come in contact with the system.
   a Prior to the design to explain the need and expected approach to be taken
   b At the end of the design phase
   c Prior to implementation
   d After implementation
5 Do not attempt to install a system which is not debugged. The new system probably causes modest traumatic change; errors may increase the level of trauma beyond tolerable limits.

A case study[3] of a problem-plagued installation is instructive in pointing out the human problems of system implementation. The Minneapolis Post Office installed an automated source data collection system to record time spent on each job and the volume of activity for each employee. The purpose was to provide better information on attendance, volume, work measurement, etc. The underlying causes for the failure were environmental factors, method of introduction, and work relations.

1 The environment for automation was poor because of the political character of management, a militant union which opposed the new system, and a history of unsuccessful automation efforts.
2 The method of introduction was essentially to install the equipment and later explain how to use it (but with very little explanation about what the system was doing). The system was initiated, designed, and implemented from Washington; follow-up interviews disclosed that the employees did not generally understand its purpose or usefulness.

---

[3]John Anderson, Gary Dickson, and John Simmons, "Behavioral Reactions to the Introduction of a Management Information System at the U.S. Post Office," working paper 72-05. The Management Information Systems Research Center, University of Minnesota, Minneapolis, 1972.

3 Work relations were disturbed. For example, the job of time-keeper was eliminated. This was a popular position, and senior employees could bid to take it when it came available. Also, the timekeeper was an important part of the informal communication system. Another disturbance was the discontinuation of posting sick leave status and accrued vacation time on a bulletin board. This report had been a focus of informal discussion—eliminating it disrupted a social function as well as doing away with information that was considered important by the employees.

Human Problems in Using Computer-based Systems

In addition to the problem of overcoming resistance to change, the information system analyst and designer must take into account human factors in the design. Some of these considerations have been mentioned in prior chapters and are summarized here. As an example of human problems in system design, it was found that the source data recorder design in the Post Office system created a difficulty. The employee inserted a badge and pressed a button to record the transaction. However, in the prototype system, the source recorder made no response to indicate receipt of the transaction. This lack of feedback frustrated the employees, who were also bothered by the lack of a visual record of their transactions.

Job assignments between man and machine should not always reflect processing advantage; other factors such as the need to have the human perform an interesting set of tasks should be considered. In other words, tasks which may be performed by the computer may need to be assigned to the human in order to keep the human stimulated and alert.

The way humans view their job may influence their use of an information system. There is evidence that managers will not use computer-access terminals directly but will make use of them if their secretaries or assistants are trained in their use. For example, at one company, the difference in terminal use by managers for analysis and decision-making purposes is explained by the ability of their assistants to use the terminal.

Managers will tend to not use systems they do not understand. This does not mean a technical understanding of, say, the program structure or modular design, but an understanding of the logic of the process they are asked to rely upon. This problem is especially acute in models for analysis, decision-making simulation, planning, etc. A model that is so complex that the user cannot understand why his or her inputs result in certain outputs will most probably never be utilized. This suggests the need for simple models which grow as more complex features can be accepted by the users.

SUMMARY

There are alternative approaches to the development of an information system. Two important alternatives are the evolutionary or bottom-up approach, which focuses on growth in response to the requests for additions to the system, and the top-down approach, which attempts to arrive at an overall design by deriving information requirements from the goals, activities, decisions, etc., of the organization. Elements of both approaches may be used with the relative emphasis dependent on organizational philosophy and current information system characteristics.

The master plan defines the individual applications. Two significant approaches to the determination of information requirements for applications are the decision analysis approach and the data analysis approach. The decision method derives information requirements by an analysis of the decisions and decision algorithms. The data analysis approach arrives at information requirements by an investigation of data already being collected and data that managers claim should be available. The decision approach is most applicable for decision support modules; the data analysis is most suitable for transaction processing, but a combination of methods is often applied to the information analysis phase of application design.

The life cycle for the development of an information system consists of three main stages—definition, physical design, and implementation. The main stages can be divided into smaller phases. The life cycle approach is useful in the management and control of application development because it provides a structure for planning and for identifying development progress.

The state of the art with respect to information system design technology is described mainly by manual methods involving, for example, forms, check lists, and processes to follow. There are a few well-developed manual systems in use such as SOP and ADS, but most installations use less-structured manual methods. There have been various attempts at quantitative and automated systems analysis, but to date these are research developments rather than operational systems.

Human factors are very significant in the success of information system development. Communication and participation are the primary methods for reducing resistance to new systems. The system design should take into account the human problems in using computer-based systems; otherwise the system will be likely to fail from lack of use.

EXERCISES

1 What are the weaknesses in a data base approach to MIS design?
2 How does an organization chart approach differ from a functional approach to overall information system design?
3 Describe the advantage and disadvantages of:
   a The bottom-up approach to the MIS master plan
   b The top-down approach to the MIS master plan
4 Describe how the approach taken to MIS development might affect a manager of a function.
5 Describe the major steps each of the following organizations might take in designing an MIS using a top-down approach and using a bottom-up approach:
   a A large wholesale florist (makes sales to retail florists)
   b A rural bank serving a farming area
6 Explain how the effectiveness of an information system is influenced by the decision maker. Explain the advantages and disadvantages of individualized information systems.
7 Explain the difference between the data analysis and decision analysis approaches to definition of information requirements for an application.
8 Explain the use of the decision analysis and data analysis methods for the following applications:
   a Payroll processing
   b Personnel selection, advancement, and retention
   c Inventory management (safety stock, reorder point, reorder quantity, disposal of obsolete items)
9 Explain the phases in the development life cycle.
10 Describe the outputs (reports, documents) from each phase of the development life cycle.
11 Various "life cycles" have been proposed, but they are all very similar. Show the similarity between the following life cycle and the life cycle in the text:
   Problem definition
   Preliminary survey
   Detailed business systems
   Detailed computer systems
   Programming specifications
   Programming
   Programming tests
   System tests
   Installation

12 Laden and Gildersleeve[4] describe the phases of a system project as:
Survey
Systems investigation
Systems design
Programming
Filemaking
Clerical procedures
Systems testing
Parallel running
Compare this listing with the phases outlined in the chapter.

13 It is sometimes said that there is both a logical design and physical design for an information system application. Explain in the context of the life cycle.

14 Explain the use of manual techniques involving special forms and specified processes. Identify some examples of these systems.

15 Why is it difficult to automate information analysis?

16 How is resistance to new information systems overcome?

17 "If he's being resisted (the MIS designer), it's partially because he invites resistance in the way he goes about trying to get line management to adopt MIS." Explain and evaluate this statement by Argyris, 1970.

18 Prepare a report comparing various descriptions of the information system development life cycle. See Benjamin, 1971, p. 29, and also "Education Related to the Use of Computers in Organizations," *Communications of the ACM*, September 1971, p. 57.

19 Read more details of two process- and forms-driven methods for analysis. Compare them as to scope, forms, and steps.

20 Read the reference for Homer, 1960, and evaluate the utility of matrix methods.

SELECTED REFERENCES

General References

Ackoff, Richard L.: "Management Misinformation Systems," *Management Science*, December 1967, pp. B147–B156.

Argyris, Chris: "Management Information Systems: Challenge to Rationality and Emotionality," *Management Science*, February 1971, pp. B275–B292.

——: "Resistance to Rational Management Systems," *Innovation*, no. 10, 1970, pp. 28–35.

Bauer, James B., and J. Bruce Sefert: "Humans Factors in Systems Design," *Management Services*, November-December 1965, pp. 39–50.

Benjamin, Robert I.: *Control of the Information System Development Life Cycle*, John Wiley & Sons, Inc., New York, 1971.

---

[4]H. N. Laden and T. R. Gildersleeve, *System Design for Computer Applications*, John Wiley & Sons, Inc., New York, 1963, pp. 223–225.

Blumenthal, Sherman C.: *Management Information Systems*, Prentice-Hall, Inc., Englewood Cliffs, N.J., 1969.

Bubenko, J., Jr., B. Langefors, and A. Solvberg: *Computer-Aided Information Analysis and Design*, Studentlitteratur, Lund, Sweden, 1971. A report of research in Scandinavia on computer-aided analysis and design.

Burch, John G., Jr., and Felix R. Strater, Jr.: *Information Systems: Theory and Practice*, Hamilton Publishing Co., Santa Barbara, Calif., 1974.

Dickson, G. W., and John K. Simmons: "The Behavioral Side of MIS," *Business Horizons*, August 1970, pp. 1–13

Head, Robert V.: "Automated System Analysis," *Datamation*, Aug. 15, 1971, pp. 22–24.

McFarlan, Warren F., Richard L. Nolan, and David P. Norton: *Information Systems Administration*, Holt, Rinehart and Winston, Inc., New York, 1973.

Mumford, Enid: "Planning for Computers," *Management Decisions*, vol. II, 1968, pp. 98–102.

———, and Olive Banks: *The Computer and the Clerk*, Humanities Press, New York, 1967.

Nolan, Richard L.: "Systems Analysis for Computer-based Information Systems Design," *Data Base*, Winter 1971, pp. 1–10.

Pedler, C. S.: "New Variables in the Data Processing Equation," *Computers and Automation*, May 1969, pp. 28–30.

Rubin, M.: *Introduction to the System Life Cycle*, Auerbach Publishers, Inc., Princeton, N.J., 1970.

———: *System Life Cycle Standards*, Auerbach Publishers, Inc., Princeton, N.J., 1970.

Shaw, J. C., and W. Atkins: *Managing Computer Systems Projects*, McGraw-Hill Book Company, New York, 1970.

Teichroew, Daniel: "A Survey of Languages for Stating Requirements for Computer-based Information Systems," *Proceedings of the Fall Joint Computer Conference*, 1972.

Zani, William: "Blueprint for MIS," *Harvard Business Review*, November-December 1970, pp. 95–100.

Special References for Techniques and Technology in Information System Development

General Couger, J. D.: *Systems Analysis Techniques*, John Wiley & Sons, Inc., New York, 1973. A book of readings and a commentary on the major systems analysis techniques.

ADS Lynch, H. J.: "ADS: A Technique in System Documentation," *Data Base*, Spring 1969, pp. 6–18.

ADS *Study Guide for Accurately Defined Systems*, National Cash Register Company, Dayton, Ohio, 1968.

ARDI Hartman, W., H. Matthes, and A. Proeme: *Management Information Systems Handbook*, McGraw-Hill Book Company, New York, 1968.

AUTOSATE Butler, D. D., D. M. Fairbrother, and O. T. Gatto: *Data Systems Design and Control Using Autosate—An Automated Data System Analysis Technique*, Rand Corporation, Santa Monica, Calif. RM3976-PR, February 1964.

AUTOSATE Gatto, O. T.: "Autosate," *Communications of the ACM*, July 1964, pp. 425–432.

BISAD *Business Information Systems Analysis and Design: Student Reference Guide*, Honeywell, Inc., Electronic Data Processing Division, Wellesley Hills, Mass., 1968.

Hoskyns system Rhodes, J. J.: "Beyond Programming," in J. Daniel Cougar and Robert W. Knapp (eds.), *Systems Analysis Techniques*, John Wiley & Sons, Inc., New York, 1973.

Industrial dynamics Forrester, J. W.: *Industrial Dynamics*, The M.I.T. Press, Cambridge, Mass., 1961.

Industrial dynamics ———: "Industrial Dynamics—After the First Decade," *Management Sciences*, March 1968, pp. 398–415.

Industrial dynamics Pugh, Alexander L.: *Dynamo User's Manual*, 2d ed., The M.I.T. Press, Cambridge, Mass., 1961.

ISDOS Teichroew, Daniel, and Hassan Sayani: "Automation of System Building," *Datamation*, Aug. 15, 1971, pp. 25–30.

Matrix models Homer, Eugene G.: "A Generalized Model for Analyzing Management Information Systems," *Management Sciences*, July 1960, pp. 500–516.

Matrix models Lieberman, Irving J.: "A Mathematical Model for Integrated Business Systems," *Management Science*, July 1956, pp. 327–336.

SOP The following six IBM manuals describe the Study Organization Plan approach: *Basic Systems Study Guide*, SF20-8150-0, 1963; *IBM Study Organization Plan: The Approach*, SF20-8135-0, 1963; *IBM Study Organization Plan: The Method Phase I*, SF20-8135-0, 1963; *IBM Study Organization Plan: The Method Phase II*, SF20-8137-0, 1963; *IBM Study Organization Plan: The Method Phase III*, SH20-8138-0, 1963, reprinted August 1970; *IBM Study Organization Plan: Documentation Techniques*, FC20-8075-0, 1960, 1961.

SOP Glans, Burton Grad, David Holstein, William E. Meyer, and Richard N. Schmidt: *Management Systems*, Holt, Rinehart and Winston, Inc., New York, 1968.

Systems algebra Langefors, Borje: *Theoretical Analysis of Information Systems*, vol. I & II, Studentlitteratur, Lund, Sweden, 1970.

TAG *The Time-automated Grid System*, Sales and Systems Guide, International Business Machines Corporation, 420-0358-0, 1966.

EVALUATION OF THE INFORMATION SYSTEM FUNCTION
EVALUATION OF THE EXISTING HARDWARE/SOFTWARE SYSTEM
    Operation of Performance Monitors
    Evaluation by Use of Performance Monitors
    Evaluation by Use of System Logs and Observation
    Scheduling Analysis
EVALUATION OF A NEW OR REPLACEMENT
  HARDWARE/SOFTWARE SYSTEM
    The Study Group
    The Feasibility Study
    Preparation of Specifications and Obtaining Proposals
    Evaluation of Proposals
EVALUATION OF INFORMATION SYSTEM APPLICATIONS
    Technical Evaluation
    Operational Evaluation
    Economic Evaluation
QUANTIFYING BENEFITS FROM INFORMATION SYSTEMS
  APPLICATIONS
    Direct Estimate of Value of Application
    Less than/Greater than Cost Method
COST/BENEFIT ANALYSIS OF DESIGN ALTERNATIVES
    Response Time
    Display Detail
    Data Quality
SUMMARY
EXERCISES
SELECTED REFERENCES

434

Chapter 16

Evaluation of
Information Systems

The evaluation of information systems can be performed in different ways and at different levels, depending on the objectives of the evaluation. The purposes can be to assess technical capabilities, operational performance, and utilization of the systems. These evaluations define how well the system performs; they do not tell whether the organization is spending too much or too little on the system. Evaluation of performance therefore needs to be combined with cost/benefit evaluation. Such evaluation should be performed not only for the system as a whole but also for individual applications and major design alternatives. This chapter reviews major forms of evaluation for computer-based information systems.

EVALUATION OF THE INFORMATION
SYSTEM FUNCTION

The evaluation of the information system function covers the management and operation of information processing. Most of the topics have been described in Chapters 14 and 15. Areas covered by this evaluation are:

- Management of the information processing function
  - Development and maintenance of a master development plan
  - Budgets and other procedures for resource allocation and control
  - Procedures such as management reports to identify and correct unsatisfactory performance
- Staffing of information processing
  - Quality of the staff in terms of qualifications
  - Training and updating processes
- Development process for new applications
  - Standards for the development cycle
  - Project management control
- Operations
  - Operational standards
  - Scheduling of jobs
  - Supervision
- Control and security
  - Quality control procedures
  - Security for computer room, files, programs, etc.
  - Backup provisions for files
  - Contingency planning for equipment failure

The evaluation of the information system function may be conducted by one of the following:

1 A special audit team assembled for this purpose from among the executives of the organization
2 An internal audit team which performs operational audits
3 An outside consulting organization

The objective of the evaluation is to measure the quality of current performance in order to improve future performance. The evaluation report should therefore focus not only on determination of weaknesses and strengths but also on suggested improvements.

EVALUATION OF THE EXISTING HARDWARE/SOFTWARE SYSTEM

The purpose of existing hardware/software system evaluation is to determine if all resources are needed, if some resources should be replaced with improved hardware or software, if a rearrangement of resources would improve effectiveness, and if additional resources would increase the effectiveness of the system. Some examples of actions resulting from performance evaluation of the existing hardware/software system are:

- Addition of a new data channel
- Replacement of a low-speed data channel with a high-speed channel
- Dropping of a data channel not being used
- Addition to main memory capacity
- Change in disk storage units
- Change in disk storage organization
- Change in data management software
- Addition of spooling software

The methods and tools for evaluation of the hardware/software system are hardware monitors, software monitors, system logs and observations, and scheduling analysis.

Operation of Performance Monitors

Hardware monitors are sensing devices attached to selected signal lines in the computer hardware to measure the presence or absence of electrical impulses. For example, a sensor might be attached to collect data on the time that the CPU is in wait state. Another sensor might measure channel activity. The monitoring device does not affect the operation of the computer hardware. It requires no CPU storage and no cycle times. The data from the sensor probes is routed to counters. Periodically, the data in the counters, together with the time determined by an internal clock, is written onto magnetic tape or other output medium. The data on the magnetic tape is in computer-readable format. It is periodically summarized by use of a computer program and reported in an analytical format.

The monitors can collect data on both CPU and peripheral device activity. The major shortcoming of the hardware monitors is that they cannot identify the program which is being measured unless the location of the program in memory is known. Most computers of reasonable size use relocatable programs and have more than one program in memory at a time; this reduces the effectiveness of hardware monitors for measuring specific program efficiency. The operating system normally resides in a fixed partition in memory, and so its activity can be measured.

Software monitors are computer programs. They reside in main memory and require execution time; they interrupt the program being executed to record data about the execution. They therefore slow down the execution of the programs they are monitoring. One approach to reduce the amount of interruption is to sample the activities rather than to measure them continuously. Software monitors can identify particular programs or program modules. They can measure the performance of each application program within the operating system environment. Peripheral device activity is not measured directly but can be estimated from the CPU commands.

Evaluation by Use of Performance Monitors

Hardware and software monitors can be used to detect idle resources, bottleneck facilities, and load imbalance. Inefficient use of resources due to excessive wait time can be measured. This wait time may be caused by insufficient channel capacity, excessive seek time by disk storage devices, inefficient overlapping of input/output and processing, etc. The monitors assist in identifying the causes of inefficiency.

The remedies to be applied following performance monitoring and analysis of the results include:

- Changes in equipment
- Recoding of program segments
- Redesign of disk storage files
- Restructuring of access to disk storage records

There is agreement that monitoring is most effective when there is some idea or conceptual model of how the major jobs utilize resources. Once the conceptual model is defined, useful data may be collected and analyzed. The following is a suggested procedure[1] for improvement of the performance of a hardware/software system using a conceptual model plus monitors:

1 Understand the system—the way it is managed, the workload, the configuration.

2 Analyze operations—reported utilization, operational objectives, operational characteristics, system characteristics, job characteristics, and current accounting and evaluation data.

3 Formulate hypotheses about the characteristics causing inefficiencies.

4 Analyze probable cost-effectiveness of possible system modifications.

5 Test hypotheses about problems and potential improvements by collecting data.

6 Implement changes and test effectiveness.

[1]T. E. Bell, B. W. Boehm, and R. A. Watson, "Framework and Initial Phases for Computer Performance Improvement," *Proceedings of the Fall Joint Computer Conference,* 1972, pp. 1141–1154.

The results from such "tuning" of hardware/software systems have been significant. A 25 percent reduction in execution time for the few jobs which normally take most of the processing capability is not unusual.

Evaluation by Use of System Logs and Observation

The system log may provide data useful for evaluation. This is especially true of small installations which maintain simple logs of jobs, job times, etc. An analysis of the system log may indicate problems with reruns, variations in running times for jobs caused by operator inefficiency, or excessive machine failure. The log may also be used to develop a distribution of jobs by time required. This may yield a simple list of jobs ordered by time required (say, per month). Such a list generally reveals the impact of, for example, a few large jobs or a stream of small jobs.

Observation of computer operations is useful in detecting inefficient scheduling of resource use and inefficient applications. The signs of inefficient scheduling or poor operating procedures are:

- Processing delays for operator to locate files, mount tapes or disks, load forms, or perform similar functions
- Excessive requirements for operator response at console
- Delays due to lack of training in proper restart procedures when processing is interrupted

The observation of the computer console often provides an indication of efficiency of utilization. For example, a console light on many computers will signal when the CPU is in wait state. An excessive percentage of time in that state indicates possible program or file access inefficiency. Observing the disk storage arm movements is sometimes useful in identifying unsuitable file storage organization. Rapid and continuous arm movements in and out may suggest that related records are not stored in related locations.

Scheduling Analysis

When programs are run in multiprogramming mode, the scheduling of the programs into memory may affect the processing time. The scheduling of the jobs efficiently can be quite complicated because factors to be taken into account include system resources required by each job, time constraints, input/output demands, and priorities.

A manual analysis of usage may provide some indication of scheduling efficiency. An alternative is the use of scheduling algorithms which seek to optimize the operations of the computer in multiprogramming mode.

EVALUATION OF A NEW OR REPLACEMENT HARDWARE/SOFTWARE SYSTEM

The process of evaluation for a new or replacement hardware/software system will vary depending on the level of experience by the organization in using computers, the urgency of replacement, and other factors. A generally recommended approach consists of steps such as the following:

    Feasibility study
    Preparation of specifications
    Obtaining of equipment proposals
    Evaluation of proposals

These steps are carried out or supervised by a study group.

The Study Group

A committee or task group is formed to direct the evaluation study. For most organizations, the committee should consist of middle-management personnel who represent the principal functions of the business, plus an executive from the systems function. One of the major problems in systems design is understanding the requirements of the different portions of the organization. The use of middle-management personnel who are reasonably high in the organization and can speak authoritatively about the requirements of their functions gives authority and scope to the work of the group. Members of the study group should be freed from part of their responsibilities in order to allow adequate time for this assignment. Although they do not have to be technically proficient, they should have a reasonable overall understanding of data processing. The study group must be provided with technical staff support.

For an organization that already has a computer installation and is studying the value of a new or expanded system, the staff support can come from the data processing systems staff. For an organization without prior experience, the use of outside consultants is frequently advisable. If used, consultants should work with, guide, assist, and otherwise aid the study group by providing the experience and technical expertise which the committee may lack. It is not usually advisable to turn the entire evaluation process over to outside consultants.

The Feasibility Study

The purpose of the feasibility study is to investigate the present system, evaluate the need for a new or replacement hardware/software system, select a tentative system, evaluate the cost and effectiveness of the proposed system, and evaluate the impact of the proposed system on the organization.

To evaluate the need for a new or replacement system, the study group must understand the information requirements of the organization. This understanding may be obtained by the dual process of examining the existing data processing system to determine what is currently being done and of investigating through interviews and analysis what information is needed but is not being furnished by the existing system. Data on the cost of operating the current system must be collected in order to make a cost/benefit analysis for a new system.

From the information obtained in the feasibility survey, the study group formulates one or more tentative systems, then makes rough estimates of cost and ability to meet performance objectives. From these tentative systems, one of which should usually be a modified version of the system in use, a system is selected as the best solution and is then analyzed further in terms of personnel impact, cost/benefit, and suitability to the firm's needs.

The feasibility study assembles data on the impact on company personnel of the proposed system. Rough plans are formulated for orienting, training, counseling, and adjusting the work force to the computer system. Estimates are made of the cost of the adjustment.

The cost/benefit study summarizes the benefits to be expected from the computer, the expected cost, and expected savings, if any. Figure 16-1 shows a summarized analysis. This would be supported by an analysis showing more detail. The figures are rough because specific equipment has not yet been selected. For the purposes of an investment analysis, the life of a system is probably about five to eight years, with six years probably a satisfactory compromise unless added facts dictate otherwise.

The results of the feasibility study together with the recommendations of the study groups are summarized and presented for top management approval. If the project is approved, the next step is to prepare a manual of specifications for use in procurement.

Preparation of Specifications and Obtaining Proposals

The *manual of specifications* is a statement of requirements which defines specifically what is to be accomplished by the proposed hardware/software system. It is a fairly detailed document. Most of the data needed for it is collected in the feasibility study. The document serves both as a summary of the proposed system for internal purposes and as a statement for use in inviting equipment proposals from vendors of data processing

---

COST ANALYSIS

Estimated initial cost of new computer system
    Cost of site preparation $xx
    Analysis and programming of basic applications   xx
    Cost of training, file conversion, parallel
        operations, etc.   <u>xx</u>
    Total one-time costs   <u>$xx</u>

Estimated annual operating costs
    Computer and related equipment rental or
        amortization and maintenance $xx
    Software rental   xx
    Analysts and programmers   xx
    Operating personnel   xx
    Space charges, supplies, power, etc.   xx
    Total operating costs $xx
Annual savings (displaced costs plus value of
   operation efficiencies less annual operating
   costs)   <u>$xx</u>

Rate of return (rate at which present value of
   savings equals present value of one-time
   costs)   xx%
Other intangible benefits (list)

Figure 16-1   Preliminary cost/benefit analysis.

equipment. The system specifications will usually include the elements listed in Figure 16-2.

On the basis of a preliminary screening, four or five vendors may be invited to submit proposals. Each vendor is provided with a copy of the manual of specifications and the rules for submitting proposals. There may be followup interviews with vendors to clarify any misunderstandings or uncertainties in the specifications. The manufacturer's representative is usually provided with an opportunity for a presentation to the study group, and at this meeting will summarize the proposal and answer questions. The manufacturer's proposal should normally contain the points listed in Figure 16-3.

The contract for the system is usually based on the manufacturer's standard contract form, but this still leaves many points for negotiation. For example, the assistance to be provided by the manufacturer—such as number of system analysts who will get the system going and number of hours of free test time—may vary from installation to installation, depending on the negotiations.

Evaluation of Proposals

Evaluation may be simple if only one manufacturer can satisfy specifications, but in general several manufacturers will respond with proposals worthy of consideration. Since there are a number of considerations, both

1 Introduction
  a Description of organization and what it does
  b Summary of requirements
  c Current equipment
  d Selection process—criteria to be used, form of responses, etc.
2 System requirements
  a Hardware features required
  b Software required
    (1) Compilers (FORTRAN, COBOL, RPG, etc.)
    (2) Utility packages (e.g., sort routine)
    (3) Application packages (e.g., linear programming)
    (4) Operating system
    (5) Data management system
  c Support required
    (1) System designers provided by vendor
    (2) Backup facilities
    (3) Test time and facilities
  d Constraints
    (1) Planned delivery date for equipment and software
    (2) Time constraints on processing
  e Desirable features not required to meet specifications
  f Capability for future growth
3 Major applications (for each application, the following apply)
  a System description
  b File description including current size and growth rate
  c Input data specifications and volume of input
  d System flowcharts for each run and run descriptions giving the following:
    (1) Frequency of processing
    (2) Volume of transactions
    (3) Suggested method of processing

Figure 16-2 Elements in a manual of specifications.

1 Proposed equipment configuration
   a Equipment units
   b Equipment operating characteristics and specifications
   c Options or alternative configurations
   d Ability of the system to expand (modularity)
   e Special requirements as to site and other installation costs
2 Cost of proposed configuration
   a Rental and purchase price by unit
   b Extra-shift rental
   c Maintenance contract if a unit is purchased
   d Software rental
3 Software availability for specified software and special software packages
4 Systems support
   a Systems analysis included; cost for added services
   b Programming services included; cost for added services
   c Customer maintenance engineer availability
   d Education support and schedule of rates
   e Backup availability
5 Terms
   a Acceptance of specified delivery date or proposed alternative delivery date
   b Payment terms
   c Lease-purchase and other options
   d Amount of test time to be provided
6 System performances for specified applications
   a Changes in design if different from that specified in requirements
   b Timings (how long each application takes)
   c Changes in timings using optional equipment
7 Other information

Figure 16-3 Outline of information normally found in a manufacturer's proposal.

quantitative and subjective, one evaluation method is to rank each supplier by a point system. For each criterion for evaluation, a number of points is assigned as a potential total, and then each manufacturer is rated by being awarded part of or all the potential points. A summary for such an analysis is given in Figure 16-4. There is a supporting analysis for each of the summary criteria. For example, software evaluation might include such subcriteria as:

Operating system evaluation
COBOL evaluation
FORTRAN evaluation

RPG evaluation
Data management system evaluation
Storage requirements
Other software evaluation

When the evaluation is made, different criteria will receive different weights with different users. The major questions are whether the proposed equipment will perform the job in the time allowed, what its relative cost will be, and whether it has flexibility to expand as more applications are added. A system should allow for growth—in file size, in number and scope of applications, and in volume of transactions. Most systems can provide for growth by the addition of equipment options. For example, a stripped-down, minimum-memory computer may have its power increased by addition of faster input/output units, more storage, or special instruction packages. A compatible family of computers allows the user to move from one computer in the family to a larger size without reprogramming. An evaluation should be made not only of the existing software but also of the probability of promised software being available on schedule.

	Criteria for evaluation	Possible points	Proposals A	B	C
1	**System performance (42%)**				
	a Hardware performance	60	60	41	42
	b Software performance	60	39	43	31
	c Expansion capabilities	55	41	48	30
2	**Vendor capabilities (25%)**				
	a Vendor performance	40	25	32	21
	b Maintenance and backup	20	14	18	13
	c Installation support	20	12	18	12
	d Staff preference	25	15	20	5
3	**Cost (33%)**				
	a Rental price	50	35	23	40
	b Terms for extended use	20	17	5	18
	c Ongoing educational cost	25	21	9	17
	d Maintenance and backup cost	20	15	10	14
	e One-time system and education cost	20	18	11	14
		415	312	278	257

Figure 16-4 Summary sheet for point-ranking method of computer evaluation.

In evaluations of hardware and software, it is frequently desirable to program and run a test problem to try out the effectiveness of the software and to appraise the operating problems. The manufacturer will usually provide time for testing. Frequently, an order must be placed before any test machine is available, but the practice in the industry is to use the initial sales order as a basis for scheduling machine delivery. When the delivery time comes close (say, six months), the order is firmed. Thus, there is usually sufficient time to evaluate by test runs the equipment which may not have been available when the initial order was placed.

When equipment is being evaluated, the alternative of a mixed system should be considered. Several firms offer plug-in compatible peripherals (say, a disk unit) which have higher performance at a lower cost than the manufacturer's units. The main disadvantage of these independent peripherals is in the added management problems of dealing with more than one vendor and coping with responsibility for equipment-caused failures.

The study group should make an analysis of the applications timings furnished by the manufacturer and conduct an independent analysis of the computer capabilities. In doing this, it should keep in mind that the real criterion for measuring system performance is throughput. The comparisons that are made are in lieu of the complete throughput analysis, which cannot be made in advance because all programs would have to be written and running. The following are frequently used methods of comparison and are listed with comments on their effectiveness:

Comparison techniques	Comments
Core cycle time	Extremely gross measure. Unreliable because systems differ in organization. Useful only for systems with same organization.
Instruction times	Very gross measure, since the frequency of instruction use must be considered.
Instruction mix times (average for a mix of instructions)	An average instruction time based on the expected frequency with which each instruction is used for different types of applications. Gross measure, but better than unweighted instruction time. At best, it is a measure of raw internal computing power.
Kernel problem	Sample problems are coded with the system's own instructions and timed. Especially useful for standardized mathematical applications. Gives a measure of internal performance, but does not reflect the effect of input/out-

Comparison techniques	Comments
	put, multiprogramming, operating system, etc.
Standard benchmark problems	Standard problems of a type normally performed. The problem is coded, and time to perform the standard task is estimated or measured by running it. Standard benchmark problems usually reflect typical jobs but are not a sample of the complete processing system as it will operate. Most commonly used method.
Simulation	The characteristics of the proposed system are compared with the characteristics of available computers, and the performance of the different systems is simulated by a computer program.

EVALUATION OF INFORMATION SYSTEM APPLICATIONS

An information system application may be evaluated in terms of three measures: technical, operational, and economic. For new applications, these are feasibility measures; for existing applications, they represent performance measures.

Measure of feasibility/performance	Comments
1 Technical feasibility/ performance	Can application be accomplished with existing technology? Has technology proved to be capable of supporting the application? For example, a realtime system requires special hardware for effective operation.
2 Operational feasibility/ performance	Can (does) the system operate successfully? Will it be used? Is it being used?
3 Economic feasibility/ performance	Will (does) the benefit from the system exceed the cost?

New proposals should be subjected to the three tests of feasibility; existing applications should be evaluated in terms of the three tests of performance.

Technical Evaluation

The technical evaluation of new applications examines whether it is technically feasible to perform the proposed information processing. Many applications are beyond the technical capabilities of the hardware and software available for use. The following are examples of technical evaluation questions:

- Is the data transmission rate fast enough to handle the data?
- Is there sufficient auxiliary storage to keep the necessary files?
- Can the CPU respond to all requests within the specified time period?
- Are there known computational methods for solving the problem?
- Will the operating system support the proposed operational approach?

When applications are installed, subsequent evaluation may disclose that they operate ineffectively because the technical capabilities of the hardware and software cannot support them properly. An online realtime operation may work but be very slow because the computer involved has insufficient capability to handle the workload.

Operational Evaluation

Operational feasibility considerations relate to whether the input data can be provided and the output will be usable and used. For example, it may be technically feasible for sales representatives to telephone in every sale, but operationally it may be impractical. It is technically feasible to issue 100-page computer-generated reports, but it is operationally infeasible for them to be utilized effectively. It is technically feasible to place a terminal in every manager's office, but, as discussed previously, there are considerations which suggest such terminals will receive little use.

Evaluation of applications after implementation should examine how well they operate with special reference to input, error rates, timeliness of output, and utilization. Some research on utilization of output suggests the need for periodic evaluation of applications.[2] In the study of Gee,[3] 64 line managers at the middle management level of manufacturing companies were interviewed and asked to evaluate control information items they received as having substantial use by them or as being irrelevant or background information. Of 579 items, 46 percent (267) were considered to be irrelevant or useful only for background. In a further investigation, 49 middle managers were asked to classify items of control information as vital (admitting no delay), important (used for reference but delay or inaccuracy generally not

[2]John K. Simmons and Michael J. Barrett, "A Behavioral and Technical Investigation into the Utilization of Accounting Reports by Middle Managers," in Thomas J. Burns (ed.), *Behavioral Experiments in Accounting*, College of Administrative Science, Ohio State University, Columbus, 1971, pp. 351–414.

[3]Kenneth P. Gee, "Specifying and Satisfying the Control Information Requirements of Middle Management," unpublished paper, University of Manchester, England.

significant), or background (items rarely used). The results from 383 items were as follows:

Vital	32%
Important	36%
Background	32%

There is a tendency to not terminate a report once it is started. Even though it may not be used, there often is a feeling that it might have utility in the future. This is consistent with the concept of the value of unused information described in Chapter 3. Various methods are used to spot unused reports:

- Termination of the report to see if anyone asks for it when it does not arrive
- Periodic review of all reports by a task force
- Transfer pricing to provide incentives for managers to eliminate unnecessary reports

Economic Evaluation

When a project is proposed, it should be subjected to tests of economic feasibility; after it is installed, it should be periodically reviewed for continuing cost/effectiveness.

In assessing economic feasibility of new projects and evaluating the economic benefit of the MIS system (or major subsystem), it is useful to categorize costs and benefits as follows:

Costs
    Measured or estimated with low variance
    Estimated with medium or high variance
Benefits
    Measured or estimated with low variance
    Estimated with medium or high variance

Some examples of costs and benefits in each category are shown in Figure 16-5.

The measured or estimated costs with low variance are the outlays to operate an application. Examples are personnel, supplies, equipment, and equipment maintenance. These can usually be identified with reasonable certainty because there are specific uses of resources—such as salary payments and equipment rental payments—that are clearly associated with information processing. The identification of the costs of operating a single application is somewhat more difficult because some

	Costs	Benefits
Low variance in estimate	Hardware Purchased software Installation Operating personnel Supplies Application maintenance	Cost displacement such as reduction of personnel
Medium variance in estimate	Application development	Reductions in assets employed, such as reduced inventory Improvements in asset management, such as increased rate of collections and reduced borrowing.
High variance in estimate	Implementation problems Reduced efficiency such as from employee resistance Error handling outside data processing Loss of revenue due to errors	Increased revenue from reduction in time of service, improvement in data availability, improvement in delivery time Reduced costs from improved accuracy Improved performance from improved data, more timely reports, and extended decision-making capabilities

Figure 16-5 Costs and benefits from computer-based information system applications.

costs are shared with other projects. The methods for deciding how much to associate with an individual application are imprecise and depend somewhat on the purpose of the allocation. Allocation was discussed in Chapter 14.

Costs of application development can be estimated, but experience suggests that there is a medium variance in these estimates. For example, the variance for the cost of developing an application can be expected to be in the range from 25 to 100 percent. Several significant costs have a high variance in estimation and are frequently ignored because their incidence is in user areas rather than in data processing:

Example	Comments
Implementation costs	The costs of changeover to a new system may be substantial but largely unreported. Examples are on-the-job training for employees of the user and reduction in efficiency during training.
Employee resistance	Employee resistance to or irritation with the information system may reduce effectiveness of job performance.
Error handling	The cost of error handling—examination, correction, and reentry—is substantial yet difficult to measure because it is diffused throughout the organization.
Error losses	Customers can become dissatisfied because of errors in data processing. Customer goodwill is reduced, but measuring the revenue loss is difficult.

The benefits most easily measured are those of cost displacement. A computerized payroll system displaces payroll clerks, for example; this type of saving can be reasonably well documented. There are benefits that can be identified but which have a medium variance (say, less than 100 percent in 90 percent of the cases) in the estimated value. Applications which result in reduced inventories of raw materials or inventory in production because of improvements in ordering and scheduling yield a real benefit, but the precise amount cannot be identified. Information system applications which result in improved management of assets by improved collections or reduced borrowing through better planning also yield a specific benefit which is not easily measured because of the interaction of other variables as well.

There are other real benefits that have a high variance attached to estimates. The problems of estimating benefits in such cases are described in the next section.

A major question which arises in evaluation of information resources is how much a company should spend. There have been studies showing the percentage of sales utilized for information processing in various industries. In general, it has been found that leaders in various industries tend to spend more on computer resources than the followers, but there are still wide variations in the wide amount spent and the success that comes with it. An executive may obtain some useful feel for the ratio of cost that is appropriate to devote to information processing cost, but it is only a very rough measure. The MIS master plan is useful in answering the question of "how much" because of the interrelation between estimated benefits and the estimated cost for the applications in the master plan.

QUANTIFYING BENEFITS FROM INFORMATION SYSTEMS APPLICATIONS

The value of an information system application may be both economic and noneconomic. Economic benefits are those that cause improvements in revenues or reductions in costs. Noneconomic benefits are related to quality of life. A reduction in uncertainty which has no economic impact may nevertheless be desirable because humans tend to value uncertainty reduction for its own sake. Closely allied is improved confidence in decision making because of improved quality and quantity of information (even when the decisions themselves do not change). Another example is a reduction in frustration due to improved access to information. Even if the noneconomic benefits do not affect revenues or expense, they can be assigned a dollar value because organizations are willing to pay for these advantages.

This section addresses the benefits previously classified as "estimated only with a large variance." For these benefits, quantification is especially difficult. Benefits are not easily measured or are so interconnected with other factors that it is difficult to separate the effects of each. According to the theoretical exposition in Chapter 7, the value of an information system application for decision-making support is the value of the improvement in results caused by the improvement in information. According to this concept, information which does not change a decision has no value. This concept presents two difficulties. It is often difficult to identify the causal relation and to measure the change resulting from the information. Also, information is not isolated in its effect. Information for one decision may be significant months later in another, even unrelated, decision. The strict mathematical approach is therefore useful conceptually, but its application is very restricted.

The problem of quantifying benefits is even more difficult for benefits not related to the value of information for decision making. One useful approach is to have users or knowledgeable executives estimate the value of an information system application. This estimation process can be a direct estimate of value or can be a greater than/less than cost method.

Direct Estimate of Value of Application

In a research study by Gallagher,[4] managers of a medium-size firm responded to a questionnaire asking them to estimate the value of a report used in nonprogrammed decisions. The key question was, "What is the maximum amount you would recommend paying for the xxx report for your use?" Some of the conclusions of the study were:

- Managers who participated in the design of the application gave higher estimates of value than managers who had not participated.
- Managers in upper-middle, line, operating positions placed a higher value on the application than other managers.
- The managers were able to make dollar estimates of the value of the application (i.e., the maximum amount the company should pay for the report). These ranged from $176,000 to $404,000.

The study suggests that a reasonable estimate of the monetary value of a specific application system can be obtained by asking each user for an estimate.

Less than/Greater than Cost Method

Humans tend to be not especially adept at estimating value without some standard based on alternative prices, customary prices, or other criterion. It is generally easier for the human estimator to answer a less than/greater than question than to generate a point estimate. For example, it is probably easier to obtain an answer to the second question below than to the first.

1 What is the value of the report analyzing past-due accounts?
2 Is the value of the report analyzing past-due accounts greater than $200 per month?

This suggests an alternative approach to benefit estimation which seeks to determine not the exact benefit but only if the benefit is sufficient to justify the expenditure. The procedure might be as follows:

Estimated cost (including expected rate of return on investment)	xxx
Less: Benefits from displaced costs and benefits estimatable with low or medium	

---

[4]Charles A. Gallagher, "Measurement and Analysis of Managers' Perceptions of the Value of Selected Management Information," unpublished doctoral dissertation, Florida State University, Gainsville, December 1971.

variance	−xxx
Estimated costs in excess of easily estimated benefits	xxx
Benefits to be evaluated	
Improved decision making	
Improved response time to customer inquiries	

Users, or executives having responsibility for the users, would be asked if the benefits to be judged have a value in excess of the cost assigned to them.

The estimation approaches are applied at the level of applications. The benefits of an information system can be viewed as the sum of the benefits from individual applications. This presents some conceptual and measurement difficulties because several applications operating together may result in a greater benefit than each of them singly. This aggregation problem is best handled by those responsible for the master development plan because they must evaluate the entire system.

COST/BENEFIT ANALYSIS
OF DESIGN ALTERNATIVES

In the design of computer-based information system applications, there are a number of tradeoffs to be made. These tradeoffs represent design options and should be analyzed as to cost and benefit and presented to management for decision making.[5] Examples of design options relate to response time, display detail, and data quality.

Response Time

Response time is the time for the information system to respond to a stimulus. Three major types of stimuli require responses:

    1 Transaction processing request
    2 Input which results in updating of the data base (transactions, corrections, new records, deletions, etc.)
    3 Retrieval request

The response may be immediate (realtime), or it may be subject to a variety of processing delays. The response requirements differ depending on the application and the input stimulus. The following are some considerations affecting the response time for these three types:

[5]James C. Emery, "Can We Develop Cost-Effective Information Systems?," *Management Informatics*, no. 6, 1972, pp. 243–249.

Stimulus requiring response	Considerations in response time
Transaction	The transaction that needs to be completed at once (while the customer waits) will generally need fast response supported by an updated data base.
Updating data base	An up-to-the-minute data base is generally useful in operational decisions; it is less important at a high level such as in strategic planning. It is desirable as support for on-line transaction processing.
Retrieval requests	The retrieval of data required for operating decisions tends to need fast response; higher-level decisions can generally tolerate some delay.

Thus, fast processing and response time is usually most useful for certain types of transactions and updating situations. Retrieval requests are generally less critical with respect to response time. However, in some decision situations, prompt and effective decision making depends upon fast response. Fast response is also useful in allowing decision makers to "browse" through the file to work through an ill-structured problem.

The typical cost analysis will show cost per application (both development and operation) increasing as the system displays fast-response characteristics. This is due to extra hardware and software, more complex application design, and communications and terminal costs.

Display Detail

In Chapter 4, research was described which indicates that users make better decisions with summarized information but are less confident than when they have worked with the detailed data. Studies of humans as information processors suggest that they have a very limited processing capability. The tradeoff for display made might be:

1 Paper report versus CRT display
2 Summary versus detailed report
3 Substantial analysis to compress the detail versus minor aggregations

There is a tendency for decision makers to desire more information than they can effectively use. The tradeoff is therefore the danger of obscuring of some important result via aggregation and reduction in confidence versus the reduction in file requirements and output requirements.

Data Quality

In a research study, Carl Adams interviewed 75 top and middle managers in 10 major corporations to determine their attitudes toward information. The managers were asked whether (given a choice) they would prefer an improvement in quality or an improvement in quantity. Almost 90 percent preferred an improvement in quality.[6]

There is a tendency to request higher quality of data than is required. Accounting data on cash, customer billing, etc., needs to be very exact; data on sales by product by area can be less exact and yet be completely satisfactory. The cost of data increases with the quality requirements. Additional accuracy and completeness are achieved with a cost of redundant data and controls at a variety of points in the processing cycle. This suggests the need to examine the quality requirements for an application rather than to attempt achieving a single level of quality across all applications. In some cases, the existence of the data base concept will make quality differentiation more difficult because the use of data is not specified in advance.

SUMMARY

Evaluation of an information system may be conducted at a number of different levels: the overall function, the hardware/software system, and the application. The evaluation of the management and operation of the function was discussed in Chapters 14 and 15; Chapter 16 concentrates on the hardware/software system and the application.

The evaluation of hardware/software systems can be divided into the evaluation of an existing system for improvement and evaluation of a new or replacement system. The evaluation of the existing hardware/software system can use a variety of techniques ranging from observation to hardware and software monitors.

The evaluation of new or replacement hardware/software systems generally follows a process in which a study group studies feasibility, prepares specifications for approved systems, and obtains vendor proposals. The proposals may be evaluated by assigning point values to various features that are important and judging each proposal on each point.

[6]Carl R. Adams, "How Management Users View Information Systems," working paper 14, The Management Information Systems Research Center, University of Minnesota, Minneapolis, 1973, p. 16.

A difficult problem is the quantifying of benefits from information system applications. The cost displacement benefits are fairly easy to measure; the less-measurable benefits come from, for example, response time, customer service, improved quality, and a better data base. These factors do have a value which may be estimated either directly or by using a less than/greater than approach.

In evaluation of information systems, various alternative designs are considered. They should be analyzed as to cost and benefit. Examples of design factors are response time, display detail, and quality.

EXERCISES

1 Outline the scope of an evaluation audit of the information system function.
2 Describe how an evaluation of the information system function might be conducted.
3 Describe the operation of a hardware monitor. How does a hardware monitor differ from a software monitor?
4 Describe the process of "tuning" a processing application.
5 Some organizations have used monitors to collect data on hardware performance, but have not been able to use the data effectively. Why might this occur?
6 An evaluation team observing operations in the computer center noted the following. Explain the possible evaluative interpretation the team might make.
   a The operator could not find the forms for job 104.
   b The computer was idle while the tapes for job 107 were loaded. The prior job had not used tapes.
   c The tape reels from the runs for the previous day were stacked in the corner.
   d The operator was being helped by a friend who had the day off.
   e Rerun time was not logged separately from regular run time.
   f The scheduling of jobs seemed to be a random process.
7 When a team was asked to evaluate the applications being run, the data processing manager pointed out that 1,000 different programs were being run. How might the installation approach this task efficiently?
8 Why does proper scheduling of jobs make a difference in throughput in the following:
   a A single program environment?
   b A multiprogramming environment?
9 Describe the process for evaluating a new or replacement hardware/software system.
10 What is the purpose of the manual of specifications?

11 Describe the strengths and weaknesses of the point-ranking method. How should the point values be arrived at?

12 Describe methods for comparing the performance of different computers.

13 Benchmark problems are frequently used. What will a benchmark provide? What are the weaknesses of the method?

14 Explain the three measures for evaluation of an application.

15 What incentive does a manager have to eliminate unnecessary processing or unused reports in the following instances:

  a When there is no charging system?

  b When computer costs are charged to using units on a cost basis?

16 Describe the hidden costs of implementation, employee resistance, and error handling.

17 Why is it difficult to measure loss of customers or sales due to problems in computer processing?

18 A top executive exclaimed, "I don't know whether we are spending too little, too much, or just the right amount on computer data processing." How might this problem be settled?

19 Explain how use of a computer-based information system could have noneconomic consequences. Can these be assigned a dollar value?

20 Explain how the dollar value of difficult-to-measure benefits might be derived.

SELECTED REFERENCES

Bedford, N., and M. Onsi: "Measuring the Value of Information—An Information Theory Approach," *Management Services*, January-February 1966, pp. 15–22.

Bell, T. E., B. W. Boehm, and R. A. Watson: "Framework and Initial Phases for Computer Performance Improvement," *Proceedings of the Fall Joint Computer Conference*, 1972, pp. 1141–1154.

Boyd, D. F., and H. S. Krasnow: "Economic Evaluation of Management Information Systems," *IBM Systems Journal*, March 1963.

Canning, Richard G.: "Get More Computer Efficiency," *EDP Analyzer*, March 1971.

————: "Savings from Performance Monitoring," *EDP Analyzer*, vol. 10, no. 9, September 1972.

Carlson, G.: "How to Save Money with Computer Monitoring," *Proceedings of the ACM Annual Conference*, 1972, pp. 1024–1040.

Chervany, Norman L., and Gary W. Dickson: "Economic Evaluation of Management Information Systems: An Analytical Framework," *Decision Sciences*, vol. 1, 1970, pp. 296–308.

Diebold, John: "Bad Decisions on Computer Use," *Harvard Business Review*, January-February 1969.

Freiberger, Walter (ed.): *Statistical Computer Performance Evaluation*, Academic Press, Inc., New York, 1972.

Gallagher, Charles A.: "Measurement and Analysis of Managers' Perceptions of the Value of Selected Management Information," unpublished doctoral dissertation, Florida State University, Gainesville, December 1971.

IBM Systems Journal, vol. 8, no. 4, 1969. Seven papers on the subject of performance measurement.

Lucas, H. D., Jr.: "Performance Evaluation and Monitoring," *Computing Surveys*, September 1971, pp. 79–91.

————: "Performance Evaluation and the Management of Information Services," *Data Base*, Spring 1972, pp. 1–8.

McFarlan, F. Warren: "Management Audit of the EDP Department," *Harvard Business Review*, May-June 1973, pp. 131–142.

Simmons, John K., and Michael J. Barrett: "A Behavioral and Technical Investigation into the Utilization of Accounting Reports by Middle Managers," in Thomas J. Burns (ed.), *Behavioral Experiments in Accounting*, College of Administrative Science, Ohio State University, Columbus, 1971, pp. 351–414.

Warner, C. D.: "Monitoring: A Key to Cost Efficiency," *Datamation*, Jan. 1, 1971, pp. 40–42, 49.

CURRENT ISSUES
    Extent of Integration
    Man/Machine Division of Labor
    Information Quality Control
    System and Data Security
SOCIETAL IMPLICATIONS
    Changing Patterns of Employment
    Changing Job Characteristics
    Nonresponsive Systems
    Reduction in Privacy
    Concentration in the Computer Industry
FUTURE INFORMATION SYSTEM DEVELOPMENTS
    Future Hardware and Software
    New System Design
SUMMARY
EXERCISES
SELECTED REFERENCES

Chapter 17

Current Issues, Societal Implications, and Future Developments

CURRENT ISSUES

The development of management information systems has been very rapid. The major developments have occurred in the period beginning in the mid-1960s. There have been differences of opinion about how computers should be used in information systems. Some of these issues have been resolved; others still remain. This section describes some of the current issues and problems of information systems for organizational use.

Extent of Integration

An early concept in organizational information system design was the total system in which the entire information system was designed as a single unified system. This concept has largely been abandoned, primarily because integrating the entire system was found to be too difficult and also unnecessary. Instead, the idea of a federation of systems (or a number of large subsystems) has gained currency. This is consistent with the system concepts explained in Chapter 4. A current issue is still, however, the amount of integration that should be applied to the organizational information system. Integration may occur in two ways—processing integration and data integration. Processing integration refers to the size of the processing subsystem, i.e., how many somewhat independent subsystems should be combined for processing purposes. Data integration refers to the combining of files into data bases. The issue is the extent of this combining of files. Decisions on these integration issues are currently being made by trial and error judgment. Experience over the next several years may develop a clearer approach.

Man/Machine Division of Labor

The management information system tends to be a man/machine system in which some activities are performed by the computer and some by the human operator or manager. The technology has been advancing so rapidly that an increasing number of human functions can be performed faster, more accurately, and with greater scope by the computer. However, humans have certain inherent advantages. They can reason from incomplete information. They can operate in a trial-and-error environment and can apply the entire range of their experience to problems. At the same time, humans require challenge and variety in their jobs in order to remain motivated. This means that an optimal technical solution to division of labor might result in an unsatisfactory job environment for the human operator or manager. The major issue, therefore, is how to structure the different tasks in a man/machine environment so that the technology is used effectively while a satisfactory job environment for the human is still maintained.

Information Quality Control

In a manual system many people look at the results of processing as documents flow through the system. Errors can be spotted by any of the various people who work with these documents. The fact that more than one person works on the processing or handles a document also adds to the control against unauthorized, improper, or fraudulent transactions. In other words, an unauthorized person cannot easily initiate a transaction in a manual system because of the human review which will generally identify the unauthorized initiation.

Separate files and separate processing systems localize errors. The redundancy in the manual system often results in similar files being maintained by different parts of the organization. In the event of errors, this redundancy often makes it possible to identify correct data. The integration of processing and integration of data means that much of the redundancy is removed. An error which might have been localized to one function may now affect a variety of functions because the data item is prepared and processed only once. All applications access the single recording.

The quality measures in information processing have historically been oriented toward the manual, nonintegrated systems which could allow a larger error rate than the integrated systems where the errors can compound. A major problem in information processing is therefore the upgrading of the quality of input and processing in computer-based information systems.

System and Data Security

System and data security is not just a conceptual issue; it is a practical problem because the consequences of inadequate security can be serious. Consider some examples of computer-based fraud.

- Union Dime Savings Bank in New York, over a three-year period, lost approximately $1.5 million to an embezzler. The embezzler, a teller supervisor at the bank's Park Avenue branch, used the supervisor's override feature of the online system to make fraudulent entries.
- The management of Equity Funding Corporation Of America, a large insurance company, utilized the computer to cover a fraud involving $110 million in nonexistent insurance policy loans.
- Arrests were made of individuals attempting to sell the name and address files of a large marketing organization.

In computer-based information systems the concentration of processing and files in a limited area using a small number of operations personnel increases the risk from fraud, destruction, theft, etc. A continuing problem in information system management is to provide adequate system and data security by such measures as:

Computer center access protection
Terminal access security
Data access security
Special fire and theft provisions
Off-premises backup for files and programs
Provision for backup processing
Internal and external audits

SOCIETAL IMPLICATIONS

The use of computers for organizational information systems affects the quality of life outside the organization and therefore has implications for society in general. Some major considerations are changing patterns of employment, machine-paced management, nonresponsive systems, reduction in privacy, and concentration of industry.

Changing Patterns of Employment

The use of computers for clerical processing tasks has displaced employees who perform these duties. This change has been significant enough that growth in numbers of clerical jobs has declined in recent years. However, the computer industry has created new jobs—systems analyst, programmer, computer operator, to name a few. The clerical jobs being displaced have generally been menial, repetitive, and uninteresting. The new jobs are, on balance, well paid and challenging. Because the computer is extending the scope of work performed, total employment may not have changed drastically—the jobs displaced by computers are probably offset by jobs created by the computer industry. At the same time, however, the jobs created require education and training at a fairly high level; the jobs displaced used fairly low-level, minimally trained people. In other words, the computer is reducing job opportunities for the poorly trained. However, because many of the displaced jobs are not challenging, society is probably better off to apply its human energies to other tasks. This is a long-run view; in the short run, computers have compounded the problem of employment for the marginally educated and unskilled.

There have been many predictions that management information systems would have an employment impact on middle managers by reducing the need for them. In Chapter 5, it was suggested that human information processing is a severe constraint in organizational design. Therefore, an information system might reduce the need for middle managers to act as filters and communicators among organizational units. The predictions have also suggested that the middle manager's job would be reduced in scope as information/decision systems made it possible for more decisions to be made at higher levels. The predicted effects have not been observed to any great extent. There may be a trend in the direction indicated; it is not as evident as is the impact on clerical jobs. The reason may be that a large proportion of a middle manager's job is not programmable. Personnel decisions, leadership and motivation, opportunity search, and other such duties still need the human touch.

Changing Job Characteristics

The assembly line is a very efficient mechanism to produce standardized manufactured products. However, in certain ways it is detrimental to human values. The human job content is made so invariant that it becomes boring and the human workers cannot set their own pace; they must perform at the rate of the assembly line. These factors have led to dissatisfaction and disruption of production. Any attempt to increase the speed of the assembly line meets with strong opposition. A potential danger in computer-based systems is that the computer will result in machine-paced clerical and managerial operations. The clerical employee is paced by the "demand" for prompt input of transaction data; the manager is paced by the system "demand" that decisions be made in a defined time period.

The use of computer-based systems is most efficient if standard methods and procedures are used. This concept extends to management levels. The computer-assisted management approach provides standard methods for analysis of decisions, planning, and control. The computer is thus a force in standardization of some elements of both clerical and managerial jobs.

The computer-based MIS is changing the environment for decision making. The organization at all levels is richer in information. When the data is combined with decision support software, the ability to make good decisions is enhanced. However, the system characteristics tend to favor the analytic decision style over the heuristic style.

The computer-based systems may be changing the amount and location of power in organizations. Control of information resources represents an element of power similar to control of cash and other organizational assets. The use of dispersed processing and local files decentralizes power based on information resources. The use of data base systems centralizes certain types of information power even though access is broadened.

Nonresponsive Systems

To paraphrase the nursery rhyme, when computer data processing systems are good, they are very, very good; when they are bad, they are horrid. The problem is generally not in the computer hardware but in the system design and operation. Almost everyone is aware of experiences with computer-based processing systems which were nonresponsive. For example:

- A department store sends its customer statements out 10 days late, but still charges customers a late-payment fee if the payment is not received by the regular billing date. Instead of the normal 25 days to pay without penalty, customers have only 15.

- A company error in an account by a credit card company takes six months to correct. During this period, delinquent charges are assessed. The computer sends out increasingly threatening messages.
- A request for a correction is answered with, "Our computer system won't allow it."

The concept of individual dignity suggests that systems be designed to be responsive to the individual. The problem of errors and the nonresponsiveness of systems to correction requests has resulted in proposed legislation to protect customer rights in such cases.

The credit reporting area illustrates the social need for responsive systems. The Fair Credit Reporting Act provides that a person refused a job, refused credit, charged more for credit or insurance, etc., because of a credit report must be informed of the report. The person can see the files without charge, dispute the contents if not true, and obtain reinvestigation. If a disputed item cannot be verified, the agency must so notify those who have received prior reports (for six months to two years, depending on the type of report). A person must be informed that such an investigation is being made. Adverse information older than three months cannot be used unless verified. Data on charges such as arrests or lawsuits must include the record of the final disposition. Bankruptcies must be purged from the file after four years.

Reduction in Privacy

The existence of data bases has added a new dimension to the problem of privacy, a problem to be found within organizations as well as within the larger context of government and society. Within an organization, the problem is that of general access to files that were formerly more or less unavailable except to the part of the organization which maintained them. For example, a financial institution such as a savings and loan association might establish a single file containing all information about a customer instead of maintaining separate files for his different activities with the association, e.g., as depositor, savings account holder, mortgagee, borrower on auto loan, safety deposit box renter. Prior to the existence of the data base, the people dealing with the savings account had no ready access to the fact that the account holder also had a loan with the association. After the data base is developed, not all persons in the organization should have free access to it, because of the internal organizational consideration based on "no need to know" and also because of the societal consideration that data furnished to an organization was furnished for specific purposes and should not be available for unrelated purposes except by permission of those concerned.

The privacy problem of a data base in a single organization is compounded when organizations form networks to exchange information. Credit reporting is an example of such sharing of data. There have been suggestions that governments centralize data to develop more coherent and complete files about, for example, persons receiving government assistance. It would be possible to match welfare recipients, who are not supposed to have more than one car, against auto registrations to identify those who do have more than one car. Such centralization has been rejected because of the fear of the eventual impact of complete computer-based dossiers. Also, information furnished to a governmental agency such as a motor vehicle bureau is provided for one legal purpose; to use it for another is an expansion of governmental authority which is generally considered not to be desirable. The problems of privacy related to both public and private data bases have prompted legislation at various levels of government and in various countries.

Concentration in the Computer Industry

The computer industry presents a problem to the United States economic/social system. Unlike many countries which encourage monopolies, the United States views concentrations of economic power as inconsistent with the political system, and the policy of the government under the antitrust laws is to promote competition by "breaking up" giant companies which dominate an industry. The computer industry is under continuous scrutiny in this regard because IBM dominates, with about 70 percent of the market. Most of the remainder of the business is divided among five companies having market shares of from 3 to 7 percent (Honeywell Information Systems, Inc., Univac Division of Sperry Rand Corp., Burroughs Corp., The National Cash Register Co., and Control Data Corporation). There is then another set of companies with even smaller shares of the total market.

IBM has been very profitable; its competitors have not. This is not due to lack of economic power. The computer divisions of large, powerful companies (General Electric Co. and RCA Corporation) were not able to obtain profitability. Yet IBM does not quote unduly low prices. In the industry, there is agreement that IBM provides a price umbrella under which the other companies have a chance of making a profit. The economies of scale in hardware and software favor IBM (it costs the same to develop a compiler for one machine as for 10,000), but IBMs sales are usually made because of marketing skill and level of support (such as software) rather than on the basis of hardware price. Should IBM be "broken up" into independent, smaller companies? The answer is not obvious, and the debate will likely continue for some time.

Recent court decisions suggest that IBM will be required to accept greater competition. In 1973, Telex Corp., a manufacturer of replacement peripherals, obtained a large judgment against IBM because IBM had carried out certain marketing practices that made it difficult for Telex to sell its peripheral units.

FUTURE INFORMATION SYSTEM DEVELOPMENTS

Technology in the computer field has tended to change very rapidly; information system concepts have evolved more slowly. A major influence (perhaps the major influence) on information system development is the changing capabilities and changing cost of the hardware and software used in the systems. This section summarizes hardware and software trends and projects some of the ways that information systems may develop.

Future Hardware and Software

There have been some strong trends in computer hardware; these are expected to continue. Hardware will be faster, smaller, and less expensive. Storage will have larger capacity and faster access and be less expensive. The input and output of data will be faster, more available to the user, and less expensive. The hardware will continue to decline as a percentage of the total cost of a computer-based information system.

These conclusions are based primarily on changing technology which is reducing the size and cost of hardware. Some of these developments are summarized below.

Computer subsystem	Technology
Central processor	The densities of computer circuits are increasing (number of circuits for a given area) and yields are improving (percentage of circuits produced without a fault). One 1970 forecast was for central processor cost in 1980 of from one-fifth to one-tenth the 1970 cost.[1] The reliability of the central processor is expected to improve.
Memory	Unlimited online storage (say, 10^{13} to 10^{14} bits) is expected to be available at very modest cost. A hierarchy

[1]Frederic G. Withington, "The Next (and Last?) Generation," *Datamation*, May 1972, p. 11.

Computer subsystem	Technology
	of memory devices having different cost/access characteristics will be available.
Input/output devices	By 1980 perhaps 80 percent of hardware cost will be for peripherals. A growth in use of terminals for direct entry and retrieval is expected.
Data communications	Estimates are for an explosive growth during the 1970s. The Bell system plans a telephone network by 1980 four times the size of the 1970 network. Transmission speeds will be significantly higher. Competitive data communications systems will be available.

Software developments have tended to lag behind hardware. There is some trend to provide hardware for traditional software functions. Compilers (or at least significant parts) will be implemented by circuitry or microprogramming of the circuitry. The trend is toward more standard, off-the-shelf software because of the quality that can be designed into such systems. One of the significant trends may be for organizations to purchase substantial parts of the software for the MIS system rather than making the software in-house.

New System Design

The design process is still very judgmental, and very little use has been made of technology in the design of new applications. Current research suggests that there will be significant developments in automation of system design which will reduce the cost of new system design.

Most new organizational information systems will be based on the concepts described in the text. The implementation of such management-oriented information systems will be slow, primarily because of the long development times. Most large systems have a development period of several years. At the same time, there is an evolution in design based on experience and in response to changes in technology and cost factors. The directions in design are likely to be toward individualized systems.

The preceding chapters have emphasized the need to identify information needs and to then build a system to meet these needs. There is evidence that individuals differ in their need for and utilization of information. This suggests individually tailored systems, but such systems are costly, given existing technology. Future developments in information system hardware, software, and design methods may allow each manager a system tailored to the critical decisions that individual must make and able to change as managerial needs and experience change.

The use of tailored systems may be extended to the management of executive time. It has been suggested that executives be provided with a personalized system to assist in planning and controlling their calendar and their extraorganizational contacts.[2]

SUMMARY

There are differences of opinion in the design and application of information systems for organizational use. Some major issues and problems were surveyed. Also explored were societal implications of information systems with respect to employment, privacy, industry concentration, and responsiveness to individual dignity. Future developments were identified with respect to hardware and software as they affect information systems. System design is expected to evolve rather than to change radically, with the direction of change toward more individualized systems.

EXERCISES

1   Read various articles about the Equity Funding fraud which was referred to in this chapter. Identify how the computer was used as an instrument of fraud. Discuss implications for society. (Hint: Useful articles to start with are Wyndham Robertson, "Those Daring Young Con Men of Equity Funding," *Fortune*, August 1973, pp. 81–85, 120, 122, 124, 128, 132; and Christopher Podgus, "Outwitting the Computer Swindler," *Computer Decisions*, September 1973, pp. 12–16.

2   Read the Swedish law on privacy with respect to computer data processing. Discuss its application in your country. (The law is published in *Computer Decisions*, November 1973, pp. 50, 51.)

3   Define how a computer might be used by a family if it were in the price range of color television sets. Assume a complete system with:

   CPU.

   Storage (say, 5 million characters or about enough to store two or three complete textbooks).

   Input/output (CRT display with hardcopy output if desired).

   Software provided on plug-in modules. Some unique functions programmable if desired.

4   What are the implications of "breaking up IBM" into several companies? Look at users, the other vendors, society, shareholders, etc.

5   Discuss the tradeoffs for permitting versus prohibiting interchange of data by different governmental agencies.

6   Why is dealing with computer-processed customer statements different than with bills processed by humans?

[2]Richard F. Sprague, *Information Utilities*, Prentice-Hall, Inc., Englewood Cliffs, N.J., 1969.

7 Discuss the following statements:
   a The computer has relieved mankind of computational and data processing drudgery.
   b The computer has reduced opportunities for clerical employees.
8 It is proposed that technology innovations be required to "pay their own way" not only in the organization adopting them but also in society. What are the social costs of computers? How might users be required to pay for these social costs?
9 Investigate the Luddite movement in England from 1811 to 1816, organized to destroy manufacturing machinery in the belief that its use reduced employment. Draw parallels in the use of computers.
10 Explain the differences in the use of processing integration and data integration.

SELECTED REFERENCES

Boonin, Lawrence I.: "Who Should Pay for 'Risk of Revolution' in New Techniques?," *Wharton Quarterly*, November-December 1969, pp. 38–40.

Freed, Roy N.: *Materials and Cases on Computers and Law*, available from the author, 33 Poplar Road, Wellesley, Mass., 1971.

Hoffman, L.: "Computers and Privacy: A Survey," *Computing Surveys*, 1, 2, 1969.

Kriebel, Charles H.: "MIS Technology: A View of the Future," *Proceedings of the Spring Joint Computer Conference*, 1972, pp. 1173–1180.

"Legal Aspects of Computerized Information Systems," *Honeywell Computer Journal*, vol. 7, no. 1, 1973 (entire issue).

Martin, J., and A Norman: *The Computerized Society*, Prentice-Hall, Inc., Englewood Cliffs, N.J., 1970.

Parker, Donn B., Susan Nycum, and S. Stephen Oüra: *Computer Abuse*, Stanford Research Institute, Menlo Park, Calif., 1973.

Pylyshyn, S. W. (ed.): *Perspectives on the Computer Revolution*, Prentice-Hall, Inc., Englewood Cliffs, N.J., 1970.

Rosenberg, N. (ed.): *The Economics of Technological Change*, Penguin Books, Inc., Baltimore, 1971.

Taviss, I. (ed.): *The Computer Impact*, Prentice-Hall, Inc., Englewood Cliffs, N.J., 1970.

Viavant, W. (ed.): *Readings in Computers and Society*, Science Research Associates, Palo Alto, Calif., 1971.

Westin, A. F.: *Privacy and Freedom*, Atheneum Publishers, New York, 1967.

—— (ed.): *Information Technology in a Democracy*, Harvard University Press, Cambridge, Mass., 1971.

Withington, Frederic G.: "The Next (and Last?) Generation," *Datamation*, May 1972, pp. 71–74.

——: *The Real Computer: Its Influences, Uses and Effects*, Addison-Wesley Publishing Company, Inc., Reading, Mass., 1970.

Index